THE DEVELOPMENT
OF MILITARY THOUGHT

THE DEVELOPMENT
OF MILITARY
THOUGHT:

The Nineteenth Century

AZAR GAT

CLARENDON PRESS · OXFORD
1992

Oxford University Press, Walton Street, Oxford OX2 6DP
Oxford New York Toronto
Delhi Bombay Calcutta Madras Karachi
Petaling Jaya Singapore Hong Kong Tokyo
Nairobi Dar es Salaam Cape Town
Melbourne Auckland
and associated companies in
Berlin Ibadan

Oxford is a trade mark of Oxford University Press

Published in the United States
by Oxford University Press, New York

© Azar Gat 1992

British Library Cataloguing in Publication Data
Data available

Library of Congress Cataloging in Publication Data
Gat, Azar.
The development of military thought: the nineteenth century/
Azar Gat.
p. cm.
Includes bibliographical references and index.
1. Military art and science—Europe—History—19th century.
2. Military art and science—United States—History—19th century.
I. Title.
U41.G38 1992
355'.0094'09034—dc20 92–11907
ISBN 0–19–820246–6

Typeset by Cambrian Typesetters, Frimley, Surrey
Printed and bound in
Great Britain by Biddles Ltd.,
Guildford and King's Lynn

To Ruthie and the newborn Tamar

PREFACE

IN many ways this volume is a sequel to my previous book, *The Origins of Military Thought from the Enlightenment to Clausewitz* (Oxford, 1989). It picks up where the latter ended, in the aftermath of the Napoleonic era, and traces the evolution of military ideas up to the outbreak of the First World War. As before, within its time-span and thematic definition, this book claims to be neither comprehensive nor exhaustive. Technological and tactical developments, for example, as well as many other important subjects, are mentioned, if at all, only as part of the background. At the focal point of the book stand the wider conceptions of war, strategy, and military theory which dominated Europe and the West in the period concerned. It seeks to bring out the intellectual assumptions and picture of the past which underlay military outlook, and the major influences which went to shape them.

Two main themes developed in my previous book run through this one as well. Nineteenth-century military theory was dominated and given its distinctive character by the advent of national, all-out war and it correlative strategy of destruction. The new mode of war which had emerged with the French Revolution and Napoleon was revived, updated, and made the rule by the Prussian mass armies led by Moltke. By the turn of the twentieth century, it had evolved into total war under the added impact of increasing popular, nationalist, and imperialist pressures and the new resources injected into war by industrial society.

Military thought was, equally, dominated by two contending conceptions of the nature of military theory, formulated during the age of Enlightenment and the Romantic period, in the eighteenth and early nineteenth centuries respectively. The continued and, indeed, continuing relevancy of those conceptions need not be surprising. Broadly defined, they represent the two fundamental positions towards the study of man and human institutions which emerged in the wake of the scientific revolution of the seventeenth century. One of these looked to the exact and natural sciences as a model to be adopted and applied. The other, by contrast, maintained that the humanities were different in nature from the sciences and could never be studied by the same methods. Taking many forms and reflected in numerous and often diverging currents of thought, the struggle between these two fundamental approaches has characterized all human and social sciences in the modern period.

There are also some marked differences between the present book and its predecessor. While the eighteenth century was intensely philosophical in outlook, in the nineteenth century, other disciplines, such as history, economics and biology, deposed philosophy from its position of prominence in the shaping of educated public opinion. Correspondingly, the focus of this book widens. In addition, while no comprehensive study of nineteenth-century military ideas exists, I have also been able to benefit from the much greater number of specialized works written on nineteenth- as oppoed to eighteenth-century military history, very many of which are of excellent quality. This in turn induced me to make the structure of the present book more panoramic. The first, introductory, chapter of the book provides a cross-European (and American) overview; the second deals with Prussia-Germany; the third with France; the fourth with Britain and the United States; the fifth with the Marxist tradition which would come to dominate Russia. Together these chapters were intended to throw light on the same themes from various angles.

I would like to take this opportunity to extend warm thanks to Professor Sir Michael Howard, previously of Oxford University and now at Yale, who took the trouble to read the greater part of the draft upon which this book is based. As always, I benefited greatly from his thoughtful suggestions. For the many faults that still remain in this book, I alone am to be blamed. I am also grateful to the editors of the *Journal of Contemporary History* and editors of *War and Society* for granting me permission to incorporate material which first appeared in those publications. Tel Aviv University generously covered the various costs involved in the composition of successive drafts of the book.

CONTENTS

1
Positivism, Romanticism, and Military Theory 1815–1870

MODERN views on the nature of military theory originated from the most intensely philosophical period in European history. They were formed in response to the all-pervasive, epoch-making, and bitterly conflicting intellectual climates of the Enlightenment on the one hand, and the Counter-Enlightenment or Romanticism on the other.

The very idea that something called military theory existed—or rather was very much lacking—was the product of the intellectual gospel of the Enlightenment. Stimulated by the spectacular successes of the natural sciences, the men of the Enlightenment sought to bring everything under the domination of reason by creating orderly sciences and disciplines in all spheres of human endeavour. Dominating Europe from the middle of the eighteenth century, the military school of the Enlightenment was burning with an overriding sense of vocation to form a universal theory of war, based on immutable rules and principles, systematically taught, and applied to changing circumstances by the general's creative genius.

By the turn of the century, however, a new sweeping intellectual movement, largely hostile to the ideas of the Enlightenment, was emerging throughout Europe. Particularly active in Germany, the Romantics stressed the complexity and diversity of human reality, which could not be reduced to abstract formulas and which was dominated by emotions, creativity, and the historical conditions of each period. It was in this framework that a new outlook on the nature of military theory was formed, in the works of writers such as Berenhorst and, above all, Clausewitz, breaching the hitherto absolute hegemony of the military school of the Enlightenment.

At the beginning of the nineteenth century, therefore, the transforming experience of Napoleonic warfare, made possible by the social energies unleashed by the French Revolution, was subjected to theoretical formulation in terms of two conflicting intellectual paradigms. The theoretical legacy of the Enlightenment, which in the eighteenth century had been applied mostly to the relatively limited and cautious warfare of the *ancien régime*, was now adapted to reflect the new crushing mode of warfare. To be sure, the older, battle-shy theories of Lloyd and Bülow were also carried into the Napoleonic age by military thinkers such as August Wagner and, most notably, Archduke Charles of Austria. Under the immediate impact of Napoleon's downfall, these theories were even reinforced for a while in some minds by misgivings regarding the adventurous nature of the emperor's strategy, which was blamed for the loss of whole armies in the Russian and Saxon campaigns of 1812 and 1813.[1] But for most of the generation which had undergone the shattering trial of Napoleonic warfare, eighteenth-century strategy was totally discredited, while Napoleon was the 'god of war'. And it was Jomini who won fame by updating the theoretical outlook of the Enlightenment to produce a striking schematization of Napoleon's aggressive rationale of operations. He emphasized the overthrowing of the enemy's army in rapid manœuvring to cut its communications or to penetrate between and overwhelm each of its fractions separately. At the same time, in Prussia—the focal point of the fierce reaction against the world-view of the Enlightenment—Clausewitz combined another inter-pretation of the Napoleonic war of destruction with a completely new formulation of the concept of military theory, constructed from the materials of Romanticism.[2]

Thus it is important to realize that, in general, there was little difference in military outlook *per se* between Clausewitz and Jomini; both reflected the spirit and outline of Napoleonic strategy. Clausewitz's highly polemic rhetoric against the military theory of his day and against Jomini (which recent commentators have surpassed each other in paraphrasing) can only be understood in its cultural context, namely the all-out attack of the new German Movement on the world-view of the Enlightenment, which

---

[1] See Baron Rogniat, *Considérations sur l'art de la guerre* (Paris, 1816). The book aroused a public sensation and sparked a literary skirmish with the exiled emperor himself; Napoleon's counter-attack from St Helena in Montholon's *Mémoires* (Paris, 1823) provoked Rogniat's *Réponse aux notes critiques de Napoléon* (Paris, 1823). For one favourable reaction in Germany see Carl von Decker, *Ansichten über die Kriegführung im Geist der Zeit* (Berlin, 1817).

[2] See Azar Gat, *The Origins of Military Thought from the Enlightenment to Clausewitz* (Oxford, 1989).

rendered his predecessors' intellectual assumptions totally unacceptable to Clausewitz. Hence also the background for the subsequent
development of military theory. The conventional picture of a
struggle between Jominian and Clausewitzian ideas and influences
is oblivious to the wider context. The shift in the centre of military
power from France to Germany after 1870–1 marked a decisive
change in the fortunes of the two contending conceptions of
military theory; but, both before and after this, their fortunes were
equally tied up with the fortunes of the cultural traditions from
which they had emerged. They could only take root and flourish
where they found the climate of ideas favourable. Their spread and
influence matched remarkably the contours of the intellectual map
of Europe, shaped by those currents of thought which had their
origins in the Enlightenment and Romanticism and which formed
people's outlook on the world in the nineteenth century.

Although Romanticism had indigenous expressions everywhere
in Europe, it was the wealth and depth of German literature and
philosophy that attracted the minds of the élite in all countries from
the late 1810s to the 1830s, exerting a profound and lasting
influence even on the intellectual opponents of the movement. By
the 1840s, however, the tide of Romanticism was ebbing throughout
Europe, and it was the descendants of the Enlightenment who
dominated the mid-century. Favoured by a remarkable scientific
and technological advance which spread the culture of science,
positivism, in its broadest sense, became the prevalent *état d'esprit*.
The progressive application of the scientific methods of observation
and induction to the more complex sciences of man and society
would elevate these disciplines too from their state of infancy; this
was the mood most characteristically articulated in France by
Auguste Comte, whose doctrines found equally receptive ground
on both sides of the Channel. Needless to say, this climate of ideas
was favourable to the theoretical legacy of the military school of the
Enlightenment.

It was not that soldiers in the nineteenth century were either very
interested in, or knowledgeable about, the major intellectual
currents that dominated their times, although most military
thinkers—by nature people of intellectual inclination—were remarkably conscious of them. The all-encompassing philosophical
ideal of the eighteenth century was a thing of the past, and with it
had gone much of the enthusiastic sense of vocation to lay the

foundations of military theory, the discipline which during the Enlightenment had always been there to be discovered. All the same, the intellectual frameworks remained, and military outlook was in some important respects almost predetermined by the prevailing cultural perspectives.

There were, of course, many other important factors at work. No great war took place in Europe between the fall of Napoleon and the German Wars of Unification. The predominance of domestic politics and social developments resulted in a long period of reduced international and military tensions, as the autocratic regimes of the Restoration struggled with the rising middle classes, with nationalism, and with the effects of the expanding Industrial Revolution and urbanization. Governments were therefore more concerned to employ their armies as a weapon in internal affairs, and indeed to crush the seeds of revolution within the armies themselves, than to use them in war against allied governments with similar interests. While the guns were silent, however, the products of industrialization, such as the rifle and the breach-loader, the steam engine and the electric telegraph, were quietly transforming war, with military theory following in their wake.

In a previous book, I traced the emergence of the two dominating conceptions of military theory within their centres of origin up to the late 1830s. This introductory chapter will therefore begin by widening the angle of vision to two countries of the periphery— Britain and the United States—before again picking up the threads of development in France and Germany.

It is well known that the British army of the Napoleonic era was fundamentally an eighteenth-century institution. Being the least-affected of all European forces by the military innovations which Revolutionary France had introduced and which all her continental rivals had had to adopt to a greater or lesser degree, it remained a professional force which drew its officers from the privileged, and its rank and file from the lowest classes of society. With the coming of peace, in a rapidly changing society and gradually reformed political system which had traditionally regarded the army as a potential danger and as alien to British values, the neglected army was to become increasingly anachronistic.[3] This, however, was

[3] See Gwyn Harries-Jenkins, *The Army in Victorian Society* (London, 1977); Edward M. Spiers, *The Army and Society 1815–1914* (London, 1980); Hew

hardly the reality for the proud veterans of the Peninsula and of Waterloo in the generation after 1815. Nor was the philistine image which later became associated with the British officer-corps applicable to them. Indeed, when certain of those gentlemen turned their attention to military writing, they produced some fascinating expressions of the major trends vying with each other in British society in the early nineteenth century.

The prevailing approach to military theory—in Britain as everywhere else—had been derived since the eighteenth century from the ideas of the Enlightenment. Jomini synthesized the intellectual legacy of the military school of the Enlightenment with the characteristics of Napoleonic warfare, and outside France— where the vain Swiss was not very popular among his former comrades-in-arms—his pre-eminence was readily acknowledged. A disciple of Jomini and the best-known military author in Britain was Sir William Napier (1785–1860), famous for his masterful, voluminous *History of the War in the Peninsula*. At the age of fourteen, Napier followed his two elder brothers into the army and, under Moore and Wellington, he actively participated in the Peninsula campaigns from 1808 to 1814, rising to the rank of lieutenant-colonel. Retiring from the army on half pay in 1819, he first looked for an outlet for his considerable artistic talents in painting and sculpture, and finally found his vocation in the research and writing of his great work.

Napier's attitudes in politics, philosophy, and military theory all converge in one central core of beliefs; his upbringing made him a radical Whig, sympathetic to France, and an intellectual child of the Enlightenment. His father had always condemned the war against Revolutionary France, and the son was equally critical of Tory war-policy in his *History*. Throughout his life he was an enthusiastic and unreserved admirer of Napoleon, whom he regarded not only as the greatest military genius there had ever been but also as an enlightened ruler.[4] Domestically, by 1805 he strongly favoured the

Strachan, *Wellington's Legacy: The Reform of the British Army* (Manchester, 1984). John W. Fortescue, *A History of the British Army* (London, 1930), vols. xi–xiii is still the only comprehensive narrative. Two brief accounts are Michael Howard, 'Wellington and the British Army', in his *Studies in War and Peace* (London, 1970), 50–64; and Geoffrey Best, *War and Society in Revolutionary Europe* (Leicester, 1982), 231–43.

[4] See H. A. Bruce (ed.), *Life of General Sir William Napier* (London, 1864), i. 29; the author was General Sir Patrick MacDougall who, like Bruce, was Napier's

radical efforts to democratize the British political system and to protect the poor against the growing effects of the Industrial Revolution. He married the niece of the radical Whig leader Charles Fox. Later, like most of the radicals, he became increasingly alienated from Whig politics and, after the Reform Bill of 1832, he denounced the party for betraying the popular cause by denying the franchise to the masses.[5] The writings of William Cobbett, which he read in his youth, made him a life-long critic of commercial circles and of *laissez-faire* economists. Employing his pen with his usual zeal, he fiercely objected to the Poor Law Amendment in the 1830s and to the repeal of the Corn Laws in the 1840s.[6]

Napier's Whig starting-point was closely associated with the development of British thought from the seventeenth century on. He was thoroughly familiar with the 'writings of the English philosophers . . . from Lord Bacon down to Adam Smith and Dugald Stewart'.[7] Not surprisingly, when he turned his attention to military theory, he found the main themes familiar enough.

His earliest work was the first review of Jomini's *Treatise on Grand Military Operations* to be published in Britain. It appeared in 1821 in the *Edinburgh Review*, the leading liberal journal in the country. Whereas in conquered Germany, where people had been eager to grasp the secret of Napoleonic warfare, the young Jomini had already been a celebrity by 1808, it took longer for him to penetrate the parochial British scene.[8] Napier's review was un-

son-in-law. Two brief accounts are T. R. E. Holmes, 'Sir William Napier', in his *Four Famous Soldiers* (London, 1889), 227–59; and J. Fortescue, 'Napier's "Peninsular War" ', in his *Historical and Military Essays* (London, 1928), 219–35. Finally, an excellent work to which this section is greatly indebted is Jay Luvaas, *The Education of an Army: British Military Thought, 1815–1940* (London, 1965); for Napier see 7–38.

[5] Bruce, *Napier*, i. 346–8; Holmes, *Four Famous Soldiers*, 249–50. For Napier's close association with the radical MPs John Arthur Roebuck and Joseph Parkes (which in 1832 involved his name in talks of radical revolution) see William Thomas, *The Philosophic Radicals* (Oxford, 1979), 234, 239, 257, 295.

[6] Bruce, *Napier*, i. 346–8; also see Napier's *Observations on the Corn Laws* (London, 1841), an excellent piece of political and economic pamphleteering against the Cobdenites.

[7] Bruce, *Napier*, i. 26; for a reference to Locke's epistemology, see Napier's 'Essay on Education of the Deaf and Dumb', ibid., ii. 523.

[8] In Britain, as everywhere else in Europe, the *Traité* was read (when it was read) in the original French, widely understood by the educated classes. But it was even better-known through numerous comments, reviews, abstracts, and second-hand references. After all, the principal ideas of the work could be summarized on the back of a postcard. Large extracts from the historical parts of the *Traité* were

reservedly admiring, presenting the *Treatise* as 'one of the most profound, original, and interesting [works] that has appeared in our day'.[9] He reproduced fully the theoretical outlook developed by the military thinkers of the Enlightenment and faithfully accepted Jomini's view of himself as the one who finally succeeded in supplying his predecessors' confused ideas with true content. Indeed, for the men of the post-Napoleonic period, eighteenth-century warfare (and hence military theory) appeared not as the outgrowth of eighteenth-century society and politics but as an erroneous system put right by Napoleon.

According to Napier, the art of war was advancing: 'Till the middle of the last century the greatest and most distinguished leaders had seldom been able to free themselves from the shackles of the wretched system of warfare which they found established.'[10] They had depended totally on magazines and had dispersed their forces to defend their frontiers, rather than keeping them united. A brilliant exception, wrote Napier, had been Marlborough, and the truth regarding the proper way of conducting operations had been gradually revealed since the time of Frederick the Great. However, Frederick's genius had been predominantly tactical and had fallen short of a true grasp of strategy. It was Napoleon who had brought the art of war to the pinnacle of perfection, by crushing the tyranny of the magazines, concentrating his forces, moving them on interior lines, and substituting battle for manœuvre.[11] 'This last', wrote Napier, 'was the period in which the principles of the military art were brought to all the perfection of which they appear to be capable . . . Napoleon incontestably surpassed all who preceded him and left nothing in which he could himself be surpassed.'[12]

According to Napier, the true principles of the art of war, as practised by Napoleon, had been unveiled by Jomini. The advancement of the art had thus been matched by the advancement of military theory. While historical works had traditionally contained only tiresome memoirs and unprofitable details, wrote Napier, Lloyd had begun to discover the principles of the art in the

published in *The History of the Seven Years War* (London, 1808?); the theoretical parts were abstracted in J. A. Gilbert, *An Exposition of the First Principles of Grand Military Combinations and Movements, Compiled from the Treatise upon Great Military Operations* (London, 1825).

[9] Napier, 'Traité des grandes opérations militaires', *The Edinburgh Review*, 35 (1821), 377. [10] Ibid. 378.
[11] Ibid. 378, 380, 383–4, 387–91. [12] Ibid. 380.

philosophical manner. Tempelhoff had followed suit, and Guibert, whose books Bonaparte is said to have carried with him to the field, had produced many illuminating ideas which, if they had not established the art, were at least free from the prejudices of their day. 'Jomini however', says Napier, 'has been the first to give a complete exposition of the principles of war. His powerful and original mind enabled him to far outstrip the authors who had preceded him.'[13] His principles 'do not depend upon the particular institutions of any country or age, but . . . in great part are applicable to all times and places'. Starting from a broad survey of the military events of the last 70 years, Jomini 'elicits by a sort of *induction* the true causes of their failure and success'.[14]

Napier met Jomini in Paris in 1824 whilst he was carrying out the extensive preparatory research for his *History*.[15] The great work that made him famous appeared in six volumes and took twelve years to publish (1828–40). The theoretical outlook of the Enlightenment and Jomini's principles of the art of war underlie the book, which masterfully reveals those principles at work in the conduct of the great military geniuses Napoleon and Wellington. Napier's theoretical outlook is again strikingly manifested in a letter which he wrote in 1847 and in which he rejected the idea of composing a work on 'The Philosophy of War'. The following lines could equally well have been written (in fact had been) by Guibert, Lloyd, or Jomini:

Such a work involves a preliminary investigation of the human mind as to why men engage in warfare at all. Then would come the distinction between religious wars, civil wars, wars of aggression and aggrandisement, wars of defence, wars of folly, and wars of necessity. Then the progress of the art! its varying phases in different degrees of civilisation, how far it can be carried on by barbarous nations, how far it depends upon civil institutions and the progress of the sciences; how much it depends on such extraneous matters, and how much upon original genius in general. And all reasoning on this point must, to carry weight, be supported by illustrations taken from history and experience . . . I believe the greatest genius would shrink from it, as beyond the power of man to treat with accuracy and authority. Bacon, who has considered all things belonging to philosophy, has not touched upon it.[16]

---

[13] Napier, 377–8.   [14] Ibid. 379; my italics.
[15] Bruce, Napier, i. 240–3; to his wife he wrote that Jomini reminded him of Tom Paine.   [16] Ibid., ii. 277–8.

A typical exponent of the Whig interpretation of history, Napier crusaded for the truth as he saw it, and was categorical, almost hysterical, in his judgement of people.[17] Commanding a brilliant, seemingly effortless style, he engaged in endless literary battles with the victims of his *History*, against political targets, and on many other issues. The bitter personal skirmishes around the *History* alone produced a forest of pamphlets. One of those with whom he crossed swords was another veteran of the Napoleonic wars, Major John Mitchell, who, like Napier, reached the rank of major-general while on the reserve list. Their open dispute concerned mostly matters of tactics, but they also had a deeper symbolic significance. Mitchell was, to my knowledge, the only non-German military author in pre-1871 Europe to be decisively influenced by the new winds which had been blowing from the German cultural scene from the late eighteenth and early nineteenth centuries.

Romanticism was an all-European movement. It was most notably represented in Britain by the Lake Poets—Wordsworth, Coleridge, and Southey; and its religious aspects found characteristic expression in the Oxford Movement and the Roman Catholic revival. But nowhere were its intellectual manifestations in the spheres of philosophy, history, politics, and the arts so comprehensive, profound, and stimulating as in Germany. All the leading ideas of the day, wrote Hippolyte Taine in the middle of the nineteenth century, were produced in Germany between 1780 and 1830.[18] From the 1810s, German ideas were imported everywhere in Europe, to extremely fertile effect. Madame de Staël's *De l'Allemagne* (1813) introduced them into France, and in Britain it was mainly Coleridge and Carlyle who in the 1820s and 1830s, brought German philosophy and literature before the dazzled educated public. The Romantics emphasized emotions and inner life and rejected any reduction of the wealth and totality of experience to dead abstractions and principles. Striking as they did at the foundations of the accepted tenets of the Enlightenment, these ideas profoundly impressed the young John Stuart Mill, at the centre of the enemy camp. As he recalled in his *Autobiography*, they showed him the way out of a severe mental crisis and marked a turning-point in his relationship with his towering father and with Benthamite doctrines, rooted in the eighteenth century. In the

---

[17] See Luvaas, *The Education of an Army*, 16, 42.
[18] Cited by John Dewey, *German Philosophy and Politics* (New York, 1915), 14.

military field in Britain, these ideas hardly had any effect at all, but where they did appear, the story could not have been more characteristic. John Mitchell (1785–1859) brought them from Germany and found his main forum in the Tory *Frazer's Magazine*, dominated by Coleridge, in the company of such authors as Carlyle himself.[19]

In 1797 Mitchell accompanied his father on a four-year diplomatic mission to Berlin. During this period, he attended the Ritterakademie at Lüneburg. At sixteen, he tells us, he read Klopstock to his first love, and she read Goethe's *Werther* to him.[20] He returned to Britain in 1801, but his German period determined his intellectual career for life. He joined the British army in 1803 and during the war served in the West Indies, Spain, and the Low Countries. Before and after Napoleon's final defeat, he was often used by Wellington as an interpreter in the negotiations with Austria, Prussia, and the smaller German states. Retiring on half pay in 1826, he too turned to historical and journalistic writing.[21] Under the pseudonyms 'Captain Orlando Sabertash' and 'Bombardino', he wrote in *Frazer's Magazine* several series of light, humoristic, and perceptive pieces on military affairs, on social news from the European salons—in which he was a welcome and frequent visitor—and on many of the great men he met there. The latter pieces mainly comprised admiring portraits of Romantic artists and conservative politicians: Heine, Hugo, Berryer, Guizot, David, Thiers, Lamartine, and Chateaubriand.[22] He wrote two large military biographies of Wallenstein and Napoleon and several smaller ones. His *Thoughts on Tactics* presented in a systematic manner the ideas he had expressed in numerous articles on military affairs, mostly published in the *United Service Journal*. Like Napier's writings, all these were united by a common intellectual

[19] On *Frazer's Magazine* see Miriam Thrall, *Rebellious Frazer's. No. 1 Yorke's Magazine in the Days of Maginn, Thackeray and Carlyle* (New York, 1934); Mitchell is mentioned on 27–8, 30.

[20] *Frazer's Town and Country Magazine*, 26 (1842), 347.

[21] The principal source on Mitchell's life is Leonhard Schmitz's introductory memoir to Mitchell, *Biographies of Eminent Soldiers of the Last Four Centuries* (London, 1865), pp. vi–xviii; based on this is the sketch in *DNB*, xii. 519–20. The only comprehensive study is to be found in Luvaas, *The Education of an Army*, 39–64.

[22] 'Reminiscences of Men and Things', *Frazer's Magazine*, 26 (1842), 733–6, 740–2; 27 (1843), 99–106, 145–151, 298–301, 454–64, 687–704. Mitchell writes that he loves David despite his being a republican: ibid. 27, 151.

framework, evident in Mitchell's politics, cultural orientation, and military theory. They were all strikingly dominated by a German point of view.

Mitchell's Napoleon is the infamous tyrant portrayed by the German nationalists. The story of his fall is dominated by the rising of the peoples, particularly the awakening of the German national spirit which culminated in the German War of Liberation of 1813. This was a very unusual perspective in early nineteenth-century Britain.[23] Mitchell's France was the detested power that subjugated other nations in the name of so-called universal doctrines of reason. In his highly sympathetic essay on Metternich, containing barely veiled criticism of contemporary Whig attitudes, Mitchell denounced the

multiplied attacks made [in the last fifty years] by what are falsely called liberal goverments upon the rights, liberties and independence of peoples and states. . . . To the conservative principle [many European countries] . . . are indebted for all the national institutions they continue to possess. . . . If the people of a country love the unity and strength of an absolute monarchy, they are much oppressed by having what is termed among us a liberal and constitutional monarchy forced upon them.[24]

This was no mere reaction. Mitchell's view reflected the intellectual position that had developed in Germany since the days of Herder and Möser in response to the threatening ideas of the French Enlightenment, and which had turned into a form of national resistance against French imperialism after 1806. Every society, it was argued, bore the source of its happiness within itself. The delicate fabric of its peculiar institutions, woven by long historical evolution, could not simply be torn down and replaced by some ingenious scheme based on abstract principles.

The influence of the German Movement determined every aspect of Mitchell's military thought. If Napier's theoretical outlook was totally derived from Jomini, Mitchell's military writings were from beginning to end no more than an English transplantation of Berenhorst's *Reflections on the Art of War* (1796–9). For Mitchell, Jomini added nothing to military theory, although, for a Frenchman, he was 'a pretty fair relater of events'. The French military authors were, he claimed, much inferior to the German.[25] It was 'Berenhorst

[23] J. Mitchell, *The Fall of Napoleon* (3 vols.; London, 1845).
[24] *Frazer's Magazine*, 29 (1844), 333.
[25] Id., *Thoughts on Tactics and Military Organization* (London, 1838), 121.

of whom the present writer avows himself a humble follower'.[26] And to Berenhorst, Mitchell added a bright new star when, in the late 1830s, he became familiar with Clausewitz's collected works.[27]

From Berenhorst's *Reflections*—a characteristic product of the 'Storm and Stress' period in German culture—Mitchell drew both his reliance on the military thinkers of the Enlightenment and a light-hearted, sardonic attitude towards their theoretical efforts. Military theory, he wrote, had made very little progress from its glorious origins with the Greeks through the darkness of the Middle Ages to the various achievements of the modern era. Despite all the talk about the advance of military science and art, no general principles had been established.[28] Why this was so, 'the late General Clausewitz tells us in a very able, though lengthy, and often obscure book on War': unlike any other science or art, in war the object reacts.[29]

The two main tactical points forcefully championed by Mitchell derived from the same source. Regarding cavalry he believed—against recent experience and accepted opinion—that it could and should be trained to charge and break infantry formations. Here too he was strictly expressing the opinions of Berenhorst and those of Bismark, the Württembergian cavalry specialist.[30] Regarding infantry he argued, provoking a lively and ultimately very unpleasant exchange with a brilliantly polemic Napier, that the bayonet was an absolutely useless weapon. To create a real shock-effect, half of the soldiers ought instead to be armed with the pike, abandoned more than a century earlier. This, of course, was a late episode in the famous controversy of the eighteenth century over the

---

[26] *Thoughts on Tactics and Military Organization*, 12.

[27] For the very few but respectful references to Clausewitz in Britain upon the publication of his works, see H. Strachan, *From Waterloo to Balaclava: Tactics, Technology and the British Army, 1815–1854* (Cambridge, 1985), 8–10.

[28] See mainly ibid. 1–7, 111–21. Cf. Berenhorst, *Betrachtungen*; for Berenhorst's intellectual background and ideas, see my *Enlightenment to Clausewitz*, 150–5.

[29] *Thoughts on Tactics*, 8; a footnote explains that Clausewitz was 'a general in the Prussian service lately deceased. His posthumous work, "Vom Kriege", was published in Berlin in 1832.' In 1840, in the course of his literary debate with a sarcastic Napier, Mitchell compared Napier unfavourably with 'General Clausewitz whose writings have since attracted so much notice in Germany'; Clausewitz's masterly history of the wars in Europe since 1792 'shows us at last how military history should be written': *United Service Journal* (1840), 264. For further, increasingly admiring comments by Mitchell, see Strachan, *From Waterloo to Balaclava*, 8–10.

[30] See esp. ibid. 73–110, 177–212. Bismark was translated into English: *Lectures on the Tactics of Cavalry*. (London, 1827, 2nd. edn. 1855).

ordre profond and the *ordre mince*, and again Mitchell was strongly adhering to the ideas advocated by Berenhorst, in the footsteps of Folard and de Saxe.[31]

These tactical points assumed their fuller significance in the context of Berenhorst's comprehensive criticism of the Frederickian system. Voicing the Counter-Enlightenment's intellectual opposition to Frederick's bureaucratic, machine-like state, Berenhorst totally rejected the principles of the Prussian military system, which was based on brutal discipline, inhuman drill, and automatic performance on the battlefield. Instead of suppressing individuality, argued Berenhorst, the army's main aim must be to inflame the soldiers with an unbeatable fighting-spirit. This required, of course, a complete reversal of attitude towards the soldier. Rather than being regarded as cannon-fodder, he had to be treated as a human being. After the military successes of the French Revolutionary armies, Berenhorst became the leading figure in the growing intellectual ferment in Prussia. His most notable ally was the controversial military thinker A. H. D. von Bülow, who criticized the class basis of the Prussian army and state and urged that the Frederickian system be abolished and that advancement be determined according to merit. Indeed, following the disaster of 1806, these were the ideas that were to find their consummation in the Prussian reform movement.[32]

The criticism which had been levelled against the Prussian army of the *ancien régime* remained perfectly applicable to the only army that retained its eighteenth-century form well into the nineteenth century. More than thirty years after the Prussian reformers, Mitchell was fiercely campaigning on the very same battlegrounds against the distinct social characteristics of the British army. He called for a human attitude towards the soldier, for the abolition of corporal punishment, and for the improvement of the troops' appalling living-conditions. He was the principal public opponent of the purchase system of officer commissions, which he denounced as hindering talent and military proficiency.[33] Like the Prussian

---

[31] Ibid. 25–72, 123–76; for his exchange with Napier on this matter see *United Service Journal*, 3 (1839), 103–6, 531–36; 1 (1840), 262–8.

[32] For Bülow see my *Enlightenment to Clausewitz*, 79–94; for Mitchell's acknowledged debt to Bülow see, for example, *Thoughts on Tactics*, 12.

[33] Again Mitchell's arguments in the *United Service Journal* from the mid-1830s are recapitulated in *Thoughts on Tactics*, esp. pp. v–viii, 239–90.

reform movement itself, this demonstrates that, contrary to their reactionary image, the German Movement and Romanticism, on account of their fundamental evolutionist approach, could be either reformist or conservative, depending on the circumstances and the opponent. Indeed, when from the 1840s the political and public urges for reform finally reached the army, it was the radical Napier who, with his customary zeal, opposed any talk of reform.[34] His position derived not only from a sense of pride in the British army of the Peninsula, symbolized by the towering figure of the Duke of Wellington, but also from deeper intellectual sources. If, as Napier maintained, 'this last was the period in which the principles of the military art were brought to all the perfection of which they appear to be capable', could any change be a change for the better? Like Jomini, Napier was not very receptive to change. It is no coincidence, for example, that for both men the introduction, in the middle of the century of the rifle as the standard infantry-weapon came as unwelcome news; it posed a threat to a universalist conception of war.[35]

Mitchell's intellectual origins made him a highly interesting exception, but an exception he was. British officers may have had little time to consider their profession, and even less to reflect on military theory, but inasmuch as they were exposed to any such speculation, it was derived entirely from the military thinkers of the Enlightenment. This exposure increased after the Crimean débâcle, when the neglected army suddenly found itself at the centre of public interest and facing calls for a comprehensive overhaul. When, in response to this demand, Napier's son-in-law, Lieutenant-Colonel—later Major-General—Sir Patrick MacDougall, composed *The Theory of War, Illustrated by Numerous Examples from Military History* for the education of his fellow officers, he humbly stated that he was merely digesting Jomini, Archduke Charles, and

[34] See esp. Napier's pamphlet *Six Letters in Vindication of the British Army, Exposing the Calumnies of the Liverpool Financial Reform Association* (London, 1849); this is Napier at his best in an exchange with Gladstone, the association's secretary.
[35] After the devastating use of the rifle in the Crimea, Jomini in the new edn. of the *Précis de l'art de la guerre* (1855), 2nd. app., still denied that tactics could ever radically change. For an exchange between Jomini and a French critic on this matter, see 'General Jomini and the "Spectateur Militaire" ', *United Service Journal* (1856), 201–5. The railway was, of course, an even greater challenge. For the attitude of Charles and William Napier toward the Minié rifle see Luvaas, *The Education of an Army*, 34–5.

Napier.[36] The book went through three editions within six years. It made MacDougall the natural choice for the post of first commandant of the staff college which was founded in 1858.[37]

Similar in character to the *Theory of War* but of much wider influence was the famous *The Operations of War* (1866). It was composed by Sir Edward Bruce Hamley (1824–93), the first professor of military history at the staff college and, in the 1870s, its fourth commandant.[38] Hamley had one foot in the world of literature and contributed regularly to *Blackwood's Magazine*, one of the most popular periodicals in the country. He was a man of the London salons, a member of the Athenaeum, the famous scientific and literary club, and a friend of the circle of philosophers who made the club their centre, Herbert Spencer being the most famous of them.[39] His mastery of style and exposition made the *Operations of War* one of the most successful military textbooks ever. Based entirely on Jomini's rationale of operations and Archduke Charles's geographical analysis, the book demonstrated the principles of strategy in the clearest and most didactic manner through descriptions of a variety of modern military campaigns. It soon became the official textbook both at Camberley and at West Point and went through five editions in Hamley's own lifetime alone.

However, as mentioned before with respect to all Jominian military literature which turned the characteristics of Napoleonic warfare into the universal principles of war, Hamley's writings were difficult to adapt to the sweeping changes brought about by

[36] P. L. MacDougall, *The Theory of War, Illustrated by Numerous Examples from Military History* (London, 1856); see esp. v–vii. For another, condensed exposition of Jominian principles with an introductory congratulating letter by Napier, see Edward Yates, *Elementary Treatise on Strategy* (London, 1852); the author was a fellow of St John's College, Cambridge. Also see his *Elementary Treatise on Tactics*. (London, 1853).

[37] For MacDougall see the sketch in *DNB* Supplement, 993–4; Luvaas, *The Education of an Army*, 101–29; and Brian Bond, *The Victorian Army and the Staff College 1854–1914* (London, 1972), 83–4.

[38] See Alexander Innes Shand, *The Life of General Sir Edward Bruce Hamley* (2 vols.; London, 1895); E. M. Lloyd in *DNB* Supplement, xxii. 807–10; Luvaas, *The Education of an Army*, 130–68; Bond, *The Staff College*, 84–8, 131–3; A. R. Godwin-Austin, *The Staff and the Staff College* (London, 1927), esp. 112–14, 133–4.

[39] Shand, *Sir Edward Bruce Hamley*, esp. i. 23, 43–8, 181. An interesting picture of Hamley's attitudes, despite his Toryism, is given in his sharp critique *Thomas Carlyle: Mirage Philosophy* (London, 1881) and, on the other side, his highly sympathetic biography *Voltaire* (London, 1877).

steam and advanced metallurgy.[40] Not surprisingly, the fortunes of Jomini and Hamley were closely linked. Despite being formulated in a period of revolutionary change, Hamley's tactics, like Jomini's, never departed from the Napoleonic model, and in the sixth edition of the *Operations of War* (1907), published after Hamley's death, the original part on tactics was therefore omitted altogether. The First World War, with its long, continuous fronts, made the Napoleonic strategic model largely irrelevant and marked the final eclipse of both Jomini and Hamley. In 1923 the *Operations of War* was reprinted for the last time.

It has been observed, however, that a reaction against the book had already been setting in during the 1890s, though the reason for this has never been properly explained. In 1894 the book lost its monopoly as the set text in military history for the staff college entrance-examination. In 1898 it was subjected to comprehensive criticism by Lieutenant-Colonel G. F. R. Henderson, then the professor of military history at Camberley.[41] In criticizing Hamley for being schematic and for ignoring the spirit of war, the commander's intentions, and moral forces, Henderson was voicing the classical themes of the German military school. His criticism reflected a decisive shift in the direction in which the world now looked for military theory.[42]

The intellectual world of the founding fathers of the American republic was grounded in the ideas of the British and French Enlightenment. In the military field this meant strong aversion to the institution of standing armies, mistrusted as a potentially dangerous instrument of despotism and selfish interests and as alien to the values of civil society. The natural preference—reflecting both the prevalent sentiment among the *philosophes* as well as existing American institutions—was for a militia of free citizens, called up in time of danger to defend their country. All the same,

---

[40] See Luvaas, *The Education of an Army*, 141–50.

[41] Ibid. 150–1; Bond, *The Staff College*, 87–8.

[42] As was the custom with many of the military thinkers of the Enlightenment, Hamley stressed the importance of moral forces but excused himself from discussing them. In the introduction to later editions of *The Operations of War*, he named Clausewitz as their most notable student. With the Prussian army beginning to attract universal attention after 1866, Hamley sent a copy of his book to Moltke. But Moltke's reply was polite and formal rather than complimentary as it is sometimes presented, and indeed could not have been different: Shand, *Sir Edward Bruce Hamley*, i. 183–4.

when the War of Independence, and later the defence needs of the young republic, almost forced the creation of a small regular army, it was again Europe and European organization, tactics, and military thought that constituted the formative influence, bringing the military outlook and literature of the Enlightenment with them.[43]

The most notable manifestation of this was the founding of the United States Military Academy at West Point. The origins of the Academy, the ideas behind it, and its curriculum reflected and paralleled the story of the military academies pioneered all over Europe in the second half of the eighteenth century in response to the Enlightenment ideal of military education. Early discussions about an academy had been prompted by the War of Independence, and they continued thereafter, largely under the influence of French and German officers. As in Europe, the military schools for the professions of artillery and engineering were the first to appear, established by Washington at West Point in 1794 to remedy the acute lack of technical expertise in the young army. In 1799 the prolific Hamilton submitted to Secretary of War McHenry a complete scheme for the establishment of five military schools: one Fundamental School and four Schools of Application for engineering and artillery, cavalry, infantry, and the navy. Secretary McHenry presented the scheme to Congress with only minor modifications. 'The art of war', he told Congress, 'is subjected to mechanical, geometrical, moral and physical rules; it calls for profound study; its theory is immense; the details infinite, and its principles are rendered useful only by a happy adaptation of them to the circumstances of place and ground.' As evidence of the importance of military professionalism and science, he cited the military authors of Antiquity as well as Machiavelli and Marshal de Puységur, who had left, he wrote, an 'excellent treatise on war'.[44]

Nothing came of the proposal. But, significantly, it was none other than President Jefferson—the arch-enemy of state machinery

---

[43] For the militia vs. standing army and for the general view of war, see Russell F. Weigley, *History of the United States Army* (Bloomington, Ind., 1967), 29–94; Marcus Cunliffe, *Soldiers and Civilians: The Martial Spirit in America 1775–1865* (London, 1969); Reginald Stuart, *War and American Thought from the Revolution to the Monroe Doctrine* (Kent, Oh., 1982).

[44] Hamilton to McHenry, 23 Nov. 1799, in Henry Cabot Lodge (ed.), *The Works of Alexander Hamilton* (New York, 1886), vi. 265–72; Documents 39, 40, 14 Jan. and 13 Feb. 1800, in *American State Papers, Military Affairs* (Washington, DC, 1832), i. 133–5, 142–4.

and military professionalism—who took action to open the Military Academy in 1802.[45] Historians who found this puzzling forgot that he was also one of the greatest exponents of the American Enlightenment.[46] The man he chose to organize the institution was Jonathan Williams, a civilian and grandnephew of Benjamin Franklin. Williams was a man of wide scholarly pursuits who had collaborated with his famous relative in several scientific projects and was himself a member of the American Philosophical Society and a contributor to its *Transactions*. Having long been an enthusiast for fortification and military science, he was commissioned by Jefferson as a major in the artillery in 1801. It is characteristic of the age and the man that one of Williams's first initiatives was to found the United States Military Philosophical Society—with Jefferson himself as its first patron—to discuss and 'promote military science'.[47]

Like the Woolwich Academy, West Point emphasized the technical professions, an approach which was also in line with the desire to integrate the army into society. From 1817, following the war of 1812, the academy was thoroughly reorganized under the command of Captain Sylvanus Thayer with a view to making it the seedbed of an increasingly professional, though miniature, army. Thayer, who made an extensive tour of study in France and brought with him some thousand books on the military art, looked to the French military schools, especially the École polytechnique, and to French military teaching as a model. Again, it was the legacy of the Enlightenment that lay behind American military education. From 1818 the academy's standard text for the study of the

---

[45] See R. E. Dupuy, *The Story of West Point: 1802–1943* (Washington, DC, 1943), 27–31; Sidney Forman, *West Point* (New York, 1950), 16–19; Weigley, *History of the United States Army*, 105–6. For the wider intellectual and institutional context see my *Enlightenment to Clausewitz*, esp. 59–63.

[46] See for example Weigley, in Paret (ed.), *Makers of Modern Strategy from Machiavelli to the Nuclear Age* (Princeton, NJ, 1986), 412–3. Theodore J. Crackel in 'The Founding of West Point: Jefferson and the Politics of Security', *Armed Forces and Society*, 7 (1981), 529–43, dismisses the Enlightenment background without bothering with either evidence or argument (p. 532). Also see Reginald C. Stuart, *The Half-Way Pacifist: Thomas Jefferson's View of War* (Toronto, 1978), which does not refer, however, to the creation of West Point.

[47] For Williams and the Military Philosophical Society and its proceedings see esp. Forman, *West Point* 23–31; also Dupuy, *The Story of West Point*, 27–31; M. E. Lombard, 'Jonathan Williams', *Dictionary of American Biography*, xx. 280–2. Scharnhorst's *Militärische Gesellschaft*, springing from the same intellectual sources and strikingly similar in orientation, was also founded in 1802.

science and art of war was Captain J. M. O'Connor's translation of Gay de Vernon's *Traité élémentaire d'art militaire et de fortification* (1805). The French original, composed by an engineering officer and professor of fortifications at the École polytechnique for the students of that school, concentrated on the technical services, but the translator added an extensive summary of

the best principles and maxims of such writers as Guibert, Lloyd, Tempelhoff and Jomini, particularly of the latter, whose work [the *Treatise*] is considered a masterpiece and as the highest authority. Indeed no man should pretend to be capable of commanding any considerable body of troops unless he has studied and meditated on the principles laid down by Jomini.[48]

From the 1830s Vernon's book was replaced by the widely circulated notes of Denis Hart Mahan (WP 1824). As Thayer's protégé, Mahan was sent to study in France. In his capacity as the professor of civil and military engineering and of the art of war and later as chairman of the Academic Board, he became the leading figure in the academy for four decades. He also wrote a little book, *An Elementary Treatise on Advanced Guard, Out-Posts and Detachment Service of Troops . . . with a Historical Sketch on the Rise and Progress of Tactics* (1847), which was typical of the Enlightenment genre of military literature.[49] But the first major American treatise on the conduct of operations was written by one of Mahan's closest pupils, Lieutenant Henry Wagner Halleck (WP 1839). It was entitled *Elements of Military Art and Science, or Course of Instruction in Strategy, Fortifications, Tactics of Battles etc.* (1846). Halleck was a widely read military writer, and his vast knowledge found full expression in his comprehensive book. In the fields of strategy and tactics the book was totally dominated by Jomini, as well as by the work of August Wagner and Archduke Charles.[50]

[48] S. F. Gay de Vernon, *A Treatise on the Science of War and Fortifications . . . to which is Added a Summary of the Principles and Maxims of Grand Tactics and Operations* (2 vols.; New York, 1817); the summary of Jomini's work appears in ii. 385–490; the quotation is from i. v.

[49] On Mahan see Dupuy, *The Story of West Point*, 133–47, 165–72, 195–204; Forman, *West Point*, 58, 82, 87.

[50] For the strategic teaching see esp. *Elements of Military Art and Science* (New York, 1846), 35–54; the recommended bibliography for the strategic section alone includes the theories and histories of Jomini, Charles, Wagner, Rocquancourt, Jacquinot de Presle, Gay de Vernon, Lloyd, Tempelhoff, Grimoard, Fuché, Saint-Cyr, Laverne, Beauvais, Kausler, Gourgaud, Montholon, Napoleon, Foy, Dumas,

In the Napoleonic Club, founded at West Point in 1848, officers met under Mahan's chairmanship to discuss Napoleon's campaigns, largely through the medium of Jomini. One of the most notable participants was George B. McClellan (WP 1846) who thought Jomini was 'the ablest of military writers and the first author in any age who gathered from the campaigns of the great generals the true principles of war'.[51] Another occasional participant may have been Robert E. Lee. His class at West Point (1825) had studied Gay de Vernon as the text for the subject of Grand Tactics, one of the five military subjects taught at the academy. When he became the superintendent of the academy in 1852, his small private library included Jomini's *Précis de l'art de la guerre* in the original French.[52] Halleck, McClellan, and possibly also Thomas J. (Stonewall) Jackson visited Jomini in Europe.[53] E. T. Hitchcock and P. G. T. Beauregard were his disciples. William T. Sherman said in 1862 that 'should any officer . . . be ignorant of his tactics, regulations or even the principles of the art of war (Mahan and Jomini), it would be a lasting disgrace'.[54] All the translations of Jomini's major works into English were done in America. Indeed, and this had not been fully recognized, in no other country was Jomini translated so extensively. The *Précis* was translated (badly) in 1854. It served as the official text of a new course, the 'Theory and Practice of Strategy and Grand Tactics', introduced into West Point in 1860.[55] The Civil War produced not only a new, better translation of the *Précis* but also full translations of Jomini's multi-volume *Traité des grandes opérations militaires* (the only one

Ségur, Pelet, Koch, Clausewitz, Guibert, Thiers, and Napier (p. 58–60); compare with the bibliographical introduction to Jomini, *Summary of the Art of War* (New York, 1854), 14–21.

[51] McClellan, 'Jomini', in *The Galaxy*, 7 (1869), 874–88, cited in David Donald, 'Refighting the Civil War', in his *Lincoln Reconsidered* (New York, 1956), 89, 194.

[52] For the curriculum and for Lee's private library and borrowing-list from the academy's library, see Douglas S. Freeman's thoroughly documented *R. E. Lee* (4 vols.; New York, 1934), i. 76–7, 352–3, 358. Freeman is right in pointing out that 'Grand Tactics' included what has later been called strategy; this was still the French usage in the early nineteenth century, before the term 'strategy' was fully accepted from the German (Gat, *Enlightenment to Clausewitz*, 40–2, 114). The currently accepted opinion that no 'strategy' at all was taught in the academy is, therefore, based on a misunderstanding. Also see Eben Swift, 'The Military Education of Robert E. Lee', *Virginia Magazine of History and Biography*, 35 (1927), 97–108; Donald, 'Refighting the Civil War', 88–9.

[53] Swift, 'The Military Education of Robert E. Lee', 151.

[54] Donald, 'Refighting the Civil War', 90.   [55] Ibid. 89.

existing in any language) and of *Vie politique et militaire de Napoléon*, the latter done by Halleck himself, the Union's general in chief.[56]

All this is known well enough because of the climatic events that followed. The Civil War was conducted by West Pointers, and it has justly been said that generals on both sides went into the war with a sword in one hand and Jomini's *Summary of the Art of War* in the other.[57] Opinion regarding the exact nature of both Jomini's teaching and influence had undergone some noticeable changes, however. Strangely enough, while early commentators had a good grasp of what Jomini stood for and a balanced picture of his influence, later ones seemed no longer to have either. The reason for this is not difficult to trace; as Clausewitz was reconquering the West from the 1950s, interpretations reflected Jomini's deteriorating image.

To understand what Jomini's teaching was, it must not be forgotten that he won fame by successfully schematizing Frederickian and Napoleonic warfare. He emphasized initiative, aggressive conduct, mobility, and concentration of force, and regarded the destruction of the enemy army as the principal aim of military operations. This was to be achieved either by manœuvring against his rear and cutting off his lines of operations and retreat or, if the enemy divided his forces, by operating from a central position and crushing each of these fractions separately. Excellent studies regarding Jomini's influence in America perceived this clearly.[58] However, from the late 1950s a new note crept in. Since it was known that Clausewitz opposed Jomini, military historians could no longer regard Jomini as an adequate interpreter of Napoleon. It was not enough that he was regarded as too deeply rooted in the eighteenth century and thus too moderate and remote from the idea of the nation-in-arms; the tendency to distinguish clearly (and unfavourably) between Clausewitz and Jomini has now somehow

---

[56] Jomini, *Summary of the Art of War* (New York, 1854), trans. by Maj. O. F. Winship and Lieut. E. E. McLean; *The Art of War* (Philadelphia, 1862), trans. by Captain G. W. Mendell and Lieutenant W. P. Craighill; *Treatise on Grand Military Operations* (2 vols.; New York, 1865), trans. by Col. S. B. Holabird; *Life of Napoleon* (4 vols.; New York, 1864), trans. by Major-General H. W. Halleck.

[57] J. D. Hittle's introduction to *Jomini and his Summary of the Art of War* (Harrisburg, Pa., 1947), 2.

[58] Swift, 'The Military Education of Robert E. Lee', esp. 150–4; Donald, 'Refighting the Civil War'. Also see my *Enlightenment to Clausewitz*, esp. 131–5.

given rise to the erroneous notion that the latter even failed to grasp the essence of Napoleonic strategy and regarded the occupation of territory rather than the enemy army as the object of military operations.[59] Clausewitz's own writings make clear that this was totally untrue. What ever shortcomings he found in Jomini, Clausewitz thought his great merit was that, in contrast to his predecessors in the eighteenth century (Lloyd, Bülow, Archduke Charles, etc.), he maintained that 'the engagement is the only effective means in war'.[60] Indeed, from the early 1970s, a much-called-for correction finally redressed the picture.[61]

The same tendency also found expression in the assessments of Jomini's influence on the conduct of the Civil War generals, an influence which everyone agrees existed. Early interpreters were aware of the different aspects of the matter inherent in the nature of Jomini's theories. They noted the Jominian leading theme behind the classical campaigns of central position and interior lines masterminded by Lee in 1862; one was brilliantly carried out by Stonewall Jackson in the Shenandoah Valley, and another was conducted by Lee himself against the armies of McClellan and Pope, culminating in the great enveloping battle of the Second Manassas.[62] On the other hand, the shortcomings of Jomini's teaching were also clearly pointed out. Changing circumstances were everywhere rendering parts of what Jomini had regarded as a universal theory of war obsolete. The rifle was transforming tactics,

[59] A series of military historians seem to have followed in each other's footsteps here; see esp. T. Harry Williams, 'The Military Leadership of North and South', in D. Donald (ed.), *Why the North Won the Civil War* (Baton Rouge, La., 1960), 28–47, esp. 30; Stephen E. Ambrose, *Halleck: Lincoln's Chief of Staff* (Baton Rouge, La., 1962), esp. 5–7; John R. Elting, 'Jomini: Disciple of Napoleon', *Military Affairs*, 28 (1964), 17–26, which is otherwise the best biographical study of Jomini in English; Weigley, *The American Way of War: A History of United States Military Strategy and Policy* (London, 1973), 82–3, 84, 88.

[60] Carl von Clausewitz, *On War*, trans. Michael Howard and Peter Paret, (Princeton, NJ, 1976), ii. 2, 136.

[61] The turning-point was Archer Jones, 'Jomini and the Strategy of the American Civil War: A Reinterpretation', *Military Affairs*, 34 (1970), 127–31; further elaborated in Jones and Thomas L. Connelly, *The Politics of Command, Factions and Ideas in Confederate Strategy* (Baton Rouge, La., 1973), esp. 6–30; and Jones and Herman Hattaway, *How the North Won* (London, 1983), esp. 12–14, 21–4. Also see Joseph L. Harsh, 'Battlesword and Rapier: Clausewitz, Jomini and the American Civil War', *Military Affairs*, 38 (1974), 133–8. T. H. Williams in effect admitted the mistake in 'The Return to Jomini: Some Thoughts on Recent Civil War Writing', ibid. 39 (1975), 204–6.

[62] Swift, 'The Military Education of Robert E. Lee'; Donald, 'Refighting the Civil War', 91–5.

and, more fatal to Jomini, the ability to transport troops quickly by railway over vast distances was calling into question the advantage of the interior lines in strategy.[63] Moltke's campaigns of 1866 and 1870–1 were later to prove this decisively, but the new developments were still difficult for Jomini's disciples in North America to grasp. Lincoln, no professional soldier, intuitively reproduced the Allies' strategy against Napoleon in 1813, suggesting that the North could best deny the initiative to the enemy and make effective use of its own numerical superiority by launching a closely co-ordinated concentric attack on the whole periphery of the South. But Halleck was dismissive: 'To operate on exterior lines against an enemy occupying a central position will fail, as it has always failed, in ninety-nine cases out of a hundred. It is condemned by every military authority I have ever read.'[64]

Indeed, later commentators tended to associate Halleck's and McClellan's indecisiveness with Jominian pedantry. At the same time, since Jomini had now come to be seen as moderate and as one who had regarded the occupation of territories rather than the destruction of the enemy army as the object of operations, his reputation as the inspiration behind the crushing campaigns of the brilliant generals of the Confederacy became problematic. As a result, several historians tied themselves in some curious knots. One stated that Jomini had regarded the occupation of territory as the object of operations, but later argued that the South won its initial successes through the application of Jominian doctrines, which led to a decisive battle.[65] Another historian purged Jomini altogether of responsibility for Confederate strategy, leaving him to share indirect responsibility only for the Union's blunders. While arguing that Civil War generals on all sides, and especially Lee, were obsessed with the climactic battle, he attributed this to the Napoleonic model, forgetting that he himself maintained that it had been predominantly through the medium of Jomini that these generals had studied Napoleon.[66]

In truth, Jomini's was a striking interpretation of Napoleonic

[63] Donald, 'Refighting the Civil War', 96–7.
[64] *The Collected Works of Abraham Lincoln*, ed. Roy P. Basler (New Brunswick, 1953), v. 98–9; *The War of the Rebellion: A Compilation of the Official Records of the Union and Confederate Armies* (Washington, DC, 1880–1901), Series One, xi, pt. 2, 497; cited by Weigley, *The American Way of War*, 493.
[65] Williams, 'The Military Leadership of North and South', 30, 38.
[66] Weigley, *The American Way of War*, 82–3, 92–127.

generalship, and without attributing to the Civil War generals excessive bookishness or theoretical preoccupation, one can say that, on both sides, they could only operate—for better or for worse—on the basis of the strategic concepts which they had acquired in the course of their common education. Significantly, the only notable exception was the very mediocre student at West Point (1843) who had resigned from the army in 1854. When asked by a young officer about Jomini after he had become famous, Grant answered that he had never paid him much attention. 'The art of war', he said, 'is simple enough; find out where your enemy is, get at him as soon as you can, strike at him as hard as you can, and keep moving on.'[67]

In their handling of the French army, the returning Bourbons faced their usual dilemma. They had to uproot the legacy of the Revolution and Empire in one of the most typical and glorious institutions of those regimes, while accommodating some of their achievements and avoiding an all-out confrontation with their wide circles of sympathizers and beneficiaries. Here too, the result was an uneasy compromise which brought together Napoleonic veterans and returning *émigrés*, and incorporated limited conscription, and (until 1824) a reserve, with long-service army. Codified in the Saint-Cyr Law of 1818, these were the institutional principles of the French army from the Restoration throughout the period of the July Monarchy and Second Empire.

Reaffirmed by the Soult Law of 1832, these principles now reflected the satisfaction of the middle classes with the professional army, which enabled them to exempt their sons from military service by finding replacements, and whose base was limited enough to prevent it from becoming an instrument of popular revolution. Correspondingly, the prevailing mood in the army itself changed from widely held Bonapartist sympathies to detached conservatism. When called upon to do so, it could be relied on to crush radical disturbances, from the ominous silk-weavers insurrection in Lyons in 1831 to the great June 1848 uprising in Paris. The army too came to prefer long-term service as a remedy for notoriously undisciplined character of the French conscript.[68]

---

[67] Louis A. Coolidge, *Ulysses S. Grant* (Boston, 1922), 54.
[68] See J. Monteilhet, *Les Institutions militaires de la France (1814–1924)* (Paris, 1926), ch. 1; Raoul Girardet, *La Société militaire dans la France contemporaine*,

These principles of organization also matched the limited scope of the army's military tasks. During the Restoration the army was employed in the two semi-political interventions in Spain (1823) and Greece (1827), and began the long conquest and pacification of Algeria (1830). Despite some sabre-rattling over the Eastern Question in 1840, Louis-Philippe recoiled from any military confrontation with a highly suspicious Europe. Only Napoleon III's revisionist and opportunist politics resulted − apart from world-wide colonial adventures − in two large-scale, but strictly contained wars, in Crimea (1854–1856) and Lombardy (1859), against major European powers.

Thus there was little in the military experience of post-Revolutionary France to match its glorious past. Nor did the poor living-conditions, dull routine, and social as well as cultural isolation of the French officer-corps, many members of which came from a very humble background, provide much intellectual stimulation.[69] During the Restoration, Napoleon's retired marshals and generals satisfied the public's nostalgic thirst for an account of the nation's and their own glorious days in the most popular literary genre of the Romantic period—history. Their memoirs and such theoretical works as Marshal Marmont's *De l'esprit des institutions militaires* (1846) reflected the prevailing synthesis of the Enlightenment's conception of military theory and Napoleonic strategy.[70] There was, however, very little that was original and significant in French military thinking during the July Monarchy and Second Empire. Colonial experience could produce anti-guerilla doctrines, such as those of Marshal Bugeaud, the veteran of

---

1815–1939 (Paris, 1953), pt. one; Pierre Chalmin, *L'Officier français de 1815 à 1870* (Paris, 1957); Douglas Porch, *Army and Revolution; France 1815–1848* (London, 1974). For a brief account see Best, *War and Society in Revolutionary Europe*, 215–222.

[69] See previous note and William Serman, *Les Origines des officiers français 1848–1870* (Paris, 1979).

[70] For a characteristic popular example see Gouvion Saint-Cyr, *Mémoires pour servir à l'histoire militaire sous le directoire, le consulat et l'empire* (4 vols.; Paris, 1831), esp. the foreword and the introductory essay: 'Pensée sur la guerre'. Marmont, *De l'esprit des institutions militaires* (Paris, 1846), discusses the '*positivist* principles of war' (my italics) and their application; as mentioned, Jomini is often deliberately ignored. For an overview of authors and works see P. G. Griffith, *Military Thought in the French Army, 1815–1851* (Manchester, 1989), 57–62; E. Guillon, *Nos écrivains militaires* (2 vols.; Paris, 1898), ii. 142–236; and E. Carrias, *La Pensée militaire française* (Paris, 1960), 226–62.

the Peninsula and conquerer of Algeria.[71] The conduct of operations in relatively small and isolated forces in a hostile environment reinforced the tendency of the French army to promote cohesion and morale as the paramount military qualities.[72] But the use of light, independent, mobile units against irregulars was scarcely relevant—indeed was probably downright alien—to the needs of a large-scale European war.

Thus, when the army under the Second Empire regained some of its former glory and cultivated a professional reputation and heroic mystique—built up outside the fortifications of Sebastopol and on the battlefields of Magenta and Solferino—it did so with much bravery, panache, and *esprit de corps*. But equally characteristic was the administrative and logistic chaos, influenced by long experience of improvisation and leading to an almost ideological spirit of contempt for orderly staff-work, as well as a lack of training in it. Only the emergence of a major challenge to French military supremacy in Europe introduced a new sense of alarm and apprehension into the military establishment and generated considerable intellectual ferment.

Prussia was the only one of Napoleon's rivals to adopt the principle of the nation-in-arms after her defeat in 1806 and to retain it after 1815. It was the revival of this principle later on that made possible the decisive victory of her mass armies over the Austrians in 1866. In the early 1860s the King of Prussia transformed the main legacy of this experiment, the independent Landwehr militia, which had been both politically and militarily unreliable, into a mere second-line reserve of a large army of short-term universal conscription. In a remarkable reversal of political fronts between king and parliament, the autocratic ruler thus created a well-trained and disciplined national army of unprecedented size. After the Prussian victory of 1866, the newly created North German Confederation possessed about one and a half times as many front-line troops and double the overall number of men in arms as the considerably more populous France. This was the fundamental problem that the French army had to confront.

In late 1866 Napoleon III, concerned by these developments, set

---

[71] H. D'Ideville, *Memoirs of Marshal Bugeaud, From his Private Correspondence and Original Documents* (2 vols.; London, 1884); A. T. Sullivan, *Thomas-Robert Bugeaud* (Hamden, Conn., 1983).
[72] See Griffith, *Military Thought in the French Army*, 117–22.

a one-million-man target for the French army, in order to match the estimated strength of the Prussians. However, the idea of adopting the Prussian military system was rejected by most of the emperor's advisers on both military and political grounds. The army had got used to believing that universal short-term conscription with a large reserve could only create half-trained mobs. Civilians objected to universal conscription as disruptive of their way of life and socially dangerous. In early 1868 a compromise measure was carried through the Corps législatif by Marshal Niel, Napoleon's newly appointed Minister of War. It maintained the principle of a long-service regular army based on limited conscription, but established a first-line reserve and a second-line militia (the Garde mobile) which, unlike their German counterparts, were mostly composed of those exempted from conscription and were therefore almost totally untrained. Thus, although the basis of the regular army itself was expanded and the target of one million men in arms was secured on paper, the new reserve and militia were militarily useless. Both military and civil authorities regarded them with contempt and made sure they would never materialize.

The public controversy over the problem of defence was fuelled by General Trochu's best-selling book *L'Armée française en 1867*, based on the confidential recommendations of a military commission set up by the emperor, of which the author was a member. Trochu was blunt about the army's mystique, sacred traditions, and practices. He argued that in order to meet the new challenge, the army had to expand along the lines put forward by Niel, and reform thoroughly its administration, military education, system of promotion, and tactics.[73]

The debate over the two conflicting forms of military-social institutions was complicated by a tactical element. From the middle of the century, the paramount military question preoccupying soldiers all over Europe was the tactical significance of the new, accurate, long-range rifle. Replacing the smooth-bore musket and widely used for the first time in the Crimean War, the rifle threatened to revolutionize tactics by calling into question the feasibility of mass charges, carried out by dense infantry- and

---

[73] Trochu, *L'Armée francaise en 1867* (20th edn., Paris 1870); Michael E. Howard, *The Franco-Prussian War* (London, 1961), ch. 1; also see Lynn M. Case, *French Opinion On War and Diplomacy during the Second Empire* (Philadelphia, 1954).

cavalry-formations. The war of 1866 introduced a new factor into the problem and, in this respect too, was the cause of much excitement in France. The Prussians employed a breech-loader, the 'needle-gun', which was given much of the credit for their success. The French responded quickly by adopting an even more advanced breech-loader, the *chassepot*.

Great military literature has always been produced in response to great challenges and stimuli, whether military, intellectual, or other. The acute challenge to the tradition and ethos of French professionalism, the controversies surrounding the proposed reform of the French military system, and the problem of the modern battlefield created a more than adequate stimulus. They drove a rather obscure but highly perceptive colonel, who as a junior officer had distinguished himself under Trochu in the Crimea, to explore the essence of fighting-performance. The result was *Battle Studies*, one of the most fascinating and original works on military affairs ever to be written, and widely acclaimed as a classic. As it happens, however, the book has received remarkably little serious scholarly attention and attracted no full-length study. Much about its origins and influence has thus remained either unrecognized or shrouded in myth, and deserves closer scrutiny.

The little we know about the man Charles-Jean-Jacques-Joseph Ardant du Picq is derived from army records and from a short biographical letter that his brother was requested to write for the second edition of his works. Ardant du Picq was born in 1821 and graduated from Saint-Cyr in 1844. He fought in the Crimea, where he was taken prisoner while storming the central bastion at Sebastopol. He then took part in the campaigns in Syria (1860–1) and Algeria (1864–6), rising steadily in rank and receiving the customary decorations and medals. He was likeable and was respected as an honest man of independent mind. He was mortally wounded while leading his regiment near Metz in the opening stage of the Franco-Prussian War.[74]

The man's writings are more enlightening than this sketch of a rather undistinguished life-story. Versed in modern, predominantly French, military literature, du Picq cites Montecuccoli, Folard, de Saxe, Guibert, Napoleon, Jomini, Saint-Cyr, Bismark (the military

[74] Introductory material to Ardant du Picq, *Battle Studies* (Harrisburg, Pa., 1947; 1st edn. New York, 1921; based on the 2nd edn. of *Études sur le combat*, ed. Ernest Judet), 25–31.

writer), Decker, Thiers, and Bugeaud. Like all proponents of the current of military thought that had its roots in the Enlightenment, he sought to advance military science. However, both his mode of thinking and his concerns were quite different and novel. He did not share the traditional preoccupation with the conduct of grand operations. Finding military theory too mechanistic, materialistic, and dominated by mathematical reasoning,[75] he quoted Marshal de Saxe's famous saying that the human heart was the starting-point of all matters pertaining to war.[76] Fighting-performance, he believed, was rooted in the most elementary instincts of man's individual and group psychology.

The human heart is the constant element in war: 'Centuries have not changed human nature . . . at bottom there is always found the same man.'[77] After the Romantic onslaught on the philosophers of the eighteenth century, du Picq needs no reminder of the varied particular manifestations of human nature, to which he is ever attentive; and in the age of progress he is fully aware of historical change: ·

The art of war is subjected to many modifications by industrial and scientific progress. But one thing does not change, the heart of man.[78]

I have heard philosophers reproached for studying too exclusively man in general and neglecting the race, the country, the era, so that their studies of him offer little of real social or political value. [However] the opposite criticism can be made of military men of all countries. . . . They fail to consider as a factor in the problem man confronted by danger.[79]

It was du Picq's belief that military theorists not only missed the vital element in war but also neglected the really important data in their preoccupation with grand strategies. 'The smallest detail, taken from an actual incident in war,' he wrote, 'is more instructive for me, a soldier, than all the Thiers and Jominis in the world'; more instructive than 'the plans and general conduct of the campaign of the greatest captain'.[80] Indeed, he believed that ground-level information about actual fighting constituted the basis for a truly scientific study of war.

Commentators have noted but never dwelt on du Picq's

---

[75] *Battle Studies*, 40, 50, 192.   [76] Ibid. 39.
[77] Ibid. 39–40.   [78] Ibid. 109.
[79] Ibid.   [80] Ibid. 5, 7.

scientism.[81] Yet it constitutes a major source of his inspiration. His was not the enthusiastic but loose theoretical ideal of the eighteenth century but the rigorous programme and research-method of positivism, the dominating intellectual current during the Second Empire.[82] According to du Picq, military science was to be produced through a careful analysis of the vast data of experience, systematically gathered:

From a series of true accounts there should emanate an ensemble of characteristic details which in themselves are very apt to show in a striking, irrefutable way what was necessarily and forcibly taking place at such and such a moment of an action in war. Take the estimate of the soldier obtained in this manner to serve as a base for what might possibly be a rational method of fighting. It will put us on guard against *a priori* school methods.[83]

Du Picq insisted that copious evidence regarding the soldier's real behaviour in the past is the key to his conduct in the future.[84] This would produce 'prescribed tactics', which, while not being too dogmatic, would lay down with mathematical logic 'some clearly defined rules, established by experience' to serve as a guiding doctrine.[85] Against the notorious gulf between theory and practice in war which existed in his day, he wrote, 'let us gather carefully the lessons of . . . experience, remembering *Bacon's* saying, "Experience excels science".'[86]

In his search for primary data on the fundamental characteristics of fighting man, du Picq first went to Antiquity, where 'battle was simple and clear', and where, in the case-studies of Cannae and Parasalus, he believed he could trust 'the clear presentation of Polybius, who obtained his information from the fugitives of Cannae', and 'the impassive clearness of Caesar in describing the art of war'.[87] The result was the pamphlet *Étude du combat d'après*

---

[81] See almost the only scholarly article on du Picq, Stefan Possony's half of 'Du Picq and Foch: The French School', in E. Earle (ed.), *Makers of Modern Strategy* (Princeton, NJ, 1943), 208.

[82] Throughout this chapter the term positivism is used in its broadest sense— almost interchangeably with scientism—rather than in the stricter one as the teaching of Auguste Comte. Two good works in English are: D. G. Charlton, *Positivist Thought in France during the Second Empire 1852–1870* (Oxford, 1959); and W. M. Simon, *European Positivism in the Nineteenth Century* (New York, 1963).   [83] *Battle Studies*, 7–8.

[84] Ibid. 103–4.   [85] ibid. 138–40.
[86] Ibid. 260; my italics.   [87] Ibid. 39, 55.

l'antique, 'Ancient Battle', completed in 1868 and distributed privately. He then addressed himself to modern battle, in a study which he did not live to finish. Here he had no intention of relying on 'the accounts of historians alone'. In all but a very few cases, he wrote, historians 'show the action of troop units only in a general way. Action in detail and the individual action of the soldier remain enveloped in a cloud of dust, in narratives as in reality.'[88] Historians tend to impose order upon the chaos of war, and their heroic rhetoric is often misleading as to man's true behaviour in battle. Fortunately, argued du Picq, for modern battle we possess another source of information, incomparable in wealth—the first-hand experience of soldiers. For the man who advocated Baconian methods—which had been canonized in D'Alembert's famous introduction to the *Grande encyclopédie* and had ever since been the archetypal model for positivist thought—the problem was how to get to this source, pose the right questions, and have the findings gathered and assessed on a grand scale.

In 1868 du Picq composed a highly detailed questionnaire and had it distributed among his fellow officers of all ranks. This striking example of positivist behavioural research—which ended with the above-quoted warning against a priori school methods—is worth quoting at some length. In a copy intended for the commanding general at Limoges, one reads:

Concerning a regiment, a battalion, a company, a squad, it is interesting to know: The disposition taken to meet the enemy or the order of the march towards them. What becomes of this disposition or this march order under the isolated or combined influences of accidents of the terrain and the approach of danger?
Is this order changed or is it continued in force when approaching the enemy?
What becomes of it upon arriving within the range of the guns, within the range of bullets?
At what distance is a voluntary or an ordered disposition taken before starting operations for commencing fire, for charging, or both?
How did the fight start? How about the firing? How did the men adapt themselves? (This may be learned from the results: So many bullets fired, so many men shot down—when such data are available.) How was the charge made? At what distance did the enemy flee before it? At what distance did the charge fall back before the fire or the good order or good dispositions

[88] Ibid. 103.

of the enemy, or before such and such a movement of the enemy? What did it cost? What can be said about all these with reference to the enemy? The behaviour, i.e. the order, the disorder, the shouts, the silence, the confusion, the calmness of the officers and men whether with us or with the enemy, before, during, or after the combat?
How has the soldier been controlled and directed during the action? At what instance has he had a tendency to quit the line in order to remain behind or to rush ahead?
At what moment, if the control were escaping from the leader's hands, has it no longer been possible to exercise it?
At what instant has this control escaped from the battalion commander? When from the captain, the section leader, the squad leader? At what time, in short, if such a thing did take place, was there but a disordered impulse, whether to the front or to the rear carrying along pell-mell with it both the leaders and men?
Where and when did the halt take place?
Where and when were the leaders able to resume command of the men?
At what moments before, during, or after the day, was the battalion roll-call made? The results of these roll-calls?
How many dead, how many wounded on the one side and on the other; the kind of wounds of the officers, non commissioned officers, corporals, privates, etc. etc.[89]

Replies were slow in coming, but this, as du Picq's brother remarks, was due to indifference rather than to ill will. However, from mid-1868 to early 1869, du Picq did receive a few of the accounts he was seeking. These were based on personal experience on the battlefields of the Second Empire and some of them proved to be of considerable interest.[90] He continued to seek out first-hand information among his comrades-in-arms, but it would be an exaggeration to say that this was absolutely essential for him. Positivist notions aside, his mind had, in fact, long been made up. Until the outbreak of the war of 1870, he immersed himself in the writing of a 'Study on Battle', compiled posthumously under the title 'Modern Battle'. Together with 'Ancient Battle', it comprises a unity of supreme stylistic beauty, perceptive power and originality.

---

[89] *Battle Studies*, 5–7.
[90] Introductory material to *Battle Studies*, pp. xvi–xvii, 28; for extracts from some of the most detailed and interesting accounts, including du Picq's re-questioning, which were kept by du Picq's family, see ibid. 263–273. Of course du Picq composed the questionnaire for the study of modern battle in 1868, after finishing 'Ancient Battle', and not the other way around, as Possony's confused chronology seems to suggest: 'Du Picq and Foch', in Earle (ed.), *Makers of Modern Strategy*, 209.

'Man does not enter battle to fight but for victory. He does everything that he can to avoid the first and obtain the second.'[91] This is du Picq's main thesis. Man is dominated by the instinct of self-preservation, whose agent is fear. Therefore, he may be induced or forced to fight for something, but fighting itself is unnatural to him.

Primitive man almost never fights face to face. He ambushes in order to kill his enemy in a moment of surprise. If attacked, he flees. The Arabs in Algeria provide a clear example of this.[92] It is only civilized societies that produce long-drawn-out battles. They do so by imposing collective duty and cohesive organization on human nature. This is the function of discipline and tactics. They can never overcome human nature, and mass formations are always liable to flee in panic; but the better conceived they are, the better are the results.[93]

The Greeks achieved considerable results in this respect, but in Antiquity it was the Romans who excelled all others. They showed profound understanding of morale, combining rigorous discipline with masterly tactics. The Greek phalanx was a mass formation in deep order, based on the notion that the rear ranks would push the front ones into battle and replace the casualties. Yet the truth of the matter was that, placed so close to the sounds and sights of battle, the rear ranks were all-too-exposed to the terrible psychological exhaustion of the face-to-face clash, which man can stand only to a very limited extent. Thus, if something went wrong, they were the first to fall back. Conversely, the Romans protected their reserves against the tremendous moral fatigue of the front line by placing them at a sufficient distance from the turmoil of battle. The legion was formed in three separate lines, with the veteran troops waiting calmly in the rear. Detached in this way, they were able to counter any adverse development in the front rather than be engulfed in it themselves.[94]

Fighting in a disciplined formation was the secret of the Greek and Roman victories over the Asiatic hordes and of the Romans' victories over the fearful Gauls and Germans, far more warlike than themselves and greatly superior in number. Living before the development of the critical study of ancient military sources that

91 *Battle Studies*, 43, 94.   92 Ibid. 43.
93 Ibid. 47–9.   94 Ibid. 50–4.

was to be rigorously undertaken by Delbrück—du Picq was unaware of the often wildly inaccurate and partisan nature of the numbers given by the ancient accounts, even though he was remarkably sceptical of the modern ones.[95] Thus he was convinced that ancient battle strikingly demonstrated that collective cohesion by far outweighed not only individual valour but also great numerical superiority. The Romans won because in a disciplined formation man's natural aversion to fighting was counterbalanced by the fact that he was both physically and morally protected by his fellows.

Hence the nature of ancient battle. In the clash, says du Picq, the soldiers took great care not to get separated from their friends. The front lines therefore very rarely mixed, and casualties at this stage were not heavy. Only a moral collapse could really cause an orderly formation to fall apart. This was why a surprise attack, especially against the flank or rear of an army, had always been such a decisive act, regardless of its actual strength. It created terror and, therefore, disintegration. The encircled Romans in Cannae, almost double the number of their Punic enemies, put down their weapons only for that reason.[96] There are, says du Picq, many examples of armies who swore to conquer or perish, but very few of them kept their oath. Leonidas' three hundred at Thermopylae were immortalized for a good reason. There is a moment when horror prevails, discipline and collective unity break down, and the army dissolves into a terrified mob running for its life.[97] It is only at that stage, when the army disintegrates and during the pursuit, that the real killing occurs. This was why in ancient battles the vanquished suffered casualties much greater than the victor, whose losses were usually light. In turn, this was one of the reasons for the unbeatable fighting-spirit of troops with long experience of triumph; they knew they were not only invincible but also practically invulnerable.[98]

---

[95] *Battle Studies*, 134.
[96] Ibid. 81–5.   [97] Ibid. 94–5.
[98] Ibid. 99, 113. Du Picq's analysis remarkably anticipated Victor D. Hanson's insightful *The Western Way of Warfare: Infantry Tactics in Classical Greece* (Oxford, 1990); indeed, his approach anticipated the whole modern school of writers who, like S. L. A. Marshall and John Keegan, concentrated on the experience of battle and on individual and group psychology. See Roger J. Spiller, 'S. L. A. Marshall and the Ratio of Fire', *RUSI Journal* (1988), 63–71; incidentally, this article demonstrates that in Marshall's case too his ideas predated his famous researches, whose scientific character and whose conclusions he to a large extent fabricated.

The lessons of ancient battle supported the dominating legacy of the African school in the French army, which believed it beat off hordes of savages by force of superior cohesion, discipline, and tactics.[99] Indeed, for du Picq, ancient battle was only a means to reveal man's nature and the root causes that made him fight in spite of it. The purpose of the work was to illuminate the study of modern tactics, although modern battle was considerably different from the ancient type; the introduction and perfection of firearms had brought some fundamental changes. Du Picq called attention to the highly conspicuous fact that, although firearms were much deadlier than the weapons of Antiquity, casualties had, proportionately, diminished. Since 'man is capable of standing only before a certain amount of terror', he kept himself at a distance. Battle was now waged from afar. According to du Picq, firearms had actually given man a choice to act in accordance with his nature and avoid a face-to-face encounter as far as he possibly could.[100] Furthermore, since the bullet was blind to bravery, the victors now also suffered heavily and had lost what was previously one of the major stimuli of their moral strength. At the same time, with the increased distance between the opposing forces, breaking contact and retreating had become easier and a greater temptation.[101] Enforcing discipline, keeping the dispersed men under control, and making them fight had become more difficult than ever.

The urgent problem now was to discover what tactics were needed in the era of the accurate and long-range rifled breech-loaders such as the Prussian 'needle gun' and the French *chassepot*. It was du Picq's contention that the days of the dense formation were over. Taking up the great doctrinal controversy of the eighteenth century regarding the *ordre profond* and the *ordre mince*, du Picq maintained that the belief in the shock power of the column had always been mythical and mechanistic. Physical shock, claimed du Picq, was only a word, since real contact and the glorified bayonet-charge to the end almost never happened. The effect of a charging column was predominantly moral and was successful only against a wavering enemy who disintegrated because he could not bear face-to-face fighting. When the defenders kept calm and steady, as the British did in the Peninsula, it was the

[99] Griffith, *Military Thought in the French Army*, 117–22.
[100] *Battle Studies*, 112–14.
[101] Ibid. 99–100, 113.

attackers' turn to waver and retreat before actual contact was made.[102] With the modern rifled breech-loader, claimed du Picq, the employment of the deep formation was finally doomed. So also was the prevailing two-men-deep line, using the inherently inaccurate fire-by-command. In its place, the French army ought to adopt an open formation. Most of the soldiers ought to disperse and operate in a single loose line of skirmishers, leaving large intervals between them, taking advantage of the terrain, and using aimed fire at will. Strong reserves ought to be kept concentrated behind, and the easy-to-control column should be used only for manœuvring.[103] Rapid-firing arms had given the advantage to the *defensive* and rendered an advance under fire almost impossible: 'This is so evident that only a madman could dispute it.' (So much for Foch's alleged mentor.) For the attack, the army should look for the right opportunity and try to outflank the enemy or manœuvre him out of his position.[104] These highly perceptive insights were very similar both to Moltke's trend of thought from the late 1850s and to the actual tactics employed by the Prussians after their initial costly attacks on French defensive positions in the early battles of the war of 1870–1.

The great enigma that remained was whether men, when faced with the horrors of the modern battlefield and dispersed out of effective control, would be willing or could be made to fight at all. According to du Picq, many were in effect already hiding inside the battlefield. What was the value of an army 200,000 strong, if only half that number were fighting and the other half disappeared in a hundred ways? It was better to have 100,000 men who could be counted upon. Gideon, wrote du Picq, preferred the three hundred he knew would fight to the thirty thousand he sent home. It was Napoleon who had created the false theory of the 'big battalions', and he was the one responsible for the modern preoccupation with numbers. In modern battle, more than ever before, one needs morally reliable troops, and these, said du Picq, were created only by discipline, training, and *esprit de corps*, welded by experience.[105]

---

[102] *Battle Studies*, 143–55.

[103] Ibid. 115, 160–75.

[104] Ibid. 155, 162, 180. Du Picq failed, however, to appreciate the significance of the challenge facing cavalry. He thought that its problem was no bigger than the one facing infantry. Like almost everyone in Europe, he did not believe that the American experience of long-range cavalry-raids was applicable to Europe: ibid. 179–204.   [105] Ibid. 106, 111, 121, 131–3.

As mentioned before, all this was a direct response to the challenge of the Prussian mass armies and to Marshal Niel's controversial reforms. There is no doubt where du Picq's sympathies lay. When finishing 'Ancient Battle', which was based on a largely erroneous evaluation of numbers in Antiquity, he wondered if a small cohesive army might not even in his day gain the upper hand against a larger one.[106] Yet later he effectively became resigned to the idea that France had no choice but to create a large army.[107] The problem was that Niel's compromise reforms were not going to provide her with one. That was what complicated matters in the pre-1870 debate in France. Du Picq shared the almost universal scepticism in the army about the proposed reforms. 'Our projected organization', he wrote, 'will give us four hundred thousand good soldiers. But all our reserves will be without cohesion if they are thrown into this or that organization on the eve of battle.'[108] The 'second portion' of the recruits, serving only for five months before passing over to the reserve, were of dubious military value, while the Garde mobile was practically useless. Neither was at all comparable with the Prussian reserve and Landwehr, and du Picq was quick to point this out. King William's military reforms in Prussia were sound. 'The Prussians conquered at Sadowa with made soldiers, united, accustomed to discipline. Such soldiers can be made in three or four years now.'[109] The Prussian army was a far cry from a shapeless mass. 'An army is not really strong unless it is developed from a social institution.'[110]

From the time of the Enlightenment, every military thinker in France knew that military institutions were very much the product of racial differences and social institutions. In stressing such national characteristics as French enthusiasm and restlessness, British calmness and perseverance, and German flock-like discipline and order, du Picq was reiterating views that were a century old and were prevalent not only in France but all over Europe.[111] His ideas about contemporary developments in European society and politics and their relationship to war were also highly characteristic

---

[106] Ibid. 105–6.
[107] See, for example, ibid. 230.
[108] Ibid. 131; compare, for example, with Marshal Randon, the Minister of War: 'It [the proposed organization] will only give us recruits. What we need is soldiers,' quoted in Howard, *The Franco-Prussian War*, 32.
[109] *Battle Studies*, 217, 131; also 123.
[110] Ibid. 222.   [111] See, for example, ibid. 40, 129, 223.

of the time. Like the proponents of all trends of thought that traced their origins to the Enlightenment, he believed that traditional societies admired military virtues and that aristocracies were by nature bellicose and acted as a spur to war. 'Peace spells death to a nobility,' he wrote. 'Consequently nobles do not desire it, and stir up rivalries among peoples, rivalries which alone can justify their existence as leaders in war, and consequently as leaders in peace.'[112] Like Renan in *La Réforme intellectuelle et morale de la France* (1871), du Picq argued that, with the advance of society and of democratic values, the military spirit was waning: 'This is why the military spirit is dead in France.' Militarily, however, this posed a problem. Surrounded as she was by the still-aristocratic societies of Prussia, Austria, and Russia, France was at a disadvantage.[113] Like many post-Revolutionary Europeans, at whatever end of the political spectrum, du Picq was convinced that the historic trend towards democracy was universal and unstoppable. But unlike Tocqueville or Thiers, he did not look upon it with apprehension; the cause of democracy was in line with French interests. With Revolutionary France defeated,

democracy takes up her work in all European countries. . . . This work is slower but surer than the rapid work of war which, exalting rivalries, halts for a moment the work of democracy within the nations themselves. . . . Thus we are closer to the triumph of democracy than if we had been victors.[114]

It was only a matter of time 'until the Russian, Austrian and Prussian states became democratic societies, like ours'.[115]

In the meantime, the ruling classes struggle to maintain their supremacy. Du Picq's analysis of the decade's events in Prussia is highly perceptive, even if it is not entirely original. 'The King of Prussia and the Prussian nobility, threatened by democracy,' he writes, 'have had to change the passion for equality in their people into a passion for domination over foreign nations. . . . They have succeeded. They are forced to continue with their system.' Using Machiavellian doctrines, they arouse German jingoism.[116] Another great menace is that arch-enemy of the French and of progressive forces all over Europe—tsarism, which had only recently created a

[112] *Battle Studies*, 216–17.   [113] Ibid. 217–21.
[114] Ibid. 218.   [115] Ibid. 221.   [116] Ibid. 217, 221–2.

wave of indignation in the West by ruthlessly suppressing the Polish revolt of 1863; tsarism 'calls for a crusade to drive back Russia and the uncultured Slav race'.[117]

'French democracy rightfully desires to live', writes du Picq.[118] And since France can no longer depend on the military spirit of a social warrior-class, she must constitute her army on the only basis that counts in a commercial society. 'Good pay establishes position in a democracy . . . M. Guizot says "Get rich".' Existing conditions must be changed and the officers and NCOs must be paid well.[119] In addition, the officers must not be troubled with too much study or work. Leisure in peacetime is one of the main attractions of the military profession. While voices in France were urging the emulation of Prussian excellence, du Picq was equally hostile to the idea of intensive military education and to the armchair scholars of the general staff.[120]

The shattering defeat in the war of 1870–1 (in which Ardant du Picq was killed) caused much intellectual ferment among the French military and led to a marked intellectual revival. Contrary to popular belief, however, du Picq's work had no influence on this development. 'Ancient Battle' and 'Modern Battle' were published posthumously in two succesive issues of the *Bulletin de la Réunion des officiers* (1876–7), followed by the first edition in book form of *Études sur le combat* in 1880. However, these obscure publications had no apparent impact. One modern commentator, expecting to find evidence for an opinion everyone takes for granted, has recently noted this with surprise.[121] The simple fact is that du Picq and his work are cited by none of the major exponents of the new French military school which emerged from the mid-1880s around the École supérieure de guerre: Maillard, Cardot, Gilbert, Bonnal, Langlois, and the young Foch. Nor are they mentioned in E. Guillon's extensive survey of French military literature, published in 1898.[122] Reviews of the second edition of *Battle Studies* (1903)

[117] Ibid. 222.   [118] Ibid. 218.
[119] Ibid. 218; this was the common argument in the army; cf. Griffith, *Military Thought in the French Army*, 15.
[120] *Battle Studies*, 219, 212. Howard, *The Franco-Prussian War*, 38. On the French staff-corps, its isolation from, and tense relationship with, the officers of the line see Griffith, *Military Thought in the French Army*.
[121] Joseph Arnold, 'French Tactical Doctrine', 62.
[122] Guillon, *Écrivains militaires*.

leave the unmistakable impression that the work was, for all practical purposes, new.[123] Indeed, du Picq's work became so popular after the publication of the second edition precisely because its emphasis on moral forces could then be enlisted to support the already established and powerful trends which had developed independently over the previous decade and a half.

The reasons for du Picq's sudden success after 1903 will be elaborated in Chapter 3. It is a fact, however, that the second edition of *Battle Studies* had an immediate impact and turned it into a much-admired classic. The book sold five more editions before the outbreak of the First World War. It was cited by everybody from both the older and younger generations of French military authors. Although du Picq had believed that the strength of the defence had been growing, had rejected close formations and bayonet charges, and had never advocated the *offensive à outrance*, his psychological and moral teaching none the less served as one of the main sources of inspiration for the 'Young Turks' in the French general staff, who advocated the offensive in the decade before the war.

However, later commentators and historians—who anyway tended to confuse the views of the 'Young Turks' and the offensive school with their predecessors' Clausewitzian and Napoleonic teachings—erroneously projected du Picq's influence further back to the first, obscure, publication of his work. In 1912 a survey of military literature indicated that the ideas which Cardot had begun to teach at the École de guerre in 1885 had first been mooted by du Picq. No claim for historical links between the two was made, however.[124] All the same, relying on this work, Irvine's pioneering study in English of French military ideas (1942), already strongly associated the appearance of the first edition of *Battle Studies* in 1880 with the emergence of the new wave in French military thinking in the mid-1880s.[125] This notion has been widely accepted ever since, even though no evidence has ever been produced. It is easy to understand why it grew and took hold. Both the

[123] See, for example, Pierre Lehautcourt, 'Le Colonel Ardant du Picq', *La Revue de Paris* (May–June 1904), 347–66.

[124] Jean Dany, 'La Littérature militaire d'aujourd'hui', ibid. (Mar.–Apr. 1912), 612.

[125] Dallas Irvine, 'The French Discovery of Clausewitz and Napoleon', *Journal of the American Military Institute*, 4 (1942), 151.

chronological proximity and the obvious similarity between Clausewitz's and du Picq's emphasis on morale made the mistake almost natural.

The 'du Picq connection' became particularly significant and interesting in relation to Ferdinand Foch. As we shall see, Foch's military thinking was formed during his professorship at the École de guerre (1894–1900) and was composed totally of the exciting ideas his older and more senior colleagues had developed in the school in the decade before his arrival. However, Foch was the only member of that remarkable group of professors not to have reached retirement age yet when the First World War broke out. Thus, because of his subsequent career, his pre-1914 role was blown out of proportion and became the subject of great interest. It was the naïve and enthusiastic translators and editors of the American edition of *Battle Studies* (1921) who presented du Picq as the spiritual mentor of the new French school headed by Marshal Foch, who had just led the Allies to victory in the Great War. They solicited an introductory congratulatory letter from Foch, which was in fact very brief and formal and, furthermore, mentioned absolutely no debt to du Picq.[126] Still, the image they created was accepted—and received a scholarly stamp, from E. M. Earle's authoritative and widely read *Makers of Modern Strategy* (1943), which carelessly, though with more restraint, coupled du Picq and Foch together as the 'French school'.[127] The false impression was again created mainly by means of strong insinuations, because no evidence existed. But there was also the casual remark by du Picq's American editors, anxious to stress his importance, that his book was referred to in such works as Foch's famous *The Principles of War*, translated into English the year before. In fact no such reference exists. Foch, the great name-dropper, cites everyone except du Picq.[128] His book, published in 1903, comprised the lectures he had delivered at the École de guerre a few years earlier, when practically no one knew of du Picq.

Indeed, the origins of the French school, including Foch's

---

[126] Frank Simonds, Colonel John Greely, and Major Robert Cotton in the introductory material to *Battle Studies*, pp. v–xii.

[127] Stefan Possony and Étienne Mantoux, 'Du Picq and Foch: The French School', in Earle (ed.), *Makers of Modern Strategy*, esp. 218.

[128] Introductory material to *Battle Studies*, p. xiii.

teaching, lay elsewhere. Fifteen years after the defeat of 1870–1, the main influence came from across the German border. It introduced an entirely new military outlook, which replaced the traditional concepts and the positivist notions that such military authors as Lewal, Berthaut, Jung, Derrécagaix, and Pierron had continued to propound after 1871.

Only in Germany was the reaction against the Enlightenment so profound and all-encompassing as to influence military theory decisively and produce a new conception of its nature. Berenhorst and, later, such pupils of Scharnhorst's as Rühle von Lilienstern, Lossau, and, above all, Clausewitz, who in their formative years went through the Romantic revolution, fiercely rejected what they regarded as Enlightenment abstractions. They called for a comprehensive theory of war which would reflect the diversity of human reality, and emphasized creative genius, moral forces, and the factors of uncertainty and chance. Even here, however, the new conception of military theory no more than compromised the dominance of the military school of the Enlightenment. The general intellectual struggle in Germany between the legacy of the Enlightenment and what was increasingly becoming a distinctive German Movement was as yet far from conclusive in its results. Moreover, in the military field in particular, the theoretical legacy of the Enlightenment was closely tied up with one of the few useful analytical tools in the profession—the rationale of operations, especially in its updated Napoleonic-Jominian formulation.

Thus, even during the height of Romanticism, some of Clausewitz's associates in Prussia, such as Decker and Valentini, were paraphrasing the theories of Bülow, Wagner, and Archduke Charles.[129] This was certainly the case in the smaller German states, which were much less touched by the emotional wave that so deeply affected large sections of the Prussian intellectual and political élite

---

[129] Decker, *Kriegführung* and *Grundzüge der praktischen Strategie* (2nd edn., Berlin, 1841). Decker was instructor in the *Allgemeine Kriegsschule* when Clausewitz was the director; on their attitude towards each other see Peter Paret, *Clausewitz and the State* (Oxford, 1976), 313–14. Georg Wilhelm von Valentini, *Die Lehre vom Krieg* (2nd edn., Berlin, 1833); there was a mutual antipathy between Valentini and the reformers, including Clausewitz: Paret, *Clausewitz and the State*, 192. Both Valentini and Decker were prolific and successful authors, best known for their works on the 'little war'.

at the beginning of the nineteenth century.[130] By the 1840s, as Jomini was outliving his contemporaries' resentments and criticisms and consolidating his early meteoric success into a European pre-eminence with the publication of his *Summary of the Art of War* (1837), it was his bold, Napoleonic theories that dominated the scene. After a characteristically German conceptual analysis, these were compactly summarized by Wilhelm von Willisen (b. 1790) in his *Theory of Great War* (1840): 'apply strength against weakness, front against flank, masses against a stretched front, superior against inferior force.' Napoleon himself had indicated how this was to be achieved: 'the secret of victory lies in the secret of communications'.[131]

Willisen's career came under a shadow when, in 1850, he failed to defend Schleswig-Holstein on behalf of the German Confederation against the Danish army. But his book, based on his lectures at the Kriegsschule, was an accepted text both in Prussia and abroad. In 1866, commenting on the development of the campaign in Bohemia, he hardly concealed his indignation at Moltke's dispersed strategy, which broke the Jominian golden rule. 'All that can be said of the movements now being executed', he wrote, 'is that they repair the worst fault that could have been committed—dissemination of forces in two widely separated groups'.[132]

A disciple was Wilhelm Rüstow (1821–78), the most prolific and diverse military scholar in Europe after 1850 and a man of unusual biography, whose significance transcended the military sphere. Rüstow was a lieutenant of engineers in the Prussian army when the revolution of 1848 broke out. Like Heinrich von Bülow during an earlier great revolutionary crisis, he was a committed and vocal enemy of Prussia's political and social system.[133] A staunch republican, he was one of the very few Prussian officers who openly

---

[130] See for example J. von Theobald, *Die Kunst der großen Kriegs operationen nach den besten Quellen frey bearbeitet* (Stuttgart, 1820).

[131] Karl Wilhelm von Willisen, *Theorie des großen Krieges* (Berlin, 1840), 81, 76, and also 105. On Willisen see R. von Caemmerer, *The Development of Strategical Science during the 19th Century* (London, 1905), 131–56.

[132] Quoted by F. E. Whitton, *Moltke* (London, 1921), 119. Willisen also opposed the adoption of the 'needle gun' by the Prussian army: Dennis Showalter, *Railroads and Rifles: Soldiers, Technology and the Unification of Germany* (Hamden, Conn., 1975), 90, 97–8.

[133] Rüstow was co-editor of Bülow's *Militärische und vermischte Schriften* (Leipzig, 1853).

sided with the revolution, speaking and writing in favour of the replacement of the regular army—the instrument of absolutism and mirror of the class system—with a true popular army.[134] When the army finally put an end to the revolution, Rüstow had to resign and leave Prussia. He settled in Switzerland and became a freelance military writer, publishing more than two dozen books on all aspects of the military profession. He wrote some scholarly military histories, scientific studies of ancient warfare (in collaboration with H. Köchly, a professor of Classics in Zurich), campaign histories of all the wars of his day, and highly technical works on fortification. In 1860 he joined Garibaldi and acted as his chief of staff with the effective rank of major-general in the famous campaign of liberation through the Kingdom of the Two Sicilies.[135] After returning to Switzerland, he was accepted into the Swiss general staff with the rank of colonel and taught military history for a short while at the University of Zurich.[136]

Rüstow had a profound understanding of the way war was shaped throughout history by political and social conditions. This should not be attributed too narrowly to an intellectual bequest from either Clausewitz or Willisen and Jomini, although Rüstow was influenced by the writings of both in this regard.[137] All expressed nineteenth-century historicism, which dominated this age of social transformation and revolutionary change. A deeply

[134] Wilhelm Rüstow, *Der deutsche Militärstaat, vor und während der Revolution* (Königsberg, 1850), repr. with a brief biographical introduction by G. Oestreich, (Osnabrück, 1971). During the constitutional crisis of the early 1860s Rüstow was again intensely involved in the campaign against the subjugation of the Landwehr, the people's army, to the Junkers' regular army. He wrote several pamphlets on this subject in 1862–3.

[135] See Rüstow's account from the field of battle, 'Die Brigade Milano', in Ludwig Walesrode (ed.), *Demokratische Studien* (Hamburg, 1860), in the company of some of the most famous names of German and European radicalism. Visiting in Garibaldi's headquarters were, among others, Lassalle and the revolutionary poet Georges Herwegh. Incidentally, Rüstow was later instrumental in causing Lasselle's death, when, for romantic reasons, he pushed him into the duel in which he was killed: Shlomo Na'aman, *Lassalle* (Hanover, 1970), 763–84.

[136] For Rüstow see also the preface to the English edition of his book *The War for the Rhine Frontier 1870* (3 vols.; London, 1871); Marcel Herwegh's *Guillaume Rustow: Un grand soldat, un grand caractère* (Paris 1935); see also two unpublished doctoral dissertations: R. von Steiger, 'Der Rüstow Prozeß 1848–1850' (Berne, 1937); P. Wiede, 'Wilhelm Rüstow' (Munich, 1958).

[137] See Rüstow, *Der Krieg und seine Mittel* (Leipzig, 1857), bk. 1, 13–124; and esp. *Die Feldherrkunst des neunzehnten Jahrhunderts* (2 vols.; Zurich, 1857), i. 5–43, 505–66. Here (p. 506) he made his famous remark that 'Clauzewitz is much quoted but little read'. He himself had a reserved respect for Clausewitz.

historical approach characterizes Rüstow's excellent *Generalship in the Nineteenth Century* (1857), which traces the development of military practice and theory from the age of absolutism through the Revolution up to the Restoration. That the book never received the attention it deserved must have been due to Rüstow's position as an outsider in both the military and the academic world. It was his *History of Infantry* (1857) that first kindled Delbrück's interest in military history and led to the latter's great life-work, which integrated military history into German historical scholarship.[138]

Yet his universalist outlook, set limits on Rüstow's historical approach. As we have seen, by the middle of the nineteenth century, disciples of Jomini everywhere were facing the same problem, as the rifle and the railway threatened to revolutionize both tactics and strategy. Writing in 1857, Rüstow maintained that the principles of the art of war were eternal, varying only in the forms they took, and that the rifle would make no fundamental change in tactics and certainly not in strategy, where Napoleonic principles could not be superseded. By 1872, in his treatment of the German Wars of Unification, the argument was unchanged but the position was defensive. The breech-loader and Moltke's concentric strategy overtaxed the flexibility of the theoretical framework.[139]

In the consultations which took place during the preliminary stages of the war of 1866, Moltke had to overcome the opposition of the Adjutant-General, von Alvensleben, and of Colonel Düring of the general staff to his proposed deployment and advance on exterior lines.[140] But the campaigns in Bohemia and France established his military pre-eminence. They also marked the ascent of a formidable Prussian-German military school, with a highly distinctive and dominating theoretical outlook, to match the new German Reich, with its acute political and cultural self-awareness.

[138] Rüstow, *Geschichte der Infanterie* (Gotha, 1857).

[139] Rüstow, *Die Feldherrnkunst*, i. 2; *Strategie und Taktik der neuesten Zeit* (3 vols.; Zurich, 1872–4), i. pp. vii, 109. His problem was well pointed-out by Caemmerer, *Strategical Science*, 220–1.

[140] Walter Goerlitz, *The German General Staff* (London, 1953), 85; Showalter, *Railroads and Rifles*, 62.

2
The German Military School:
Its World-View and Conception of War
1815–1914

THE German Wars of Unification transformed the political and military map of Europe. For two centuries, since the days of Louis XIV, France had been, despite some reversals, the predominant power on the Continent; henceforth this position was taken by the new German Empire. Prussia accomplished this in a remarkable feat of military proficiency, and it was to her that the world now looked in military affairs. All armies remodelled themselves on her system of conscription and reserve, general staff and military education, organization and tactics. But behind German might they also discovered a formidable and cohesive military school, possessing a highly distinctive view of war. Flowing from Germany, this view of war decisively influenced people's approach to military theory, doctrine, and history from the late nineteenth century; in many respects it still does. Indeed, the military approach of the Prussian-German military school did not merely consist of a body of operational doctrines; these took their place in a much wider outlook on politics, history, and human nature which dominated German thought from the turn of the nineteenth century.

The characteristic ideas of the Prussian-German military school were shaped by the meeting of two revolutions: one intellectual, the other military. 'German thought', wrote Ernst Troeltsch, 'whether in politics or in history or in ethics is based on the ideas of the Romantic Counter-Revolution' against the ideas of the Enlightenment;[1] and military thought was no exception. In the first place, the new intellectual currents introduced a new understanding of the role of war in human reality. In response to the acute threat of

---

[1] Ernst Troeltsch, 'The Idea of Natural Law and Humanity in World Politics', app. to O. Gierke, *Natural Law and the Theory of Society 1500–1800* (Cambridge, 1934), 203.

French Revolutionary ideas and political imperialism, the cosmo-politan, cultural humanitarianism of eighteenth-century Germany gave way to a general awakening of nationalism in a highly political form. Fichte and Adam Müller, Schleiermacher and Hegel only articulated and further disseminated sentiments and ideas which had developed and become prevalent among large sections of the Prussian élite during the patriotic struggle against Napoleon. Old Prussian *étatisme* and the new Romantic emphasis on the organic unity of the *Volk* now merged into a highly influential set of beliefs: the state is the dominating agent in human development, enforcing law and morality at home but subjected to no higher authority in its relations with other states; consequently, in the international arena, war is not accidental or abnormal but an unavoidable and natural means of arbitration, not to be judged by the moral standards derived from intra-state reality; furthermore, war actually plays an important positive role in countering corruption and softness within nations and in strengthening the social fabric. This new outlook, which gradually gained currency, was also reflected in the private and public writings of many of the military reformers, among them the still-almost-anonymous Clausewitz.[2]

The Romantic world-view also produced a new conception of the nature of military theory, in stark opposition to the theoretical outlook of the Enlightenment. To recapitulate: military writers in Germany held that, like all spheres of human activity, war was not susceptible to the methods which had proved so successful in the natural sciences; war was the sphere of clashing wills, rising emotions, uncertainty, and confusion; no universal rules and principles could in any real sense reflect its diverse complexity and endless contingencies; these could only be mastered by the general's practical genius and iron will.

Finally, the effects of Romanticism blended well with the overwhelming impact of the French and Napoleonic revolution in the military field. Even before the catastrophic defeat of 1806, but

---

[2] For all this, including Clausewitz's view on the moral status of war, which was far from being non-existent as modern commentators have assumed, see my *The Origins of Military Thought from the Enlightenment to Clausewitz* (Oxford, 1989), 236–50 and the authorities cited. See also the first and best volume of Gerhard Ritter's monumental study *The Sword and the Scepter* (4 vols.; Miami, Fla., 1969; German original 1954), the ideas in which closely parallel my own, both here and regarding Moltke. I was not sufficiently aware of this at the time I wrote my previous book.

much more strongly after it, a new conception of war was emerging in shattered Prussia. The German cultural scene, which since the late eighteenth century had been highly sensitive to the inter-dependence of all elements of the social fabric, provided military observers with a unique insight into the social origins of the revolution in war. Critics of the Frederickian military system at the turn of the century and, later, the reformers, traced the sources of French power to the total mobilization of patriotic energies and popular masses, which made possible the pursuit of great objectives by means of bold and crushing strategy. Prussia's grave condition, which made the struggle against Napoleon one of national survival, called for a similar commitment. The relatively limited warfare of the *ancien régime* was totally discredited. The reformers' work and plans for a general insurrection, come what may, envisioned all-out war. This became the characteristic mark of the Prussian military around the symbolic figure of Blücher, 'Marshal Vorwärts', and Gneisenau, his chief of staff, during the campaigns that brought down Napoleon in 1813–15. Prussian headquarters became the major advocate of aggressive strategy and the most vocal and insistent force pushing for a total overthrow of French power. These were the attitudes which received their most striking theoretical formulation from Clausewitz. He believed that they expressed the true and lasting nature of war, and that one could not depart from them with impunity—a belief which he began to qualify only during the last years of his life.

This view of war, conception of military theory, and approach to the conduct of operations became the intellectual creed of the Prussian-German military school because they were intertwined with the major trends which dominated German thought in the nineteenth century. Here too lies the key to the understanding of 'Clausewitz's influence'. Ideas do not just appear out of thin air; nor do individual thinkers get hold of people's minds single-handedly by sheer abstract appeal. Clausewitz had given expression to the ideas and attitudes that had dominated his intellectual environment; and his work was canonized by later generations in Germany, who named him as their classic authority, because they could find in his writings a sophisticated formulation in the military field of the way they themselves saw their world. After the Second World War, with the start of German national self-examination and ideological reorientation, historians inside, and then outside,

Germany sharply contrasted a 'good' and largely sterilized Clause-witz with his 'bad' successors. But in truth, while developing in a more aggressively nationalist and militarist direction, the Prussian-German military school was both historically and intellectually far closer to him than our period could ever be.[3]

Thus, as its title indicates, this chapter adopts a particularly wide point of view, more so than any other chapter of the book. It attempts to outline the German 'military mind' and place it in the context of the German 'public mind', or *Weltanschauung*, as a whole. No aspect of the former, it is suggested, can be properly understood without reference to the latter. Inevitably, this involves a broader survey of German history in the period concerned than would normally be regarded necessary in a work of this nature. All the more so since the distinctive German tradition which had its most powerful and creative period in the nineteenth century was far from being monolithic or unaffected by the passage of time. The cosmopolitan, non-political age of Goethe gave way, after the reform era, to the awakening of German national consciousness. The liberal struggle against the Restoration was disappointed in the revolutions of 1848 and shattered after the Prussian constitutional struggle of the 1860s, when Germany was united from above by Prussia's most conservative forces. The creation of the German Empire by Bismarck in 1871 turned Germany into the strongest power on the Continent and was followed by rapid industrial and demographic growth, economic expansion, and urbanization. However, with these came the shadows and anxieties of grave domestic and foreign threats and challenges, amplified by growing secularism and materialism. All these shifts in conditions and concerns, experiences and perspectives found expression in the military field too. Indeed, spanning almost the entire century, no life-story reflected this more strikingly, or was more closely associated with determining the course of events, than that of Helmuth Carl Bernard von Moltke (1800–91).

MOLTKE AND THE ERA OF GERMAN UNIFICATION

From the time of the earliest historical appraisals of Moltke it has been widely agreed that he personified the transformation of the

---

[3] See Gat, *Enlightenment to Clausewitz*, 168–254.

German public mind during the nineteenth century.[4] The post-humous publication of his youthful writings and letters not only provided further evidence of his outstanding intellectual faculties and moral integrity; they also revealed a wealth and liveliness of personality which added new dimensions to the Olympian remote-ness and silent austerity which characterized his public image in old age. Indicating the diversity and breadth of his interests, these early writings also revealed an outlook and attitude to life which had been free from bias, humanist, cosmopolitan, undogmatic and tolerant in regard to religion, and almost entirely non-political. While Moltke had emerged from anonymity to world fame only in his sixties, there now appeared a new and quite unexpected 'young Moltke'. Indeed, the change went deeper than variations in temperament between young and old age and transcended the mere personal level.

Moltke's father was an impoverished former lieutenant of the Prussian army, who found employment in Denmark. The young Moltke was sent to the Royal Danish Academy for Cadets in Copenhagen, where he graduated in 1818 as first in his class. In 1822, armed with excellent recommendations, he transferred to the Prussian service. His achievements during his studies at the Prussian War School (1823–6) under the directorship of Clausewitz (who had little contact with the students) were also considerable.[5] In 1828 he was assigned to the topographical branch of the general staff, of which he became a member in 1832, and in which he was to remain.[6] At the same time, however, his extra-military activities played at least as important a part in his life. He was born into the later phase of that great age which gave Germany its reputation as 'the nation of poets and thinkers'.

During the 1820s and early 1830s, Moltke, poverty-stricken, shy, and socially withdrawn, occupied himself with a variety of intellectual pursuits. When he left the Kriegsschule, he already

---

[4] See the nationalist historian Dietrich Schäfer on the tenth anniversary of Moltke's death: *Zu Moltkes Gedächtnis. Rede* (Jena, 1901).

[5] For his record in both services see *Moltke, His Life and Character, Sketched in Journals, Letters, Memoirs, a Novel and Autobiographical Notes* (New York, 1892; vol. i. of *Gesammelte Schriften und Denkwürdigkeiten des General Feldmarschalls Grafen Helmuth von Moltke*, Berlin, 1892), 28–36.

[6] The standard biography is Eberhard Kessel, *Moltke* (Stuttgart, 1957); earlier ones include those by Max Jähns (1894–1900), Wilhelm Bigge (1901), Fritz von der Goltz (1903), Wilhelm von Blume (1907), and, in English, Spenser Wilkinson (1913) and F. E. Whitton (1921).

spoke German, Danish, and French. He then taught himself English and took lessons in Russian and Italian. In his later travels he also picked up Turkish. In 1832 he was competent enough in English to undertake the translation of Gibbon's monumental *Decline and Fall of the Roman Empire*, on which he worked after duty for two years in an attempt to supplement his income. In the course of their long years of correspondence, he and his brother Ludwig often discussed their translations of English poets, as well as German poetry and their own poetic efforts. Helmuth loved music, had a considerable talent for drawing, read extensively, and wrote as much. In 1828 he wrote a short novel, *The Two Friends*, in the style of German classicism. The revolutions of 1830–1 stimulated two small historical studies, which were both published in book form: *Holland and Belgium in their Mutual Relations from their Separation under Philip II* (1831), and *The Internal State of Affairs and the Social Condition of Poland* (1832).[7]

In 1836 Moltke took six months' leave to travel to Vienna, Constantinople, Athens, and Naples. At the request of the Turkish government he stayed in the Ottoman Empire for three years as a military instructor. The trip produced a volume of letters, some of which were published in book form; a collection of his surveys of the Dardanelles, Constantinople, and the Bosphorus; a book on the Russo-Turkish campaign of 1829; and various articles.[8] Tours of the interior of Asia Minor and the Mesopotamian desert produced further cartographical works and some valuable geographical information. These were sent to Professor Karl Ritter, the pioneer of the discipline of natural and historical geography and Moltke's former teacher at the Kriegsschule.[9] After marrying and working several years on the staff of the IV Army Corps, Moltke spent

[7] For the novel see *Life and Character*, 37–91. The two historical works were reprinted in *Essays, Speeches and Memoirs of Field-Marshal Count Helmuth von Moltke*, i (New York, 1893; vol. ii of *Gesammelte Schriften*), 1–163.

[8] *Briefe über Zustände und Begebenheiten in der Türkei 1835–39* (1841, 4th edn., Berlin, 1882), with an introduction by Karl Ritter; Norbert Fischer (ed.), *Moltke als Topograph* (Berlin, 1944); *The Russians in Bulgaria and Rumelia in 1828 and 1829* (London, 1854); 'Essays upon the Eastern Question (1841–1844)', repr. in *Essays, Speeches and Memoirs*, i. 267–308. Also see Jehuda L. Wallach, *Anatomie einer Militärhilfe: Die preußisch-deutschen Militärmissionen in der Türkei 1835–1919* (Düsseldorf, 1976), 17–29.

[9] 'Autobiography', in *Life and Character*, 20–3; Ernst Curtius, 'Memorial Speech at the Royal Academy of Sciences at Berlin', 2 July 1891, in *Essays, Speeches and Memoirs*, ii. (New York, 1893; vol. vii of *Gesammelte Schriften*), 221–31; Mutschke, *Moltke als Geograph* (Freiburg, 1935).

another year abroad as aide-de-camp to Prince Henry of Prussia, during which time he lived in Rome (1845–6). This year produced a number of geographical and historical notes, strongly influenced by Niebuhr's *Römische Geschichte*, the seminal work of modern critical historiography, which Moltke admired deeply. A topographical map of the environs of Rome, surveyed and drawn by Moltke, was published (1852, 1859) and led to an exchange of letters with Alexander von Humboldt.[10] Moltke also took great interest in the development of the railway, at first primarily as a great instrument of economic development and for private financial reasons. Between 1841 and 1844 he sat on the board of the company constructing the Hamburg–Berlin line. His 'Considerations on the Choice of Railway Routes' (1843) is impressive both in its command of the economic and technical details and in its mastery of exposition.[11]

All of Moltke's works make splendid reading. The beauty of his narrative is matched by keen powers of observation, strong judgement, and a comprehensive view of his subject-matter. The author's sympathetic character also shines through, and his intellectual approach was clearly equally sympathetic.

Both Moltke's religion and his politics were typical of the age of Goethe. Throughout his life he was permeated with a deep sense of cosmic religiosity which recognized no strict form or dogma and gave almost equal status to all historical religions as different expressions of the same spiritual and moral truth.[12] His treatment of political issues was similarly unbiased. His work on Holland and Belgium and his study of Polish history, society, and politics offer excellent proof of this. Both works were written against the turbulent background of the revolutions of 1830–1, and in both cases Prussia's vital interests were deeply involved. Yet not only was Moltke's point of view unaffected by the political tensions and concerns of his day; it was also remarkably devoid of national

[10] See previous note and *Life and Character*, 144–78; *Letters to Mother and Brothers* (vol. iv of *Gesammelte Schriften*), 263, 276.

[11] The article was reprinted in *Essays, Speeches and memoirs*, ii. 223–63; also see *Letters to Mother and Brothers*, 249; Showalter, *Railroads and Rifles*, 29–30.

[12] See Moltke, 'Thoughts on this Life and Trust in a Future Life', *Life and Character*, 325–32; see also his repudiation of any established church: *Field-Marshal Count Helmuth von Moltke as a Correspondent* (New York, 1893; vol. v of *Gesammelte Schriften*), 257–8; and an interest in Strauss's famous *Life of Jesus*, the controversial critical study of the Scriptures: ibid. 174.

chauvinism. Clausewitz's articles from these very same years, dealing with the problem of Belgian and Polish independence in the light of German and Prussian interests and European position, were typical of the new attitudes and concerns of the German nationalists and provide a remarkable contrast to Moltke's works.[13] Quite apart from being openly hostile to Polish political aspirations, Clausewitz was full of contempt for the Poles, 'a people that had remained half-Tartar in the midst of civilized European states'. Even more strongly did he despise and detest the Jews in Poland, those 'dirty German Jews, swarming like vermin in the dirt and misery'.[14] By contrast, Moltke's treatment of the Poles and the Polish Jews was highly sympathetic, trying to convey the inner feeling and form of their social and communal life with a kind of anthropological delight more in keeping with an earlier generation of German cultural and cosmopolitan nationalism than with the new political one.[15] Rather than being personal, the differences here—which reverse the roles into which Clausewitz and Moltke have been typecast in recent historiography—are symptomatic of the changing intellectual climate in Germany.

Nowhere is this and Moltke's early outlook more strikingly expressed than in one of his articles on the Eastern Question (1841):

We candidly confess our belief in the idea, on which so much ridicule has been cast, of a general European peace. Not that long and bloody wars are to cease from henceforth, our armies be disbanded, and our cannons recast into nails; that is too much to expect; but is not the whole course of the world's history an approximation to such a peace? . . . Wars will become rarer and rarer because they are growing expensive beyond measure; positively because of the actual cost, negatively because of the necessary neglect of work. Has not the population of Prussia, under a good and wise administration, increased by a fourth in twenty-five years of peace? And

---

[13] Clausewitz, 'Die Verhältnisse Europas seit der Teilung Polens' and 'Zurück-führung der vielen politischen Fragen, welche Deutschland beschäftigen, auf die unserer Gesamtexistenz', in *Carl von Clausewitz, Politische Schriften und Briefe*, ed. Hans Rothfels (Munich, 1922), 222–38. Also see Peter Paret, *Clausewitz and the State* (Oxford, 1976), 406–9, 419–20.

[14] Cited by Paret, *Clausewitz and the State*, 420, 212. The rising national chauvinism was by no means shared by the majority of the reformers; compare with Boyen's observations on the Poles and Galician Jews: ibid. 212.

[15] See Frederick Hertz, *The German Public Mind in the Nineteenth Century* (London, 1975), 228.

are not her fifteen millions of inhabitants better fed, clothed and instructed today than her eleven millions used to be? Are not such results equal to a victorious campaign or to the conquest of a province, with this great difference, that they were not gained at the expense of other nations, nor with the sacrifice of the enormous number of victims that a war demands? . . . When we consider the milliards which Europe has to spend every year on her military budget, the millions of men in the prime of life who are called away from their business in order to be trained for a possible war, it is not hard to see how these immense powers might be utilized and made more and more productive.[16]

In view of things to come, this was an astounding profession of political faith.

Indeed, the 1840s saw clouds gathering on both the foreign and the domestic horizon. The system of Vienna was beginning to waver. New threats and anxieties were growing everywhere. Political attitudes were changing. In 1840 Thiers's demand for the annexation of the left bank of the Rhine to France shook Europe and aroused German public opinion to a pitch of national fervour. A new note crept into Moltke's writings. The calm and scholarly objectivity of his works on Holland, Belgium, and Poland gave way to passionate nationalist polemic.[17] The cataclysmic events of 1848–50 generated crises of unprecedented gravity. Moltke's letters to his brothers, which had been totally apolitical in spirit, were now suddenly charged with politics as both Prussia's character as a state, Germany's fate, and his own personal future became the subject of uncertainty and concern. Previously, he had held a moderate reformist position, respecting both historical roots and the necessity for further development.[18] In the early 1840s he believed that Prussia stood in the forefront of reform and reasoned liberty.[19] The situation in 1848, however, was revolutionary, not reformist. Like members of the propertied classes everywhere,

[16] Moltke, 'Germany and Palestine', *Essays, Speeches and Memoirs*, i. 276–7.

[17] Moltke, 'The Western Boundary' (1841), ibid. 165–220. While French pamphleteers evoked the image of Romanic civilization, recovering lost territories from the Germanic world, Moltke contrasted the ancient traditions of Romano-French despotism with German freedom, and unfolded the story of the French violations of the territorial integrity of the German Reich since the fifteenth century.

[18] See Moltke's notes on the Hungarian nobility (1835), perceptively indicating both its glorious historical role and its patent anachronism in 'the epoch of steam-ships, militia, spinning and printing machines, constitutions and reform': 'Journal Written on his Way to Constantinople', *Life and Character*, 103.

[19] Cited by Goerlitz, *The German General Staff* (London, 1950), 71.

Moltke was fearful that the liberal revolution would be taken over by a democratic 'red republic' led by skilful demagogues, in a general rebellion 'of those who own nothing against those who own something'.[20] After the autumn of 1848, when the Austrian and Prussian governments had recovered their nerve, Moltke regarded the reaction which was setting in as inevitable.[21]

For the 'shriekers in Frankfurt', the professors and lawyers of the National Assembly with their presumptuous schemes and empty gestures, Moltke had little respect.[22] But their principal aim, German unity, and the emotions and forces they set in motion were the very things that he himself grew to cherish most.[23] While the king of Prussia rejected the imperial crown when it was offered to him by the Frankfurt assembly, Prussia moved on her own initiative to create a German union under her leadership. Moltke was thrilled.[24] From mid-1850 Prussia and Austria faced each other in arms. Moltke's corps was mobilized for twenty-four weeks. Then Prussia backed down in the humiliating settlement of Olmütz, and Moltke exploded with indignation. 'The worst government cannot ruin this nation,' he concluded bitterly; 'Prussia will stand yet at the head of Germany.'[25]

The experience of 1848–50 marked a turning-point in modern German history. The public mood and perceptions were transformed, and so were Moltke's. The disillusion with the impotent liberal leadership and liberal ideals, which had crumbled before real power both at home and abroad, turned into contempt and a new emphasis on the role of power and determined action in politics. 'There will be an age of heroes after the age of shouters and writers,' wrote Moltke at the end of 1849.[26] He had changed and was aware of it.[27] His letters were now dominated by politics. Calm and sympathetic understanding gave way to passionate conviction and cold determination. The moderate reformist turned into a staunch conservative. From his position of responsibility—he

---

[20] The quotations are from 17 Feb. 1850, 17 Nov. and 9 July 1848, *Letters to Mother and Brothers*, 135, 125, 115.
[21] 9 Sep. and 17 Nov. 1848, 27 Sept. 1849, 29 May 1850, ibid. 120, 125, 268, 141.
[22] The quotation is from 9 July 1848, ibid. 115; also see, for example, 21 Sept. 1848, ibid. 122.   [23] 27 Sept. 1849 and 21 Mar. 1850, ibid. 268, 138.
[24] As early as Sept. 1848 this had become his guiding ideal; ibid. 123.
[25] 25 Feb. 1851, ibid. 145.
[26] 27 Sept. 1849, ibid. 268.   [27] 15 Jan. 1850, ibid. 269.

became chief of staff of an army corps in August 1848—he viewed an increasingly destabilized European system: an adventurous emperor in a revisionist France; an arrogant Austria, determined to keep Prussia down and block the unification of Germany; and a Denmark who exploited German disunity to change the status quo in Schleswig-Holstein. His point of view was completely transformed. Now it was totally Prussian- and German-oriented, imbued with a sense of self-righteousness and a distaste for Prussia's adversaries. Reflecting the change of course in German historical scholarship as a whole, Ranke's older universal historicism was supplemented among Moltke's favourite readings with the new nationalist perspective and preoccupation of Droysen and his successors in the influential Prussian historical school. These boiled down to the doctrine that from her origins it had been Prussia's historical mission to unite Germany, and her cause was therefore the true and moral cause of Germany.[28] The man who a decade before had professed his belief in a general European peace, now repeatedly saw war on the cards, both before the German Wars of Unification and in the subsequent two decades until his death.

From the mid-1850s he was beginning to rise to positions of national significance, and then, thanks entirely to his outstanding personal qualities and remarkable achievements, he shot to national and international prominence. In 1855 he was appointed senior aide-de-camp to Prince Frederick William of Prussia, and a year later he was promoted to major-general. In 1857 he became acting chief of the Great General Staff and in the following year chief of staff. His great creative and analytical powers and mastery of exposition were now channelled into his own professional sphere, producing a massive output of operational plans, staff studies, and memoranda. His successful role in the Danish war of 1864, and especially his masterminding of the Bohemian campaign of 1866, won him the confidence of the king. They transformed the general staff from a mere planning-bureau of little authority into

[28] For Moltke's admiration for Ranke, see ibid. 276, and *Moltke as a Correspondent*, 263. It was with Ranke's solicitation that Moltke was accepted in 1860 as an honorary member of the Prussian Royal Academy of Sciences: *Essays, Speeches and Memoirs*, ii. 233. For Moltke's recommendation of Droysen's *History of Prussian Politics* right after its publication, see *Letters to Mother and Brothers*, 16 Mar. 1856, 280–1. For the Prussian historical school and Droysen in particular, see Georg Iggers, *The German Conception of History* (Middletown, Conn., 1968), 90–123 and 104–15 respectively.

the effective high command of the army in time of war, and promoted its chief from a position of secondary significance to the role of war-lord. In 1867 Moltke was elected as a Conservative member both to the Prussian Upper House and to the Reichstag of the newly created North German Confederation; this latter position was to be replaced after 1871 and until his death by a seat in the Reichstag of the German Empire. He now saw only one solution to the German problem: 'For fifty years German unity has been extolled in prose, in verse, in song, and in toasts.' These years 'have shown that union can never be achieved by means of peaceful understanding . . . It is God's will that Prussia should solve the problem' with her sword.[29] A full circle had been closed with the early enthusiasts for the ideal of German unification among the Prussian reformers. It had been around 1820 that Clausewitz had written: 'Germany can reach political unity in *one* way only, through the sword, when one state subdues all the others.'[30]

Germany was united by the sword. The formative experience of 1848 was reinforced by the collective lessons of the era of unification. The story is familiar enough. The liberals' defeat had been completed in the Prussian constitutional crisis of the 1860s, when they had opposed the government on the very reforms of the army that made the victories of 1866 and 1870–1 possible. The German Reich was created in war by force of arms and state power. Not only did this determine the political and social structure of the new empire; it also shaped the dominating outlook shared by its political, social and intellectual establishment. It reinforced older intellectual trends which had been building up the distinctive German tradition since the Romantic revolt and the political and ideological struggle against the 'ideas of 1789'. Moltke's world-view, crystallized after the creation of the empire into a hard core of convictions, typified this comprehensive outlook.

First, there was the nature of international relations and the role of war. United Germany was the strongest power in Europe and, under Bismarck, during the first two decades of her existence, she was also a power of the status quo. Yet from his post at the general

---

[29] There are two virtually identical formulations of this idea in early 1868; the quotations are from 'Drafts of Undelivered Speeches in the Parliament of the Customs Union', *Essays, Speeches and Memoirs*, ii. 18, 14; also see 26 May 1866 and 24 Jan. 1868, *Letters to Mother and Brothers*, 178, 184–5.

[30] 'Umtriebe', in Rothfels (ed.), *Clausewitz, Politische Schriften*, 171.

staff, Moltke saw no reason for complacency. Called to defend the
government's military budgets in the periodical highly contentious
parliamentary debates on these, he repeatedly declared Germany's
peaceful intentions, based on her satisfaction with the existing
European order, and candidly professed that she had no interest in
further territorial expansion that would compromise her ethnic
integrity.[31] However, the apprehensions of Germany's neighbours
were only natural and, owing to her special geopolitical position,
Germany, in her turn, had an endemic security problem. 'We are
placed right in the midst of all the Great Powers,' Moltke told the
Reichstag; 'Our Eastern and Western neighbours have only to form
front in one direction, we in all directions.'[32] From 1859 he had
repeatedly expressed his concern at the possibility of a gigantic
clash between the great European races: a Germanic centre caught
in the middle between an 'alliance of the Slavic East and the
Romance West'. After 1871 this became a leading theme in his
plans for war.[33] On the western border lay a humiliated and
revanchist France, whose remarkable recovery and rapid rearmament
caused much alarm across the Rhine. On the eastern border lay the
Russian Empire, lured by Bismarck's masterful diplomacy, but
always bound to be alienated by her conflicts in the Balkans with
Germany's other ally, the Habsburg monarchy. Were France and
Russia to co-operate, Germany would find it extremely difficult to
win a war. Before 1870 Moltke had continuously pressed for an
immediate war against France, before her army had had time to
reform. The intended purpose of war at that time had been to
change the status quo and bring about the unification of Germany.
Now, in every major international crisis—with France in 1875 and
1887 and especially with Russia in 1887–8—Moltke and the
general staff urged a preventive war, although the political motive
of such a war was fundamentally defensive.[34] How the temporary
weakening of the defeated enemy was to be maintained without

---

[31] Sitting of the Reichstag on the Imperial Military Bill, 16 Feb. 1874, *Essays,
Speeches and Memoirs*, ii. 114–15; Debate on the Imperial Budget, 24 Apr. 1877,
ibid. 120.

[32] Debate on the Imperial Military Law, 1 Mar. 1880, ibid. 124–5.

[33] See the many references in Ferdinand von Schmerfeld (ed.), *Die deutschen
Aufmarschpläne 1871–1890* (Berlin, 1929), cited by Ritter, *Sword and Scepter*, 229;
313, n. 59.

[34] Walter Kloster, *Der deutsche Generalstab und der Präventivkrieg-Gedanke*
(Stuttgart, 1932), 6–33; Ritter, *Sword and Scepter*, 227–38; Rudolph Stadelmann,
Moltke und der Staat (Krefeld, 1950), 279–334.

periodic wars is a question to which Moltke appeared to have no real answer.[35] In fact, what he most probably had in mind was the imposition of peace terms that would set permanent restrictions on the enemy's armed forces, and indeed on its independence.

The lessons of the era of unification and the problems of European power-politics reinforced the legacy of German culture since its reaction against Enlightenment liberalism and cosmopolitanism. Travelling the same intellectual road himself, Moltke now arrived at exactly the same view of war which had been developed by Adam Müller and Rühle von Lilienstern, Hegel and Clausewitz. 'What sensible man would not wish that it were possible to apply to peaceful objects the enormous expenditure incurred by Europe for military purposes?' he asked the Reichstag in 1868; yet 'war is, in reality, but the carrying on of diplomacy by different means'.[36] The phenomenon of war is embedded in the nature of the international system. While 'within a country, the law protects the rights and liberty of the individuals, without as between state and state might is the only right'. No tribunal of international arbitration exists, and were it to exist, it 'would lack the power of executing its decrees'.[37] The only practical guarantee against war is not an international agreement but a strong and peaceful Germany which would impose peace on her neighbours.[38]

These remarks before the Reichstag were more fully elaborated in the famous replies that Moltke wrote in 1880–1 to two activists campaigning in favour of international law and peace who had approached him for his opinion and support. It was as if his ideas from forty years before regarding a general European peace had been written by another man. He now believed not only that war was natural and necessary, and thus impossible to eliminate by kind-hearted visionaries, but that it also had a positive, and even a sublime, role to play in human life:

Permanent peace is a dream and not even a beautiful one, and war is a law of God's order in the world, by which the noblest virtues of man, courage and self-denial, loyalty and self-sacrifice, even to the point of death, are developed. Without war the world would deteriorate into materialism.[39]

[35] Ritter, *Sword and Scepter*, 227–8.
[36] 15 June 1868, *Essays, Speeches and Memoirs*, ii. 50.
[37] 16 Feb. 1874, ibid. 105.　　　　　　[38] Ibid. 50, 115.
[39] Moltke to Prof. Dr. Bluntschli, 11 Dec. 1880, *Moltke as a Correspondent*, 272.

Rising social-Darwinist notions found their place in the framework of Lutheran political realism and spiritual non-worldliness:

Is not the life of man, his whole nature, a battle of that which is to be with that which is? And so it is in the life of nations. . . . Who is able to escape misfortune in this world, or who can even run away from the burdens of life? Are not both by God's providence conditions of our earthly existence?[40]

In most of this, Moltke practically saw eye to eye with a man whom he befriended in the Reichstag, Heinrich von Treitschke.[41] A Berlin history professor, editor of the *Preußische Jahrbücher* and the most vigorous public spokesman for the new merger of Prussianism and German nationalism, Treitschke became the most notable and influential representative of the German school of political philosophy in Imperial Germany. The competition and struggle between states, the higher agents of human development, was for Treitschke the very stuff of which history was made:

The features of history are virile, unsuited to sentimental or feminine natures. Brave people alone have an existence, an evolution or a future; the weak and cowardly perish, and perish justly. The grandeur of history lies in the perpetual conflict of nations, and it is simply foolish to desire the suppression of their rivalry.[42]

War, therefore, will endure to the end of history as long as there is multiplicity of states. The laws of human thought and of human nature forbid any alternative, neither is one to be wished for. . . . War is the one remedy for an ailing nation. Social selfishness and party hatreds must be dumb before the call of state when its existence is at stake.[43]

Treitschke's *History of Germany in the Nineteenth Century* took its place on the short-list of Moltke's favourite readings. Composed in 1890 for the *Revue des Revues*, this list reflects Moltke's—and Germany's—intellectual evolution: the Bible, Homer, Shakespeare, Schiller, and Goethe appear side by side with Clausewitz, Ranke, Carlyle, and the nationalist historians Sybel and Treitschke.[44]

The publication in the newspapers of Moltke's replies regarding

[40] Moltke to M. Goubareff, 4 Feb. 1881, *Moltke as a Correspondent*, 279–80.
[41] Stadelmann, *Moltke und der Staat*, 366–8.
[42] Treitschke, *Politics* (2 vols.; London, 1916), i. 21. The book was compiled after the author's death, from the notes of lectures he had delivered in the early 1880s.
[43] Ibid., i. 65–6; also see ii. 395–6.
[44] *Moltke as a Correspondent*, 262–3; also see *Life and Character*, 228.

perpetual peace incited attacks in the Berlin press accusing the field-marshal of militarism.[45] The German Empire had been the creation of Prussia, shaped in the image of her authoritarian political system and dominated by her old ruling classes. But the political and social structure of the Reich, as well as its ruling ethos, was widely opposed. In the Reichstag, in order to push the government's legislation through, Bismarck was manœuvring opportunistically but with increasing difficulty between the conservative parties, the National Liberals, and even the Catholic Centre Party. While the Reichstag had been given very limited authority in the German constitution, and virtually none at all in foreign and military affairs, it still voted the Imperial budget. The government fixed the term of the military budget at seven years and usually got its way, but Moltke was not alone in finding the endemic political and ideological haggling with the parliamentary opposition depressing. Here again was the rule of empty talk, challenging the integrity and stability of the Reich at home, and inspired by irresponsible and dangerous illusions in treating the Reich's military needs. Delegates had to be reminded: that the milliards that Napoleon I had extracted from defeated Prussia were a permanent lesson to a country which tried to economize on its vital defence-expenditure; that universal military service was the school of the nation, implanting a sense of duty and obedience in its citizens; that the alternative to the regular army, the militia, promoted by the Left against Prussian militarism, had never succeeded and could never succeed.[46]

The most distressing political development, however, was the rise of the Social Democratic Party. For Moltke, this was an old mortal enemy. During the campaign of 1870–1, he had been constantly preoccupied with the spectre of radical and socialist revolution and sought to make the defeat of the popular armies raised by Gambetta for the defence of the French republic a lesson for the whole of Europe.[47] The horrors of the civil war in France confirmed his worst fears. During his long membership of the Reichstag, the only occasion on which he rose to speak on other

[45] *Moltke as a Correspondent*, 285–6.

[46] These were recurring themes in Moltke's parliamentary polemics. See *Essays, Speeches and Memoirs*, ii. 106, 138 for Napoleon's milliards; p. 14 for universal military service; pp. 111–12 for the militia.

[47] 1 Feb. 1871, ibid. 254; 21 Sept., 27 Oct., 23 Nov. 1870, and 1 Mar. 1871, *Letters to Mother and Brothers*, 193, 200, 203, 213.

than military issues was when the government introduced the Socialist Bill in 1878, a measure which marked the start of twelve years of struggle to suppress the Social Democratic Party by legal means. Against the socialist idea, he directed arguments which were very akin to the ones he used a little later against the idea of a permanent peace. Want, misery, and privation were inseparable conditions of human existence. Although they might slowly improve in time, their abolition was both unattainable and undesirable for the development of the human race.[48]

This striking similarity was significant. The idea both of permanent peace and of socialism conflicted with the very concept of the state which had been developed in Prussia from the turn of the nineteenth century and which was consecrated with the establishment of the German Reich: the definition of the state as power (*Macht*) without, and law and justice (*Recht*) within.[49] Those who threatened either, whether foreign rivals or domestic political forces like Catholicism or socialism, were proclaimed enemies of the state (*Reichsfeinde*).[50]

Indeed, for Moltke, the government was the rock of stability both in domestic and foreign affairs. In contrast to the liberal and socialist ideas that wars were incited by governments in the interest of the old ruling classes, Moltke maintained throughout his life that in the age of the masses, the passions of the people were a far greater stimulus for the outbreak of wars and were directly responsible for the out-and-out character they had assumed. 'In these days', he wrote to his mother as early as 1831, 'war and peace and the relations of nations are no longer cabinet questions; in many countries the people themselves govern the cabinet, and thus an element is introduced into politics on which it is impossible to reckon.'[51] After the out-and-out struggle with French national resistance in 1871, and in his polemic with the Left on matters of peace and war, this became a recurring theme: 'Strong governments are a pledge of peace. But the passions of the populace, the

---

[48] *Essays, Speeches and Memoirs*, ii. 76–7. Also see on the similarity between war and social deprivation: Mar. 1879, 18 Feb. 1878, 10 Feb. 1881, *Moltke as a Correspondent*, 270, 269, 279, 292.   [49] Cf. Treitschke, *Politics*, i. 19.

[50] See Wolfgang Petter, ' "Enemies" and "Reich Enemies": An Analysis of Threat Perceptions and Political Strategy in Imperial Germany, 1871–1914', in Wilhelm Deist (ed.), *The German Military in the Age of Total War* (Worcester, 1985), 22–39.

[51] 1831 Feb. 13, *Letters to Mother and Brothers*, 47.

ambition of party leaders, and public opinion led astray both in speeches and by the press—all these, gentlemen, are elements which may prove stronger than the will of those who rule.'[52] In 1890, rising to defend the expansion of the German army in one of his last appearances before the Reichstag, Moltke saw equally bleak consequences at home and abroad from the rising of the masses: '. . . these elements take the form of national and racial aspirations, and, above all, dissatisfaction with the existing state of affairs'. 'The days of the cabinet wars are past,' he told the Reichstag, 'now we have only the people's war.'[53] His famous vision of the resulting character of war was prophetic:

If war breaks out, one cannot foresee how long it will last or how it will end. It is the great powers of Europe which, armed as they never were before, are now entering the arena against each other. There is not one of these that can be so completely overcome in one or even in two campaigns that it will be forced to declare itself vanquished or to conclude an onerous peace; not one that will be unable to rise again, even if only after a year, to renew the struggle. Gentlemen, it may be the Seven Years War, it may be the Thirty Years War; and woe to him who sets Europe in flames, who first casts the match into the powder-barrel.[54]

Indeed, views on the nature of international relations and on the place of war within human reality were closely related to the outlook on the conduct of war itself. Moltke's remarkable insight into the future foresaw the ultimate military consequences of the politicization of the masses, brought about by the combined effects of nationalism, urbanization, mass education, and mass communications. But the process had begun exactly a century before; people's wars had been taking the place of cabinet wars since the French Revolution and the emergence of the modern nation-state. By centralizing power and establishing the principle of popular sovereignty, France had been able to mobilize and throw into war social resources and human masses on an unprecedented scale and had managed to generate immense moral energies. These in turn had found their strategic corollary expressed in Danton's famous formula: 'L'audace, et encore de l'audace, et toujours l'audace.' Developed and refined by Napoleon, the new system of war had

---

[52] 11 Jan. 1887, *Essays, Speeches and memoirs*, ii. 133; also see, for example: Mar. 1879 and 10 Feb. 1881, *Moltke as a Correspondent*, 270, 280.
[53] *Essays, Speeches and Memoirs*, ii. 136.   [54] Ibid. 137.

consisted of a massive concentration of force and crushing strategy, aiming at the enemy's total overthrow. After Prussia's catastrophic defeat, both these new sources of power and the resulting mode of war had been highlighted and celebrated by the Prussian reformers. Whereas the reformers had been thrown out of power after Napoleon's downfall, both their institutional and their doctrinal legacy remained. With her Landwehr militia, Prussia remained the only power in Europe of the Restoration to base her military system on the mobilization of her people. This system was later turned by King Wilhelm I and his Minister of War, von Roon, into an effective nation-in-arms. Similarly, the reformers' new, uniquely aggressive operational conception, modelled on Napoleonic strategy and emphasizing determined action and the destruction of the enemy army in battle, had found expression in the tremendous zeal of the Prussian army in the campaigns of 1813–15 and persisted thereafter. When the reorganization of the 1860s gave the Prussian army the numerical superiority over its rivals formerly enjoyed by the armies of Revolutionary France, the crushing strategic concepts had again found their natural counterpart.

The belief that no rigorous system of military theory was possible was fundamental to the new currents of military thought in Prussia. Ever since the Romantic revolt against the ideas of the Enlightenment, the doctrine of universal natural law had been rejected in each and every department of German culture. No sphere of human activity, conditioned as it was by its historical setting and dominated by a multitude of acts of volition, could ever be compressed into a formal system of rules and principles; this cultural premiss, introduced into the military field by Clausewitz, was widely disseminated by Moltke: little could be said about war theoretically. After Moltke's death, in publishing his extensive military memoranda, correspondence, and staff studies in the multi-volume *Militärische Werke*, the general staff took the liberty of piecing together under systematic headings passages which had been written in different circumstances, often even without referring to their source. But Moltke himself only summarized his strategic teaching—in a brief essay composed for direct practical purposes between his two great wars: 'Instructions for Superior Commanders of Troops' (1869), supplemented after the war in France by the even briefer 'On Strategy' (1871). 'The doctrines of strategy', he wrote, 'hardly go beyond the first propositions of common sense; one can hardly call them a science; their value lies almost entirely in their concrete application.'[55] From the beginning of operations, only the general's will and force of action can prevail over the moral and physical complexity of war, 'Strategy is [but] a system of expediences.'[56] For example, 'one reads much in theoretical books about the advantages of "operating on the interior lines". Yet one will have to ask oneself in each particular case what at the moment will be the most advantageous thing to do.'[57]

Indeed, the celebrated principle of the interior lines is a case in point. Moltke faced unanimous criticism when in 1866 he chose to disregard what was widely accepted as the advantage of interior lines, deploying his armies on a front extending from Saxony to Silesia. Military commentators all over Europe disapproved and, until the campaign of 1870–1 silenced them for good, they attributed Prussian success to poor Austrian generalship.[58] The high priest at Jomini's altar, his friend and biographer Lecomte, did not mince words:

Since war was first waged seldom have such masses been placed in a more ghastly situation. The historical blunder of the Austrian commanders advancing in 1796 to the relief of Mantua in three columns—a blunder so thoroughly punished by Bonaparte—was at any rate a strategic masterpiece compared with the Prussian plan of 1866.[59]

Moltke also had his critics in the Prussian army itself, but here his innovative strategies could at least be explained by appealing to prevailing intellectual notions. First, the particular circumstances of each case always take priority over any established rule: *individuum est ineffabile*. In 1866 the extended deployment was dictated by the special circumstances of the earlier Austrian mobilization, which imposed a defensive position on the Prussians at the initial stage of the campaign, and which had to be countered by rapid mobilization and deployment, using all available railway-lines. However, Moltke's case went far beyond the claim of special circumstances. It is no

---

[55] 'Verordnungen für die höheren Truppenführer' (1869), in *Militärische Werke*, ii, ii (1900), 172.

[56] 'Über Strategie' (1871), ibid. 219–3.

[57] 'Taktische Aufgaben', Nr. 58 (1878), ibid., ii, i. (1892), 133.

[58] For a selection of commentaries see Gordon Craig, *The Battle of Königgrätz* (London, 1964), 176–7.

[59] Quoted by Whitton, *Moltke* (London, 1921), 118–19.

accident that, while disciples of Jomini everywhere found the strategic as well as the tactical effects of the railway, the electric telegraph, and the rifle indigestible, it was in Prussia that their revolutionary significance was more readily accepted. Its deep historicist roots made military thought in Germany inherently more conscious of, and receptive to, historical change. Compared with the military theories of Jomini and his fellow thinkers, wrote Rudolph Caemmerer, the enormous advantage of the German conception of military theory 'lies in its *capacity for further development*'.[60]

It is this quality that accounts for Moltke's theoretical flexibility. The 'progress of technology,' he wrote, 'easier communications, new weapons, in short completely altered conditions, make it appear that the means by which victory was gained formerly, and even the rules laid down by the greatest generals, are frequently inapplicable to the present'.[61] If massed together from the opening of a campaign, the huge new armies would choke communications, and prove difficult to operate and impossible to supply. But by initially deploying over vast spaces, they could make full use of existing railway-heads for rapid mobilization and supply, and march on converging routes to achieve massive concentration on the field of battle.[62] 'March divided, strike united' was the new dictum. From the time of his appointment as chief of the general staff, Moltke advanced far-reaching proposals for the systematic preplanned use of the railway.[63] Prussia's exposed geographical position and system of reserves provided the most favourable ground for the acceptance of such ideas. The electric telegraph greatly facilitated the co-ordination of the entire process of mobilization and deployment, and the largely increased fire-capability of the rifle, by enhancing the power of defence, made it considerably more difficult for the enemy to overwhelm each of the army corps separately, before effective support could arrive.

Even before, but especially after, the Italian campaign of 1859, Moltke keenly observed the far-reaching effects of the rifle on tactics and strategy. Though not directly the responsibility of the

[60] Caemmerer, *The Development of Strategical Science during the 19th Century* (London, 1905), 54; italics in the original.
[61] 'Verordnungen', *Militärische Werke*, ii, ii, 172.
[62] Ibid. 173.
[63] Dennis Showalter, *Railroads and Rifles, Soldiers, Technology and the Unification of Germany* (Hamden, Conn., 1975), 39–43.

general staff, this subject was at the top of the European military agenda and was intensely discussed in the Prussian army. Moltke produced a series of memoranda which constituted perhaps the most accurate and comprehensive assessment written at the time. He clearly foresaw that the ability of cavalry to operate against infantry was considerably weakened, and that mass infantry bayonet-charges were a thing of the past. Attacking infantry would have to advance in small columns, thickly protected by skirmishers, take full advantage of the ground, and always seek to avoid frontal engagements by turning the enemy's flank.[64] The remarkable strengthening of fire-power from defensive positions, claimed Moltke, rendered the strategic offence which made maximum use of tactical defence the most advantageous form of war at that time.[65] Upholding circumstantial analysis against all formal assertions, Moltke consciously disregarded Clausewitz's insistence that defence was intrinsically stronger than attack. No general answer existed to the question of which of them was stronger, he wrote in his 'Instructions' of 1869. While the attack enjoyed the advantage of initiative, defence could make better use of the cover of ground. The individual case must always decide.[66] Similarly, it was more than just his utter humility that prevented Moltke from crowning his operations on exterior lines as a new 'strategic system'. The debate on the differences between Napoleon's and his own systems of war was one that was conducted by others at a later stage.[67]

Significantly, on both sides of this debate a consensus prevailed that, while the forms (*Formen*) of war may change with time, its spirit (*Geist*), or essence (*Wesen*), remains unchanged.[68] Indeed, the rejection of any formal system and the strong awareness of circumstantial differences and historical change must not mislead;

[64] 'Taktisch-strategische Aufsätze', 12 July 1858, 5 Jan. 1860, Apr. and May 1861, 1865, ibid., esp. 7–9, 19–24, 27–41, 49–65. See also Showalter, *Railroads and Rifles*, 110–13.

[65] Ibid., esp. 7, 31, 56, 65.   [66] Ibid., 208.

[67] See Colmar von der Goltz, *The Conduct of War* (London, 1899, first publ. in German 1895), 135–44; Hugo Baron von Freytag-Loringhoven, *Die Heerführung Napoleons und Moltkes* (Berlin, 1897); S. W. L. von Schlichting, *Taktische und strategische Grundsätze der Gegenwart* (3 vols.; Berlin, 1897–9); id. *Moltke und Benedek* (Berlin, 1900); id. *Moltkes Vermächtnis* (Munich, 1901); Alfred Krauss, *Moltke, Benedek und Napoleon* (Vienna, 1901); Carl Bleibtreu, *Napoleon'sche und Moltke'sche Strategie* (Vienna, 1901); Fritz von der Goltz, *Moltke* (Berlin, 1903), 182–95; Caemmerer, *Strategical Science*, pref. and ch. 8.

[68] For each side of the argument, see most strikingly: Krauss, foreword; F. von der Goltz, 182–6.

in the tradition of nineteenth-century German idealism these notions were always matched by a strong claim to capture the inner essence of reality.[69] The Prussian-German military school had an overriding and highly prescriptive conception of the conduct of war. While Clausewitz and his friends had argued that the dominating Napoleonic mode of warfare could not be reduced to rules and principles, they had still believed that it represented the universal nature of war and exhibited the true implications from its concept (*Begriff*); this is an ambivalence which nowadays has been the cause of much misunderstanding. The essence of war was fighting, which implied the destruction of the enemy forces in battle. In the 'Instructions' Moltke presented this conception of war, and his own innovative contributions, with his customary brevity and comprehensiveness:

The victory in the decision by arms is the most important moment in war. Only victory breaks the enemy will and compels him to submit to our own. Neither the occupation of territory nor the capturing of fortified places, but only the destruction of the enemy fighting-power will, as a rule, decide. This is thus the primary object of operations.[70]

Acting boldly and aggressively, the army must seize the initiative and seek the enemy army wherever it may be found. Since the uncertainty and confusion of war, the severe shortage of information, and enemy activities work against all operational planning, there is no point in devising detailed schemes beyond the deployment (*Aufmarsch*) phase. Only the aim and the general line of advance are to be clearly stated. During the course of the campaign, effective co-operation between the separate units must depend on the initiative of local commanders and on their having been trained to leave everything and rush towards the sound of the guns. For the battle itself, one cannot be too strong. Once the enemy is located and engaged, all forces converge to achieve overwhelming superiority, strategic envelopment, and tactical encirclement. A decisive battle of destruction would be the desirable result. 'The operations against France', stated Moltke's memorandum of 6 May 1870 to the general staff,

will simply consist in our advancing in as close a formation as possible for a few marches on French soil, till we meet the French army and then fight a

---

[69] See, for example, Iggers, *The German Conception of History*, esp. 111.
[70] 'Verordnungen', *Militärische Werke*, II. ii. 173.

battle. The direction of this advance is in general towards Paris, because in that direction we are most certain to hit the mark we are aiming at, the enemy's army.[71]

Carried out with considerable numerical advantage and with greatly superior railway, mobilization, and staff systems, this operational conception produced absolutely decisive results. In 1866 the Prussian First, Second, and Elbe Armies managed to unite on the battlefield of Königgrätz, and while the Austrian army under Benedek did succeed in escaping their pincer movement—and total annihilation—it was no longer capable of effective resistance. In 1870, after some confused and bloody clashes on the frontier, one half of the French army was shut up in the fortress of Metz and the other pushed against the Belgian border near Sedan. The two capitulations that ensued sent virtually the entire French regular army, some 300,000 men in all, as prisoners of war to Germany.

However, while Königgrätz, Metz, and Sedan destroyed the Austrian and French armies, both wars still had to be brought to an end. This is where the famous disputes between Bismarck and the military broke out. In 1866 the king and his military advisers wanted to give the Austrian army no time to rally, occupy Vienna, and dictate peace terms which would include war indemnities and the annexation of Austrian Silesia, the Sudeten, and the Kingdom of Saxony to Prussia. Bismarck, however, was mostly concerned about the prospects of French intervention. Having achieved what he regarded as Prussia's principal aim, which was the exclusion of Austria from German affairs, as well as extensive annexations and the creation of a Prussian-led confederation in north Germany, he virtually forced a moderate peace on his enraged sovereign. In 1870–1, the picture was even more complicated. After the destruction of the French regular armies, war went on. The republican government prepared the capital for siege and, raising the banner of 1792, began to mobilize huge armies in the provinces, while *francs tireurs* harassed the advancing Prussian columns and lines of communication. On the other side, Bismarck was again primarily concerned about possible intervention by the other powers, and was manœuvring to find a suitable French partner and the means by which pressure could be exerted on him to negotiate a favourable peace. This required careful control over the direction

[71] *Militärische Werke*, I. iii. 131–2.

and aims of military operations. Tensions between Bismarck and the military began to mount over the fate of Bazaine's besieged army in Metz, which Bismarck thought he might use to reinstitute a Bonapartist ruler in Paris. These tensions developed into a head-on confrontation with Moltke and the general staff concerning the occupation of Paris, which Bismarck regarded as nothing more than a political bargaining-card for the attainment of peace. The army strongly resented any political interference in its business, while Bismarck acted with customary ruthlessness to impose his will.

This conflict has been dissected by historians ever since.[72] It has been presented as the first instance of a bid by the general staff for autonomy from, and equal status with, civil authority in the German Reich—one that was destined to have far-reaching influence on German history. With the army free from parliamentary control and responsible only to the person of the king, its claim was deeply rooted in the Prussian, and later German, political structure and ethos. 'Up till now', wrote Moltke to the King after being called to order, 'I have considered that the Chief of the General Staff (especially in war) and the Federal Chancellor are two equally warranted and mutually independent agencies under the direct command of Your Royal Majesty.'[73]

The positions of the military both in 1866 and 1870–1 have been presented as totally divorced from political considerations and have been widely attributed to a narrow military point of view, only to be expected of generals. This explanation, however, hardly gets to the bottom of the matter, as some leading historians have noted.[74] Contrary to popular belief, soldiers as such are no more naturally disposed to radical military measures than other parts of the political community. To understand their attitudes, one has to examine the political and cultural environment in which they operate. The Prussian military had a highly distinctive conception

---

[72] For the latest and most comprehensive accounts see Stadelmann, *Moltke*, 212–64; Ritter, *Sword and Scepter*, i. 219–25; Gordon Craig, *The Politics of the Prussian Army* (Oxford, 1955), 196–216; Michael E. Howard, *The Franco-Prussian War* (London, 1961), 271, 352–7, 436–43.

[73] 29 Jan. 1871, Craig, *The Politics of the Prussian Army*, 214; Stadelmann, *Moltke*, 437, where the full document is printed.

[74] See Ritter, *Sword and Scepter*, i. 193–4; his acute analysis goes partly against the general drift of his own work, which blames Germany's later historical course on the improper place of the military. For Stadelmann see below.

of war, at once military and political, developed during the great struggle against Napoleon: crushing strategy was to bring the enemy to his knees in the pursuit of great political objectives. The similarity between the attitudes of the reformers in 1814–15 and the positions of the military and the King (himself a veteran of 1815) in 1866 and 1870–1 is striking. Stein and the Prussian headquarters of Blücher and Gneisenau, in almost open defiance of Frederick William III, had been passionately demanding extensive territorial annexations to Prussia, including the whole Kingdom of Saxony, and had been willing to go war with Austria, supported by the other European powers, if their demands were not met. Similarly, both in 1814 and 1815, they forcefully pressed for a total overthrow of French power, for the occupation of Paris and France, and for a punitive peace, treating with open hostility, and trying by all means at their disposal to pre-empt and frustrate, the alternative, subtle political schemes that Metternich had been entertaining.[75] When the tsar had expressed the opinion that the king of Prussia might need help against his Jacobine army, he had hit the nail right on the head. The conflict in 1814–15, as in 1866–71, was not so much between political and military points of view. Stein allied with Blücher and Gneisenau; Schwarzenberg with Metternich. The conflict was more between the old cabinet conception of politics and war and the one emerging in the age of nationalism and all-out strategy. As pointed out by Stadelmann, it was Metternich's world in collision with Clausewitz's. While Bismarck was a classical representative of *raison d'état* and the five-power order, Moltke developed into an exponent of state nationalism and national war.[76]

In 1870–1 Moltke was adamant that French resistance must be crushed. He recommended that the activities of the *francs tireurs* be suppressed by the most severe reprisals and regarded the fall of Paris mainly as a means to free the German armies to deal with the French popular forces. In the heat of his debate with Bismarck the Prussian crown prince observed that 'Count Bismarck desired peace, but General Count Moltke a war of extermination.'[77] Moltke's conversation with the crown prince concerning the future

[75] See Ritter's excellent analysis in ch. 4 of *Sword and Scepter*, i.
[76] Stadelmann, *Moltke*, 176 and foreword respectively.
[77] 13 Jan. 1871, *The War Diary of the Emperor Frederick III, 1870–1871*, 258.

course of the war after the fall of Paris puts Moltke's plans squarely in the context of his overall conception of strategy's means and ends:

MOLTKE: We shall push forward into the south of France in order finally to break the enemy's power.
THE CROWN PRINCE: But what will happen when our own strength is exhausted, when we can no longer win battles?
MOLTKE: We must always win battles. We must throw France completely to the ground.
THE CROWN PRINCE: And what then?
MOLTKE: Then we can dictate the kind of peace we want.[78]

Moltke always stressed that war was but a political means.[79] His insistence that politics must not interfere with the aim and conduct of strategy cannot, therefore, simply be dismissed as a soldier's effort at a clear demarcation of his professional sphere. His attitude was the outgrowth of an expansive and sweeping conception of the nature of war and strategy, which could never be violated with impunity. After his experience in 1870–1 he worked out the following formula:

Diplomacy avails itself to war to attain its ends, crucially influencing the beginning of war and its end. It does the latter by reserving to itself the privilege of raising or lowering its demands in the course of the war. In the presence of such uncertainty, strategy has no choice but to strive for the highest goal attainable with the means given.[80]

Since this position is often contrasted with Clausewitz's, it must be made clear that it is almost identical with Clausewitz's own formulations in his notes on strategy of 1804 and in the period until 1827, when he began to undergo the intellectual transformation which was terminated by his death.[81] Both expressed a new and highly pronounced conception of war and strategy which had been developed in Prussia in the era of national war.

Indeed, the experience of French popular resistance in 1870–1 demonstrated the scale of resources mobilized when two great

---

[78] 8 Jan. 1871, quoted by Goerlitz, *The German General Staff*, 92, from H. Uncken (ed.), *Großherzog Friedrich I von Baden und deutsche Politik von 1854–1871, Briefwechsel, Denkschriften, Tagebücher* (Berlin and Leipzig, 1927), 300–1.
[79] See, for example, 'Verordnungen' (1869), *Militärische Werke*, II. ii. 206
[80] 'Über Strategie', ibid. 291; Ritter, *Sword and Scepter*, i. 194–5.
[81] Gat, *Enlightenment to Clausewitz*, 203–5.

modern nations were locked in a life-and-death struggle. The destruction of the enemy's armies was no longer sufficient. In his letter to Professor Bluntschli, in which he denounced the idea of a permanent peace, Moltke made this clear: 'I cannot at all agree with the "Déclaration de St. Pétersbourg" that the "weakening of the hostile fighting power" is the only right proceeding in a war. No; all the resources of the hostile government must be affected, her finance, railways, victuals, even her prestige.'[82] This type of war, he told the Reichstag in 1890, might take seven or even thirty years. National war and all-out strategy in a modern industrial setting and on a modern industrial scale were breeding total war.

'WORLD-POWER OR DECLINE'

In rapid succession between 1888 and 1890, Kaiser Wilhelm I, Bismarck, and Moltke—the three men with whose names the era of unification and the establishment of the German Reich were most intimately connected—either died or departed from public life. This was a coincidence which corresponded only too aptly to deeper trends that were transforming both German society and the international system in the late nineteenth century. A younger generation, which had grown up in a formidable German Empire with a sense of Prussia's great triumphs, now faced two fundamental and largely parallel developments. Internally, from the mid-1890s, German industrialization, hand in hand with urbanization and demographic growth, which had begun seriously in the 1850s and had taken off after the unification, entered a continuous period of outstandingly rapid expansion. Far outstripping the other great powers of Europe in her growth-rate, Germany now emerged from a position of rough equality in population and production to assume a marked and consistently widening superiority over all her major potential rivals. In the process, the country was transformed from a predominantly rural to a predominantly urban one, while her traditional social and political order was here struggling to keep its own and here forced to recede before modern capitalist mass society. Externally, Germany's fast-growing dependence on, and interest in, foreign trade and markets coincided with the general

---

[82] *Moltke as a Correspondent*, 274.

expansion of the Western industrial powers over the undeveloped world. The partitioning of Asia and Africa injected great instability, fierce competition, and tremendous new tensions into the old European power-system. In the age of imperialism, the European power-struggle was assuming global dimensions.

It is the interweaving of Germany's political, social, and intellectual traditions with these new conditions and challenges that accounts for all aspects of her development, including that of the military. This has been argued and demonstrated in the vast volume of works which have flowed, since the 1960s, from the Fischer controversy and from the reorientation of the German historical approach to Imperial Germany in the era before the world wars. Of this most contentious and massively documented period, the following passages can present only an overview.

It is customary to begin from the economic and demographic data, and with good reason. Between 1870 and 1914 German population grew 66 per cent, from 41 to 68 million. By comparison, France, Germany's major military rival, grew only 11 per cent, from 36 to 40 million. Thus German advantage grew from 13 per cent to 70 per cent. Moreover, when production figures are considered, Germany's advantage over France in 1910–13 was sixfold in coal production, more than threefold in pig-iron production, and fourfold in steel production. Overall, her manufacturing production was two and a half times that of France.

Between 1870 and 1913 German coal production increased by a factor of 6 and pig-iron production by a factor of 9.36. By comparison, in Britain, Germany's major economic contender, figures increased by only 2.25 and 1.5 times respectively. Whereas in 1870, Germany's industrial production was only a fraction of Britain's, by 1900 she had almost caught up with her in absolute terms, and by 1913 she had overtaken her, narrowing the gap in per capita production. In 1913, while being 10 per cent inferior to Britain in coal production, Germany was more than 50 per cent superior in pig-iron production and 134 per cent superior in steel production. Her overall manufacturing production was some 9 per cent greater.

In Europe, only the Russian growth-rate compared with the German, but starting from total backwardness, Russia was still very far behind Germany in 1913 by all indicators except population. Although Germany was less than half as populous as

Russia, her coal production was more than eight times as great and her pig-iron and steel production almost four times as great. Her overall manufacturing production was twice as great as Russia's. Yet her vast resources and fast growth-rate made Russia Germany's major potential rival.[83]

All in all, Germany was becoming at least as strong as France and Russia put together, and more powerful than Britain. On a global level, only the colossal United States was greatly superior to Germany by all indicators and potentially was already becoming the greatest power.[84]

All sections of Germany's ruling élite and of public opinion at large were highly conscious of these underlying trends. Not only was the balance of European power tilting in Germany's favour; the shift coincided with the dawn of a new era in world history. In a new global industrial and commercial system, Western expansion indicated that the future lay with world empires—politically, economically, and militarily. The opening-up and shrinking of the world were dwarfing the old continent of Europe. One could either take the step forward to the status of a world power in a new international system or be relegated to insignificance and decline. The new generation seemed to be facing a historic mission which was as demanding and magnificent as their fathers', and was in many ways similar to it. Then, the need had been to unite Germany and make her a great European power despite enormous domestic obstacles and against the opposition of some of the long-established great powers. Now, she had to be made a world power and expand to new continents already largely possessed by older colonial empires. Whereas under Bismarck, during the first decades of her

---

[83] Carlo M. Cipolla (ed.), *The Fontana Economic History of Europe* (Glasgow, 1973), iv. 747, 770–5; A. J. P. Taylor, *The Struggle for Mastery in Europe* (Oxford, 1954), pp. xxv–xxxi; H. J. Habakkuk and M. Postan (ed.), *The Cambridge Economic History of Europe (CEH)* (Cambridge, 1966), vi. 25; Paul Kennedy, *The Rise and Fall of the Great Powers* (London, 1988), 199–203. The figures vary slightly between these sources.

[84] Estimates of European state power on the basis of economic and demographic data in L. L. Farrar's stimulating *Arrogance and Anxiety: The Ambivalence of German Power, 1848–1914* (Iowa City, 1981), 10–39, are found crude in comparison with Kennedy's sophisticated set of measurements. If share of world manufacturing production is taken as a rough measure of state power in the industrial period, the percentages for 1913 are: Germany 14.8; Britain 13.6; Russia 8.2; France 6.1; Austro-Hungary 4.4; the USA 32.0: Kennedy, *The Rise and Fall of the Great Powers*, 202. The figures in *CEH* are slightly different, esp. regarding Russian production, estimated at 5.5 per cent.

existence, the German Empire had been a power of the status quo, she was now set against it, as Prussia under Bismarck had been before unification. Once again she seemed to need those qualities and resources that were held responsible for her glorious past ventures: great ambition and determination, boldness, and a spirit of dedication and self-sacrifice. Once again no great changes could be affected without the necessary modicum of ruthlessness and—as the other powers were unlikely to give way willingly—without the risk, indeed almost the inevitability, of war.

About all this a fundamental consensus prevailed almost across the board in German public life. The ethos of the old ruling class in the ministerial, administrative, and military establishment was matched, if not surpassed, by the enthusiasm of the bourgeoisie. The upper echelons of the bourgeoisie—the new magnates of business and industry and the political parties which spoke for them—in effect already shared in the leadership of Germany and could not be more aware of the prospects that lay ahead. The left-wing liberals may have opposed the grip of the old ruling class on the Reich's political, social, and military system, but many of them regarded precisely the creation of a German world-empire as a means of mobilizing the great popular energies of modern mass society, thus bridging the fearful divide between the working classes and the rest of society. The most distinguished university professors articulated this vision. By the eve of the Great War, even the Social Democratic Party, ideologically a mortal enemy of imperialism and military might alike, was beginning to feel the pressure for a more patriotic stand both within its rank and file and among its voters. Nobody personified the various trends, forces, and hopes that characterized Germany more forcefully than the man who aptly gave the period its name. This was the young and brilliant, but erratic and complex, Kaiser Wilhelm II, who by the turn of the century had led his country off on the two complementary courses of *Welt-* and *Flottenpolitik*.[85] On the whole, it would be fair to say that, within the prevailing consensus regarding Germany's future, differences, as important as they may have been, were mostly a matter of degree and were concerned with means.

This consensus also accounts for the views in the army. The latter, and especially the legendary Prussian Great General Staff,

[85] See the lively contributions to John Röhl and Nicolaus Sombart (eds.), *Kaiser Wilhelm II: New Interpretations* (Cambridge, 1982).

was regarded and feared by contemporaries as the bastion of German militarism and as the evil spirit of international politics. A more sophisticated version of this view influenced early historical works both inside and outside Germany, which sought to find in the peculiar position of the army within the state much of the reason for Germany's history and fate in modern times.[86] However, with the historical reappraisal of the trends and mood which dominated German policy and public opinion in the Wilhelmine era, a new picture emerged. While the army certainly had an important and largely independent position within the Reich's political and administrative structure, and, like each of the other bodies in this structure, certainly possessed its own characteristic professional and social point of view, this point of view was on the whole indistinguishable from the prevailing consensus.[87] Nor was it, of course, monolithic within this consensus. In this respect, opinions in the army, and the army's military orientation, mirrored the attitudes ruling the Reich and the general direction of German policy almost theme by theme.

In comparison with any of the other great powers, the dominating intellectual traditions in Germany needed remarkably little adaptation to the age of imperialism. The ideas which had found their most famous expression with Treitschke and Moltke were commonplace. In the military field, one could find them stated at the opening of almost each and every treatise. They were intended to provide the necessary foundation for any realistic appreciation of the essence of war and of its function in the relations between states.[88] Moltke's views were echoed by such disciples as Colonel, later General of Infantry, Wilhelm von Blume, whose book *Strategie* (1882) was based on a course of lectures delivered at the *Kriegsakademie*. The state, wrote Blume, was the highest form of organization in humanity's course of self-education towards ethical, intellectual, and material elevation. As such, each state constitutes a distinct cultural entity, whose interests may sometimes conflict with those of other states. Although civilized nations try to settle their differences peacefully, war, despite its horrors, is often

---

[86] See esp. Ritter, *Sword and Scepter*; Craig, *The Politics of the Prussian Army*.

[87] See esp. L. L. Farrar, *The Short-War Illusion* (Oxford, 1973), 20; id. *Arrogance and Anxiety*, 146–8, 176, 198–9.

[88] See Detlef Bald, 'Zum Kriegsbild der militärischen Führung im Kaiserreich', in J. Dülffer and K. Holl (eds.), *Bereit zum Krieg: Kriegsmentalität im wilhelminischen Deutschland, 1890–1914* (Göttingen, 1986), 150–3.

the unavoidable result. No state can forget this without risking destruction.[89] The prolific military author Lieutenant-General Albrecht von Boguslawski reiterated Moltke's opinions to the letter in his book *War in Its True Significance to the State and People.* War, he wrote, was the law of nature, while perpetual peace, advocated by the philosophers of the eighteenth century, was a dream, and not even a beautiful one.[90] It is therefore not surprising that, in comparison with its counterparts in the other European countries, the German peace-movement never gained any public stature. Its ideal went against the national ethos and was widely seen as naïve, undesirable, and dangerous.[91] Its activists, together with all other sorts of pacifists, were regarded with a mixture of contempt and despair by broad-minded men of the world, who saw them as 'political children'.[92] When the Hague Conferences convened in 1899 and 1907, they were regarded with cynicism, scepticism, and suspicion by all powers. But in Germany they were regarded with almost open hostility as a plot to tie the country's hands.[93]

In his international best seller *The Nation in Arms* (German orig. 1883), which in Germany alone ran through five editions by 1898, Major, later Field-Marshal, Colmar von der Goltz propounded the accepted ideas with greater zest: 'Wars are the fate of mankind, the inevitable destiny of nations.'[94] The various nations confront each other like individuals in the state of nature. No tribunal or arbitration has the power to curb their selfish interests and impose peace upon them. Individual good will notwithstanding, the

[89] Wilhelm von Blume, *Strategie: Eine Studie* (Berlin, 1882), 1–9; a 2nd edn. was published in 1886, and a 3rd, rev. one in 1912.

[90] Albrecht von Boguslawski, *Der Krieg in seiner wahren Bedeutung für Staat und Volk* (Berlin, 1892). For practically identical ideas see Wilhelm Balck, *Modern German Tactics* (London, 1899; first publ. in German 1892), 1–5; and Freytag-Loringhoven, *Krieg und Politik in der Neuzeit* (Berlin, 1911), esp. 268–80. During the war, as deputy chief of the general staff, Freytag-Loringhoven found the time to issue a collection from Treitschke's works: *Heinrich von Treitschke: Auswahl für das Feld* (Leipzig, 1917).

[91] For this and other opinions on the role of war, see Roger Chickering, *Imperial Germany and a World Without War: The Peace Movement and German Society 1892–1914* (Princeton, NJ 1975), esp. 183, 392–6.

[92] The quotation is from A. Boguslawski, *Betrachtungen über Heerwesen und Kriegführung* (Berlin, 1897), 89–90.

[93] A recent study is Jost Dülffer, *Regeln gegen den Krieg? Die Haager Friedenskonferenzen von 1899 und 1907* (Frankfurt a.M., 1981).

[94] Colmar von der Goltz, *The Nation in Arms* (London, 1906), 470.

dynamics of their position allows them no relaxation in their military efforts.[95] This is particularly true in the age of national war. The experience of French popular resistance in 1870–1, about which von der Goltz wrote his first book, is ominous:

The advent of future war is regarded with anxious expectation. Everyone seems to feel that it will be waged with a destructive force such as has hitherto never been displayed. War is now an exodus of nations and no longer a mere conflict between armies. All moral energies will be gathered for a life-and-death struggle; the whole sum of the intelligence residing in either people will be employed for their mutual destruction. . . . If obstinacy and persistency were displayed equally by both sides, the end of the struggle would only be conceivable after general devastation and pauperisation had completely exhausted the physical, and long suffering the moral, forces . . . it may be necessary to literally flood a country with troops and to exert extreme pressure upon the population for years on end.[96]

Behind this picture of war lay an overpowering perception of human history: 'a nation, like an individual, has to fulfil a certain mission in the time given it. The discharge of the duties of civilisation brings nations into conflict.'[97] Nineteenth-century historicism, an acute sense of unified human development and cultural growth, and intense nationalism came together with German idealism in the idea, most famously formulated by Hegel, that great historical nations dominated and personified the various stages of humanity's development. In the age of imperialism, hardly any other view in Germany was as influential in shaping popular perception of humanity's past, present, and future. 'The destiny of nations is like that of men,' wrote von der Goltz, 'nations rise, they grow, they bloom, they decay, and cease to be.' Germany, exploding with vigour, was now destined to take the place of older, decaying empires; her hour had come and she must rise to the challenge. 'The star of the young Empire has only just risen on the horizon; its full course lies still before it.'[98]

Predominance, of course, is never surrendered; it always has to be won. By the turn of the century, political realities and historical perspectives were everywhere receiving a timely reinforcement from the teaching of biology and the all-pervasive cultural impact of the Darwinian revolution. Human evolution was the scene of a

[95] Ibid. 10–11.　　　[96] Ibid. 463–5.
[97] Ibid. 463.　　　[98] Ibid. 474.

perpetual life-and-death struggle between races, peoples, and nations over space, resources, and power; only the fittest survived, while the others were doomed to extinction, disintegration, or subjugation.[99] Side by side with scientific racism, a very powerful culture of popular racism developed, which in Germany ran from the Kaiser himself downwards. The theories of the French Count Gobineau were transmitted and popularized by Wagner and developed by his son-in-law, Houston Stewart Chamberlain, in his widely read *Foundations of the Nineteenth Century* (1899). The book presented the racial struggle as the motive power of history and postulated the superiority of the Germanic peoples, and the Germans in particular, over all other races.[100] Representatives of the scholarly community cautioned that there was no scientific basis for biological demarcations between the various ethnic groups within the white race, and pointed out that all modern European nations, the Germans not excepting, were ethnically mixed.[101] Yet it was precisely here that much of the popular attraction of racism lay. By 1897 Boguslawski, while acknowledging the limited applicability of racial distinctions to Europe, went on to delineate the combination of racial and national qualities that characterized each of the major European armies.[102]

By the first decade of the twentieth century, the popular perception was that the Germanic race was gaining the ascendancy, while the inferior Latin and Celtic nations, particularly France, were declining. Things were more disturbing on Germany's eastern frontier. This was the scene of the historic and gigantic clash 'between Germandom and Slavdom' led by Russia, which so troubled Helmuth von Moltke the younger, nephew of the great Moltke and chief of the general staff from 1906 to 1914.[103] In his

---

[99] For the overall cultural impact, see Alfred Kelly, *The Descent of Darwin: The Popularization of Darwinism in Germany, 1860–1914* (Chapel Hill, NC, 1981).

[100] Two standard works are Léon Poliakov, *The Aryan Myth: A History of Racist and Nationalist Ideas in Europe* (London, 1974); and George L. Mosse, *Toward the Final Solution: A History of European Racism* (London, 1978). A good brief account for Germany is Roger Chickering, *We Men Who Feel Most German: A Cultural Study of the Pan-German League* (Boston, 1984), 237–45.

[101] See, for example, Max Weber, *Economy and Society* (New York, 1968), i. 385–98; Hans Delbrück, *Government and the Will of the People* (New York, 1923; first publ. in German 1914), 3–4. See also Fritz Fischer, *War of Illusions* (London, 1975), 255–7.   [102] Boguslawski, *Heerwesen und Kriegführung*, 21–35.

[103] The quotation is from a letter to the Austrian chief of staff, 10 Feb. 1913, in Conrad von Hötzendorf, *Aus meiner Dienstzeit, 1906–1918* (5 vols.; Berlin, 1921–5), iii. 146–7.

worried mind, the strong racial overtones which had always overlain his predecessors' preoccupations with the strategic problem of war with Russia, now assumed the more modern character of a racial life-and-death struggle for survival and world leadership. From 1912, with the rising tensions in the Balkans, the slogan of the coming 'racial war between the Teutons and the Slavs' was on everyone's lips, both in government and amongst the public.[104] Japan's spectacular defeat of Russia in 1904–5—the first victory of a modernized oriental nation over a great Western power—gave much food for thought. There was universal admiration for the young, vigorous race of warrior spirit, with whom the Germans felt a special affinity. 'How did the racial character of the Japanese bear up under the pressure of war against superior numbers?', ran the topic of one year's final essay in the Kriegsakademie.[105] Yet admiration was mixed with phobias concerning the growth of the 'Yellow Peril' that threatened white racial and political supremacy.[106] Blacks, of course, were regarded as subhuman and did not count at all. In 1904 the revolt of the Herrero nation in South West Africa was answered with a systematic policy and strategy of extermination, exceptional even by colonial standards. Anti-Semitism was increasingly prevalent from the 1870s and assumed a racial character.

National pride, rapid economic growth, the sight of a new world being opened up, a sense of historical and cultural mission amplified by racial overtones, and considerations of domestic politics—all these helped bring about the formation of German *Weltpolitik* by the turn of the twentieth century. Admittedly, in the long-drawn-out argument over the 'German problem' in modern European history, it has long been contended that in all these respects Germany was far from unique. As we shall see, similar views and ambitions prevailed throughout the Western world and motivated all the great powers in the age of imperialism.[107]

[104] For a rich selection of such comments see Fischer, *War of Illusions*, 190–5.
[105] Cited by Arden Bucholtz, *Hans Delbrück and the German Military Establishment: War Images in Conflict* (Iowa, 1985), 58.
[106] See, for example, Fritz von der Goltz, *Die gelbe Gefahr im Licht der Geschichte (The Yellow Peril in the Light of History)* (Leipzig, 1907). Fritz was Colmar's son and himself a general staff officer and military adviser to the Argentinan army.
[107] The most notable ideological defence is that by Ritter, *The German Problem* (Columbus, Oh., 1965). Outside Germany an authority like A. J. P. Taylor doubted in the wake of the Fischer controversy, that German power-politics was fundamentally

Yet it has also been pointed out that, because of her great strength and aspirations, Germany was the only great power whose aims and view of the future ultimately involved the destruction of the European balance of power and the virtual domination of Europe. Furthermore, German history and national ethos had been shaped in sharp and conscious rejection of the traditions of Enlightenment liberalism which in the West at least tempered the practices of *Realpolitik*. This gave German ambitions and conduct a particularly ruthless and menacing quality and appearance.

The Naval Laws of 1898 and 1900, which inaugurated the massive build-up of the German battle-fleet—soon to become the second most powerful in the world and a challenge to British naval supremacy—signalled the German intent to break out of the continent of Europe. While formerly measuring herself by continental standards mainly against France and Russia, Germany now measured herself by world standards against England, Russia, and the United States. Given Germany's new economic and global orientation, and with French power declining, England was assuming the position of Germany's arch-rival in the eyes of German decision-makers and the public at large. The prospect of a preventive continental war against France and Russia, which had dominated German military thought in the 1880s, was now overshadowed (at least in perception) by the prospect of war against England.

The realignment of the international system to face the growing German challenge took Germany completely by surprise. In 1904, having tried and failed to reach an agreement with Germany, England overcame her deep traditional rivalry with France and came to a settlement with her over their colonial differences. In another surprising move for Germany, the Anglo-French Entente was expanded and consolidated when, in 1907, England resolved the historical disputes in which she had been engaged with the Russian Empire, France's ally, in central Asia. Germany found herself isolated, with only Austria-Hungary on her side. Her attempt to undermine the Entente by forcing a show-down over Morocco in 1905–6, when Russia was paralysed by defeat and revolution, only brought England and France closer together. A second crisis over Morocco, in 1911, and successive Balkan crises

different or unique. See also David Calleo, *The German Problem Reconsidered* (New York, 1978), introduction and 49–53.

in 1908 and 1912–13, raised tensions in Europe to unprecedented levels and further strengthened the coalition against Germany. In turn, Germany felt politically contained and militarily encircled by what she perceived as a concerted effort to block her development into a world power. Enthusiastic expansionism now blended with deep anxieties over German security and survival. It was widely felt among the German ruling élite that what it regarded as Germany's necessary and legitimate growth was being gravely threatened: the hostility directed at her, and the formidable odds ranged against her, were jeopardizing her fundamental security. The impressive revival of Russian power in the years preceding the First World War, manifest in continuous economic expansion, massive military build-up and rapid railway-construction, seemed to be tipping the scale irrevocably against Germany in a matter of a few years.[108] The growing Russian strength made both Chancellor Bethmann-Hollweg and Chief of Staff Moltke profoundly pessimistic about Germany's future. It played a dominant role in steering German policy in the direction of pre-emptive or early war, an idea that was first mooted in the war council of December 1912 and figured prominently in German thinking until the July crisis of 1914.[109] Indeed, following the great debate over Germany's motives and aims on the eve of the First World War, it has been argued that neither expansionism and aggression nor insecurity and desperation were sufficient to explain German behaviour; only the highly dangerous combination of both could do this.[110]

The open confrontation between Germany and the Entente powers, which created an atmosphere of perpetual world-crisis in the decade preceding the Great War, charged German ambitions with intense public emotion and magnified the country's sense of being faced with decisions of fateful historical significance. No book expressed the views, unspoken assumptions, and hopes that prevailed in Germany more bluntly, or shocked foreign public opinion more deeply, than Friedrich von Bernhardi's famous *Germany and the Next War* (German orig. 1912), written in the wake of the second Moroccan crisis. The book won its author, a recently retired general of cavalry and one of Germany's foremost

---

[108] See Norman Stone, *The Eastern Front, 1914–1917* (London, 1975), chs. 1–2.
[109] See Fischer, *War of Illusions*, 161–4, 370–88.
[110] See esp. Farrar, *The Short-War Illusion*, pp. xvi, 33–7; id. *Arrogance and Anxiety*.

military writers, international renown. His even more shocking *Our Future* (1912), written after the Second Balkan War, further enhanced his reputation. In the Entente's war-propaganda he was to occupy an especially notorious place—together with Treitschke and Nietzsche—as the epitome of the German spirit and as one of its most influential representatives.[111]

The titles of the first five chapters of *Germany and the Next War* speak for themselves: 'The Right to Make War', 'The Duty to Make War', 'A Brief Survey of Germany's Historical Development', 'Germany's Historical Mission', and 'World Power or Downfall'.

... nations do not form a single society ... all real progress is founded upon the struggle for existence and the struggle for power prevailing among them. That struggle eliminates the weak and used-up nations and allows strong nations possessed of sturdy civilisation to maintain themselves and to obtain a position of predominant power until they too have fulfilled the civilising task and have to go down before young and rising nations.[112]

Thus 'war is a biological necessity'. Darwin and modern science corroborate Heraclitus' dictum that 'war is the father of all things'.[113]

Relying extensively on Fichte and Treitschke, Bernhardi exalted the cultural role and historical function of the state.[114] Its existence, he wrote, like that of the individual, 'is valuable only when it is consciously and actively employed for the attainment of great ends'.[115] Celebrating the glorious past of the German people as the exponent of reasoned liberty, Bernhardi rallied his countrymen to their future mission.[116]

In the new partitioning of the world, says Bernhardi, Germany started off belatedly and badly. A nation of 65 million people cannot be treated as inferior to a France of 40 million and an

---

[111] See J. A. Cramb, *Germany and England* (London, 1914); Charles S. Terry, *Treitschke, Bernhardi and Some Theologians* (Glasgow, 1915); Anon., *Bernhardi Converted* (London, 1915); James Crichton-Browne, *Bernhardi and Creation* (Glasgow, 1916).

[112] Friedrich von Bernhardi, *Britain as Germany's Vassal* (London, 1914; trans. of *Unsere Zukunft*), 27–8.

[113] Bernhardi, *Germany and the Next War* (New York, 1914), 18; also see *Britain as Germany's Vassal*, 106–7, 111–12.

[114] *Germany and the Next War*, 24–5, 45.

[115] Ibid. 56–7.   [116] Ibid. 58–65; *Britain as Germany's Vassal*, 30–46.

England of 45 million, of whom only part are of Germanic origin. In the coming realignment of the world, France must agree to, or be forced to acknowledge, German hegemony in Europe. Germany will consolidate her already massive economic control over Central Europe and the Balkans into an economic union and political alliance of Mitteleuropa, led by herself and through her sister-empire and proxy, Austria-Hungary. This union will extend to form a wider sphere of influence in the Ottoman Empire and the Near East. The major effort, however, should be made in the colonial sphere. Here, the first target is the formation of a huge German Mittelafrica, created by welding Germany's existing colonies to Portugal's old colonies and to the Belgian Congo, both ready for re-partition. England may either agree to the direction of German policy and form an alliance with her against the United States, the Slavs, and the Yellow Peril, who are the true future rivals of the European powers, or come to a collision with Germany.[117]

The main contribution of the massively documented works of Fritz Fischer was to show that Bernhardi's ideas and views of Germany's political aims were not shared only by the political Right but in fact reflected the wider consensus growing among Germany's ruling élite. While government circles and the liberal press denounced Bernhardi's book as irresponsible and harmful to Germany's foreign relations, the political vision to which he gave expression was actually the one which was to guide Germany during the Great War.[118] Helmuth von Moltke the younger, the chief of the general staff whose perception of Germany's position made him one of the major 'hawks' in the years preceding the war, delivered this characteristic statement in late 1914:

The Latin peoples have passed the zenith of their development, they can no longer introduce new fertilising elements into the development of the world as a whole. The Slav peoples, Russia in particular, are still too backward culturally to be able to take over the leadership of mankind. Under the rule of knout Europe would be led back to the state of spiritual barbarism. Britain pursues only material objectives. Germany alone . . . can at present take over the leadership of mankind into higher goals. . . . This war will

---

[117] *Germany and the Next War*, 132–55, 207–8; *Britain as Germany's Vassal*, 94–5, 104–7.
[118] Fischer, *Germany's Aims in the First World War* (New York, 1967; first publ. in German 1961), 34–5. See also, for various segments of German society, the essays compiled in Dülffer and Holl (eds.), *Bereit zum Krieg*.

lead to a new development in world history and . . . determine the direction in which the whole world will move for the next centuries . . .[119]

The German outlook on the future was mainly dynamic and optimistic. Equally, however, Bernhardi's famous slogan, 'world power or decline', captured the grave doubts and pessimistic thoughts which were depressing and tormenting the minds of Germany's ruling élite. 'Mighty deeds raised Germany from political disruptions and feebleness,' wrote Bernhardi; but was Germany still capable of living up to her present and future challenges?[120]

The rapid modernization of Germany, while doubling and redoubling her power and wealth, also bred a deeply felt cultural malaise. The disintegration of traditional society and of community life brought about massive social dislocation and urban alienation. Secularization, together with capitalist commercialism and materialism, eroded the old system of values and beliefs. To be sure, the development was European-wide. By the turn of the nineteenth century it gave rise throughout the Continent to the second of the great waves of anti-modernism which, since the late eighteenth century and in remarkably regular centennial intervals, have followed periods of great modernist enthusiasm. But in Germany in particular, where modernization was exceptionally rapid, this wave coincided with the major themes of the country's cultural tradition, which formed its distinct self-identity after the Romantic revolt.

Side by side with overflowing optimism regarding Germany's future, and great enthusiasm for technological advances, there was widespread unease at the present and nostalgic yearning for the qualities of a lost past.[121] The meteoric rise to fame experienced by Nietzsche's works in the late 1890s was symptomatic of an age which tried to escape from the uniformity, conformity, and mechanization of mass society by appealing to individual creativity, elementary forces of life, and aesthetic experience. In Germany in particular, these feelings blended well with the tendency to equate the ailings of modernity with Western liberalism, false rationalism, and the Judaeo-Roman tradition of Christian morality, all regarded as alien to the natural free spirit of ancient and historic Germandom.

---

[119] Helmuth von Moltke (the younger), *Betrachtungen und Erinnerungen* (Hamburg, 1914), 11; quoted by Fischer, *War of Illusions*, 549.

[120] Bernhardi, *Germany and the Next War*, 9.

[121] See the excellent introduction in Fritz Stern, *The Politics of Cultural Despair* (Berkeley, Calif., 1961).

Works—like those of popular authors such as Paul de Lagarde and Julius Langbehn—which propounded these ideas were enormously successful from the 1890s.[122] In addition, there were widespread fears that, historically, prosperity eroded organic unity and public virtue and spelt decadence and disintegration for great civilizations. Spengler's *Decline of the West* was published at the end of the Great War but conceived before it.[123] Was Germany losing her edge?—that was the disturbing question. During the second Moroccan crisis the younger Moltke—the spiritualist, cultural pessimist, and admirer of Paul de Lagarde—[124]wrote to his wife:

If we again creep out of this affair with our tail between our legs, if we cannot be aroused to an energetic demand which we are prepared to enforce by the sword, then I am doubtful about the future of the German Empire. Then I shall resign. But before, I will propose that we abolish the army and place ourselves under the protectorate of Japan. Then we will be able to make money without disturbance and make fools of ourselves.[125]

In the military field, no one expressed the prevailing mood and concerns more forcefully than Field-Marshal von der Goltz. His works reveal great attention to, and an acute grasp of, the rapid technological advances that were transforming war. But at the same time he was anxious that modernity should not lose the Germans their simple ancient warrior vigour. The cycle of civilization was obvious:

Victory brings might, might riches, but prosperity luxury. . . . The more civilized, the more wealthy a nation becomes, the greater the capacity for pleasure and indulgence. It shrinks from effort and comes gradually to estimate property and ease more highly than the brutal pursuit of war.[126]

---

[122] Felix Dahn's *Moltke als Erzieher* (Breslau, 1892) emulated Langbehn's famous *Rembrandt als Erzieher* (1890) which opposed an imaginary Rembrandt, personifying the true German spirit, with present-day philistinism. Dahn, a history professor and popular novelist who exalted pagan and medieval Germandom, also made Moltke the hero of a play (1890) modelled on Schiller's *Wallenstein*, and participated in the editing of Moltke's *Gesammelte Schriften*: George Mosse, *The Crisis of German Ideology* (London, 1966), 69–70; *Moltke as a Correspondent*, 307–8.

[123] H. Stuart Hughes, *Consciousness and Society: The Reorientation of European Social Thought 1890–1930* (London, 1959), 378.

[124] For a good brief portrait of Moltke, see Isabel Hull, *The Entourage of Kaiser Wilhelm II* (Cambridge, 1982), 239–42.

[125] Moltke, *Betrachtungen und Erinnerungen*, 19 Aug. 1911, 362.

[126] Colmar von der Goltz, *Jena to Eylau* (London, 1913), 74; see also *The Nation in Arms*, 8.

Germany . . . has become rich, and her riches increase daily. She grows in culture, but this growth in culture is unfavourable to the warlike development of her people. . . . Present-day philosophy teaches free development of personality. Everything which stands in its way should be put aside . . . Involuntarily the question arises; will the spoilt multitudes . . . be willing to respond to the stern call to sacrifice life and property in defence of the Fatherland?[127]

In his historical journey to the great scene of Prussia's downfall and regeneration, von der Goltz found a remarkable degree of analogy with the conditions and problems of his own age, with a clear warning attached. The reformers had traced Prussia's collapse before Napoleon predominantly to the inadequacy of her old political, social, and military system in the Revolutionary age of popular participation, and this line of explanation was re-emphasized in the great biographical histories of the military reformers written after the unification by Max Lehmann, Georg Heinrich Pertz, Hans Delbrück, and Friedrich Meinecke. However, for von der Goltz, the radical implications of this conclusion for his own time were unacceptable. He set out to rehabilitate the old army and state.[128] The main problem, he argued, was not a social one; the difficulty lay rather in a false conception of the nature of both politics and war, also pointed out by the reformers. Prussia had fallen victim to 'cosmopolitanism, the love of peace, humanitarian twaddle, and the deteriorated pre-Jena methods of warfare'.[129] False intellectual doctrines, generated during the Enlightenment, spoiled the natural moral strength of the army.[130] Now as then, one must guard against

half-heartedness in our military effort, the hidden working of heresies which hypnotize our common sense by a parade of pseudo-scientific arguments, against any adulteration or dilution of the warlike spirit and of warlike passion, against diplomatic generals, against the interference of political considerations with strategical and tactical decisions, and above all against the tendency to value more highly the art of war and perfection of technical training than the soldierly virtues.[131]

---

[127] *Jena to Eylau*, 70–3.

[128] Ibid. v–viii; *Von Rosbach bis Jena* (Berlin, 1906; earlier version, *Rosbach und Jena*, 1883). For Delbrück's criticism of the party-political and present-oriented character of von der Goltz's analysis see his *Historische und politische Aufsätze* (Berlin, 1886), iii. 113–30.

[129] Colmar von der Goltz, *Jena to Eylau*, 329.

[130] *The Nation in Arms*, 17–19.   [131] *Jena to Eylau*, 76.

Absorbed by the idea of an impending war with England for world position, von der Goltz worked with governmental support to foster traditional values among the younger generation.[132] Another widespread cause for concern in Germany was domestic politics. The rapid transformation of the country from a traditional agrarian society into an industrial and urban mass-society was becoming increasingly more difficult to accommodate to the Reich's authoritarian and semi-feudal regime. The Wilhelmine era was thus characterized by the chronic and worsening problem of securing a stable Reichstag majority for the government, as well as by an ever growing divide between the propertied classes and a continually expanding working class.[133] In the army, people looked upon the domestic situation no differently from their peers in the rest of the Reich's political community. General Waldersee, Moltke's deputy between 1882 and 1888 and chief of the general staff until 1891, was politically active and was widely talked of as the best appointee if the Reichstag became totally ungovernable and a royal *coup d'état* took place.[134] But otherwise, soldiers, even in higher ranks, were rarely more than involved spectators.[135] Like Moltke, they shared the widespread disgust with the parliamentary haggling and the 'rule of talk', and were concerned at the government's difficulties and at the 'irresponsible attitude' of the Reichstag, which compromised national unity and interests.

As before, in the periodical parliamentary debates on the military budget, the Reichstag was repeatedly reminded of the animosity, threats, and military build-up of the other great powers, and of the need for responsible defence-preparations. A war scare was exploited by Bismarck in 1887 to push through an increase in the

[132] Von der Goltz became chairman of the semi-military Young German League, which registered 750,000 members in 1914. See Mosse, *The Crisis of German Ideology*, 171–89; and for von der Goltz's outlook and concern his *Denkwürdigkeiten* (Berlin, 1929), 325–39; the testimony of his Turkish friend, Pertev Demirhan, *General-Feldmarschall Colmar von der Goltz* (Göttingen, 1960), esp. 90–1; Hermann Teske, *Colmar Freiherr von der Goltz* (Göttingen, 1957), 68–70; Bernhardi, *Britain as Germany's Vassal*, 245; Martin Kitchen, *The German Officer Corps 1890–1914* (Oxford, 1968), 103, 139–42.

[133] See esp. Hans-Ulrich Wehler, *The German Empire.* (Leamington Spa, 1985; first publ. in German 1973).

[134] See Alfred von Waldersee, *Denkwürdigkeiten*, ed. H. O. Meisner (3 vols.; Berlin, 1923); Goerlitz, *The German General Staff*, 103–26; Kitchen, *The German Officer Corps*, 64–95.

[135] For the politics of Wilhelm's inner military circle see Hull, *The Entourage of Wilhelm II*, 208–35.

army's strength. In 1892–3, Chancellor Caprivi, a former general himself, agreed to a reform of the army in return for Reichstag approval for its expansion. The term of active military service for the infantry was reduced from three to two years, allowing for a larger annual intake of men and, thus, for a considerable expansion of the army reserve.[136] Despite the indignant rhetoric, however, the truth of the matter was that, on the whole, the government got more or less what it wanted. The army was expanded with every successive Army Law, in line with German demographic growth and the increases in French armament (see Table 1). The standing army was kept at slightly over 1 per cent of the population during most of the Reich's lifetime. During Bismarck's time, this was regarded as sufficient. However, from the 1890s, with the formation of the Franco-Russian alliance and the growing certainty that Germany would have to fight on two fronts, the military odds

TABLE 1. *Strength of the German Army, 1874–1914*[137]

Year	Population (millions)	Active Corps	Reserve Formations	Manpower (Active)
1874	43	18		425,000
1880	45	18	18 div.	454,000
1887	48	18	18 div.	496,000
1890	49	20	20 div.	514,000
1893	52	20	20 div.	588,000
1900	56	23 + 5 sup.	20 div. (5 corps)	610,000
1911	65	23 + 2 sup.	14 1/2 corps	634,000
1912	66	25	14 1/2 corps	665,000
1913	67	25	14 1/2 corps	760,000
1914	68	25	14 1/2 corps	830,000

[136] J. Alden Nichols, *Germany after Bismarck: The Caprivi Era* (Cambridge, Mass, 1958) 192–64; Stig Förster, *Der doppelte Militarismus: Die deutsche Heeresrüstungspolitik zwischen Status-quo-Sicherung und Aggression 1890–1913* (Stuttgart, 1985), 36–74.

[137] Data on strength and organization can be found in Reichsarchiv, *Der Weltkrieg 1914–1918, Kriegsrüstung und Kriegswirtschaft* (Berlin, 1930), i. supp., 357–534. Also based on the Reich's archieves and useful are Ludwig Rüdt von Collenberg, *Die deutsche Armee von 1871 bis 1914* (Berlin, 1914); Kurt Jany, *Die königlich-preußische Armee und das deutsche Reichsheer, 1807 bis 1914*, iv (Berlin, 1933), 214–338.

changed drastically for the worse. Chief of Staff Waldersee and Minister of War Verdy du Vernois tried to push for the enforcement of universal military service for all eligible men, which existed only in law.[138] Only a fixed quota from the age-group due for conscription was actually being called for active service each year, leaving a considerable portion untrained. Waldersee's successor, Schlieffen, continued to press for the expansion of the army to meet the growing threat. However, the War Ministry and the government itself flatly rejected his requests.[139] In the first decade of the twentieth century, when German policy was becoming more aggressive, when the international tensions were mounting and the Reichstag was becoming more responsive, the German army's growth-rate was declining in relative terms. There were two main reasons for this apparent paradox. First, and most important, as German attention was shifting from the continent of Europe to the world scene, the army requests were overshadowed by the grandiose naval build-up.[140] Secondly, the army's growth was kept in check by social considerations which served partly as an excuse to avoid the financial problem, but were none the less real enough.

The social transformation of Germany worried the army deeply, affecting as it did the composition of both the officer corps and the rank and file. Reluctantly, the expanding army had to open itself to officers from the growing and prospering middle class. There were simply not enough candidates from the nobility.[141] Middle-class

[138] For Verdy's proposed reforms see Förster, *Der doppelte Militarismus*, 28–36; and for the army and parliament Manfred Messerschmidt, 'Die politische Geschichte der preußisch-deutschen Armee', in Militärgeschichtliches Forschungsamt (ed.), *Handbuch zur deutschen Militärgeschichte 1648–1939*, (Munich, 1979), ii. 232–48; Wiegand Schmidt-Richberg, 'Die Regierungszeit Wilhelms II', ibid., iii. 116–22. Also see Wilhelm Deist, 'Die Armee in Staat und Gesellschaft 1890–1914', in M. Stürmer (ed.), *Das kaiserliche Deutschland; Politik und Gesellschaft 1870–1918* (Düsseldorf, 1970), 312–39.
[139] Alfred von Schlieffen, *Briefe.*, ed. E. Kessel, (Göttingen, 1958), 13 Nov. 1892, 297; Reichsarchiv, *Der Weltkrieg*, i. supp., 57–72, 77–9, 84–7; Ritter, *Sword and Scepter*, ii. 206–16; Förster, *Der doppelte Militarismus*, 112–16, 129–34; Kitchen, *The German Officer Corps*, 31–3.
[140] By 1902 the naval estimates already amounted to 30 per cent of the army's. By 1911 they were half their size: Reichsarchiv, *Der Weltkrieg*, i, supp., 530. After 1905 the size of the regular army dropped below 1 per cent for the first time: H. von Kuhl, *Der deutsche Generalstab in Vorbereitung und Durchführung des Weltkrieges* (Berlin, 1920), 110.
[141] In 1860 the ratio of aristocrat to middle-class officers in the Prussian army was 2 to 1 in favour of the nobility. By 1913 this ratio had been reversed. In the same years, the ratio in the highest ranks of general and colonel changed from 86 per cent

officers were anxious to adopt the ruling ethos of their society and profession, and therefore totally assimilated their values and outlook. Yet army authorities feared that the traditional spirit of the officer corps would be eroded by democratization, liberalism, and penetration by bourgeois mentality.[142]

A much more threatening product of industrialization and urbanization came, however, from further below. In 1871 the ratio of rural to urban population in Germany was 2 to 1; by 1914 this had almost been reversed, with parity being reached in the mid-1890s.[143] The creation of huge concentrations of workers in the large cities was reflected in the steady rise in the power of the Social Democratic Party. From the military point of view, the most serious problem was the prospect of socialist ideas penetrating the rank and file. This would have compromised the loyalty and reliability of the army as the ultimate weapon of the government and of the existing order against domestic threats, as well as undermining its discipline, patriotism, and fighting-spirit as a military instrument. The army indoctrinated its members heavily against social democracy and suppressed any sign of socialist subversion, but it could hardly have expected to counter the social and political realities.[144]

The only remedy lay in the army's conscription-policy, which

and 14 per cent in favour of the nobility to parity. Karl Demeter, *The German Officer-Corps in Society and State 1650–1945* (London, 1965), 28–9, 267; Kitchen, *The German Officer Corps*, 24–5; W. Deist, 'Zur Geschichte des preußischen Offizierkorps, *1888–1918'*, in H. H. Hofmann (ed.), *Das deutsche Offizierkorps, 1860–1960* (Boppard am Rhein, 1980), 47–50.

[142] Like most ideas regarding the social and economic development of Imperial Germany, all this was suggested in the late 1920s by Eckart Kehr in his seminal articles on German armament; see esp. 'Class Struggle and Armament Policy in Imperial Germany' and 'The Genesis of the Royal Prussian Reserve Officer' in Kehr, *Economic Interest, Militarism and Foreign Policy: Essays*, ed. G. Craig (Berkeley, Calif., 1977), 63–74, 97–108. Also see Hartmut John, *Das Reserveoffizierkorps im Deutschen Kaiserreich 1890–1914* (Frankfurt a.M., 1981); Kitchen, *The Germany Officer Corps*, 22–36, 120–3.

[143] Koppel Pinson, *Modern Germany* (New York, 1966), 221.

[144] For attacks on social democracy, following closely in Moltke's footsteps, see e.g. A. Boguslawski—*nicht Scheinkampf: Ein Wort zur politischen Lage im Innern* (Berlin, 1895); and id. *Der Krieg in seiner wahren Bedeutung*. See also Reinhard Höhn, *Sozialismus und Heer* (Berlin, 1959), ii; Messerschmidt, 'Politische Geschichte', in Militärgeschichtliches Forschungsamt (ed.), *Handbuch zur deutschen Mitilärgeschichte*, ii. 248–74; Schmidt-Richberg, 'Regierungszeit Wilhelm II', ibid., iii. 111-16; Kitchen, *The German Officer Corps*, 143–86; Bernd-Felix Schulte, *Die deutsche Armee 1900–1914: Zwischen Beharren und Verändern* (Düsseldorf, 1977), 258–90, 535–47.

favoured the rural and country population and discriminated against the city proletariat.[145] However, when, in 1905, France passed the Two Years Service Law and rigorously abolished all exemptions from conscription, this remedy started to look most unsatisfactory. Whereas France was calling up 82 per cent of those liable for service, in Germany the figure was only 53 per cent.[146] In 1909, whilst urging the expansion of the army to meet the demands of a two-front war, Schlieffen pointed out that France, with a population of 40 million, was taking into her army 220,000 men annually and was keeping them with the colours for 25 years, thus creating a wartime establishment of 5.6 million; at the same time, Germany, with a population of 62 million, was calling up an annual contingent of 250,000 men and was keeping them with the colours for 19 years, thus possessing a wartime establishment of only 4.75 million.[147]

Especially for people like von der Goltz and Bernhardi, who called for the total mobilization of national resources for the eventuality, indeed the inevitability, of war, this was an agonizing and intolerable waste and it called for radical measures.[148] However, while denouncing the neglect of universal military service, upon which Germany's greatness had been built, both von der Goltz and Bernhardi were very ambivalent about mass armies, raising doubts as to their actual necessity and military effectiveness.[149] Less aristocratic minds were needed to draw the full conclusions from

---

[145] In 1911 64.15 per cent of the conscripts came from rural areas which, according to the census of 1905, comprised only 42.5 per cent of the population. Small and country towns, which comprised 25.5 per cent of the population, added another 22.34 per cent of the conscripts. The medium-sized towns, comprising 12.9 per cent of the population, provided only 7.37 per cent of the conscripts. From the large cities, the strongholds of social democracy, which comprised 19.1 per cent of the population, merely 6.14 per cent of the conscripts were drafted: Bernhardi, *Germany and the Next War*, 243–4.

[146] Reichsarchiv, *Der Weltkrieg*, i. supp., 168–9.

[147] 'Der Krieg in der Gegenwart', in Schlieffen, *Gessammelte Schriften*, i. 14. Of course, Schlieffen was, at least partly, fixing the figures; he counted the French territorial reserve but left out the equivalent German Landsturm. In both countries people served 2 years in the active army, 10 or 11 years in the first-line reserve (reserve and the Landwehr First Portion in Germany, reserve in France), and 12 or 13 years in the second and third-line reserve (territorials and territorial reserve in France, the Landwehr Second Portion and Landsturm in German).

[148] Ibid. 68–71; *Britain as Germany's Vassal*, 64, 169–70.

[149] Colmar von der Goltz, *The Nation in Arms*, 5; Bernhardi, *Britain as Germany's Vassal*, 169; id., *On War of To-Day*, i. 11, 79–101, ii. 438–56.

the character of modern war and from Germany's political and military aims, and to disregard class problems.[150]

Indeed, the initiative for a massive expansion of the army, which would make Germany a real nation-in-arms, came from the middle-class head of the deployment section in the general staff, Lieutenant-Colonel, later Colonel, Erich Ludendorff. He began pressing in this direction from 1910. In highly characteristic memoranda composed for the chief of the general staff, the younger Moltke, and sent to the Minister of War, he wrote:

Every state fighting with every fiber for survival must strain its every resources to live up to its highest obligations.[151]

Our enemies are so numerous that it may in certain circumstances become our inescapable duty to oppose them with our entire able-bodied manpower.[152]

We must again become the nation in arms great men in great times once made us. Germany must ever advance, never retreat.[153]

The political atmosphere after the Second Moroccan Crisis and during the Balkan Wars awoke new urgency in his superior, and also made the Ministry of War and the chancellor much more attentive. Disillusionment with the naval race again tipped the balance in the army's favour. In December 1912 the general staff asked for the addition of some 150,000 conscripts to the army's annual intake (an increase in the regular army of 300,000 men or about 50 per cent over two years of service). This would effectively have established universal military service. In addition to the raising of three new active army corps, more regular cadres were to be provided for the creation of more, better organized and better-equipped reserve divisions and corps. Supplementing the large numbers of reservists who brought the active corps to war-strength, these reserve formations were greatly to increase the number of reservists intended for front-line action. An effort was also made to create more effective formations for the multitude of largely untrained reservists, who had not been called for active service but had been massed together in replacement (*Ersatz*) units.

The enormity of the request startled the War Minister, von

[150] Fischer, *War of Illusions*, 105–6.
[151] 20 Aug. 1910, *Der Weltkrieg*, i, supp. 124; Ritter, *Sword and Scepter*, ii. 221.   [152] 1 July 1910, ibid. 119; Ritter, ii. 221.
[153] 25 Nov. 1912, ibid. 147; Ritter, ii. 223.

Heeringen, and the Chancellor, Bethmann-Hollweg, especially as the army had been expanded twice in the two preceding years. In the end, however, a compromise bill was brought before the Reichstag.[154] The deliberations in the Reichstag were accompanied by the massive propaganda campaign, led by the new Army League (Wehrverein), which had been founded in 1912 by another middle-class officer, Major-General August Keim. Like the many other patriotic associations which flourished in Wilhelmine Germany, the league appealed to middle-class patriotism and urged massive armament-measures in preparation for an inevitable world war, which would establish Germany's world position.[155] The Army Act of 1913 was approved by the Reichstag at a tremendous cost. No new active corps were added to the existing twenty-five, but the army was expanded by 136,000 men, and the organization of the reserves was much improved. Ludendorff was transferred to a field command.

The plan with which Germany went to war was the famous Schlieffen Plan. It aimed at winning all-out victory in a two-front war by concentrating almost all available forces for a gigantic lightning campaign of encirclement and annihilation against France, sweeping through neutral Belgium. The eastern front, where the Russian army was slow to mobilize owing to the backwardness of the Russian railway-system, was left virtually unprotected until a decision had been reached in the west. Even more than for its strategic boldness, the plan won fame because it underwent radically different interpretations with every major shift in the view of Germany's past. It mirrors the changing attitudes to Germany's motivation, aims, and achievements before and during the First World War.

[154] For the general staff's request, see Moltke to Bethmann-Hollweg (drafted by Ludendorff), 21 Dec. 1912, ibid., i, supp. 158–73. The naval estimates which had been half as large as the army's in 1911, dropped to 43 per cent in 1912 and to 30 per cent in 1913, as the army estimates soared 75 per cent, from 931,600,000 to 1,629,600,000 RM: ibid. 530. The regular army was expanded to an all-time high of 1.2 per cent of the population: Kuhl, *Der deutsche Generalstab*, 110. Also see Hans Herzfeld, *Die deutsche Rüstungpolitik vor dem Weltkrieg*; Förster, *Der doppelte Militarismus*, 208–96.

[155] By late 1912, the Army League claimed 40,000 individual members and 100,000 corporate ones. Half a year later the numbers rose to 78,000 and 200,000 respectively. Fischer, *War of Illusions*, 107; Chickering, *We Men Who Feel Most German*, 267–77. On the patriotic associations, see Geoff Eley, *Reshaping the German Right: Radical Nationalism and Political Change after Bismarck* (London, 1980).

For most of the German military after the painful defeat, the plan became the haven of lost opportunities, the ingenious recipe for victory watered down and mishandled by Schlieffen's successor in the general staff, the younger Moltke.[156] However, with Germany's collapse in the Second World War, the old dreams of power were dashed. It was in this atmosphere that the doyen of the post-war generation of German historians, Gerhard Ritter, undertook a critical study of the plan, drawing on the original drafts which were fully disclosed only at that time. He argued persuasively that, rather than an assured recipe for victory, the plan had in fact been a reckless gamble which risked everything on one card in a desperate attempt to come up with a decisive military result in a situation in which no such result was possible. At the same time, Ritter stuck to the traditional line of the German historians who, ever since the 'war guilt' debate, had persistently denied that their country had been particularly or inherently aggressive in either her outlook or policies. For Ritter, the problem of German militarism was rooted mainly in the evolution of the German military into a position of virtual independence from the responsible civilian government of the Reich. The Schlieffen Plan reflected this problem in that it was a 'purely military' scheme, devised, in typical fashion, by a 'military technician', in total disregard of political considerations, in which he had little interest.[157] Only with the growth of a younger generation of historians in the liberal post-war years, and with the revelations coming out of the Fischer controversy, did a different view of German history in the Wilhelmine era emerge. With it the ground was prepared for yet another shift in the assessment of the Schlieffen Plan.

On the whole, despite institutional biases and personal differences, a broad political consensus prevailed throughout the history of the German Reich among its ruling élite, including its military section. Under Bismarck, Germany was a power of the status quo. Correspondingly, Moltke's plans in the event of a two-front war

---

[156] See esp. W. Groener, *Das Testament des Grafen Schlieffen* (Berlin, 1927); id., *Der Feldherr wider Willen* (Berlin, 1930); and also W. Foerster, *Graf Schlieffen und der Weltkrieg* (2nd. edn.; Berlin, 1925); id., *Aus der Gedankenwerkstatt des deutschen Generalstabs* (Berlin, 1931); Jehuda L. Wallach, *Das Dogma der Vernichtungsschlacht* (Frankfurt a.M., 1967), 305–16.

[157] Ritter, *The Schlieffen Plan* (London, 1958; first publ. in German 1956); id. *Sword and Scepter*, ii, 193–226; also see Wallach, *Das Dogma der Vernichtungsschlacht*, 58–64 *et passim*.

were fundamentally defensive. He did not believe that a quick, decisive victory was possible in this eventuality. He therefore planned to split the German army equally between the Russian and French fronts and, while opting for limited offensive operations in the east, hoped to achieve no more than a favourable negotiated peace.[158] Even the warmonger Waldersee, his deputy and successor, did not deviate from either the political or the military aspects of this assessment. The 'preventive war' which he urged was fundamentally a defensive measure. However, in the Wilhelmine era, with the growth of German power and appetites, Germany embarked on an expansionist and revisionist *Weltpolitik*. The Schlieffen Plan, aiming at an out-and-out victory, became in effect the military equivalent of this policy.[159] Initially reflecting the traditional concerns of the general staff over a two-front war, it became Germany's only hope of achieving a decisive military result. A mere military draw could no longer be accepted as sufficient.[160] This is why the plan could not have been abandoned even after its author had long gone and its chances of success had grown very slim indeed.

It is true that the German general staff enjoyed almost absolute autonomy in its war-planning and devised the plan independently without any consultation with the civilian authorities.[161] Thus the main features of the plan paralleled German policy in the decade before the war, rather than being shaped by, and co-ordinated with, it. It is also true that the Schlieffen Plan harboured grave political implications and assumed a momentum of its own during the weeks of crisis that resulted in the outbreak of the First World War. By preparing an offensive two-front war in which Germany had to take the initiative, the plan in effect made such a war an inevitability, and by allowing for the violation of Belgian neutrality,

---

[158] See again Schmerfeld (ed.), *Die deutschen Aufmarschpläne*.

[159] According to the older view this congruence could only be interpreted as 'coincidental'; see, for example, Andreas Hillgruber, *Germany and the Two World Wars* (London, 1981; first publ. in German 1967), 6–8.

[160] Even Ritter unwittingly comes to the same conclusion: *The Schlieffen Plan*, 21. However, for the new interpretation see esp. Farrar, *Arrogance and Anxiety*, 23–4, 146–8, 198–9; and also Hull, *The Entourage of Wilhelm II*, 255–6.

[161] See Jack Snyder's objections in 'Civil-Military Relations and the Cult of the Offensive 1914 and 1984', in S. E. Miller (ed.), *Military Strategy and the Origins of the First World War* (Princeton, NJ, 1985), 125–9. Snyder himself admits, however, that on the whole the Schlieffen Plan's promise of quick decisive results suited the politicians very well.

it made British participation equally inevitable. However, to put the blame on Schlieffen's 'apolitical mind' is greatly misleading. For some fifteen years, all of Germany's leading statesmen knew and approved of the Schlieffen Plan and of its political implications. Schlieffen maintained close relations with Baron von Holstein, the leading personality in the Foreign Ministry, with whom he collaborated particularly closely during the Moroccan crisis of 1905.

Schlieffen's professional preoccupation and avoidance of any political involvement are indisputable. This, however, is quite different from military isolation. A historian of the older generation was already disputing the 'strictly military' view of Schlieffen, pointing out that his conservatism, royalism, devoutness, and anti-revolutionism clearly reflected his political world.[162] Indeed, Schlieffen's political outlook was typical of his milieu. In his famous essay 'War of the Present' (1909), he outlined Germany's international situation: France, the old enemy, was driven by her desire for revenge; England, the new enemy, was motivated by fierce competition with Germany's massively expanding economy; Russian hostility was inspired by the 'inherited antipathy of the Slavs for the Germans', as well as by modern economic factors. An economic integration of Mitteleuropa was essential to combat Germany's superior enemies.[163]

Like Germany's foreign policy as a whole, the Schlieffen Plan was an almost desperate attempt to reconcile Germany's great strength and ambitions with her relative inferiority *vis-à-vis* the Entente coalition and her perception of threat and insecurity. If the plan was overstretching the limits of German power, so was German policy.[164] Both politicians and soldiers attributed their predecessors' achievements to great resolution and determination. In fact, the diplomatic isolation of the enemy, ensuring numerical military advantage, had been by far the more important cause of Prussia's successes during the unification struggle.[165] With the massive

---

[162] See Kessel's introduction to Schlieffen, *Briefe*, 49–51.

[163] Schlieffen, 'Der Krieg in der Gegenwart', *Gesammelte Schriften*, i. 20, *et passim*.

[164] For a similar argument in the naval sphere, where another 'apolitical technician', Tirpitz, was also blamed by German historians of the older generation for Germany's misfortune, see Jonathan Steinberg, *Yesterday's Deterrent: Tirpitz and the Birth of the German Battle Fleet* (London, 1965), 22–5.

[165] See note 160 above.

expansion of the Russian army and railway system in the years preceding the war, one of the most crucial assumptions and prerequisites of the Schlieffen Plan—the slow rate of Russian mobilization—had been rapidly eroded.[166] Yet, despite Moltke's growing doubts, there was no alternative to the plan if Germany was to win a decisive victory.

Of course, the German conception of the conduct of war was much more in tune with aggressive foreign policy. There was always concern among the German military that policy should not impose restrictions on war which would thwart its natural tendency to use unlimited force to destroy the enemy. Despite some reservations about his claim that defence was stronger than attack, there was unanimity with Clausewitz in regarding the offensive as the sole legitimate form of war, and defence as a temporary expedient, to be employed only when one was not strong enough to attack.[167] Only the offensive, culminating in the great battle, can bring about the destruction of the enemy's armed forces and the breaking of his will to resist, which are the sole legitimate means and end in war. This kernel of ideas, consecrated by the authority of Clausewitz and Moltke, was universally agreed.[168] For Schlieffen, the political necessity and the military ideal happily coincided. Furthermore, as Moltke had pointed out, in the age of global industrial and commercial economy the need for a quick decision

[166] During the 1890s and 1900s, Russian mobilization in the west could take place at the rate of less than 200 trains per day; by 1910 the number rose to 250 and by 1914 to 360. By 1917 the rate would have risen to 560 trains, with mobilization completed by the eighteenth day, only 3 days after the German and French mobilizations: Stone, *The Eastern Front*, 40–1. The German general staff and government were painfully aware of this development, as well as of Russian military growth. In 1912 the Germans estimated that by 1915 the war establishment of the Russian field-army in Europe would increase by more than 50 per cent, from numerical parity with the German army to a superiority of more than 30 per cent: Kuhl, *Der deutsche Generalstab*, 109.

[167] For Clausewitz's positions, which postulated the offensive whenever possible and which have been mellowed by recent interpreters, see Azar Gat, 'Clausewitz on Defence and Attack', *Journal of Strategic Studies*, 10 (1988), 20–6. For criticism of Clausewitz's definition of defence as stronger than attack, see Colmar von der Goltz, *The nation in Arms*, 254–75; Bernhardi, *On War of To-Day*, ii. 1–32. For a concurrence with Clausewitz's position see Caemmerer, *Strategical Science*, 94–109.

[168] For this all-pervasive axiom see, for example, Blume, *Strategie*, 112, 151; Colmar von der Goltz, *The Nation in Arms*, 331, 468; id., *The Conduct of War*, 5–21; Scherff, *Von der Kriegführung* (Berlin, 1883), 85 et passim; *Die Lehre vom Kriege* (Berlin, 1897), 3; Prince Kraft zu Hohenlohe-Ingelfingen, *Letters on Strategy* (London, 1898; first publ. in German 1887), 9–10; Balck, *Modern German Tactics*, 5; Bernhardi, *On War of To-Day*, ii. 209–12, 336–8, 353.

had only been strengthened. The idea that war had to be cut short to avoid economic collapse—which, with the coming of the twentieth century, was widely talked of as ruling out a general war in modern conditions—played a significant role in Schlieffen's mind.[169]

The fundamental conception of the nature of war and military theory clearly set the framework within which every military question, past or present, was approached and judged. On the one hand, all dogma was rejected, and allowance was made for great theoretical flexibility. On the other, a whole cluster of ideas was regarded as embedded in the very nature of the phenomenon of war, which was unaffected by change. 'Lasting nature' and 'changing forms' cohabited. This was not merely the bequest of Clausewitz and Moltke; it expressed the all-pervasive and fundamental tenets of German culture.

Whereas in the West positivism ruled supreme during the second half of the nineteenth century, in Germany it hardly gained any ground at all. There the intellectual legacy of the Romantic period, with its sharp distinction between *Geistwissenschaften* and *Naturwissenschaften* held sway, revived and elaborated philosophically by the work of Wilhelm Diltey and the Marburg school. This distinction implied that the methods employed and the laws formulated in the natural sciences did not apply in human affairs. Man and human phenomena are ever shaped by history and dominated by the faculties of feeling, imagination, and volition. Since Ranke, the singularity of historical events had been the first article of faith for German historians. The principles of classical British political economy were rejected by the German historical school of economy from Adam Müller, through Friedrich List and Wilhelm Roscher, to Gustav Schmoller and Werner Sombart. The doctrine of universal natural law was rejected by German political philosophers and jurists. Similarly, German military authors never tired of repudiating all formal systems of principles for military theory, and persistently stressed the overriding importance of free circumstantial study, historical change, and moral forces.[170]

---

[169] See Kehr's provocative *Economic Interest*, 53–5. Also see, for example, Moltke, 'Verordnungen' (1869), *Militärische Werke*, II. ii. 173; Ritter, *The Schlieffen Plan*, 47–8.

[170] Blume, *Strategie*, 33–5; Kraft zu Hohenlohe-Ingelfingen, *Letters on Strategy*, 4, 10–11; Schlichting, *Moltkes Vermächtnis*, 6; Verdy du Vernois, *Studien über den*

Hence the considerable opposition in the higher ranks of the army to Schlieffen's growing dogmatism. In the general staff, Schlieffen was greatly admired, almost worshipped, by his subordinates, especially the younger generation of officers. But some of the army's most distinguished and conscientious officers objected to what they regarded as crude violations of the army's most fundamental theoretical tenets. In his obsession with his great plan of war against France, Schlieffen directed the historical section of the general staff to undertake a trans-historic study of the causes of victory in history, aimed at proving that all great victories had been won purely by encirclement.[171] He constantly impressed this doctrine on his subordinates during manœuvres, staff rides, and war games.[172] Finally, after his retirement, he pursued the same line in his historical 'Cannae Studies' and the essay 'War of the Present'.[173] His most outspoken critic in this matter was Bernhardi, who left his position as head of the historical section because of disagreements with Schlieffen. He publicly and thoroughly criticized Schlieffen's anonymous 'War of the Present' (1909), arguing principally, on various grounds, that the doctrine of encirclement could not be elevated to the status of sole recipe for victory. The conduct of operations, he argued, was ever flexible, depending on the circumstances as judged by the commander in the field. A break through the enemy's front, totally repudiated by Schlieffen, had its advantages and its opportune moments.[174] This view was shared, for example, by General Karl von Bülow, who was the quartermaster-general under Schlieffen in the general staff, and who was to command the Second Army of the Germans' enveloping right wing in 1914.[175]

Krieg (4 vols.; Berlin, 1891–1909), pt. iii. (1902), 1–60; Freytag-Loringhoven, *Die Macht der Persönlichkeit im Kriege: Studien nach Clausewitz* (Berlin, 1905); Bernhardi, *War of To-Day*, i. 1–2, 30–60.

[171] Generalstab (ed.), *Der Schlachterfolg, mit welchen Mitteln wurde er erstrebt?* (1903); Freytag-Loringhoven, *Generalfeldmarschall Graf von Schlieffen* (Leipzig, 1920), 58.

[172] See Ritter, *The Schlieffen Plan*, 50.

[173] The 'Cannae-Studien' are printed in Schlieffen, *Gesammelte Schriften*, i. 25–266.

[174] Bernhardi, *On War of To-Day*, ii. 40–51, 90–8, 154–81, 286; id. *Denkwürdigkeiten aus meinem Leben* (Berlin, 1927), 223–4.

[175] Friedrich von Boetticher, 'Der Lehrmeister des neuzeitlichen Krieges', in F. von Cochenhausen (ed.), *Von Scharnhorst zu Schlieffen 1806–1906: Hundert Jahre preußisch-deutscher Generalstab* (Berlin, 1933), 317.

The intense timetable essential to the success of the Schlieffen Plan necessitated meticulous day-to-day planning of the whole course of the campaign and strict adherence to the plan by the commanding generals. This went against the army's most fundamental beliefs, bequeathed from Clausewitz and Moltke, that friction would frustrate all pre-conceived plans and that consequently only general directives should be issued beyond the deployment (*Aufmarsch*) stage, while the subordinate commanders should be given wide freedom of action and room for individual initiative during the course of the campaign. General Sigismund von Schlichting, one of the most respected officers in the army, expressed these feelings most forcefully by contrasting the practices of his day with *Moltke's Legacy* (1901).[176] Similarly, in his audience with the Kaiser, in which he was offered the position of chief of the general staff, the younger Moltke criticized the general staff's war games, telling the Kaiser he did not believe that mass armies of millions could be controlled centrally. He doubted that modern wars could be won rapidly, at a single stroke. Modern war, he said, was likely to be a 'long, hard struggle with a country which will not let itself be subdued until its whole national power is broken'.[177] The growing unease in the army made Schlieffen state more than once that he did not believe in fixed formulas for victory.

As mentioned before, the other side of the theoretical coin was the canon of ideas and doctrines which were believed to express the true nature of war. There was an obvious historical and intellectual link between the conception of war which postulated out-and-out effort to destroy the enemy, and the professional canon of the German historians and political philosophers which postulated the predominance of the state and the nation and the primacy of foreign policy. Both were perceived by their exponents not as theoretical and ideological dogmas but as a correct and realistic *Weltanschauung*, on which the Germans prided themselves in comparison with the liberal West. In both cases there was almost total commitment within the professional communities to the fundamental theoretical premisses. In both cases challenges came mostly from outside and remained well on the fringes, while, at the same time, attracting a sharp, almost unanimous, negative response

---

[176] Schlichting, *Moltkes Vermächtniss*; Freiherr von Gayl, *General von Schlichting* (Berlin, 1913), 342–50; Caemmerer, *Strategical Science*, ch. 10.

[177] Moltke (the younger), *Erinnerungen*, 29 Jan. 1905, 308.

and stirring great excitement. In the Wilhelmine era, the ideas of Karl Lamprecht had this effect on the historical profession,[178] while those of Hans Delbrück and Ivan Bloch had the same effect on the military profession. In their very different ways and propounding totally different ideas, they all had one thing in common: they were heretical in relation to the prevailing outlook. Hence the more general significance of their interesting cases. Here lay the reason why, despite the sensation they created, they had almost no practical influence and are of interest only to historians of ideas. They serve to hightlight the boundaries of established opinion.

It was 1879 and Hans Delbrück had just left his post as tutor to one of the sons of the German crown prince and was about to begin his career as a young historian at the University of Berlin, when his great controversy with military opinion broke out. It was to last intermittently for fifty years in Delbrück's lifetime alone, and it continued for another decade thereafter. Only when Germany's collapse in the Second World War precipitated the eclipse of her traditional conception of war did it finally die out.

Delbrück was deeply and actively involved in German public life. He was well-connected in Court circles and in the corridors of government, sat for the Free Conservative Party in the Prussian Landtag (1882–5) and the German Reichstag (1884–90), and was Treitschke's successor as editor of the *Preußische Jahrbücher*. Because of his scholarly pre-eminence, social sensibilities, rejection of the vulgar forms of political extremism, conciliatory positions from the later stage of the First World War, and rivalry with Ludendorff and Tirpitz after that war, historians after the Second World War cast him in a 'good guy' role. Thus, while thoroughly documenting his affinity with the existing order, his belief in the political primacy and cultural role of the state, and his anti-parliamentarianism, a post-war study in Germany chose to label him as a critic of the Wilhelmine period.[179] Similarly, in two high-quality American studies of his military work, the fact that he was

---

[178] See Iggers, *The German Conception of History*, 197–200; Fritz K. Ringer, *The Decline of the German Mandarins: The German Academic Community 1890–1933* (Cambridge, Mass., 1969), 302–4; Felix Gilbert's introduction to *The Historical Essays of Otto Hintze* (New York, 1975).
[179] Annelise Thimme, *Hans Delbrück als Kritiker der Wilhelminischen Epoche* (Düsseldorf, 1955).

one of the most important and forceful public spokesmen of German imperialism and navalism is simply not mentioned.[180]

In truth, Delbrück was in every sense a true upholder of the Reich's ethos in its progressive brand.[181] He was typical of the intellectuals and politicians who shared Max Weber's analysis of the necessity of imperialist expansion in the age of modern, commercial mass-society.[182] Whereas mercantilistic considerations of raw materials and markets were uppermost in everyone's mind, by 1912 Delbrück was prepared to accept the Manchester school's claim that colonies did not pay. However, viewing the expanding global sphere of the English-speaking nations and countries as an enviable model, he saw colonialism predominantly as a means of propagating German civilization and at the same time finding an outlet for Germany's demographic growth.[183] With sophisticated wit he found the opportunity to remind his British audience in 1913 that the decline and fall of the Roman Empire provided 'the strongest empirical proof that peace is not the highest good of humanity'.[184] Like most Germans, he was thrilled when war came in 1914.[185]

---

[180] Bucholtz, *Hans Delbrück and the German Military Establishment*; Gordon Craig, 'Delbrück: The Military Historian', in P. Paret (ed.), *Makers of Modern Strategy from Machiavelli to the Nuclear Age* (Princeton, NJ, 1986), 326–53. An older, and in this respect more balanced, essay is Reinhard Bauer, 'Hans Delbrück', in B. Schmitt (ed.), *Some Historians of Modern Europe* (Chicago, 1941), 100–29.

[181] Like Max Weber, he regarded parliamentarism as nothing more than a means of securing popular legitimacy for the state in modern mass-society. Both men mocked the Western ideas of popular sovereignty and democracy: Wolfgang J. Mommsen, *Max Weber and German Politics 1890–1920* (London, 1984); Ilse Dronberger, *The Political Thought of Max Weber* (New York, 1971); Delbrück, *Government and the Will of the People*. The similarity with the ideas of Clausewitz and his fellow reformers—the progressive wing of the German Movement a century before—is striking: cf. Gat, *Enlightenment to Clausewitz*, 244–7.

[182] Emile Daniels, 'Delbrück als Politiker', in id. (ed.), *Am Webstuhl der Zeit* (Berlin, 1928), esp. 8–10. Also see F. J. Schmidt, K. Molinski, S. Mette, *Hans Delbrück, Der Historiker und Politiker* (Berlin, 1928), 137–89. A brief, balanced introduction is Andreas Hillgruber, 'Hans Delbrück', in H.-U. Wehler (ed.), *Deutsche Historiker* (Göttingen, 1972), iv. 40–52. Specifically on his programme to harness the German working-class to the patriotic and imperial cause, see Delbrück, Schmoller, and Wagner, *Über die Stumm'sche Herrenhaus-Rede gegen die Kathedersozialisten* (Berlin, 1897), 5–7.

[183] See the third collection of Delbrück's essays, *Vor und nach dem Weltkrieg, politische und historische Aufsätze 1902–1925* (Berlin, 1926), esp. 362–6 (Mar. 1912).

[184] Delbrück, *Numbers in History* (London, 1914), 55.

[185] See his patriotic and enthusiastic pamphlet *Über den kriegerischen Charakter des deutschen Volkes* (Berlin, 1914). In *Bismarcks Erbe* (Berlin, 1915), while advocating restraint in Germany's European ambitions, he restated her need of

Delbrück's controversy with some of Germany's leading military authorities, therefore, sprang from a different source. It was in fact inherent in his great life-work, which despite the suspicion from both academic and military quarters—a suspicion he never fully overcame[186]—subjected the previously neglected field of military history to the methods and standards of German historical scholarship. This included the critical study of sources, which exposed the partisan and largely fictitious nature of past accounts, especially the greatly inflated figures for enemy strength quoted for the most famous wars of Antiquity and the Middle Ages.[187] It also included the fundamental historicist tenet that every age should be understood in its own particular terms or, conversely, that all human institutions and practices—including the military—are in a deeper sense the necessary outgrowth and expression of the conditions prevailing in their times. This was the basis on which Delbrück's monumental *History of the Art of War within the Framework of Political History* (1900–20) was founded.

In Clausewitz's case, the historicist notions which had always been present in his mind surfaced in 1827 to undermine his life-long conception of the nature of war, based on the Napoleonic model. Not without pain, he then came to recognize that, apart from all-out or 'absolute' war (as he now called it), there also existed in history a second type of war, limited in its objectives and scale, which could not just be dismissed as an aberration or perversion of the true nature of war. In trying to explain this divergence, he turned primarily to the differences in the political conditions and the aims which gave rise to war. However, the planned revision of his work was terminated by his death, and his disciples in Germany tended to interpret the confusing mixture of his old and new ideas found in *On War* as a philosophical manner of expression. They stuck to his fundamental conception of war as an out-and-out effort to destroy the enemy, which reflected the dominating experience of the age, and which they themselves shared whole-heartedly.

world policies and aims, reminding his readers that 'every great nation is a colonizing nation'; ibid. 171–2.

[186] See Delbrück's preface to the fourth and last vol. of *History of the Art of War within the Framework of Political History* (London, 1985; first publ. in German 1920), x–xi.

[187] For a brief presentation of his method and results see Delbrück's brilliant *Numbers in History*.

Delbrück came to a similar conclusion as Clausewitz, but much earlier in his life, when he was only just beginning his research into military history. While working on his biography of Gneisenau, he was struck by the fundamental difference which he found between the old, eighteenth-century mode of warfare and that of the Napoleonic era. He explained this difference by referring to the radical change which had occurred in European politics and society in the transition from the restricting conditions prevailing under the *ancien régime* to the post-Revolutionary situation, in which popular resources and energies had been mobilized. This explanation fitted well into the general historical outlook; both military institutions and the conduct of war expressed the particular conditions prevailing in their age. Relying for support on Clausewitz's later ideas, Delbrück argued that varying historical conditions gave rise to two different types of strategy—the strategy of annihilation (*Niederwerfung*) and the strategy of attrition or exhaustion (*Ermattung*). Some of the great generals of history, from Pericles to Frederick the Great, were, in his opinion, exponents of the latter.[188]

The debate which developed, and in which von der Goltz, Theodor and Friedrich von Bernhardi, Caemmerer, Jähns and Boguslawski played the leading role on the military side, raged on two related battlegrounds. First, had Frederick the Great, who had previously been regarded as a precursor of Napoleon, really sought to wear the enemy down rather than destroy him in battle? Second, what had been the exact nature of the transformation in Clausewitz's ideas? On both issues Delbrück scored only part of the points. He could easily prove that Frederick's limited resources had set very definite limits to his ambitions. Frederick, argued Delbrück, never hoped to crush or occupy the Austrian Empire completely, as Napoleon would do, but only sought to gain limited territorial advantages. In the Seven Years War, when he was pressed by a greatly superior coalition, his only aim was to survive until his enemies gave up the fight. There was also little doubt, that after his ordeal, and having suffered very heavy casualties in attacking ever stronger Austrian defences, he had grown increasingly reluctant to risk his hard-to-replace troops in costly battles. His last campaign, in the War of the Bavarian Succession, was conducted as a pure campaign of manœuvre. All these were very significant points.

---

[188] The thesis was fully elaborated in Delbrück, *Die Strategie des Perikles erläutert durch die Strategie Friedrichs des Großen* (Berlin, 1890).

However, Delbrück's opponents, who raged over the slander of the great king's name, also had a point. Could Frederick's lightning campaigns and offensive battles be appropriately termed a strategy of exhaustion? Was there really no fundamental difference between the king's strategy and that of his arch-rival, the Austrian Field-Marshal Daun? Indeed, was not Delbrück's dichotomy crude and over-simplifying?[189]

Much of the same applied to the problem of Clausewitz's development. There was no escaping the fact that in 1827 he had admitted limited war into the theory of war and had intended to revise his whole work along this line. The argument that this revision had been oriented towards the past and had had no theoretical bearing on the present or future, was easily dismissed by Delbrück, who pointed out that Clausewitz had looked for the concept of war as such, which claimed universal validity. However, Delbrück's opponents rightly contended that, unlike Delbrück, Clausewitz had been talking about limited war, not limited strategy. They argued that what Clausewitz had come to recognize had been only limited political aims, and that, at the same time, he had continued to regard the destruction of the enemy forces, and particularly the clash of forces, as the only legitimate means in war.[190] Indeed, since Clausewitz's intellectual transformation had not been completed, on account of his death, in some of these points he remained half-way between his old and his new ideas.[191] For example, unlike Delbrück, he never came to rehabilitate eighteenth-century warfare, which he had always regarded as the most preposterous and disastrous distortion of the true nature of war. When other academic historians took up the debate in the 1920s and 1930s, they all had their reservations about the accuracy of Delbrück's observations.[192]

However, the reason why Delbrück found it so difficult to convince anybody was hardly because of these almost scholastic,

---

[189] For a summary of the debate and a list of the major contributions see Delbrück, *History of the Art of War*, vi, 378–82.

[190] Ibid.

[191] Gat, *Enlightenment to Clausewitz*, 223–6.

[192] Otto Hintze, 'Delbrück, Clausewitz und die Strategie Friedrichs des Großen', *Forschungen zur Brandenburgischen und Preußischen Geschichte*, 33 (1920), 131–77; Eberhard Kessel, 'Doppelpolige Strategie: Eine Studie zu Clausewitz, Delbrück und Friedrich dem Großen', *Wissen und Wehr*, 12 (1931), 623–31; reprinted in Johannes Kunisch (ed.), *Militärgeschichte und Kriegstheorie in neuerer Zeit* (Berlin, 1987).

albeit important, points. The sheer scale of the storm his opinions created indicates that he touched on some very deep nerve. He undermined the all-powerful conception of war and its conduct which postulated as the sole legitimate form of war out-and-out effort to achieve the total overthrow of the enemy by means of a gigantic clash of forces. As his critics put it, he violated the fundamental distinction between the 'fluctuating forms' (*Erscheinungsformen*) of war and its lasting 'inner essence' (*innere Wesensbedingungen*).[193] His ideas entailed an entirely new interpretation of the past, and especially of eighteenth-century warfare, in the fierce reaction against which the nineteenth century's conception of war had been formed. Furthermore, his ideas implied disturbing, and possibly even dangerous, conclusions for the present and future. Delbrück's problem is strikingly revealed in the solemn words of one of the younger historians who joined the debate and who never belonged to the military establishment. Even from his US exile in the late 1930s Herbert Rosinski wrote with enthusiasm:

The great tradition of decisive mobile strategy, from Scharnhorst onwards throughout the century, [was] not any infallible receipt, not a method or a system, but the very spirit of strategy—the adaptation of the changing forms and means of war to its ultimate object, the complete overthrow of the enemy's power of resistance.[194]

By contrast, when the First World War, which he regarded as defensive and imposed on Germany, persisted, Delbrück's old theoretical notions and basic political realism merged. His old controversy with military opinion now assumed a totally new practical significance. By 1916, when the desired lightning victory had failed to materialize and a war of positions and attrition set in, he was maintaining that Germany could not hope to overwhelm her strong enemies totally but should rather seek to wear them down in order to win a favourable negotiated peace. For that, she had to renounce all ambitions in regard to territorial annexation in the West (but not in the East or in Africa). Delbrück thus became the principal public opponent of the grandiose schemes of territorial expansion in Europe which grew to dominate both German policy

---

[193] Friedrich von Bernhardi, *Delbrück, Friedrich der Große und Clausewitz* (Berlin, 1892), cited in Bucholtz, *Hans Delbrück*, 38.
[194] Herbert Rosinski, *The German Army* (London, 1939), 138–9.

and public opinion during the war. In the later stage of the war, these were ruthlessly pursued by Ludendorff, who, from his position in the army supreme command, exercised a 'silent dictatorship' over Germany, in a bid for total victory in a total war. In his war-memoirs Ludendorff defined his purpose in unmistakable terms: 'concentrating all our resources and using them to the utmost in order to achieve peace on the battle-field, *as the very nature of war demands*'.[195] After the war, Delbrück became the most outspoken public critic of Ludendorff's direction of the war, both in the Reichstag committee which investigated the reasons for Germany's defeat, and in a long-drawn-out literary skirmish with Ludendorff himself, who made the imperative of total war his flag.[196]

Yet, as already mentioned, although Delbrück challenged one, albeit fundamental, aspect of the German conception of war, he wholeheartedly shared the wider premises of this conception. In terms of theory, this consisted in the historic indispensability and even desirability of war in relations between states. Practically, it meant calm acceptance of the fact that Germany's growth into a position of world power might very well involve war with other powers who would not forfeit their position willingly. Indeed, when Ivan Bloch denied the very feasibility of war in modern conditions, with clear theoretical and practical implications, Delbrück was quick to join the ranks as one of his most devastating critics.[197]

In the age in which war is being continually revolutionized by rapid technological changes, there has been little to match Bloch's remarkably prescient *War of the Future* (1898). Accurately delineating the features of what was to be the most curious and unexpected of all wars, it was composed—and perhaps this was no accident—by a complete amateur. Bloch was a well-connected Russian banker and railway magnate of Jewish-Polish origin, who after retirement immersed himself in the study of modern war. Eight years of work produced six mammoth quarto volumes, packed with fancy pictures, diagrams and tables, economic data,

[195] Erich Ludendorff, *My War Memories 1914–1918* (London, 1919), 5; my italics. This is the whole drift of his *Kriegführung und Politik* (Berlin, 1922).

[196] Delbrück, *Ludendorff, Tirpitz, Falkenhayn* (Berlin, 1920); id. *Ludendorffs Selbstporträt* (Berlin, 1922).

[197] Delbrück, 'Zukunftskrieg und Zukunftsfriede', *Preußische Jahrbücher*, 96 (1899), reprinted in *Erinnerungen, Aufsätze und Reden* (Berlin, 1902), 498–525.

and technical surveys:[198] 'He brought to the study of war an entirely new sort of mind, one in which the analytical skills of the engineer, the economist, and the sociologist were all combined. His book was in fact the first work of modern operational analysis.'[199] Analysing both the structure of world economy and the trend of modern weapons-technology, and drawing extensively on contemporary military literature and the experience of recent wars, he came out with unequivocal conclusions: war had become militarily impossible to decide and therefore also economically and socially suicidal.

In the military field, the meteoric increase in fire-power, set in motion by the Industrial Revolution towards the middle of the nineteenth century, went on after the German Wars of Unification. By the 1880s magazine-fed rifles had been adopted by all armies. In the mid-1880s, smokeless powder cleared the battlefield for both rifles and guns. The introduction of recoil-breakers produced the rapid-firing guns in the late 1890s. Finally, from the mid-1880s, the machine-gun began to make its appearance. All these doubled and trebled fire-rates, ranges, and accuracy, which had already begun to soar by 1870–1. For Bloch the implications were clear. They had been strikingly demonstrated in the first war in which magazine rifles had been used, the Russo-Turkish War of 1877–8. There, in their fortified camp at Plevna, entrenched and protected behind parapets, the Turks had repulsed three Russian assaults, with heavy losses; and since then the power of defence had been further magnified. In future war, argued Bloch, the entire front would freeze, leaving a desert of fire between the opposing armies:

At first there will be increased slaughter on so terrible a scale as to render it impossible to get troops to push the battle to a decisive issue. . . . Then, instead of a war fought on to the bitter end in a series of decisive battles, we shall have as a substitute a long period of continually increasing strain upon the resources of the combatants.[200]

---

[198] The complete work appeared in Russian (1898), French (1898), and German (1899) editions. For those confounded by this labyrinth, the English concise one-volume edition *Is War Now Impossible?* (London, 1899), is sufficient, if not better. By the same standard Bloch's interview with W. T. Stead, originally published in the *Review of Reviews*, is exquisite: *Has War Become Impossible?* (London, 1899).

[199] Michael E. Howard, 'Men Against Fire, Expectations of War in 1914', in Miller (ed.) *Military Strategy and the Origins of the First World War*, 41. If the language is no problem, there is a new biography in Polish: Ryszard Kolodziejczyk, *Jan Bloch (1836–1902)* (Warsaw, 1983).

[200] Bloch, *Has War Become Impossible?*, 6–7.

Everybody will be entrenched in the next war. It will be a great war of entrenchments. The spade will be as indispensable to the soldier as his rifle. . . . Battles will last for days, and in the end it is very doubtful whether any decisive victory can be gained.[201]

Once a stalemate is created, says Bloch, and the war turns into a struggle of attrition, the economic factor comes in. The modern industrial economies are totally interdependent because of an elaborate global division of labour and a highly developed system of trade. The disruption of war would be ruinous for them. Under these conditions, war is perhaps not impossible but is certainly suicidal. A general European war would mean 'a frightful series of catastrophes which would probably result in the overturn of all civilized and ordered government'. It would bring, 'even upon the victorious power, the destruction of its resources and the break-up of society'.[202]

In appreciating this astounding piece of prophecy and the sensation it created, one thing must be made absolutely clear: all armies and military men throughout Europe were highly aware of, and deeply concerned about, the sharp rise in fire-power and its detrimental effect on the offensive. In fact, all discussions of tactics for more than half a century had been dominated by this awareness and concern. In almost the same way, the economic consequences of a prolonged general war were widely talked about in the generation preceding the war, and the prospect of great domestic upheavals which would destroy the old political and social system was on everybody's mind. Bloch, however, won fame by drawing such radical conclusions from these common concerns.

It was not only that Bloch's conclusions were too radical to be believed on the existing evidence. His work aroused widespread objections because its implications were politically and militarily unacceptable. 'War,' wrote Bloch, 'once being regarded as unavoidable, the rulers shut their eyes to its consequences.'[203] Of course, he too had his point of view; he was a pacifist. Only he happened to be right. The objections of the military all stemmed from one source. In both detail and spirit they went back to the central conception of war. Bloch, it was argued, projected technical and tactical weapon-performance on to the picture of war as a whole; to use a later phrase, he 'succumbed to the technological imperative'. He over-emphasized the mechanical aspect of war and disregarded the

[201] Ibid. 17–18.   [202] Ibid. 21.   [203] Ibid. 37.

paramount role of moral forces. Thus he failed to see the advantages of initiative and morale inherent in the offensive.[204] Above all, his rejection of war could not be accepted. As already mentioned, this was the crux of the matter. Bloch threatened a whole philosophy of life, and such philosophies are rarely susceptible to change. As one anonymous critic put it:

As long as in . . . civilized states two 'modern' men still fight with one another for any reason . . . war between states will not be in the realm of the impossible, in spite of all the social and economic dangers and in spite of all the calculations of this ignorant theoretician.[205]

Indeed, the experience of the two subsequent major conflicts, the Boer War and, especially, the more regular Russo-Japanese War, seemed to confirm that the news about the death of war had been premature.[206] All armies noted that the strength of defence had grown enormously. Yet they also observed that victory had been gained, and that it had been gained through offensive spirit, superior morale, unwavering resolution, and the capacity to accept and sustain very heavy losses.[207] This was exactly in line with their all-powerful conception of war—past, present, and future. Writing in 1904, Lieutenant General Caemmerer, a sober and prudent soldier and a forceful exponent of the German conception of war, warned against a regression to the errors and misconceptions of the eighteenth century regarding the fundamental nature of war:

At the present moment we live in an age when an extraordinary progress in the technics of firearms exposes us to the danger of over-estimating the value of defensive positions, and where such theories of the importance of ground in strategy . . . might again become [a] serious danger for weak

---

[204] A good account of the Bloch debate in Germany can be found in Chickering, *Imperial Germany*, 388–92.   [205] Ibid. 391–2.

[206] Howard, 'The Doctrine of the Offensive in 1914', in Paret (ed.), *Makers of Modern Strategy*, 518. For Bloch's lectures during the South African War and for the British lessons, see T. H. E. Travers, 'Technology, Tactics and Morale: Jean de Bloch, the Boer War, and British Military Theory, 1900–1914', *Journal of Modern History*, 51 (1979), 264–86.

[207] See, for example, Schlieffen's close subordinate and chief of the historical section of the general staff, Freytag-Loringhoven, *Der Infantrie-Angriff in den neuesten Kriegen: Ein Beitrag zur Klärung der Angriffsfrage* (Berlin, 1905). On the responses in Germany to the South African and Russo-Japanese wars, see Schulte, *Die deutsche Armee*, 173–191, 199–233, which contains harsh criticism of the outdatedness of German tactics.

minds . . . It was therefore necessary to leave no doubts about their failure in history.[208]

To sum up, the German army possessed a close-knit conception of war, developed in the age of national war. This conception had been evolved on the basis of the Napoleonic model during the Romantic period and the era of Prussian reform, and had been fortified by Prussia's great triumphs in the era of unification. Its operational aspect postulated the complete overthrow of the enemy's power of resistance through the destruction of his field-army in great battles of annihilation. This in turn implied rapid concentration of forces, mobile strategy, and aggressive and offensive conduct. It was with this overriding view of war that the German army went to war in 1914, when it found that, with all nations armed to their teeth, in a new industrial setting, and with technology favouring the defence, the character of war had altered considerably. War as envisaged in the fundamental conception failed to materialize. No decision could be reached. A static total war of resources and attrition set in. Throughout the war, Germany struggled to win the desired decisive victory in a war which was perceived from the traditional intellectual perspective as, in a sense, nothing more than a very difficult case. For the German military, the war remained an all-out struggle of nations for survival and power in which material strength and moral greatness would be the deciding factors.[209] Indeed, the new face of war was equally surprising for all armies, who for almost half a century had taken their cue in military affairs from Germany, studying her great military authorities and assimilating at least the leading tenets of her operational concept.

---

[208] Caemmerer, *Strategical Science*, 70.

[209] And so it remained for conservative circles after the war. For some of the leading figures mentioned in this chapter, see Bernhardi, *Vom Kriege der Zukunft* (Berlin, 1920); August Keim, *Graf Schlieffen* (Berlin, 1921); Ludendorff, *Der totale Krieg* (Munich, 1935).

3

The Cult of the Offensive: The Sources of French Military Doctrine 1871–1914

THE story of French military doctrine on the eve and at the outbreak of the First World War is puzzling and has remained so despite all attempts at explanation. Rarely if ever in history had such a stark contrast developed between military doctrine, preached with an almost fanatic conviction, and the realities of war. The growth of fire-power and, correspondingly, the increasing preponderance of field-works and growing efficacy of tactical defence had been progressively demonstrated in the half century which elapsed between the American Civil War and the wars in South Africa and Manchuria. But the French army, alone of all armies, developed and went to war with the unique doctrine of unconditional offensive. Determining French war-planning in 1914, this doctrine came very close to submitting France to German invasion and was largely responsible for the terrifying human cost incurred by the French in their futile attacks on German positions during the early phase of the war. Within five months, France had suffered almost one million casualties, and almost another million and a half men were lost in 1915.[1] The predominance of the trench, the machine-gun, and the barbed-wire entanglement came as a surprise to all the belligerents; but, from the point of view of doctrine, it was the French army which suffered the rudest shock.

How is such a curious and gross blunder to be explained? Four independent lines of interpretation have been offered since the inter-war period. First, military historians have traced the origins of post-1871 French military theory to the French discovery of German military ideas in the mid-1880s. Coming as a revelation to

[1] The figures went down to 900,000 in 1916, 546,000 in 1917, and 1,095,000 in 1918; Paul-Marie de la Gorce, *The French Army: A Military-Political History* (London, 1963), 103.

a group of leading figures in the new staff college, the École de guerre, this discovery prompted an intellectual renaissance of great magnitude and influence. The doctrine of the offensive, it has been argued, was a further outgrowth of this formative development.[2]

Secondly, another school of historians has attributed the army's doctrines to its political leanings and sociological traits. Proceeding in the tradition of the Left's sweeping campaign in the 1900s to republicanize the army after the Dreyfus Affair and expressing the deep antagonism which prevailed between Left and Right in France in the 1920s and 1930s, these historians have viewed the army as one of the last strongholds of conservatism and anti-republicanism. They have argued that the army struggled desperately to maintain its distinctive spirit and character as a closed professional body against all efforts to turn it into an army of reservists, a real nation-in-arms. The cultivation of the offensive doctrine, arguably fit only for highly trained and cohesive professionals, is often regarded by these historians as one of the principal ideological products of this struggle.[3]

Thirdly, the fanaticism and divorce from reality which character-ized the advocates of the offensive and which appear to have bordered on the abnormal, if not the pathological, called for a deeper psychological insight. The French army, it has been argued, suffered from a deep-seated inferiority complex *vis-à-vis* its German counterpart. While German power was growing steadily and the disparity between the two armies was widening to hopeless proportions, the doctrine of the offensive became the means by which the French army escaped from the desperate reality of material odds into a world of fantasy and spiritual wishful thinking.[4]

[2] B. H. Liddell Hart, *Foch, The Man of Orleans* (London, 1931), 21–30; id., 'French Military Ideas before the First World War', in M. Gilbert (ed.), *A Century of Conflict 1850–1950* (London, 1966), 135–48; Dallas D. Irvine, 'The French Discovery of Clausewitz and Napoleon', *Journal of the American Military Institute*, 4 (1942), 143–61; Stefan Possony and Étienne Mantoux, 'Du Picq and Foch', in E. M. Earle (ed.), *Makers of Modern Strategy from Machiavelli to Hitler* (Princeton, NJ, 1943), 218.

[3] Monteilhet, *Les Institutions militaires de la France (1814–1924)*; Georges Michon, *La Préparation à la guerre: La Loi de trois ans (1910–1914)* (Paris, 1935); see also R. Girardet, *La Société militaire dans la France contemporaine, 1815–1939* (Paris, 1953), 193–278; Richard Challener, *The French Theory of the Nation in Arms* (New York, 1955).

[4] John Bowditch, 'The Concept of Élan Vital: A Rationalization of Weakness', in E. M. Earle (ed.), *Modern France* (Princeton, NJ, 1951), 32–43.

Fourthly, an affinity has long been discerned between the doctrine of the offensive and the French intellectual climate at the outset of the twentieth century. This intellectual climate was dominated by vitalistic notions customarily associated with Bergson's philosophy but in fact prevalent in French culture generally. It was also characterized by the yearning for spiritual and moral regeneration.[5]

Some of these lines of interpretation—almost self-contained from their beginning—have recently been restated even more vigorously, to the virtual exclusion of all other explanations.[6] Consequently, provided with remarkably coherent but mutually exclusive interpretations, historians seem to be facing a most unfortunate situation, in which it appears that the more we know the less we understand. The present chapter therefore attempts to bring together in a meaningful historical synthesis some fairly well-known materials. It will be argued that all the above-mentioned interpretations possess long lineage and appear perfectly plausible because all four are indeed well-founded. None of them, however, can stand alone. Like all historical phenomena, the doctrine of the offensive evolved from the joining-up and interweaving of several historical threads originating from separate and diverse sources.

THE FRENCH DISCOVERY OF CLAUSEWITZ AND NAPOLEON

The humiliating defeat of 1870–1 was traumatic for France. She was forced to accede to harsh peace-terms, topped by the handing-over to Germany of Alsace-Lorraine and by the payment of a huge war-indemnity, designed to cripple her finances and delay her military recovery for a generation. Furthermore, both politically and militarily, she had lost her traditional position as the predominant power in Europe. From being the terror of her

[5] e.g. ibid.; and, in his footsteps, Barbara Tuchman, *The Guns of August* (New York, 1962), 48; M. E. Howard, 'The Influence of Clausewitz', in Clausewitz, *On War* (Princeton, NJ, 1976), 37.

[6] For the second line of interpretation see J. Snyder, *The Ideology of the Offensive* (Ithaca, NY, 1984), 41–106; for the third, Douglas Porch, *The March to the Marne: The French Army, 1871–1914* (Cambridge, 1981), 213–31; id., 'Clausewitz and the French, 1871–1914', in M. Handel (ed.), *Clausewitz and Modern Strategy* (London, 1986), 287–301.

neighbours, she was now herself placed in a condition of inferiority *vis-à-vis* a powerful and arrogant Germany.

The war had been a crushing demonstration of German military superiority, but the reasons for this painful fact were not entirely clear, and explanations diverged. For Adolphe Thiers, for example, the problem amounted to no more than the criminally bad politics of Napoleon III and the related state of French military unpreparedness. Others were far more pessimistic. There was widespread gloom, and deeper concern that hierarchic and disciplined German society, respecting authority, duty, order, and hard work, was fundamentally superior to morally degenerate and politically and socially divided France.[7] On the more practical level, however, German military preponderance was widely attributed to the greatly superior Prussian reserve, mobilization, and staff systems, which enabled Prussia and her allies to deploy, supply, and control in the field, with astonishing effectiveness, vast armies that enjoyed overwhelming numerical advantage. However distasteful this fact was, the Prussian military model set the agenda for military reform in France after 1871. Considered from organizational and institutional points of view by a whole host of military pamphleteers and by the responsible governmental and army authorities, the Prussian model dictated, and generated, a sweeping restructuring of the French army during the 1870s.

The adoption of the Prussian system of short, universal military service was favoured by most generals and politicians in the wake of the defeat. It was mainly the personal position and high-handed interference of Thiers, the Republic's formidable president, that prevented it from being accepted more or less in its entirety. Adhering to the old liberal principles of the Orlean monarchy, he both feared the arming of the people and objected to the compulsory conscription of the sons of the bourgeoisie. Flaunting his authority as the foremost historian of the First Empire, he argued that the strength of the Napoleonic armies had lain in their hard core of veterans. He saw no serious fault in the old long-service professional army, which he wanted to keep as a reliable political instrument. Threatening at one point to resign, he effectively forced a compromise on the National Assembly. Thus the Law of 1872 enacted the principle of universal military service

---

[7] Ernest Renan, *La Réforme intellectuelle et morale de la France* (Paris, 1871); also see Trochu in Porch, *The March to the Marne*, 36.

and abolished paid substitution but stipulated two different lengths of service. While part of the recruits, determined by lot, were to serve for a period of five years, the rest were to serve for only six months to one year before passing to the reserve. On the model of the German one-year volunteers, high-school graduates enrolling in the universities and providing for their own uniform and maintenance served for one year only and were released to the reserve as second lieutenants. Young men training to be teachers or priests were totally exempted, and there were many other exemptions on family and social grounds.[8] In practice, however, successive ministers of war soon circumvented the law by administrative means. Regarding the shorter period of service as militarily unsound, they introduced a more egalitarian system by reducing the number of one-year conscripts and keeping them with the colours for longer periods of time. At the same time, they increased the number of long-term conscripts, while releasing them before the end of their legal term.[9] The law itself was changed only in 1889.

The army, which before 1870 had had no permanent organization above the regimental level, adopted the Prussian brigade, division, and corps structure. Like the German army, it was formed (in metropolitan France) into eighteen army corps.[10] In a great effort of construction, the railway network leading to the German border was vastly expanded, and the difference in speed between German and French mobilization was considerably reduced.[11] A new general staff was created in the Ministry of War in 1871 and reformed in 1874 to replace the old and inadequate Dépôt de guerre. Although providing a badly needed permanent and central organ of operational planning, it was still far inferior to its German counterpart. The supreme command remained with the responsible political and military authorities—the president and the minister of war—and was later entrusted to a generalissimo, a post created in

---

[8] Monteilhet, *Les Institutions militaires*, 109–153; David Ralston, *The Army of the Republic: The Place of the Military in the Political Evolution of France 1871–1914* (Cambridge, Mass., 1967), 35–48; Allan Mitchell, *Victors and Vanquished: The German Influence on Army and Church in France after 1870* (London, 1984), 20–30.

[9] Of an average annual contingent of almost 300,000, about half were fully exempted on various grounds. Of those recruited, the ratio of short- to long-term conscripts was, on average, more than 1 : 2 until 1877, and then fell to about 1 : 4 by 1880: Porch, *The March to the Marne*, 29.

[10] Ralston, *The Army of the Republic*, 49–52; Mitchell, *Victors and Vanquished*, 32–48.   [11] Mitchell, *Victors and Vanquished*, 60–4.

time of war only. Thus, as in the original Prussian command-structure before the extraordinary shifts of power in the Moltke era, the new French general staff was no more than a planning-bureau. It was officially designated the General Staff of the Minister of War to underline its subordinate role and was headed by a relatively junior general.

The staff corps was also reformed on the Prussian model. The closed staff-corps system, whose members had seen no active service with the troops and had therefore been out of touch with the rest of the army, was abolished. The Prussian system of rotating general-staff officers between staff- and field-posts was adopted in its place.[12] The old staff college was closed and a new one, emulating the Prussian Kriegsakademie, was created in 1876–8 to train the army's future command-echelon. The École militaire supérieure or École supérieure de guerre, as it was renamed in 1880, accepted officers with several years of regimental service after a competitive entrance-examination and offered a two-year course, as against three years in its German counterpart.

While the massive fortification of the eastern border carried out from 1874 by General Séré de Rivières shielded France from a swift German attack,[13] the French army was again becoming a force to be reckoned with. Although Gambetta returned from his tour in Germany in 1876 convinced that the French army was no match for the German,[14] Moltke was much impressed and alarmed by the speed and scale of the French recovery. The French, he told the Reichstag in 1874, were adopting the German military institutions under French names.[15] From the late 1870s, he assumed a defensive posture for the German army in the west in the case of a two-front war.

The instititional reforms in the French army were matched by strong intellectual ferment. The old Imperial army had been famous not only for its panache and its exaltation of the manly and martial virtues but also for its disdain of, and aversion to, all forms of

---

[12] Ralston, *The Army of the Republic*, 141–161, 89–94; Porch, *The March to the Marne*, 82–7.
[13] A. Marchand, *Plans de concentration de 1871 à 1914* (Paris, 1926), 4–9; Mitchell, *Victors and Vanquished*, 53–60.
[14] Herbert Tint, *The Decline of French Patriotism, 1870–1940* (London, 1964), 23.
[15] Moltke, *Essays, Speeches and Memoirs of Field-Marshal Count Helmuth von Moltke* (2 vols.; New York, 1893), ii. 109.

intellectualism and bookishness. Marshal MacMahon had reputedly stated that he would eliminate from the promotion list any officer whose name he had seen on the cover of a book.[16] The generals of the Empire had been baffled by the map-exercises and *Kriegspiele* on the Prussian model, which Napoleon III had tried to introduce before 1870.[17] Furthermore, in the tradition of the Revolutionary armies, the great majority of the French officers had been promoted directly from the ranks and had humble social origins, many of them barely knowing how to read or write. The contrast with their German peers in the campaign of 1870–1 was striking.[18] It was to the intellectual and professional qualities of the German officer-corps—no less than to the excellence of the German system of elementary education, shaping the rank and file—that the outcome of Metz and Sedan was generally credited. The reform of French military education, ranging from the establishment of NCO schools through the reform of the cadet academies to the creation of the École de guerre, was an acknowledgement that the French were lacking in the fundamentals of the military profession.[19] 'Before the war none of us knew anything,' admitted General Galliffet, one of the heroes of the old army.[20] New professional military journals like the *Revue militaire des armées étrangères* (1872) and the *Revue d'artillerie* (1873) were founded to promote military knowledge. Military literature proliferated.

The process of reform was accompanied in the early 1870s by the publication of a great many works devising and debating schemes for, and methods of, conscription and mobilization, staff organization, and military education. The most distinguished of the new military authors was Colonel, later General, Jules-Lewis Lewal. Chief of the historical-statistical bureau of the Dépôt de la guerre before 1870, he won renown after the war as one of the most outspoken critics of the old army and the author of the most comprehensive scheme of reform, *La Réforme de l'armée* (1871). He later became the founding father of the École de guerre (1877–80) and Minister of War (1885). In a series of books which

---

[16] Gorce, *The French Army*, 9. For more examples of the same attitude, see Irvine, 'The French Discovery of Clausewitz and Napoleon', 146–8.

[17] Porch, *The March to the Marne*, 41.

[18] Howard, *The Franco-Prussian War*, 16; Porch, *The March to the Marne*, 37–8.

[19] Porch, *The March to the Marne*, 39–41.

[20] Ralston, *The Army of the Republic*, 87.

appeared under the common title *Études de guerre* (1873–90), he gradually gravitated from questions of military organization and education towards the topic of the conduct of armies in the field. Hesitantly, French military authors were again stepping into the long-neglected field of operational doctrine. They came equipped with the concepts of positivism and scientism, which dominated their intellectual environment, as well as with the classical heritage of military theory since the age of the Enlightenment.

As noted by recent historians, Lewal's positivism was intertwined with a thoroughgoing determination to infuse the French army with a true spirit of professionalism. He believed that the scientific and systematic study and conduct of war were the secret of the success of the German education and staff system and accounted for its superiority. 'War is today a positivist science,' he preached to his readers.[21] Military organization, he maintained, was based on a number of positive principles and axioms.[22] In his *Introduction to the Positive Part of Strategy* (1892), he quoted Marmont, following in the tradition of the Enlightenment, to the effect that war had two parts: one speculative and moral, the other positive and based on principles.[23] In strategy, the latter consisted fundamentally of the Napoleonic-Jominian rationale of operations.[24]

Other military authors wrote in the same vein, presenting the classical rationale of operations in the context of modern concerns and practices in the fields of mobilization, transportation, and deployment. So did General Jean-Auguste Berthaut, Minister of War from 1876 to 1877; Colonel, later General, Victor Derrécagaix, captain in the old general staff and, in the mid-1880s, deputy chief of the École de guerre; and General Édouard Pierron.[25] Positivism, however, was most remarkably represented in the works of General Théodore Jung, who certainly deserves a separate study. His *War and Society* (1889) is a unique catalogue of positivist thought and an astonishing testimony to the author's extensive philosophical and scientific interests. He cites every prominent name in European

---

[21] Mitchell, *Victors and Vanquished*, 87.
[22] J. L. Lewal, *La Réforme de l'armée* (Paris, 1871), 3.
[23] Id., *Introduction à La Partie positive de la stratégie* (Paris, 1892), 36–7.
[24] Ibid. 49–53.
[25] J. A. Berthaut, *Principes de stratégie, étude sur la conduite des armées* (Paris, 1881); V. D. Derrécagaix, *La Guerre moderne* (Paris, 1885; trans. as *Modern War*, Washington, DC, 1888); Édouard Pierron, *Stratégie et grande tactique, d'après l'expérience des dernières guerres* (Paris, 1887).

science and positivist thought to support his main thesis:[26] that the study of war is part of that growing science of society which takes its example from the older and more established exact and natural sciences. Like mathematics, physics, and biology, it searches for uniform patterns of cause and effect and formulates them into simple, necessary, and universal laws.[27]

From the mid-1880s, however, a new note crept in. By 1892, in *The Positive Part of Strategy*, Lewal was giving Clausewitz a prominent place alongside the previously accepted authorities—de Saxe, Guibert, Archduke Charles, Jomini, Marmont, and Rüstow. By 1895 he was stressing the role of will-power, *la volonté*, in war and suggesting that 'it would appear exaggerated to argue with Jomini that, since Napoleon, strategy is fixed and incapable of further perfection'.[28] Derrécagaix was changing even more swiftly and decisively. As early as 1885 he was already presenting Clausewitz's conception of war and quoting von der Goltz and Blume. By 1901 he was totally converted.[29] Pierron wrote the introduction to the new translation of Clausewitz's *On War*. New influences were at work, and a new, vigorous group of intellectual activists was forming and taking the lead.

It took some time before the French acquired any idea at all of German military theory. As mentioned before, after their defeat and throughout the 1870s, they interpreted German superiority and success—not without good reason—almost purely in organizational and institutional terms. In regard to command, they deemed the source of German military proficiency to be in the legendary Prussian staff-corps, renowned for being meticulously recruited, methodically and scientifically trained to inhuman exactness and

---

[26] The precursors of social science—Bacon, Vico, Herder, Diderot, Condorcet, Comte, Blainville, Spencer, and Buckle—are followed in France by Coste, Littré, Taine, Laugel, Fouillée, Laffitte, Bourdeau, Moroeau, and Binet (to name only some of those cited); in England by Bagehot, Bain, Huxley, Flint, etc.; and in Germany by Hartmann, Lotze, Moleschott, Virchow, Wundt, Heckel, Buchner, Helmholtz, and others; Théodore Jung, *La Guerre et la société* (Paris, 1889), 1–3, 84. The book is dedicated to the famous Dr Charcot, Freud's teacher. See also E. Guillon, *Nos écrivains militaires* (2 vols.; Paris, 1898), 382–8.

[27] Jung, *La Guerre et la société*, esp. 1, 5, 119, 122. See also his *Stratégie, tactique et politique* (Paris, 1890).

[28] Lewal, *Stratégie de combat*, i (Paris, 1895), 6 ff.

[29] Derrécagaix, *Modern War*, 25–7 et passim.; id. *La Guerre et l'armée* (Paris, 1901), 5–8 et passim. Also see Pierron, *La Stratégie et la tactique allemande au début du XX*^*e*^ *siècle* (Paris, 1900).

co-ordination, and functioning with automatic technical perfection. Crowning this image was the grim Moltke, regarded by the French as no great general but as the technocratic and autocratic chief of a bureaucratic machine.[30] Only gradually did closer study provide more intimate knowledge and insight. After 1871 German won the status of being the sole obligatory foreign language taught at the cadet schools and the École de guerre. The *Revue militaire de l'étranger* (from 1901 *Revue militaire des armées étrangères*), which provided French officers with translated selections from foreign military publications, naturally focused on Germany. However, the most decisive change in this respect occurred only in the 1880s. Moltke remained his silent self for the French and as unpopular as ever.[31] But, with the appearance of Blume's *Strategie* (1882; trans. 1884), Hohenlohe's *Letters on Strategy* (1887; trans. 1887) and, above all, von der Goltz's *The Nation in Arms* (1883; trans. 1884), the German conception of war and its conduct was revealed for the first time with a striking clarity and impressive cohesiveness. From these books the French learned that the German military traced their lineage to a great master, Clausewitz. *On War* was translated into French in 1886–7.[32] German military authors were becoming household names. Review articles and translations abounded. The so-called 'French discovery of Clausewitz and Napoleon' got under way.[33]

In 1884 Lucien Cardot, major in the intelligence bureau of the French general staff, discovered Clausewitz, and a year later he delivered three brilliant lectures on Prussian military thought at the École de guerre.[34] In 1887, following the translation into French of

---

[30] Most characteristic is Lewal's obituary, *Le Maréchal de Moltke, organisateur et stratège* (Paris, 1891); and Caemmerer's both exacerbated and amused response in *Strategical Science*, 229. Also see E. Carrias, *La Pensée militaire française* (Paris, 1960), 281.

[31] See the citations from Bonnal, Gilbert and Foch in Witold Zaniewicki, 'L'Impact de 1870 sur la pensée militaire française', *Revue de Défense Nationale*, 26 (1970), 1331–41.

[32] Clausewitz, *Théorie de la grande guerre* (3 vols.; Paris, 1886–7). An older French translation (Paris, 1849–52) was out of print.

[33] Irvine, 'The French discovery of Clausewitz and Napoleon', though often didactic, is the only rigorous study; see 152–7. Curiously, Mitchell's *Victors and Vanquished*, whose special theme is the German influence on the French army, does not even mention the influence of German military ideas.

[34] H. Camon, *Clausewitz* (Paris, 1911), 1; J. Dany, 'La Littérature militaire d'aujourd'hui', *La Revue de Paris* (Mar.–Apr. 1912), 612; Irvine, 'The French Discovery of Clausewitz and Napoleon', 154–7.

Clausewitz's *On War*, an extensive review of the book was published in *La Nouvelle Revue* by France's leading military commentator, Captain Georges Gilbert (1851–1901). The author was an artillery officer who had distinguished himself in the first course of the École de guerre in 1876–7. He came under the patronage of General Miribel, the army's foremost strategic mind, but had to retire from the army in 1877 on account of poor health.[35]. His review was both favourable and perceptive.

Clausewitz, explained Gilbert, had expressed the spirit of Napoleonic warfare and had inspired Moltke. His work must be understood in connection with the transformation of war which had taken place between the eighteenth and nineteenth centuries. Eighteenth-century warfare, shaped by the character of the absolutist state and cabinet politics, had been indecisive and dominated by sieges, manœuvres, and finances. By contrast, the mass armies which had been introduced by the Revolution and had been infused with patriotism had enabled Napoleon to achieve decisive results against the whole of Europe. After Prussia's defeat and under Scharnhorst, Clausewitz had participated in the creation of the Prussian reserve-system which later won the day at Sadowa and Sedan. He had also rejected the old and erroneous theory of war, which had been preoccupied with geometric and geographic considerations. His philosophical volumes, said Gilbert, reveal the relation of war to society, the economy, and politics.[36] Clausewitz's theory of war consists in the ruthless subjugation of everything to one aim: the destruction of the enemy's main army in the major, Napoleonic battle, followed by a relentless pursuit. According to Clausewitz, one ought to act with all forces concentrated and strike swiftly without relaxation, while resolving all logistic problems by living off the countryside.[37] This, wrote Gilbert, was a 'simple, sound and virile' conception of war, though it was perhaps a little exaggerated in its reaction against geometry, was too direct, and was inappreciative of the significance of the lines of operations.[38]

Here already were all the elements of the French discovery of

[35] See Charles Malo's preface to Georges Gilbert's posthumous *Guerre sud-africaine* (Paris, 1902), ix–xix; Juliette Adam, *Le Capitaine Georges Gilbert* (Paris, 1924).
[36] Georges Gilbert, 'Étude sur Clausewitz', *La Nouvelle Revue*, (47), 1 and 15 Aug. 1887, 540–6; reprinted in id., *Essais de critique militaire* (2nd edn., Paris, 1890).   [37] Ibid. 547–55.
[38] Ibid. 554, 558. See also Carrias, *La Pensée militaire française*, 280–1.

Clausewitz and Napoleon, a discovery which soon acquired a powerful momentum. The French recognized that the Germans possessed a very distinctive conception of war, most vigorous, direct, and aggressive in character. The German victories and French defeat in 1870–1 were now largely attributed to this conception of war. However, it was also noted that this conception of war had been developed in Prussia after 1806, at the time of her great catastrophe, in imitation of French Revolutionary innovations and Napoleonic strategy. It therefore appeared that France had been defeated by the use of her own methods, which she herself had neglected after 1815. Hence the growth of the 'Napoleonic renaissance' in France, whose scholarly intensity has not been equalled before or since. This in turn was quickly followed by a realization that the Clausewitzian conception was in fact a simplistic, if not crude, model of Napoleonic strategy. Thus, while finding the German conception of war an astounding and influential revelation, the French could none the less recover some of their independent identity and national self-esteem.

The reason for the French attraction to the Prussian conception of warfare is obvious. Here was a clear and impressive theoretical edifice and doctrine of a kind that was lacking on their own side, and it rested on the two towering military models of the century— Napoleonic warfare and the Prussian campaigns of 1866 and 1870. It offered the French a new and invigorating sense of direction and seemed to revive their own best traditions. It called for the qualities of initiative and aggressiveness, which the French had always regarded as their peculiar national traits. Their response was overwhelming.

The focus of the new movement was, not surprisingly, the École de guerre. There was now an exciting theory to teach. The professor of infantry tactics from 1882, Major, later Lieutenant-Colonel, Maillard, propagated the new doctrine. '*The destruction of the enemy* is the aim; *the offensive* is the means', stated his *Elements of War* (1891), published upon his departure from the school.[39] The book offered a penetrating analysis of the Napoleonic manœuvre. It highlighted Napoleon's clear determination of the

---

[39] L. Maillard, *Eléments de la guerre* (Paris, 1891), p. v. The text of the lectures exists in the *École de guerre's* library. Also see Dany, 'La Littérature militaire', 614; Carrias, *La Pensée militaire française*, 278–9.

decisive point and line of advance, resolute and carefully co-ordinated marches in dispersed order, and rapid concentration of all forces to overwhelm the enemy.[40] Examining the nuts and bolts of the Napoleonic operational formation, Maillard showed how every column, and the army as a whole, had been covered by an advance guard and a rearguard which secured their freedom of operation in all directions. Moltke is often cited, but only as a disciple of the great Corsican. In his stimulating comparison of Jena and Sedan, Georges Gilbert, Maillard's friend, showed how the victor of 1870 in effect only duplicated the strategic pattern employed in 1806.[41] For the French the Prussians became merely a vehicle on their way back to Napoleon.

Maillard left the École de guerre in 1890 (he died as a general in 1901), but at the school his friends and colleagues were propounding the same ideas. The most distinguished of these was Henri Bonnal, who dominated the school and French strategic thinking for two decades. He arrived at the Écoles de guerre as a major in 1885 and rose to become the professor of military history, strategy and applied tactics (1892–6) and, in the first years of the twentieth century, the commanding general. Bonnal was a formidable military historian and thinker. The lectures which he delivered at the school in the 1890s grew into a series of monumental studies: *Sadowa* (Fr. orig. 1901), *De Rosbach à Ulm* (1903), *La Manœuvre d'Iéna 1806* (1904), *La Manœuvre de Landshut 1808–1809* (1905), *La Manœuvre de Vilna 1811–1812* (1905), and *La Manœuvre de Saint-Privat* (3 vols., 1904–1912). Based on exhaustive research in the French archives, which was characteristic of the new Napoleonic scholarship, these studies made him a leading authority on Napoleonic and Prussian strategy.

The explosion of Napoleonic research in France from the late 1880s laid bare the origins and structure of Napoleonic strategy. Pierron's pioneering essay *How Was Napoleon's Military Genius Formed?* (1889) anticipated Major Colin's classic study *The Military Education of Napoleon* (1900) in exploring the origins of Napoleon's early operational schemes.[42] At the same time,

---

[40] Maillard, *Éléments de la guerre*, pp. x–xv, 3.

[41] Georges Gilbert, 'Septembre et octobre 1806—juillet et août 1870', in *Critique militaire*, 59–378; Irvine, 'The French Discovery of Clausewitz and Napoleon', 158.

[42] Édouard Pierron, *Comment s'est formé le génie militaire de Napoléon Ier?* (Paris, 1889); Jean Colin, *L'Éducation militaire de Napoléon* (Paris, 1900); see also Irvine, 'The French Discovery of Clausewitz and Napoleon', 159.

Napoleon's campaigns and systems of operations were dissected by Bonnal, Camon, and Grouard. Like Maillard, Bonnal emphasized the flexibility of the emperor's operational formation, the so-called *bataillon carré*, screened as it had been by an advance guard and a rearguard and ready to turn and strike in all directions. More than anyone else before him, he also brought to light the imaginative qualities of Napoleon's genius: his mastery of deception, feints, and diversions to create surprise, disorientation, and miscalculation on the enemy's part.

Thus it is not surprising that Bonnal and his friends found Clausewitz's perception of Napoleonic strategy curiously crude and, in some fundamental respects, totally inadequate. Historians who tended to dismiss this affront to the great philosopher of war as nothing more than an expression of French chauvinism and wounded national pride, missed the main point here. Viewing Napoleon's strategy from distant and defeated Prussia, Clausewitz had been primarily impressed by its immense energy, boldness, and decisiveness. Fiercely reacting against the old 'strategy of manœuvre', he had portrayed Napoleonic strategy as extremely direct and vigorously simple and had missed a great deal of its subtlety of conception and manœuvre. Gilbert sensed this immediately in his seminal review of 1887, and Bonnal was as perceptive and accurate in assessing both the strength and the weaknesses of the Clausewitzian interpretation. He pointed out that, while Napoleon had always sought the great battle, he had never been as direct as Clausewitz had imagined in going about it.[43] The translation into French between 1899 and 1908 of Clausewitz's major histories of the campaigns of 1796, 1799, 1812, 1813, 1814, and 1815 made the shortcomings of the Clausewitzian interpretation even more obvious. Bonnal and Camon were astonished by Clausewitz's assertion that 'Napoleon never engaged in strategic envelopment'.[44] Both cited the many instances of Napoleon's *manœuvre sur les derrières*, the manœuvre against the enemy's rear, one of the most fundamental patterns of Napoleonic strategy. They failed to understand how Clausewitz could so misinterpret the

---

[43] L. Rousset (ed.), *Les Maîtres de la guerre Frédérick II, Napoléon, Moltke, d'après des travaux inédits de M. le général Bonnal* (Paris, 1899), 226–7 (the text of Bonnal's lectures exists in the *École de guerre*'s library); Bonnal, *De la méthode dans les hautes études militaires en Allemagne et en France* (Paris, 1902), 10–11.

[44] Clausewitz, *Principles of War* (Harrisburg, Pa., 1942), 49.

Marengo, Ulm, and Jena campaigns, to name only the most famous examples.[45]

It has been justly pointed out, however, that the problem of the French army was not Napoleonic strategy but how to fight the next war.[46] Bonnal and his friends were stepping on to less firm ground when they turned from history to evaluate Prussian strategy and consider operational doctrine. Bonnal had many sensible, and even brilliant, things to say when he extended his criticism of Clausewitz to the Prussian conception of warfare as a whole. At the same time, however, his picture of Prussian strategy was open to the same charges of oversimplification which he himself levelled against Clausewitz's interpretation of Napeolonic strategy.

In his learned study *Sadowa* (manuscript form 1894; printed 1901) Bonnal argued that the Prussian army, while emulating Napoleonic warfare, understood little of its subtleties, wagering everything on the rapid concentration of forces for battle.[47] This accounted both for its strength and for its weaknesses:

Its sword play is pre-eminently plain, and absolutely innocent of feints. Its strategic and tactical phrases consist of a few words which never vary— that is, its art is rudimentary. But it makes good of the poverty of its combinations. It is its tenacity, its energy, its attention to detail, and its unity of thought which render it so formidable an adversary.[48]

Even on the defensive, the Prussians attack everywhere and always. This gives them a moral advantage over a timorous or weak opponent, but when . . . it becomes a sealed pattern, it is highly dangerous, and over and above this it negates superior control. . . . An unbridled offensive is extremely dangerous when the adversary can manœuvre and can count . . . on the certainty that the assailants will rush upon the first bait they see.[49]

Herein Bonnal saw the opportunities for French strategy: it ought to take the form of flexible defence in a truly Napoleonic fashion, keeping all forces united and operating in full co-ordination to defeat the enemy's thrusts. The French field-commanders at all levels were not expected to act on their own initiative or exhibit the

---

[45] Bonnal, *Hautes études militaires*, 10–11; Camon, *Clausewitz*; J. Colin, *The Transformation of War* (London, 1912), 298–300. See also my *Origins of Military Thought from the Enlightenment to Clausewitz* (Oxford, 1989), 206–9.

[46] Michael E. Howard, 'The Influence of Clausewitz', in Clausewitz, *On War* (Princeton, NJ. 1976), 36.

[47] Bonnal, *Sadowa: A Study* (London, 1907), 48.

[48] Ibid. 49.   [49] Ibid. 243–4.

same degree of independence which had become necessary for the Prussians on account of their dispersed mode of operations. According to Bonnal, the Prussians had erred gravely when they had split their forces in 1866, and their loose method of command and control bordered on the effective abnegation of central war-planning.[50] A vigorous French army, acting swiftly in a well-calculated and carefully controlled strategy, would not leave then unpunished.

Thus in the 1890s, at least in partial disregard of the new conditions prevailing in the age of mass armies and railways, the French army revived the more concentrated, Napoleonic order of battle, supposedly possessing superior qualities of unity and central control. With some theoreticians this sometimes assumed absurd proportions. Caemmerer could hardly believe his eyes at Lewal's scheme to deploy and manœuvre in close order an army of one quarter of a million men, which he planned to squeeze on a front of only 16 miles. To the four French field-armies, altogether over one million men, Lewal allocated no more than 68 miles.[51] On a more practical level, however, French war-planning and official doctrine were also changing in conformity with the new military ideas.

The French war-plans conceived between 1875 and 1886 (Plans 1–7) were defensive in character. The French armies were spread along the German frontier, and their line of assembly was moved progressively forward from the rear, as the French railway- and fortress-systems were building up and the fear of an earlier German attack diminished.[52] After 1886, however, the Eastern crisis suggested the possibility of co-operation with Russia. Thus Plans 8 and 9 (1887 and 1888), while changing little in the deployment scheme, adopted the offensive.[53] At the same time, the French discovery of Clausewitz and Napoleon was changing attitudes at a

---

[50] Ibid. 52–3, 243. Foch reiterated these ideas in his staff-college lectures; *De la conduite de la guerre* (2nd edn.; Paris, 1909), see also *Marshal Foch: His own Words on Many Things*, ed. Raymond Recouly (London, 1929), 130. Colin was an exception in pointing out the changes in the road network since Napoleon, which accounted for Moltke's strategy: *The Transformation of War*, 304–6.

[51] Lewal, *Stratégie de marche* (Paris, 1893); id., *Stratégie de combat* (2 vols., Paris, 1895–6); Caemmerer, *Strategical Science*, 230–8.

[52] Marchand, *Plans de concentration*, 13–72; État-Major de l'Armée, *Les Armées françaises dans la grande guerre* (Paris, 1936), I, i. 3–12.

[53] Marchand, 73–91; État-Major, *Les Armées françaises dans la grande guerre*, 12–18.

deeper level. Serving in 1890–1 in the third (operations) bureau of General Miribel's general staff, Captain Ferdinand Foch later remembered what he regarded as defensive mentality and excessive reliance on terrain on the French part.[54] But generations and ideas were swiftly changing. Major Grouard was typical in denouncing reliance on fortified places, past and present, as 'the greatest military mistake of our epoch'. Reviewing the war of 1870–1, he argued that rather than lock himself and his army up in Metz, Bazaine should have withdrawn deep into the interior of the country and forced the Prussians to follow and overextend themselves. Prevailing doctrines, warned Grouard, were potentially as disastrous. Primaily associated with the name of the great Belgian fortress–builder Brialmont, they promoted fortresses as 'strategic pivots' for the field armies. While Grouard maintained that field fortifications might prove beneficial to a numerically inferior army, he emphasized that they never ought to rule strategy and become a substitute for active and aggressive conduct.[55]

By the 1890s (Plans 10–13, 1889–95), the French army was moving towards a more active form in defence—the so-called defensive-offensive strategy.[56] This trend reached its height when Bonnal was entrusted with the drafting of Plan 14 (1898), whose principles remained in force also in Plans 15 and 16 (1903 and 1909). A 'Napoleonic' order in depth reinforced the shallower, 'cordon-like', formation adopted, on the German example, after 1871. A whole army—incorporating the new 20th Corps posted at the exposed position of Nancy—formed the *couverture*. This was the screening and delaying force whose primary role was to protect the process of mobilization. A powerful army was deployed behind the four front-line armies, to act as a new 'mass of manœuvre'. Giving flexibility to the whole system of defence, it was ready to counter-attack in any direction at the opportune moment, at the command of the general-in-chief.[57]

[54] Ferdinand Foch, *The Memoirs of Marshal Foch* (New York, 1931), p. xxxix.

[55] A. Grouard, *La Perte des états et les camps retranchés: réplique au général Brialmont* (Paris, 1889); id. *Faillait-il quitter Metz en 1870?* (Paris, 1893); id. *Comment quitter Metz en 1870? Avec une note sure le rôle de la fortification* (Paris, 1901).

[56] Marchand, *Plans de concentration*, 92–127; État-Major, *Les Armées françaises dans la grande guerre*, I, i. 18–26.

[57] *Les Armées françaises dans la grande guerre*, 26–33; Henri Contamine, *La Revanche* (Paris, 1957), 77–9; Samuel Williamson, *The Politics of Grand Strategy: Britain and France Prepare for War, 1904–1914* (Cambridge, Mass., 1969), 117.

Official doctrine, as codified in the field regulations, followed a similar route. The Infantry Regulations of 1875 reflected the experience of 1870–1, when modern breach-loaders took a murderous toll on frontally attacking infantry. The regulations stressed the importance of fire-power and the careful use of ground for cover. A dispersed order of battle was recommended for the attack. Soon the lessons of Plevna (1877) corroborated and reinforced those of 1870–1.[58] However, with the army regaining some of its confidence and with the coming of new ideas, care was taken that the offensive spirit should not be lost in the face of stronger fire-power. The Infantry Field Regulations which were issued in 1884 stressed 'the principle of the decisive attack, head held high, with no attention to losses'. They called for energetic and vigorous advance even under heavy fire and against well-defended trenches.[59] Finally, issued in 1895, the Field Service Regulations were inspired by Bonnal and rightly considered by him as the consummation of the French military renaissance which centred on the École de guerre. Philosophically, they proudly proclaimed unity of doctrine, while denying dogmatic systems and principles. Strategically, they postulated the breaking of the enemy's will to resist, the indispensability of offensive action for the attainment of decisive results, and the total rejection of passive defence. They prescribed that the commander ought to maintain freedom of operation, hold the enemy at bay with a strong advance-guard, and choose the right moment to concentrate all forces rapidly for the decisive event. Clausewitz and Napoleon ruled supreme.[60]

The second half of the 1890s therefore marked the high point in the creativity and influence of the intellectual activists at the École de guerre. Colonel Hippolyte Langlois, the artillery professor from the mid-1880s and the commanding general between 1895 and 1902, was one of the chief proponents of the active and aggressive doctrine.[61] Major Cherfils, the cavalry professor, who stressed the

[58] Émile Mayer, *Autour de la guerre actuelle* (Paris, 1917), 106–7; E. Carrias, *La Pensée militaire française*, 275; Contamine, *La Revanche*, 44.

[59] Mayer, *Autour de la guerre actuelle*, 107–9; Carrias, *La Pensée militaire française*, p. 276.

[60] Bonnal, *Hautes études militaires*, 17–20; Carrias, *La Pensée militaire française*, 283–4; Irvine, 'The French Discovery of Clausewitz and Napoleon', 160–1.

[61] Hippolyte Langlois, *L'Artillerie de campagne en liaison avec les autres armes* (2 vols.; Paris, 1892); Dany, 'La Littérature militaire', 614–15; Irvine, 'The French Discovery of Clausewitz and Napoleon', 160.

use of the *arme blanche* and the cavalry charge, and Major Niox, the professor of military geography, were other leading activists in the new school.[62] Indeed, the group of instructors at the École de guerre earned recognition as 'the new French military school' for possessing a whole set of characteristics more accessible perhaps to sociologists of intellectual communities. Its members were concentrated around a single institution. They preached a fairly unified doctrine. And they were imbued with that fresh, pioneering sense of intellectual enthusiasm which is almost inseparable from any great enterprise. They were a church with a gospel, and soon they were bringing up a second generation. Gilbert, their friend and ally outside the army, proudly presented the team of the leading institution: Maillard, Bonnal, Langlois, Cherfils, and Niox were being followed by their pupils—Foch, Leblond, Lanrezac, and Ruffey, almost all familiar names from the Great War.[63]

Foch entered the École de guerre as a student in 1885, when the new wave in French military thinking was beginning to gather momentum. Not before 1882–3, he was later to write, was war taught in France on a rational and practical basis.[64] The school was, in his words, 'an absolute revelation' to him. The 'remarkable body of instructors' included 'Cardot, Maillard, Millet, Langlois and Cherfils'.[65] In 1895 he returned to the École de guerre as the assistant professor of military history, strategy, and applied tactics. A year later, with some understandable misgivings, he accepted the professorship itself, made vacant by Bonnal's departure.

As mentioned in the first chapter, all assessments of Foch's teaching and influence before 1914 have been influenced by the central role he was subsequently to play in the First World War. Nominated in 1918 to the supreme command of the allied armies in France, Marshal Foch became a figure of world fame and the focus of popular interest. Hence the somewhat distorted perspective dominating the scholarly literature. Retrospectively, Foch has been blown up out of his natural place in the new French military school.

---

[62] Maxime Cherfils, *Cavalerie en campagne* (2nd edn.; Paris, 1893); Dany 'La Littérature militaire', 614–5; Irvine, 'The French Discovery of Clausewitz and Napoleon', 160.

[63] Georges Gilbert, *La Guerre sud-africaine*, 534. Similarly see H. Langlois, *Lessons from Two Recent Wars, The Russo-Turkish and South African War* (London, 1909), p. vii; Mayer, *Autour de la guerre actuelle*, 109.

[64] Foch, *The Principles of War* (London, 1920; first publ. in French 1903), 2.

[65] Foch, *Memoirs*, p. xxxvii.

His teachers—the true innovators—had all retired before the Great War and thus remained rather forgotten staff-college professors. Had the war not come in 1914 and had Foch retired peacefully at sixty-four a year later, he would have ranked far behind Bonnal (and Langlois) in both intellectual and operational influence.

Foch was not a formidable military historian and critic like his predecessor. Upon being nominated professor at the École de guerre, he had to start virtually from scratch. 'What forced me to work at my profession', he was later to confess, 'was having to teach it.'[66] His course of study and teaching, however, was ready-made for him at the school. Firstly, it was shaped by German military literature, in which von der Goltz held the most influential place and, in turn, led back to Clausewitz. The German-influenced message was that war, and modern war in particular, was a life-and-death struggle between armed nations, which could only end in the breaking of the enemy's will to resist. The decisive battle, aiming at the destruction of the enemy's army, was the only legitimate means, and aggressive conduct the only legitimate mode of action. Secondly, on the operational level, Foch inherited the neo-Napoleonic teachings of Maillard and Bonnal. These emphasized freedom of operation as well as the manœuvre, secured by a strong reconnoitring advance-guard—the famous *sûreté*—and leading to a rapid concentration of forces for the decisive blow. Foch's *Des principes de la guerre* (1903), consisting of his lectures at the École de guerre (the text in the school library), blended these themes with examples taken from the wars of Napoleon and the Wars of German Unification. Nothing here was new. Both in content and form the book was fairly loosely put together. Nowhere did it approach the scholarly power and subtlety of exposition which had characterized the work of some of Foch's older associates.

But then Foch's main strength lay elsewhere. It has long been observed that he was, above all, a man of character. 'I am certain', Keynes was to write years later, 'that Foch's mind and character are of an extreme simplicity—of an almost medieval simplicity. He is honest, fearless and tenacious.'[67] It was his inner strength, inexhaustible springs of energy, conviction, devotion, integrity, and

---

[66] C. Bugnet (ed.), *Foch Talks* (London, 1929), 69.

[67] J. M. Keynes, *Two Memoirs* (London, 1949), 15; quoted in W. J. Fossati, 'Educational Influences in the Career of Marshal Ferdinand Foch of France' (unpub. doc. diss., University of Kansas, 1976), 70.

congenial manner that made him a source of inspiration both before and after 1914. As Liddell Hart has put it, he was a man of faith; 'he was convincing because he was passionately convinced'.[68] When he taught, it was the sublime concepts and phrases and the exaltation of moral forces and will-power that attracted him most. These were also the elements that most appealed to him in Clausewitz's work. A devout Catholic, he quoted de Maistre: 'A battle lost is a battle one thinks one has lost, for a battle cannot be lost physically.'[69] One contemporary eye-witness reports that his solemn lectures impressed his students but were not always entirely clear to them.[70] A secret report, drafted by the police before Foch's nomination to command the École de guerre in 1908, alleged that, 'during his professorship at the École de guerre, [he] taught metaphysics—and metaphysics so abstruse that it made idiots of a number of his pupils'.[71]

All the same, when Foch was forced to leave the École de guerre in 1901, it was for different reasons. If the second half of the 1890s marked the high point in the activity of the new French military school, the twentieth century brought in its wake grave crises. While the army as a whole was torn apart in the aftermath of the Dreyfus Affair, the teachings of the new school were seriously questioned following the experiences of South Africa and Manchuria. They were coming under heavy fire from different quarters.

MILITARY INFERIORITY, DOMESTIC PRESSURES, AND THE PHILOSOPHY OF *ÉLAN VITAL*

The professional debate over the probable effect of the magazine rifle, smokeless powder, the rapid-firing gun, and the machine-gun intensified in the 1890s, culminating in the controversy surrounding Bloch's sensational work (1898). For example, in the series of articles written between 1888 and 1891, Captain, later Major, Émile Mayer, Foch's old school-mate at the École polytechnique,

[68] Liddell Hart, *Foch*, 458 *et passim*. Liddell Hart was the first to strip off the hagiographic mystique surrounding Foch. But, as history, his book is marred by didactic rhetoric and by Liddell Hart's tendency to confuse past occurrences with his own intellectual battles in the 1920s and 1930s.

[69] Foch, *Principles of War*, 286.

[70] George Aston, *The Biography of the Late Marshal Foch* (London, 1929), 73.

[71] Quoted in Liddell Hart, *Foch*, 42–3.

argued that the growth of fire-power would render war immobile and favour the defence.[72] These concerns receded, however, from before the walls of the École de guerre. There, in the late 1890s, Foch was 'proving mathematically' that the much-talked-about improvements in firearms were, in fact, favourable to the offence.[73] Mayer was later to complain that, with the new ideas and aggressive doctrines coming out of the École de guerre (which he himself never attended), his opinions, when noted, had only provoked anger and disfavour. In the end, his articles were rejected by French journals and published only in Switzerland. With the outbreak of the South African war, however, both weapons and tactics were put to the test of war, and the results—most disquieting from the point of view of the prevailing doctrine—could not be ignored.

In 1902 Mayer, who had retired from the army and was working as a military writer, drew his own conclusions from the war. Paraphrasing Bloch, he argued that fighting would freeze along continuous and impregnable human walls. War would terminate only in total human and financial exhaustion.[74] By now, however, people in the highest ranks of the army, much more influential than an outsider like Mayer, were advancing similar ideas. The most important of them was François de Négrier, one of the leading and

[72] Mayer won his place in the historical literature because of his revealing war-time and post-war works, in which he settled accounts with pre-war doctrine in general and with Foch in particular. See esp. Mayer, *Comment on pouvait prévoir l'immobilisation des fronts dans la guerre moderne* (Paris, 1916), presenting articles he had written 25 years earlier; id., *Autour de la guerre actuelle*, 164–5; id, *La Psychologie du commandement, avec plusieurs lettres inédites du Maréchal Foch* (Paris, 1924), 5–10; id., *Trois maréchaux; Joffre, Galliéni, Foch* (Paris, 1928), 120–227 and, specifically about his articles, 127–33.

[73] Foch, *Principles of War*, 32; this was even than an extraordinary argument and has justly earned notoriety. After the war, Foch was embarrassed by Mayer's revelations and only reluctantly granted him permission to publish the old correspondence between them (Foch to Mayer, 21 Oct. 1921, in Mayer, *La Psychologie du commandement*, 6.) His brief account of his École de guerre period in his memoirs is a shameless forgery. By association, he tries to create the impression that he taught there the preponderance of fire-power: Foch, *Memoirs*, pp. xxxvii–xxxviii, xxxix. Later in the book, he criticizes the doctrine of the offensive and the excessive emphasis on morale and the decisive victory, without even hinting that he was one of the chief proponents of these approaches: ibid., pp. lvi–lxi.

[74] Mayer argues, perhaps correctly, that it was Bloch who was influenced by his article 'L'Évolution de la tactique', which had been published in *Bibliothèque universelle* in Feb. 1891; Mayer, *L'Immobilisation des fronts*, 74.

most outspoken generals in the army. In a series of anonymous but stirring articles in the *Revue de deux mondes*, he argued that the South African war demonstrated that front lines had become almost inviolable. The days of attacks in deep order were over. Infantry advance could only be carried out in thin lines and small groups. Cavalry could no longer charge and had to dismount to fight. The extension of the front to envelop the enemy's position was the only feasible method of attack. Observing German manœuvres, Négrier came to the conclusion that the Germans were extending each army's front to fifty kilometres, far beyond the width advocated by the French neo-Napoleonics. He blamed the professors of the staff college, saying that, in reintroducing dense order of battle and concentrations in mass, they had substituted the principles of Napoleonic strategy for the needs of modern tactics. He argued that the regulations of 1875, emphasizing fire-power, had been far more realistic.[75]

Similar ideas regarding the nature of modern tactics were expressed by General Kessler in his book *Tactique des trois armes* (1903).[76] In lectures delivered in 1902, Colonel Berot, chief of the operations bureau in the general staff (a predecessor of Grand-maison's), suggested that the army ought to combine the advantages of the tactical defence and of the strategic offence.[77] In late 1901, General Lamiraux, ex-vice-president of the Conseil superieur de la guerre, confessed about the prevailing confusion:

No one, or almost no one, can agree with his neighbour on tactical questions. Some say: firepower is all important . . . Others tell you: Attack! Always attack! . . . How does one create a method from such dissimilar ideas? We cannot do it. We take a bit of one, add a pinch of the other and hope that any errors . . . will sort themselves out in combat.[78]

Soon, however, the change of opinion found official expression in the new Infantry Field Regulations issued in 1904. Disperse order was adopted, and the use of terrain for cover emphasized.[79] At the École de guerre itself, the professor of infantry tactics in the mid-1900s, Colonel de Maud'huy, taught that modern firearms vastly

[75] Carrias, *La Pensée militaire française*, 288–9.
[76] Joffre, *The Memoirs of Marshal Joffre* (2 vols.; London, 1932), i. 27.
[77] Stephen Ryan, *Pétain the Soldier* (London, 1969), 28–9.
[78] 29 Nov. 1901, *France militaire*; quoted by Porch, *The March to the Marne*, 221.   [79] Carrias, *La Pensée militaire française*, 290.

increased the power of local defence. He argued that in order to succeed, the attacker would have to assemble massive concentrations of artillery and infantry in his chosen zone of attack.[80]

The members of the new military school were thrown on the defensive. Both Langlois and Bonnal responded at length to the charges levelled against them by Négrier and to the ideas he, Kessler, and others had advanced. Examining the battle of Plevna, Langlois came to the conclusion that an adequately planned and executed attack would have carried the place.[81] In concurrence with Gilbert's posthumous work, *La Guerre sud-africaine* (1902), he argued that the special conditions which prevailed in South Africa were hardly applicable to Europe.[82] He admitted that the rapidly improving firearms employed by entrenched infantry had made frontal attack increasingly difficult and costly. Yet he reminded his readers that beyond any contingent changes in armaments stood the eternal principles of war, the first of which was the imperative of inflicting a powerful blow on the enemy in order to force him to admit defeat.[83] He expressed concern that heavy artillery and field howitzers—whose adoption was urged to combat entrenched infantry—might become a means to escape from the main challenge, which was ultimately the need to assault and overthrow the enemy.[84] He conceded that better means and methods of attack must certainly be employed to deal with the new conditions.[85] But he argued that the writings of Négrier and Kessler were positively dangerous because, by influencing and confusing the minds of many young officers, they not only undermined trust in leaders and regulations but also killed the offensive spirit, which was essential for victory.[86] If anything, he argued, modern war would require even greater moral energies. Following the publication of the second edition of *Battle Studies* the same year, Langlois cited Ardant du Picq to this effect for the first time.[87]

Herein lay the core of the matter. When one ponders over the seemingly inexplicable blindness of the leading pre-1914 French

---

[80] Contamine, *La Revanche*, 168–9; Ronald H. Cole, ' "Forward with the Bayonet! ": The French Army Prepares for Offensive Warfare, 1911–1914' (unpub. diss., University of Maryland, 1975), 265–7.

[81] Langlois, *Lessons from Two Recent Wars*, 35–7.   [82] Ibid. 89.

[83] Ibid. 85, 124–5.   [84] Ibid. 85.   [85] Ibid. 125–39.

[86] Ibid. 111–12. For Bonnal's milder responses, see his *La Récente Guerre sud-africaine* (Paris, 1903); id., *L'Art nouveau en tactique* (Paris, 1904).

[87] Ibid. 124, 140.

military theoreticians to the effect of modern firearms, one ought to understand that their problem was least of all tactics itself. Mayer recounts his arguments with Niox and Foch, in which the latter stated that the impregnability of fronts is a problem recognized by all. However, he added, everyone also recognized that a decisive result would have to be achieved.[88] Pre-1914 military theoreticians, not only in France but everywhere in Europe, did not suffer from stupidity, as is often suggested. Quite the opposite. They were handicapped, so to speak, by an overdeveloped sense of history and too erudite a conception of warfare—one with which, paradoxically, many of the proponents of fire-power were not burdened.[89] Their minds were dominated by the Napoleonic and Prussian models, which had been endlessly studied and long hammered-out into the most powerful theory of war. If they tended to resist the changes in tactics and, like Langlois, defend the bayonet and the cavalry charge and doubt the ability of heavy field-artillery to crush entrenched infantry, it was mainly as a means to an end.[90] Their picture of war was principally strategic and moral. What they objected to was not so much the notion that the battlefield had become a murderous place, but the implication that grand, aggressive, and decisive strategy was no longer feasible. They feared that excessive emphasis on fire-power, cover, and the advantages of defence would lead back to the proverbial errors of the eighteenth century and the passivity of which the French were allegedly guilty in 1870, and destroy the moral willingness to advance and fight.[91] If there was anything that the accumulated wisdom of history taught them, it was that weakness was always quick to raise its head under any pretext, and that nothing important had ever been achieved without great valour and sacrifice.

As mentioned in the previous chapter, this was precisely why the Russo-Japanese War, while again demonstrating the protracted and immobile character of modern war and the strength of fire-power,

---

[88]   Mayer, *Trois maréchaux*, 135.
[89]   It is a point of interest that long before the events told here, the intellectual calibre of the vigorous Négrier, then the youngest corps commander in the French army, was called into question. See Charles W. Dilke, 'The French Armies', *The Fortnightly Review*, 1 Nov. 1891, 609: 'he is probably a general of armies of the future, but his knowledge of the science of modern war is disputed by the men of books' (referring then to Derrécagaix, Fay, and their generation).
[90]   Langlois, *Lessons from two Recent Wars*, 35, 100–1, 119–20.
[91]   See for example Foch, *Principles of War*, 31–33.

if anything only reinforced the dominating view of warfare. Despite everything, in a war between two regular, European-style armies, it was the attacker, vigorous and willing to make great sacrifices, who ultimately conquered.[92] Négrier repeated the highly perceptive observations which he had made after the previous war, but he added that only offensive tactics could bring victory, and he rejected passive 'positionism' as the 'heresy' responsible for the Russian defeat.[93] However Joffre remembered the war as a 'shining confirmation' of Langlois's views.[94] Foch though the same about the Napoelonic principles and his own work: 'In strategy as well as in tactics one attacks.' No revolution in industry has altered the fundamental principles of war.[95] 'Firepower does not weaken the offensive,' wrote General Bazaine-Hayter, commander of the 13th Corps in 1906. 'Never forget that a defensive battle will seldom bring victory. However powerful weapons become, the victory will go to the offensive which stimulates moral forces, disconcerts the enemy and deprives him of his freedom of action.'[96] Indeed, the war in Manchuria was soon followed by an entirely new reaction and line of interpretation.[97] If in the first half of the 1900s, the challenge to the prevailing doctrine was coming from the proponents of fire-power, in the second half of the decade, this was overshadowed by the growth of an even greater challenge from the other end of the spectrum. Coinciding with Bonnal's retirement from the army, the operational and strategic teachings of which he was the chief author were beginning to come under attack as equivocal and, in practice, defensive-minded.

Even in its heyday Bonnal's scheme of active and aggressive defence changing into the counter-offensive—the so-called defensive-offensive—did not win universal approval from his friends and colleagues. Georges Gilbert, for one, had called from the 1880s for the revival of the *furia française*, in line with his more comprehensive vision of French national regeneration. Much more critical was Lucian Cardot. At the same time as he revealed Clausewitz to the French, he propagated the ideas of the Russian general Mikhail

[92] See Snyder, *The Ideology of the Offensive*, 79–81.
[93] F. de Négrier, *Lessons of the Russo-Japanese War* (London, 1906; first publ. in the *Revue des deux mondes*, 15 Jan. 1906), esp. 71, 54–5.
[94] Joffre, *Memoirs*, 28.
[95] Foch, *De la conduite de la guerre* (2nd. edn.; Paris, 1909), ix–x.
[96] Cited by Porch, *The Road to the Marne*, 226.
[97] Snyder, *The Ideology of the Offensive*, 80–1.

Ivanovich Dragomirov, also an admirer of Clausewitz and very
popular with the French from the mid-1880s.[98] One of the few
Russian military theoreticians with a European reputation and one-
time head of the Russian general-staff academy, Dragomirov was
the leader of the so-called nationalist school of strategists in Russia.
In the tradition of Suvorov, he advocated mass bayonet-charges in
deep column, which would fully bring out the sweep of superior
morale which carried all before it.[99] In the guise of an imaginary
Russian officer, Loukiane Carlovitch, 'the Cossack from Kouban',
Cardot satirized contemporary French military thinking. He
criticized the 'antithesis in vogue: the defensive-offensive' as
absurd, illusive, and chimeric, attractive in theory but impossible in
practice.[100] He argued that the initial defensive posture was most
harmful to morale and left the initiative to the enemy and to the
tyranny of circumstances. It evoked the shadow of 1870.[101] He
mocked the fuss around the new firearms and, as a retired general
after the wars in South Africa and Manchuria, swore allegiance to
Dragomirov and scorned the new, 'modern style', school of battle
tactics.[102]

The publication of the second edition of Ardant du Picq's *Battle
Studies* (1903) could not have come at a more opportune moment.
The army and the country were then preoccupied by the very same
problems that had preoccupied du Picq in the late 1860s. His acute
studies of troop psychology, especially on a fire-ridden and highly
lethal battlefield, again became very relevant, and his emphasis on
group cohesion and morale excited interest and exercised great
appeal. Bonnal and Langlois quoted him in support of their own
long-held opinions concerning the paramount importance of
morale.[103] More importantly, brilliant middle-rank officers who

[98] See M. I. Dragomirov, *Manuel pour la préparation des troupes au combat* (3
vols.; Paris, 1886–8); id., *Principes essentiels pour la conduite de la guerre:
Clausewitz interprété par le Général Dragomiroff* (Paris, 1889).

[99] See Walter Pinter, 'Russian Military Thought: The Western Model and the
shadow of Suvorov', in Paret (ed.), *Makers of Modern Strategy from Machiavelli to
the Nuclear Age* (Princetown, NJ, 1986), 367. Dragomirov's rival in Russia was his
successor as director of the general staff's academy, G. Antonowitsch Leer, a
representative of the classical school: ibid. 367–8; H. A. Leer, *Positive Strategie*
(Vienna, 1871), and the various other versions of this book.

[100] Loukiane Carlovitch [Cardot], *Éducation et instruction des troupes* (3 vols.;
Paris, 1896–7), 144–7.   [101] Ibid. 147–8.

[102] Cardot, *Hérésies et apostasies militaires de notre temps* (Paris, 1908), *passim*.

[103] Bonnal, *Hautes études militaires*, 15. Langlois, *Lessons from Two Recent
Wars*, 124, 140.

later became the 'Young Turks' in the French general staff, like Captain Frédéric Culmann and the famous Major de Grandmaison, were much impressed by him.[104] Like his, their interest was mainly moral and tactical, rather than strategic. As mentioned in the first chapter, although du Picq had had no offensive bias, the problems he addressed and his psychological teaching still served as one of the main sources of inspiration for their offensive doctrine.

Thus preference for the out-and-out offensive, previously held by men like Gilbert and Cardot, was now taken up by younger minds. This was reflected in two books written after the wars in South Africa and Manchuria by the prolific military writer Captain Frédéric Culmann of the French general staff. Culmann argued that, in view of the devastating effect of modern firearms, the greatest moral forces would be needed to make soldiers rise and advance to the attack. Only a doctrine of *offensive à outrance* was capable of instilling the necessary attitude in them. The defensive-offensive, he maintained, was inherently inhibiting and bound to end in pure defence.[105]

Major François-Jules-Louis Loyzeau de Grandmaison, one of Foch's favourite pupils during his professorship at the École de guerre,[106] came to similar conclusions. In a subtlely written book on infantry training (1906), prefaced by Langlois, his logic was the one we have already encountered. Starting from an assessment of the new developments in tactics, he recognized that the attacker would now have to make use of a variety of new measures. He would have to make full use of the ground for cover, would have to attack at night, advance in open formation and small groups, and rely on close artillery support.[107] In the end, however, and especially against a resolute and well-armed enemy, there was no escaping from the final head-on assault: 'This can only be done brutally, without concern for losses, without economy.'[108] In du Picq's spirit but with an offensive point, Grandmaison argued that

---

[104] For Frédéric Culmann, see, for example, *Tactique d'artillerie; Le Canon de tir rapide dans la bataille* (Paris, 1906), 6, 17, 21, 37, *et passim.*; Grandmaison cites no one in his *Dressage de l'infanterie en vue du combat offensif* (Paris, 1906), but du Picq's influence is very apparent.

[105] Culmann, *Deux tactiques en présence* (Paris, 1904), 23–8; for his *offensive à outrance*, a phrase more commonly used in post-, rather than pre-war works, see ibid. 291; also see id., *Étude sur les caractères généraux de la guerre d'extrême-orient* (Paris, 1909), cited by Snyder, *The Ideology of the Offensive*, 79–80.

[106] *Foch Talks*, 199.

[107] Grandmaison, *Dressage de l'infanterie*, 10–29.   [108] Ibid. 30–1.

all victorious armies, including the French at the beginning of the nineteenth century and the German in 1870, had always possessed this in common: 'the spirit of all-out offensive and *sans arrière-pensée*, animating equally both chiefs and soldiers'.[109] 'To win victory, it is necessary to instil fear in the enemy; when one is afraid one is defeated. The only means to instil fear in the enemy is to *attack* him resolutely without worrying who is the stronger.'[110] According to Grandmaison, following in du Picq's footsteps, the instinct of self-preservation and the feelings of danger and fatigue dominate troops' behaviour. In modern conditions, everyone is more or less left to himself in the terrible environment of the battlefield, and the result is demoralizing. Hence the paramount importance of leadership, group cohesion, and individual initiative, fostered in common training.[111] The essence of tactical training, argued Grandmaison, lies in familiarizing the spirit with the unbearable by continually repeating the same exercises.[112]

Similar ideas were gaining ground with the younger generation of French officers after Manchuria. According to the evidence of one general, Grandmaison told him as early as 1907: 'We are a group of young officers convinced of the justice of our ideas, of the superiority of our theories and our methods, and are resolved to make them prevail despite all opposition.'[113] In 1908 Grandmaison became the chief of the third (operations) bureau of the French general staff. He was a man of 'high intelligence, ardent temperament, generous character . . . a power of considerable proportions'.[114] The strong impression he left on people was most memorably exemplified in the two famous lectures he delivered in 1911 at the Centre of High Military Education. Opened that year, the centre was intended to supplement the École de guerre by providing a third-year training for the army's best staff-officers. In those lectures, Grandmaison criticized the prevailing defensive-offensive doctrine and its emphasis on security, advance action, and reconnaissance. He argued that the regulations of 1895 carried a double message, which, in practice, allowed for a defensive and

---

[109] *Dressage de l'infanterie*, 68.   [110] Ibid. 89.
[111] Ibid. 33–4, 38–47.   [112] Ibid. 59; also 123.
[113] Cited by Cole, ' "Forward with the Bayonet" ', 222.
[114] M.-E. Debeney, *La Guerre et les hommes* (Paris, 1937), 281; Joel A. Setzen, 'The Doctrine of the Offensive in the French Army on the Eve of World War I' (unpub. diss., University of Chicago, 1972), 81; also 81–108 for a good treatment of Grandmaison.

passive interpretation by commanders anxious to play safe.[115] Against the arguments of the proponents of fire-power, he posed a series of shrewd questions: Once contact was made, could an advancing force really extend its front to avoid a frontal attack and envelop its enemy? Furthermore, assuming that both sides were extending their fronts, where would this end? Finally, would not such an extension involve the risk of the enemy's counter-attacking to pierce through one's overstretched front, in a strategic Austerlitz-like manner?[116] Victory in war, he argued, depends on superior morale and brutal aggressiveness. The enemy must be attacked immediately, with all forces united. Reconnaissance forces, flank detachments, and reserves must be reduced to the essential and must not remain idle and out of action. The attacker imposes his will on the enemy and paralyses his forces. Hit suddenly from all directions, the defender thinks only of parrying the blows. Therefore, on the offensive, imprudence is the best security.[117]

French military thought was taking a decisive turn. From the mid-1880s, it had differed little from the mainstream of European military ideas, originating from Germany. Based on a similar reading of history and dominated by a similar view of the fundamentals of war and strategy, its ethos and concept of operation had been active and aggressive but only preferably offensive, depending mainly on the relative strengths of the opposing armies. The reaction of French military thinkers to the challenge of South Africa and Manchuria was also, on the whole, indistinguishable from the standard reaction in all European armies. It was only from the late 1900s that French military thought took a distinctively independent course of its own. Henceforth, we are dealing with a peculiarly French phenomenon.

One reason for this unique development was undoubtedly the growing realization in France that the country was hopelessly losing out in her material race with Germany.[118] After 1870 French hopes of revival and *revanche* had hinged on the hope, albeit remote of building up French power and armed forces to something like parity with Germany. For years, approximate numerical

---

[115] Grandmaison, *Deux conférences, faites aux officiers de l'état-major de l'armée (février, 1911): La Notion de sûreté et l'engagement des grandes unités* (Paris, 1911), 2, 14–25.   [116] Ibid. 3–5.

[117] See esp. ibid. 3, 11, 27–8, 36, 76.

[118] See the references in notes 4 and 6 above.

equality had in fact been maintained. From the mid-1870s and throughout the 1880s, both regular armies had reached the half-million mark, with the French slightly in the lead during much of that time. However, from the 1890s, Germany expanding population and army reform were giving her an unassailable advantage. During the 1890s, this adverse development was more than compensated, both materially and morally, by the Russo-French alliance. But after 1904 Russia was devastated, and on the Continent France stood alone against an increasingly menacing and powerful Germany. After the second Moroccan crisis, Germany's renewed attention to her army and intensified mobilization of manpower pushed the German figures to 760,000 in 1913 and 830,000 in 1914. Against this, already exhausting the full potential of her stagnant population, French numbers remained static.[119] As mentioned in the previous chapter, while in 1871 the German population had totalled 41 million in comparison with France's 36 million, it grew to 60 million in 1905 and to 68 million by 1914, as against France's 39–40 million.

Financially, the French position was only a little better. Owing to France's heavy defence-expenditure—the highest among all the Great Powers—her military estimates had slightly surpassed Germany's until well into the 1890s. However, by the coming of the twentieth century, it was Germany who was taking the lead, notwithstanding her simultaneously gigantic naval programme.[120] By virtue of her considerable financial strength France could for a time keep up the race, but German industry, growing at a colossal rate, was increasingly making it an unequal one. By 1914 Germany had 6,000 field guns to France's 3,800, and 4,500 machine-guns to the French 2,500. In heavy field-artillery she possessed an almost total monopoly. Furthermore, each German gun had 2,000 rounds, as opposed to 1,390 on the French side.[121] The emergence of the doctrine of the offensive after 1905 and its adoption by the army

---

[119] See Contamine, *La Revanche*, 39, 54, 62, 64, 81, 94, 108, 136, 142; J. Revol, *Histoire de l'armée française* (Paris, 1929), 203.

[120] A. J. P. Taylor, *The Struggle for Mastery in Europe* (Oxford, 1954), pp. xxvi–xxviii; Reichsarchiv, *Der Weltkrieg, 1914–1918: Kriegsrüstung und Kriegs-wirtschaft*, i. supp. 530. The contemporary French estimates of German military expenditure, cited by Porch, *The March to the Marne*, 227, are grossly inflated but still serve as an indication of French anxieties.

[121] Charles de Gaulle, *France and Her Army* (London, 1945), 89. See also Cole, ' "Forward with the Bayonet" ' 118–19, 129.

after 1911 closely paralleled the growing awareness in France of that country's material weakness *vis-à-vis* Germany.[122] The French flight to moral strength was only natural. Here again du Picq's emphasis on quality, as opposed to numbers, came at the right moment and was very readily accepted.

We cannot . . . fight Germany nowadays with equal numbers [wrote Langlois in 1903]. Are we therefore to think that our cause is irremediably the weaker for this reason? I do not agree with this. The belief in the all power of numbers is demoralising, it has always been wrong, and it is more so now than ever. Individual training, military education and above all morale are the dominant factor in the fight.[123]

In 1907, after retiring from the army and being elected as senator of the Republic and member of the Academie française, Langlois continued to argue in the same vein. Having assessed the German material advantage, he proceeded on a happier note: 'But if we compare the value of the personnel, the individual values, we have an incontestable advantage over our neighbours'; 'Germany will always have the advantage of us in numbers . . . but we can compensate for that advantage by utilizing the precious qualities of race that are peculiar to us.'[124] Parliamentary deputy and ex-serviceman Adolphe Messimy expressed a similar opinion in 1908: 'We want an army which compensates numerical weakness with military quality.'[125] Serving as Minister of War during two crucial periods, in 1911 and 1914, he had ample opportunity to advance his views. 'Neither numbers nor miraculous machines will determine victory,' he wrote in 1913; 'this will go to soldiers with valour and "quality"—and by this I mean superior physical and moral endurance, offensive strength.'[126]

The army was losing out not only against the foreign threat but also on the domestic scene. At the outset of the twentieth century it was subjected to a devastating political onslaught. The morale of the officer corps plummeted. On the eve of the First World War, when it was trying to rebuild its shaken morale, the vitalizing doctrine of the offensive appeared as a useful tool.

[122] For a thorough analysis and comparison of the ominous demographic and economic trends, see, for example, Culmann, *Deux tactiques*, 297–328.

[123] Langlois, *Lessons from Two Recent Wars*, 141–2.

[124] Langlois, 'Notre situation militaire', *Revue des deux mondes*, (15 Oct. 1907), 780, 793; quoted by Bowditch, 'Rationalization of Weakness', in Earle (ed.), *Modern France*, 39.

[125] Quoted by Porch, *The March to the Marne*, 227.   [126] Ibid.

Perhaps more than any other country in Europe, France was divided by politics, indeed, over the very character of the regime itself. Born with the collapse of the Second Empire and the confusion of defeat, it took some time before it became clear that the Third Republic had come to stay. The so-called Moderate Republicans who had come to power in 1879 took action to make the republic truly and irreversibly republican. They thoroughly purged the administrative, judicial, and educational systems of conservative and clerical presence and influences. However, until the occurrence of the Dreyfus Affair in the mid-1890s, relations between the republic and the army were co-operative and correct, even if not entirely free from ambiguity. Attracting many sons of the families of nobles and notables, whose traditional careers in the civil service had been blocked, the officer corps in general may have inclined toward the Right. But the army as a body remained strictly aloof from politics, whereas the republic, in turn, left the army untouched as the focus and symbol of the nation's patriotic consensus.

The one point where party politics and army affairs touched each other was on the issue of conscription. Equal service for all and opposition to the law of 1872 had long been central to the Republican programme. In 1889, after a long process of legislation, a law on three-year service was finally approved by the National Assembly. In practice, it made no radical change. For budgetary reasons the soldiers of the first portion had already been serving for only four years or less, a period which had been further interrupted by long furloughs. In addition, budgetary constraints forced the deputies to swallow the retention of the second portion of conscripts, for the army could not use three full annual classes without being considerably expanded. Social and educational exemptions were also retained in somewhat amended forms. The purpose and significance of the law was thus principally political and declarative. Yet it was precisely for this reason that the attitude of the army towards it tended to be negative. As in Germany, the military objections were compounded by deep aversion and distrust of what was viewed by the soldiers as irresponsible party-political meddling in a vital business of defence.[127]

---

[127] For the law of 1889 see esp. Monteilhet, *Les Institutions militaires*, 220–35; Ralston, *The Army of the Republic*, 96–115.

All this, however, did little to interrupt the cordial relations between the republic and the army, whose golden age came to an end only with the eruption of the Dreyfus Affair. The army tried to block the efforts to clear the name of the Jewish general-staff officer, whose conviction for espionage for Germany turned out to be based on forged material. This fuelled the worst political crisis in the history of the Third Republic. In the name of justice as against the honour of the army, the differences in French politics between Left and Right surfaced and divided French society into two antagonistic camps. The polarization of the political scene resulted in a shift in government from centre to centre-left. From 1898 the Moderate Republicans relied for support on a left-wing block. From 1902 the government became dominated by the so-called Radical Democrats. The Radicals' political aim was to smash for good what they considered the anti-republican camp, exposed in the Dreyfus Affair. The army, which had previously been spared political persecution but which was now identified with the forces of reaction, was to be thoroughly and forcibly republicanized.

The Radicals' campaign rested on the assumption that the problem with the army was socially and politically rooted. They believed that the influx of aristocrats into the army after 1871 had changed the traditionally rather humble composition of the French officer-corps, and that the network of Jesuit high schools contributed out of all proportion to the entrance lists of the most prestigious officer-schools.[128] Nothing less than root treatment was therefore deemed necessary, and General Louis André, Minister of War from 1900 to 1904 and a zealous republican, attempted such treatment in the most thorough and ruthless manner. The army promotion-committees were abolished, and authority over promotions was transferred to the ministry. The minister and his assistants drew up the promotion lists, paying special attention to the candidates' political opinions and religious persuasions. Officers possessing republican sympathies were rapidly promoted. Officers known for right-wing or Catholic opinions or backgrounds were removed

---

[128] The validity of this picture is debated and the figures are open to conflicting interpretations. The accepted view is best summarized in Girardet, *La Société militaire*, esp. 186, 195–6; François Bédarida, 'L'Armée et la république: Les Opinions des officiers français en 1876–78', *Revue Historique* (1964), 119–64. That view has been challenged as exaggerated in all respects by Porch, *The March to the Marne*, 17–22.

from positions of importance and their advancement was delayed. To obtain the neccessary information, the ministry did not hesitate to employ not only the provincial prefects but also the network of Masonic lodges. The military schools were purged and liberalized. Candidates could now enrol in the cadet schools only after having served first for one year in the ranks. More officers were commissioned directly from among the NCOs. Caste practices and privileges among the officer corps were abolished. The army high command was lowered in stature and placed in closer subordination to the ministry.[129]

The effect of the political onslaught on the morale of the officer corps was devastating. The army was already losing much of the popularity it had enjoyed in the decades after the war of 1870–1. The memory of defeat, and desire for revenge were fading. Middle-class individualism and socialist pacifism and anti-militarism combined from the mid-1890s in mutual distaste for the army and army life.[130] The employment of the army in the suppression of ecclesiastical establishments and workers' strikes contributed to the collapse of morale.[131] The results were not slow to appear. The number of applicants to Saint-Cyr dropped from 1,920 in 1897 to 982 in 1907. Almost half of the artillery officers who graduated from the Ecole polytechnique between 1905 and 1907 had resigned from the army by 1910.[132] Standards, as recorded especially in the professional arms and at the École de guerre, were falling sharply.[133]

The political persecution of the army coincided with, and accelerated, the parliamentary initiative to enact a law introducing a two-year service. The shortening in Germany in 1893 of the term of service for infantry to two years gave full legitimacy to French republican and egalitarian aspirations and made a similar development in France only a matter of time. Public debate started in the mid-1890s, and legislation was completed in 1905. All social and educational exemptions were abolished. Under the law of 1889 more than a third of each annual class had escaped conscription

---

[129] See Ralston, *The Army of the Republic*, 260–301; and, in a critical vein, Porch, *The March to the Marne*, 73–104.

[130] Girardet, *La Société militaire*, 213–35.

[131] See Ralston, *The Army of the Republic*, 280–6; Porch, *The March to the Marne*, 105–33.

[132] Girardet, *La Société militaire*, 274.

[133] Porch, *The March to the Marne*, 84–5.

altogether and only three-fifths had served the full three years.[134] Under the new law all young Frenchmen were made to serve the equal term of two years. From 1905 France put under the colours no less than 83 per cent of each annual class, leaving only the physically unfit out of the army. As in 1889, the motivation for the law was predominantly political, but this time the practical consequences were none the less considerable. More exhaustive conscription for a shorter term of active service implied that, while the size of the regular army was slightly reduced, France was going to have many more trained men in case of war. It also followed that the regular army was now regarded less as a professional fighting-force of seasoned soldiers and more as a training-school for the reserves.

Harassed as it was during and after the Dreyfus Affair, the army could only see the Two Years Law as a further blow in the political campaign launched against it. Already in 1895, when the idea of the change was first brought before the Conseil supérieur de la guerre, it was totally rejected by the council. Furthermore, this time, the law found virtually no support in the army as a whole.[135] The arguments had not changed much from the 1870s and 1880s. Again, the opponents of the law argued that the short period of service did not suffice to make soldiers out of civilians. What was perhaps possible with the docile German conscript living in a hierarchic society was impossible with the indisciplined and egalitarian French. Again, they pointed out that the shorter period of service would worsen the army's already acute problem of persuading a sufficient number of old-timers to re-enlist as NCOs. Furthermore, while pressure was put on the army to rely more heavily on the reserves, many officers were convinced that the terrible effect of modern firearms would require even higher morale, tactical proficiency, and cohesion in the next war. Their attitude was somewhat reminiscent of the response of Louis Napoleon's officers to the ill-organized reserve-programme imposed on them before 1870. Langlois cited Ardant du Picq in praising the superior qualities of the smaller and highly trained army.[136]

Indeed, here as well du Picq's work suddenly became most

---

[134] Ralston, *The Army of the Republic*, 302–3.
[135] Ibid. 391. See, for example, Derrécagaix, *La Guerre et l'armée*; and, in support of the law, Émile Manceau (Mayer), *Nos institutions militaires* (Paris, 1901).   [136] Langlois, *Lessons from Two Recent Wars*, 140–1.

relevant. It is certainly no coincidence that the editor of the new comprehensive edition of *Battle Studies* (1903), who wrote the exalting introduction and solicited the biographical details from du Picq's family, was none other than Ernest Judet, the anti-Dreyfusite journalist and editor of the popular and aggressive right-wing *Le Petit Journal*. While the army came under heavy pressure to open up to society, and while the government was forcing it to accept the reduction of military service to two years, men like Judet were delighted by du Picq's profound scepticism of armed hordes, and by his assertion that the officer corps had to be by nature aristocratic.[137] The Two Years Law and the new intense political involvement radicalized positions and brought the question down to fundamentals: where did the main weight of French defence lie, with the regular army or with the whole nation-in-arms?

In the aftermath of the Dreyfus Affair and up until the 1920s and 1930s, this question became overcharged with politics and emerged as one of the main points of contention between Right and Left in France. Spilling over from the political scene, it also grew to dominate the historical profession itself; in fact, historians of French military affairs have written about little else. Their perspectives and attitudes reflected and echoed the political overtones and rhetoric, particularly those of the Left, to which many of these historians belonged. The army's preference for the regulars and its distrust of the reservists have been explained principally in non-military terms as a function of its political and social conservatism.[138] Furthermore, in the critical post-war years, the army's distrust of the reserves was added to the catalogue of blunders and examples of military thick-headedness that occurred in the First World War. In the process, however, the essence and complexity of the military problem itself, as seen at the time, was all but ignored.[139] Since the growth of the doctrine of the offensive has been linked to the French army's preference for the regulars, this

[137] *Battle Studies*, 22–3.
[138] See esp. the left-wing historians Monteilhet (1926) and Michon (1935), and also Girardet (1953), Challener (1955) and Ralston (1967). Snyder (1984) argues an organizational rather than political and social bias on the part of the army. Porch (1981) provides an important, if at times over-zealous, corrective to the historians of the nation-in-arms school.
[139] The exceptions are Porch, *The March to the Marne*, which goes a long way in this direction, and Jean-Charles Jauffret, 'L'Organisation de la réserve à l'époque de la revanche, 1871–1914', *Revue Historique des Armées* (1989), 27–37.

problem is worth looking into at some length. Armies struggled with the parameters of this problem not only in France but all over Europe, including in Germany itself.

The problem of the reserves was predominantly one of effective organization and cadres. As professional soldiers in all countries often pointed out, multitudes of trained reservists did not in themselves constitute a fighting force. In 1870–1 the Prussian solution had been simple. The active units had been kept on half strength in peacetime and, on mobilization, had been swollen with reservists, who doubled the strength of each company. This, however, had been possible only as long as the regulars and the reservists encompassed roughly the same number of annual classes—three in active service and four in the reserve. The Landwehr, encompassing five more annual classes, had been formed in separate units and assigned to second-line duties. By the late 1870s, however, the number of reservists grew beyond the capacity of the active units to absorb them, especially as the term of service in the reserve was extended to four and a half years. The active units still absorbed about two-thirds of the reservists, but a new form of organization had to be found for the excess, and none could be as satisfactory as the old system. The German solution was the creation of separate reserve divisions in the ratio of one reserve division to each active corps. But this was only the beginning of the process.

From 1893 the term of active service for infantry in Germany was cut to two years, while the number of classes serving in the reserve was correspondingly raised to five. The active units could now absorb only a minority of the reservists. In order to economize on costly overheads, the German army avoided the creation of more reserve formations and tried a different approach. It created a fourth, cadre, demi-battalion in each active regiment. This was considered unsatisfactory, however, and in 1898 the army retracted and incorporated the reservists from the fourth battalion in new, separate reserve-divisions. As their number grew, the reserve divisions were later formed into reserve corps. None the less, because of the heavy expenditure on armaments and professional cadres which would have been required in order to bring these formations up to full combat-effectiveness, they remained far inferior to their active counterparts and were intended primarily for secondary missions. As we saw in the previous chapter, only the pressure of Germany's international and strategic position in the decade before the war induced Schlieffen and his successors to assign the reserve formations to first-line duties. Even more importantly, Schlieffen's paper schemes could only materialize when the Reichstag was moved to vote the huge sums needed for the expansion and upgrading of the reserve formations.[140]

The French army experienced the same problems and experimented with similar solutions. Contrary to the popular impression, however, it went ahead of its German rival in using reservists for active field-service during much of the period concerned. The manpower trauma of 1870–1 had its effect. The army laws of the 1870s copied the various German reserve-categories in a slightly modified form. All reservists up to the age of 30 (33 from 1892) were assigned to the reserve, which was the equivalent of the German reserve plus Landwehr. As in Germany, large numbers of reservists were absorbed into the active units, doubling the size of the regular army on mobilization. However, since the mean active term of service of slightly over three years was matched, on average, by six classes of reservists, many reservists had to be directed to special fourth battalions created in each active regiment by the cadre law of 1875. Furthermore, the older classes of reservists between the ages of 30 and 35 were also used and formed into separate territorial divisions. They were thus assigned a much more active role than their comparable German Landsturm, which was not intended for field service. The French Plan 3 (1882), for example, deployed two territorial armies at the rear of the five line-armies, which were composed of the regular troops and their reserves.[141] Later plans during the 1880s went even further in joining the territorial divisions and troops more closely to the active corps.[142] The French were in fact using fourteen annual classes for active field-service, as against the German's twelve.

In 1888, when the Germans created the Landwehr's second portion, thus assigning their own older classes of reservists a somewhat more active role, the French went a step further. Actively encouraged by the able civilian Minister of War Freycinet, the

[140] See, against the general drift of his argument, Snyder, *The Ideology of the Offensive*, 228, n. 109.

[141] Marchand, *Plans de concentration*, 28; État-Major de l'Armée, *Les Armées françaises*, I, i. 6–7.

[142] Marchand, *Plans de concentration*, 53, 61, 83, 204–5; État-Major de l'Armée; *Les Armées françaises*, 8–18.

architect of the armies of national defence in 1870–1, the Conseil supérieur de la guerre adopted a grandiose scheme whereby sixteen reserve corps, composed of mixed regiments of reservists and territorials, were to be formed to supplement the twenty active corps.[143] The scheme, however, was probably too ambitious to be realized. The chorus of historians who have denounced the army's conservatism in abandoning the scheme have lost sight of the general European perspective and have taken all too lightly the enormity of the project. It is worth remembering that the German army reached something like the above-mentioned strength and composition only on the eve of the war and after huge investments. The arguments of the generals that the reserve formations would be worthless without adequate cadres and artillery and that such cadres and artillery were simply not available, should not be dismissed as mere excuses. The proposed scheme was soon abandoned for more practical arrangements. Between 1890 and 1895 the number of reserve corps was reduced to five, while each active corps received a third reserve-division.[144] In 1897 the army retreated from the system of grand reserve-formations and reverted to the fourth battalion in each active regiment, in addition to separate reserve-divisions.[145] These reserve divisions were concentrated in reserve groups and placed in the second line, close to the front.

Scepticism regarding the combat-worth of the reserve units (as opposed to the reservists incorporated in, and doubling the strength of, the active units—a distinction that is often forgotten) was particularly notable among the proponents of morale and active and aggressive conduct in the late 1880s and 1890s. They doubted that the reserve formations were adapted to this mode of warfare. Georges Gilbert, for example, argued that, lacking artillery and cohesion, Freycinet's reserve-formations would be of little value.[146] In 1893 the army attempted to stiffen the reserve units by creating a small cadre of regular officers in each regiment. However, critics argued that these posts were filled with the army's less-than-best officers and that the nature of the job allowed them to spend their

[143] État Major de l'Armée, *Les Armées françaises*, 18–19.
[144] Ibid. 20, 25.
[145] Ibid. 27; Marchand, *Plans de concentration*, 296–7.
[146] See Georges Gilbert's collection of essays, *Lois et institutions militaires* (Paris, 1895), 173–448; Contamine, *La Revanche*, 71–2.

time in total idleness.[147] Starting from the Bonnal-inspired Plan 14
(1898), the reserve units were returned primarily to second-line or
garrison duties, which was still no different from the role envisaged
by the Germans for their own comparable reserve and Landwehr
formations. Only in the decade before the war, and only to any
great extent after 1911, did the basic features of this picture change.
While the Germans were moving towards assigning their reserve
formations to a more active role, the Two Years Law and
subsequent political contentions were radicalizing positions in
France regarding the French reserves.

The Two Years Law created a multitude of trained reservists and
coincided with the mounting pressure on the army to open up to
civil society. The army was expected to rely more heavily on the
reservists and invest greater efforts in their training. However, left-
wing critics accused the army of sabotaging the law. For example, it
was argued that, even after the enactment of the law, the army,
which had been claiming that two years was too short a period for
the training of conscripts, was in fact wasting an alarming part of
conscripts' time on various non-combat jobs. Many of these jobs
took the form of traditional personal services for the officers, which
the army did nothing to abolish.[148] The reservists' training also left
much to be desired.[149] The seemingly vicious circle of the army's
distrust and neglect and the reservists' poor performance could
probably not be reduced to either component. The fact remains,
however, that many reservists avoided training, and that during
training discipline was often poor and performance unimpressive.[150]
Whereas Germany, where the army enjoyed the highest social
esteem, had no difficulty in creating a large and proud body of
reserve officers, in France reserve officers were in acutely short
supply because of unwillingness to volunteer.[151] Indeed, returning
to the fundamental problem of cadres, a comparison with Germany

[147] Monteilhet, *Les Institutions militaires*, 238; Porch, *The March to the Marne*, 26.

[148] Monteilhet, *Les Institutions militaires*, 315; Ralston, *The Army of the Republic*, 313; Porch, *The March to the Marne*, 195; Gerd Krumeich, *Armament and Politics in France on the Eve of the First World War: The Introduction of the Three Years Conscription* (London, 1984), 105–6.

[149] Monteilhet, *Les Institutions militaires*, 253; Porch, *The March to the Marne*, 204–5; Gorce, *The French Army*, 56–7.

[150] In 1907, for example, 36 per cent of the reservists called for training did not respond to the call; Jauffret, 'L'Organisation de la réserve', 35.

[151] Ibid., 33; Porch, *The March to the Marne*, 204–6.

speaks for itself. In 1902 Germany possessed some 75,000 to 80,000 NCOs to France's 22,000.[152] The extensive German army laws of 1911, 1912, and 1913 gave the German army 112,000 NCOs, as against 48,000 in its French rival. There were 215 career NCOs in a German infantry regiment as opposed to only 95 in its French counterpart.[153]

There was nothing in these deficiencies that several weeks or months of war-experience could not remedy. While some French reserve units may have performed poorly in the opening days of the First World War,[154] they quickly played a decisive role and, with the prolonging of the war, all distinctions between regulars and reservists disappeared completely. Yet the French army, like all armies, expected a short and decisive war, in which only battle-ready troops could participate effectively. It has been too easily forgotten that reserve formations had never been employed in the first line before the First World War, not even in 1870–1, as is widely assumed. They were a novelty and a great unknown factor. Nobody knew or could know exactly if and how they would perform. None other than Michel, whose famous plan for the amalgamation of reserve and regular units is discussed below, asked in 1911: 'These Reserve divisions exist on paper only, but who can guarantee their solidity?'[155] Michel, it is worth bearing in mind, had been the Inspector of Reserve Regiments in 1907–8 and one of their most ardent supporters. His own answer to his question was negative, and his scheme in fact called for the suppression of all reserve formations.[156] This fact has been ignored by modern historians. Only after two protracted total world wars could the army's pre-war distrust of the reserve units be dispelled and the short-war illusion ridiculed.

From 1905 intelligence regarding German intentions was changing French planning, while the effect of the Two Years Law was

---

[152] French parliamentary deliberations, cited in Ralston, *The Army of the Republic*, 301; cf. Reichsarchiv, *Der Weltkrieg*, i. supp. 485.

[153] Cited in Porch, *The March to the Marne*, 194; figures in the German sources are similar except that the 215 career NCOs were about 80 per cent and not all of the NCOs in a German infantry regiment: Reichsarchiv, *Der Weltkrieg*, 509, 512. See Porch, *The March to the Marne*, 196–200, for a thorough analysis of the French NCOs problem; also Setzen 'The Doctrine of the Offensive', 54–6.

[154] Porch, *The March to the Marne*, 211.

[155] État-Major de l'Armée, *Les Armées françaises*, I. i, ann., pp. 11, 8, 13; see Porch, *The March to the Marne*, 211, for basically the same argument as mine.

[156] État-Major de l'Armée, *Les Armées françaises*, I. i. ann., pp. 8, 12–13.

changing their reserves' organization. In 1904 French intelligence got hold of accurate information suggesting that the Germans planned a very strong outflanking movement through Belgium and Luxemburg, using reserve formations in an active role. Further intelligence reports supported this information but neither made clear that the German move would extend beyond the Meuse and Sambre in a deep north-westerly sweep, nor ruled out a German attack in Lorraine. In response, the French forces' centre of gravity was moved northward in a series of gradual adjustments. Plan 15 *bis* (1907) created a new army to the north of Verdun. Plan 16 (1909) supported this army by positioning behind it a new strategic 'army of manœuvre' as well as two, instead of one, groups of reserve divisions. All were ready to counter-attack in the direction of the Ardennes.[157] Plan 16 also incorporated the increasing number of reservists made available by the law of 1905. The fourth battalions were removed and concentrated in reserve brigades, which were created in most corps. The number of reserve divisions was increased by the creation of a reserve division in each corps-region. The plan thus raised the number of reserve battalions deployed from 320 to 463, in addition to the 108 battalions in the nine territorial divisions.[158]

More indications regarding the direction and scale of the German attack continued to accumulate.[159] By 1911 General Wilson, director of military operations in the British War Office, was reported to have estimated that the German offensive in the west would make extensive use of reserve divisions and extend as far as Lille.[160] On the basis of a similar assessment, General Michel, the new vice-president of the Conseil supérieur de la guerre and

[157] Marchand, *Plans de concentration*, 156–81; *Les Armées françaises*, 31–7; Williamson, *The Politics of Grand Strategy*, 53–5, 117–24; Jan Karl Tanenbaum, 'French Estimates of Germany's Operational War Plans', in Ernest R. May (ed.), *Knowing One's Enemies: Intelligence Assessment before the Two World Wars* (Princeton, NJ, 1984), 150–171; Cole, ' "Forward with the Bayonet" ', 296–300; Snyder, *The Ideology of the Offensive*, 81–90.

[158] État-Major de l'Armée, *Les Armées françaises*, i, i. 34–5; Contamine, *La Revanche*, 116–17.

[159] See Tanenbaum, 'French Estimates', in May (ed.), *Knowing One's Enemy*, 156–170; Snyder, *The Ideology of the Offensive*, 87–90.

[160] Tanenbaum, 'French Estimates', in May (ed.), *Knowing One's Enemy*, 159; Snyder, *The Ideology of the Offensive*, 88; État-Major de l'Armée, *Les Armées françaises*, 37. Gamelin's claim in 1954 that Foch held the same opinion as Wilson, his close friend, finds no support in any other source, not even in Foch's own memoirs; Gamelin, *Manœuvre et victoire de la Marne*, 42.

generalissimo designate in the event of war, felt that Plan 16 was inadequate. He worked out a radically new war-plan, which stretched the French forces from the Swiss border to the North Sea and shifted the main French effort to the Belgian sector. The French forces on the Franco-German frontier were to be reduced to no more than three corps, with a further three arriving in a second wave. No less than eleven corps were to be deployed along the Belgian frontier, while another three concentrated in reserve around Paris. The forces covering the German frontier and the Ardennes were to adopt a defensive stance. The main French effort was to take place on the extreme left and counter-attack the right flank of the German main thrust on the Belgian plains. As with the Germans, the doubling of the French front length necessitated the massive incorporation of reserve units in the first line. To accomplish this, Michel proposed another radical scheme, whereby the active and reserve units were to be totally amalgamated. All active and reserve regiments were to be coupled in new demi-brigades. Thus the strength of each corps was to be almost doubled, to forty-eight battalions.[161]

It is well known that Michel's strategic scheme anticipated to a remarkable extent the form that the French deployment ultimately assumed, after great upheavals, in the opening campaign of 1914. But both his schemes were radical enough to be received with distrust by his colleagues. Many practical objections were raised. There were serious question-marks regarding the soundness of his scheme for the reserves. The amalgamation of the active and reserve troops would also mean French mobilization would lag three days behind that of the Germans. Finally, what if the Germans did not cross the Meuse and Sambre, or carried out their main offensive in Lorraine after all? Especially in the latter case, most of the French army would have been deployed out of reach. The benefit of hindsight on 1914 must not mislead; any French plan had to provide for both contingencies.[162] However, the factor that tipped

---

[161] État-Major de l'Armée, *Les Armées françaises*, I, i. 38; and ann., pp. 7–17; Percin, *Les Erreurs du haut commandement*, 39–49.

[162] See previous note and also the general-staff study, cited in Tanenbaum, 'French Estimates', in May (ed.), *Knowing One's Enemy*, 161–2, and Snyder, *The Ideology of the Offensive*, 93–4. Joffre's claim in his *Memoirs*, 17–18, that Michel's plan would have exposed France completely if the German attack were to come from Lorraine, was far less apologetic than it has usually been presented as being. Also see his considerations regarding Plan 17, ibid. 78–9.

the scale against Michel's schemes and brought his downfall was not military but political and related to a deeper change in the French national mood. Michel was one of the republican generals promoted rapidly under the Radical government. He had little authority over his colleagues. Unfortunately for him, by 1911 the Radical agenda had exhausted itself and new concerns were emerging. In the wake of the Agadir crisis, the growing German threat prompted the so-called 'nationalist revival' in France. French politics reverted from the centre-left to the centre-right. The government was determined to bolster national defence by working more closely with the army. In effect, Michel was forced to go by the new Minister of War, Messimy, even before his scheme was totally rejected by his colleagues in the Conseil supérieur de la guerre.[163]

After two decades of preoccupation with domestic issues, the nationalist revival marked a shift in French public concerns. The international tensions which had been building up in the successive crises after 1905 focused attention on the foreign threat and the prospect of war. Nationalist feelings surged. Patriotism was back in fashion.[164] Ministers of War Messimy and Millerand revoked many of the steps taken by André.[165] The high command was reorganized and a new post created, Chief of the Army General Staff, which combined the previously separate positions of generalissimo and chief of staff. In 1912 a new cadre law for the infantry strengthened the regular staff- and command-element in the reserve regiments.[166] The most controversial measure, however, came in response to the German army laws of 1911, 1912, and 1913, which gave the German regular army a two-to-one superiority over its French rival. To counter this huge increase, the French government in 1913 saw no choice but to lengthen again the term of active service to three years.

In the fierce parliamentary debate which developed over the measure, delegates from the Left pointed out its dubious value, and historians followed in indicating the ulterior motives of both the

---

[163] For the famous incident, see also Adolphe-Marie Messimy, *Mes souvenirs* (Paris, 1937), 74–6.
[164] The standard work is Eugen Weber, *The Nationalist Revival in France, 1905–1914* (Berkeley, Calif., 1959).
[165] See Porch, *The March to the Marne*, 169–90.
[166] Ibid. 191–2.

ruling middle-class parties and the army.[167] However, while the army never liked the Two Years Law, there is little reason to doubt that the measure was a natural and genuine, if desperate, response to the growing German preponderance.[168] The law raised the strength of the standing army by keeping a third annual class with the colours. It could not, however, raise France's total war-establishment to the level achieved by the now-extensive exploitation of the much larger German age-classes. The army defended the logic of the law by inflating the danger of a German *attaque brusquée*, which would be carried out by the German regular army before mobilization and would overrun the inferior French frontier forces. In truth, however, it was much more concerned with ensuring its own ability to take up offensive operations as early as possible.[169] Left-wing critics argued that the law was a point-blank attempt to reassert the position of the regulars and the professional army at the expense of the reservists and the idea of the nation-in-arms. But a more sympathetic assessment concludes that the authors of the law believed it would strengthen the whole military system, of both regulars and reserves.[170] Adopted in 1913, Plan 17 incorporated 401 reserve battalions, somewhat less than Plan 16, but they were better staffed and better organized.[171]

The Left's charges assume their full significance only in the context of the socialists' fundamental position regarding the problem of national defence, not only in France but everywhere in Europe. From the middle of the nineteenth century, this consisted in the total rejection of both the institution of standing armies and of aggressive wars. For the socialists, the citizen militia on the Swiss model, intended for pure national defence, was the only legitimate form of military establishment. The great socialist leader Jean

---

[167] Monteilhet, *Les Institutions militaires*, 267–302; Michon, *La Préparation à la guerre, passim*. A good summary and refutation of the domestic interpretations based on ulterior motives, can be found in Krumeich's meticulous *Armament and Politics in France*, 5–20, which concludes that the principal motive for the law was after all military.

[168] Ralston, *The Army of the Republic*, pp. 353–6.

[169] Krumeich, *Armament and Politics in France* 17 *et passim*.

[170] See Porch, *The March to the Marne*, 191 *et passim*.; also Joffre, *Memoirs*, ii. app. 1, pp. 592–5.

[171] Instead of 22 reserve divisions, each consisting of 18 battalions, there were now 25 divisions of 12 battalions each. The six-battalion strong reserve brigades in the active corps were replaced by 2 regiments of 2 battalions each: État-Major de l'Armée, *Armées françaises*, 47–8, 55; Contamine, *La Revanche*, 141.

Jaurès was only elaborating on these ideas when, in the course of the parliamentary debate, he presented the comprehensive and systematic scheme he had developed in his book, *L'Armée nouvelle* (first publ. 1910). Taking issue with the teachings of Gilbert, Langlois, and Bonnal, he reminded the professors of the staff college that Clausewitz had argued that the defence was stronger than the attack, and pointed out that the popular nature of the Revolutionary armies was the true source of Napoleon's successes. His critics, who replied that Frenchmen did not quite resemble the Swiss and that France was not a little mountain-fortress but a Great Power, who needed an army comparable to that of the Germans to back up her European and global interests,[172] only demonstrated the fundamental nature of the dispute. The argument was not technical. What Jaurès had in mind was a different sort of France and a different sort of international system.

The nationalist revival worked to enhance the army's morale in both a direct and an indirect way. In the first place, the desire for moral and spiritual regeneration was one of its most characteristic features. Secondly, by resuming positive political co-operation with the army, it helped the army recover from the blows which it had suffered since the Dreyfus Affair and which had brought its morale to the lowest depth. The connection between this recovery and the acceptance of the doctrine of the offensive after 1911 has been indicated by historians. Joffre, the new head of the French army, consciously encouraged the young enthusiasts for the offensive and the force of morale in the general staff, as a means to restore the army's badly shaken sense of purpose and self-confidence.[173]

By alleviating the external pressures on the army, the nationalist revival also helped the army ward off what it regarded as unsound and dangerous pressures to incorporate reserve units in a full first-line role. Here again the doctrine of the offensive intervened favourably. The army's distrust of the reserves was reinforced by the doctrine of the offensive, while the doctrine of the offensive also possessed the merit of helping to ward off the pressures concerning the reserves. The reserves were simply not up to that type of warfare which allegedly necessitated great tactical skill and

---

[172] Porch, *The March to the Marne*, 210; Ralston, *The Army of the Republic*, 348–9, 352.

[173] Porch, *The March to the Marne*, 217–18, 223–4; Cole, ' "Forward with the Bayonet" ', 55, 225–6, 235; Snyder, *The Ideology of the Offensive*, 95.

cohesion. Indeed, the army's persistent scepticism in regard to indications that the Germans were planning a deep sweep through Belgium using reserve formations in the front line has also been explained by the emergence of a closed entrenched bias, rooted in political or organizational preference. Had evidence of a massive German attack on the Belgian plains been believed, this would have required the extension of the French front and the use of reserve formations in the first line.[174]

There is undoubtedly some truth in this explanation for French thinking and behaviour. It ought not to be pushed too far, however. The correlation in the army between either political conservativism or organizational resistance to change on the one hand and enthusiasm for the offensive on the other is far from being clear-cut. Politically, it has long been pointed out that good republican generals like Galliéni and Joffre himself were distrustful of the reserves and, together with the republican Sarrail, advocated the offensive. At the same time, a right-winger like Négrier emphasized the strength of modern defence and was one of the few who in 1904 took the possibility of a German invasion through Belgium very seriously. Another right-winger like Grouard advocated both the defence and the incorporation of the reserve units in the first line.[175] Organizational traditionalism fares no better. As it happened, Négrier was the most outspoken opponent of the reserves at the time of the deliberations on the Two Years Law, and so also was General Kessler.[176] Furthermore, the emphasis on morale and the

[174] See Monteilhet, *Les Institutions militaires*, 331–2, arguing for the existence of a politically rooted bias in the army; and Snyder, *The Ideology of the Offensive*, arguing for an organizational one.

[175] Contamine, *La Revanche*, 87; and also Porch, *The March to the Marne*, 249–50. On Sarrail, see J. K. Tanenbaum, *General Maurice Sarrail, 1856–1929* (Chapel Hill, NC, 1974), 28; and on Négrier in 1904, id., 'French Estimates', in May (ed.), *Knowing One's Enemy*, 155.

[176] On Kessler, see in Snyder himself, *The Ideology of the Offensive*, 75. Snyder's lucidly argued and skilfully documented thesis aims to explain everything by the army's 'organizationally motivated bias'. His book, however, seems to be guilty of its own 'professionally motivated bias' as a political scientist. It is one thing to suggest a syndrome within reality and quite another to explain the totality and complexity of this reality by it. To leave many lesser points aside, Snyder is dealing, by his own definition, with a pan-European phenomenon. Yet he finds no pan-European reasons for it. Such factors as the formative experiences of 1866 and 1870 and social Darwinism are mentioned only to be quickly dismissed: ibid. 29, 39–40, 199. On the other hand, while he attributes the spirit of the offensive in France, Germany, and Russia to different particular causes in each country, these causes are

spirit of the offensive went far beyond the military. Otherwise it would never have been accepted and encouraged by the civilians. Messimy is only one example. In 1912 Fallières, the President of the Republic, addressed the Conseil supérieur de la guerre in the following words: 'We are determined to march straight against the enemy without hesitation. The offensive alone is suited to the temperament of our soldiers, and it ought to assure us victory, provided we are willing to consecrate to the effort all our forces without exception.'[177] The nationalist revival was undoubtedly behind this attitude of encouragement and support. But the nationalist revival itself drew much of its driving force and spirit from a wider intellectual mood prevailing in France. With the advent of the twentieth century, that intellectual mood profoundly influenced feelings about, and perceptions of, the essentials of being and of human life. The military were playing a familiar and appealing tune.

As mentioned in the previous chapter, the yearning for moral and spiritual regeneration and for a rediscovery of the elementary forces of life was a cross-European sentiment that gathered momentum with the coming of the new century. Like its namesake a century before, so-called neo-Romanticism was characterized by a revolt against excessive and alienating rationalism and by the celebration of intuition, spontaneous action, and self-expression. In *fin de siècle* France, people associated the prevailing social and cultural *malaise* with the atomism and lack of a communal sense of purpose, belonging, and common binding values that are characteristic of modern society. The Dreyfus Affair, while dividing Frenchmen most deeply, provided a great rallying-point for the intellectuals and an outlet for their moral and idealistic energy. But in the aftermath of the affair, the years of Radical rule, the persecution of the church, and the growing strife in industrial relations with organized labour and socialism brought about disillusionment and disgust with republican petty politics. Discontent with materialism and with what was perceived as the triviality, mediocrity, and

---

somehow all revealed to be of an organizational nature. Armies are not 'naturally inclined towards the offensive'; for historical reasons, however, they tended to be so in the nineteenth century. The same criticism applies to Stephen van Evera, 'The Cult of the Offensive and the Origins of the First World War', in Miller (ed.), *Military Strategy and the Origins of the First World War* (Princeton, NJ, 1985), 58–107.

[177] Joffre, *Memoirs*, 30.

spiritual dullness of bourgeois society prompted the search for old and new unifying ideals, mystique, and sources of vitality.

For the second time in the space of a century, the first signs of the cultural change were revealed in the arts, where impressionism, primitivism, symbolism, and cubism replaced the classical naturalism which had ruled France until the 1870s. As in Germany, a cult of Nietzsche developed from the late 1890s. Admiring novelists like André Gide, Marcel Proust, and Alain Fournier concentrated on the psychological and the subconscious at the same time as Freud was independently developing psychoanalysis in Vienna. However, the cultural hero of the pre-war decade in France was Henri Bergson, professor of philosophy at the Collège de France from 1905 and author of *Creative Evolution* (1907). His mesmerizing Friday-afternoon lectures became public events, attended by statesmen, intellectuals, and celebrities of all sorts. Bergson led the philosophical attack against the mechanistic outlook of positivism. Since the late nineteenth century, this outlook had already been eroded by the developments in science, especially in the sphere of electromagnetics and the theory of fields, which were soon crowned by Einstein's theory of relativity (1905). Bergson argued that human analytic faculties artificially dissected reality into separate static units, thus fundamentally distorting its living and dynamic quality. Only the force of intuition could come to grips with the very essence of being, which was perpetual creative evolution in the flux of time, the so-called *élan vital*.

'Bergsonism' was enormously successful because it corresponded and appealed to the prevailing sentiments of the time, providing support, inspiration, and stimulus for many diverse and remote intellectual concerns. For example, one regular participant in Bergson's lectures was Georges Sorel. His *Reflections on Violence* (1908), celebrating the inspiring myth and the vitalizing force of direct action as the moving forces of history, influenced revolutionary syndicalism and was later looked upon sympathetically by both Fascism and Bolshevism. His companion to the lectures was the young poet and moralist, Charles Péguy, who called for his country's spiritual and moral regeneration and purification and who looked for a unifying mystique for all Frenchmen. Like many others at that time, he found his way to the Church, which, profiting from the general quest for faith, experienced a sudden and rather unforeseen revival. On the right, Charles Maurras and Action française called for revolutionary means to replace the decadent Republic with a monarchic France, based on integral nationalism and racial solidity. His friend, the novelist Maurice Barrès, also exalted nationalism and the unifying bonds of common ancestry, history, and culture. Finally, the acute foreign threat and shadow of war in the decade before 1914 enhanced the sense of common destiny, the feeling of moral seriousness and the willingness to act vigorously, especially among the educated young.[178] In his impressionist book *Les Jeunes Gens d'aujourd'hui* (1913), Agathon contrasted the 'generation of 1912' with the generation of their fathers in the 1890s. He characterized his young contemporaries as 'eager to act in the world [and] just as eager for a set of beliefs that would sustain them in their activity and give it direction'.[179] 'Life', wrote one student, 'is neither intellectual nor critical, but vigorous.' Other youths declared that 'France needed heroism to live', and saw 'in war an aesthetic ideal of energy and force'.[180] In this context, it is again not difficult to understand the popularity enjoyed by du Picq's work when it was republished in 1903. Readers admired his elevation of the human spirit above mechanistic considerations, which they found in harmony with their own critique of modern 'mechanistic' mass society.[181]

It is only against this background that one can assess the revolt of the so-called 'Young Turks' in the general staff against the generation of the 1890s and the answers they offered to French material inferiority and the hazards of both the modern battlefield and the international arena. Returning to command the École de guerre in 1908–11, after having been ostracized from his professorial chair in 1901 at the height of André's purges, Foch was now assuming an elevated, inspiring posture that was after his own heart. Apparently even more than before, he was emphasizing moral energy, action, and will-power. However, there is no reason to suppose that either his lofty mystique or the École de guerre as an

[178] The literature on this subject is extensive. See especially: Alexander Sedgwick, *The Third French Republic, 1870–1914* (New York, 1968), 120–9; H. Stuart Hughes, *Consciousness and Society, The Reorientation of European Social Thought, 1890–1930* (London, 1959), esp. 337–44; Ronald Stromberg, *Redemption by War: The Intellectuals and 1914* (Lawrence, Kan., 1982), *passim*.

[179] Cited in Paul Mazgaj, *The Action Française and Revolutionary Syndicalism* (Chapel Hill, 1979), 34; Agathon was a pseudonym for Henri Massis and Alfred de Tarde. Robert Wohl, *The Generation of 1914* (Cambridge, Mass., 1979), 5–18.

[180] Cited from Agathon by Gorce, *French Army*, 91–2.

[181] See Barbey d'Aureville in *Battle Studies*, 11–13.

institution played any significant role at that time in the development of the doctrine of offensive. In contrast to the accepted view, it has been pointed out that at the École de guerre there was great plurality in tactical matters in the years preceding the war.[182] Many of the professors there, especially those of infantry tactics, opposed the extremities of Grandmaison and his friends. To this category belonged the assistant professor, and later professor, of infantry tactics (1902–3, 1904–6, and 1908–11) Major, later Lieutenant-Colonel, Pétain. Like his predecessor Maud'huy, he taught the lessons of Manchuria and emphasized the strength of modern fire-power. So did his own successor, Debeney.[183] The belief that Pétain's advancement was delayed on that account is totally unfounded. His career had always been pedestrian. The new offensive doctrine was advanced by a committed avant-garde of young middle-ranking officers of the general staff, who were supported by some representatives of the older generation like generals Pau and Castelnau.[184] The doctrine was successful because it was adopted by Joffre, who admired the young group for its energy and promise, who was no strategist himself, and who regarded it as one of his primary missions to rid the army of its confusion and lack of confidence by providing it with a clear, unified, and inspiring doctrine.[185]

In the space of one year Joffre's general staff altered French doctrine and war-planning. The new Complementary Regulations

[182] Debeney, *La Guerre et les hommes*, 12, 277–8; cited and developed by Porch, *The March to the Marne*, 219. Porch is right in making this point but seems to be unaware of the decisive role the *École de guerre* had in fact played during the later part of the nineteenth century. He does not deal with the revival of French military thought and with the Clausewitzian and Napoleonic school of that period, nor does he distinguish between that school and the new offensive one. Consequently, he is right in arguing that the change in the intellectual climate could not be the reason for the adoption of Clausewitz by the French in the 1880s, because the intellectual change came only two decades later; yet he is wrong in extending his argument to the doctrine of the offensive, which developed precisely then; Porch, 'Clausewitz and the French', 291–2.

[183] See previous note and also Contamine, *La Revanche*, 164, 170, 183–4; Ryan, *Pétain*, 24–36; Herbert R. Lottman, *Pétain: Hero or Traitor?* (New York, 1985), 34, 38–9; Cole, ' "Forward with the Bayonet" ', 256–7, 262–4, 265–7; the texts of the lectures exist in the École de guerre's library.

[184] For a selection of articles favourable to the offensive, written between 1911 and 1914 mostly by young officers, see Cole, ' "Forward with the Bayonet" ', 218–21.

[185] Joffre's evidence in his *Memoirs*, 26, 29–30, is abundantly clear. Also see n. 173 above.

for the Conduct of Large Formations (issued 28 October 1913), Field Service Regulations (2 December 1913), and Infantry Field Regulations (20 April 1914) codified the doctrine of the offensive in unmistaken terms.[186] The first of these documents was drawn up by a committee headed by General Pau. Its General Remarks proclaimed:

The conduct of war is dominated by the necessity of giving to the operations the spirit of a vigorous offensive.

Of all the nations, France is the one whose military history offers the most striking examples of the great results to which the offensive in war leads, as well as of the disasters entailed by the passive defence . . . The lessons of the past have borne their fruit, the French army, returning to its traditions, admits henceforth no law in the conduct of operations other than that of the offensive . . .[187]

Chapter 1 proceeded in the same vein:

Military operations aim at the destruction of the organized forces of the enemy. The decisive battle followed by an energetic pursuit involving the destruction of his armies is the sole method of breaking down the will of the adversary . . . The offensive alone leads to positive results . . . From the very outset of operations he [the commander] will impress on the operations such a stamp of violence and tenacity that the enemy, shaken in his *morale* and paralysed in his action, will be forced to remain on the defensive . . . *Battles are beyond everything else moral struggles.*[188]

The continuity with, and divergence from, the regulations of 1895 are both obvious, and the latter is even specifically stated.[189] In operational terms, the new regulations rejected even the expediency of defence and thus also the defensive-offensive. Hence also the major difference between Plan 17, and new French war-plan drawn up under Joffre, and Plans 14–16, its predecessors during the previous fifteen years.

Approved in outline by the Conseil supérieur de la guerre on 18 April 1913 and taking force from 15 April 1914, Plan 17 strengthened the French concentration against Germany by assuming the friendly or neutral attitude of Britain and Italy. More

---

[186] Joffre, *Memoirs*, 33–5.

[187] *Conduite des grandes unités*, English trans. by the General Staff, War Office, *The Operations of Large Formations* (London, 1914), 7–8; italics in the original.

[188] Ibid. 20–1. For the regulations see also Cole, ' "Forward with the Bayonet" ', 227–34, 280–8; Carrias, *La Pensée militarie française*, 296–8.

[189] *Large Formations*, 8.

important, it continued the tilting and extension of the French deployment in a north-westerly direction, to counter a German sweep through Belgium. Joffre had already adjusted Plan 16 along these lines, before devising his own new plan. Plan 17 deployed a strong army, the Fifth, along the Belgian Ardennes and assigned it five corps, two reserve divisions, and one cavalry division. In close support were placed the cavalry corps and a group of reserve divisions, each three divisions strong. With the British Expeditionary Force to its left and the 'army of manœuvre', the Fourth, brought forward to its right, the Fifth Army was to move into Belgium, if the 'Belgian hypothesis' in the Plan materialized. Although this hypothesis was regarded as almost certain, available information still left room for doubt as to whether it would constitute the sole German offensive effort, extend beyond the Meuse and Sambre, or incorporate a large number of reserve units in the front line.[190] This ambiguity has generally been dismissed all too easily by historians. The truly distinguishing feature of the Plan was, however, its offensive nature. The possibility of a pre-emptive French offensive in Belgium had been ruled out by the politicians for obvious reasons in the preliminary stage of the planning. Yet, animated by the offensive imperative and encouraged by Russians pledges for early offensives in Poland in support of their allies, the authors of Plan 17 were determined not to lose the initiative to the Germans and to dictate the course of operations by opening the war with an immediate all-out attack in Lorraine.[191] 'Whatever the circumstances,' read the Plan's opening lines, 'the intention of the commander-in-chief is to advance with all forces united to the attack on the German armies.'[192]

Herein lay the decision strategic flaw of the Plan. Neither the issue of the reserves nor the Belgian problem, while being themselves mutually connected and inextricably influenced by the

---

[190] For the conflicting indications and considerations here, see Joffre, *Memoirs*, 61–4, 145. Also see Tanenbaum, 'French Estimates', in May (ed.), *Knowing One's Enemy*, 165–7.
[191] The text of the plan is printed in État-Major de l'Armèe, *Les Armées françaises*, I, i. ann., pp. 21–35; for its history and the considerations behind it see ibid., I, i. 44–61, 75–91; Joffre, *Memoirs*, 36–112. For the Entente's Belgian problem, see Krause, 'Anglo-French Military Planning, 1905–1914', 234–54, 333–5. Krause's assertion that the Russian factor was the major reason for the offensive emphasis adopted in Plan 17 is unsubstantiated and is greatly oversimplifying: ibid. 183–5, 377.   [192] Ibid., I. i. ann., p. 21.

offensive spirit, were as crucial to the events of 1914 as they have been claimed to be in retrospect. It is true that, before the war, the French high command had been playing down indications that the Germans might use reserve units in a full front-line role, a practice which the French themselves ruled out. Furthermore, many French reservists were left out of any combat-formation and were amassed in rear depots for later use as replacements.[193] However in 1914 the French high command fed its available reserve-units into battle very quickly, even before the German practice was fully recognized. The two new armies of Alsace and Lorraine, which were formed during the early stages of the Battle of the Frontiers to support the French offensive, were composed mainly of reserve divisions, which even previously had been deployed very close to the front. As the overwhelming strength of the German right wing was recognized, these armies were disbanded and their forces transported to join the two reserve divisions from Paris to form the French Sixth Army on the allies' far left.

This brings us to the Belgian problem. Although the strength of the forces assigned by Plan 17 to the Belgian sector was certainly inadequate, this inadequacy was not as grave as it appears in hindsight. As mentioned, the French had to prepare for various strategic options. This is justly pointed out by Joffre.[194] Before they could complete their deployment, they had to be certain of the actual direction of the Germans' major offensive efforts. However, there was no symmetry here between the various possible threats. From the first day of the operations the French had to be ready for a strong German offensive in Lorraine. However, if the attack came through Belgium, they would have had ample time to adjust. They could rely on their railway system to redeploy, once the German armies marched into Belgium. In this respect, the French deployment according to Plan 17 allowed for great flexibility. The French merely had to keep an open mind and maintain their freedom of operation. Only they did not. Rather than wait, as in previous French war-plans, until the German intentions were clarified, they committed themselves to a major offensive in Lorraine. Before this was called off, they had not merely suffered heavy losses but had surrendered the north of France to the Germans and risked total

---

[193] See Percin, *1914: Les Erreurs du haut commandement* (Paris, 1920), 10, 56, which is perhaps a little exaggerated.

[194] Joffre, *Memoirs*, 63–4, 68, 78–9.

defeat. The problem thus lay primarily in the doctrine of unlimited offensive, and indeed it was on this aspect that most contemporary critics of Plan 17 focused.

General Galliéni, the commander of the Fifth Army, resigned his command when Joffre rejected his request that his army be reinforced from five to nine corps. While being offensive-minded himself, he was not as extreme as the 'Young Turks' in the general staff. In view of the many uncertainties involved, he preferred more restraint during the opening stage of the campaign, until the German intentions were clarified.[195] General Lanrezac, Galliéni's successor as commander of the Fifth Army, expressed similar misgivings. Tactically, like many of the army's senior generals, he did not take the *offensive à outrance* too seriously. 'Bah!' he told a fellow officer, 'new ideas must not be resisted too much. Time, I hope, will take it upon itself to calm the ardour of these young men.'[196] Strategically, he feared the exposure of the Belgian sector and the commitment to attack in Lorraine, where he anyhow saw little prospect of success.[197] General Pierre Ruffey, the commander of the Third Army, was among the very few who anticipated that the main German effort would take place beyond the Meuse. He too advocated a counter-offensive strategy, with the main allied effort being developed in Belgium.[198] Galliéni, Lanrezac, and Ruffey all independently submitted memoranda presenting their points of view. Even General Castelnau, Joffre's deputy in the general staff and one of the authors of Plan 17, began to have something like second thoughts after being nominated to command the Second Army in Lorraine. He wondered if it was not advisable after all to delay the decisive battle in that theatre and adopt a 'counter-offensive' strategy until the Russians had time to intervene in force.[199]

Indeed, while the tactical aspect of the doctrine of unlimited

[195] Tanenbaum, 'French Estimates', in May (ed.). *Knowing One's Enemy*, 170; Cole, ' "Forward with the Bayonet" ', 264–5 for Galliéni's views of tactics, and 339–40 for his criticism of Plan 17; Snyder, *The Ideology of the Offensive*, 95–6, 103, 231–2; Gaëtan Galliéni, *Les Carnets de Galliéni* (Paris, 1932), 17–18.

[196] Cited in Cole, ' "Forward with the Bayonet" ', 258; also see 259.

[197] Charles L. M. Lanrezac, *Le Plan de campagne française et le premier mois de la guerre* (Paris, 1929), 30–43; cited by Cole, ' "Forward with the Bayonet" ', 343–4; Snyder, *The Ideology of the Offensive*, 103.

[198] See his memoranda, cited in Cole, ' "Forward with the Bayonet" ', 345–6.

[199] Private memoir cited in ibid. 337–8; Snyder, *The Ideology of the Offensive*, 43–4.

offensive, as codified in the new field regulations, was opposed by the proponents of fire-power and qualified by many others, its operational and strategic aspects, embodied in Plan 17, were criticized in principle by the exponents of the old defensive-offensive school of the 1890s. Bonnal, whose teaching and legacy became the target of Grandmaison's criticism, responded luke-warmly.[200] The main public spokesman of the neo-Napoleonic school in this regard was another of its representatives who, despite his importance, had always remained somewhat of an outsider.

Lieutenant-Colonel Auguste A. Grouard was one of the two men (the other being Mayer) to whom Liddell Hart gave his favourite part in his history of French military thought. It was the role—cast in Liddell Hart's own image—of the honest and far-sighted student of military affairs, who saw the truth and used his pen to warn his country but, ironically, was boycotted precisely for that by a blind and hostile establishment.[201] Later historians adopted this picture, but Grouard's real story was neither as dramatic and didactic nor as simple. Liddell Hart missed out parts of it and misrepresented or passed in silence over others. In fact, from the 1880s Grouard was one of the principal contributors to the Napoleonic revival, coupled as it was with a critical evaluation of the events of 1870–1. Like the other neo-Napoleonics, he denounced past passivity and reliance on fortresses and called for an energetic, aggressive, and crushing French strategy.[202] Like the others, he produced extensive studies of Napoleon's campaigns and elucidated the emperor's system of operations in a strongly Jominian vein.[203] He differed from the others only in that he did not go through the École de guerre, which seriously hampered his career, despite the favour shown to him by General de Miribel. He retired from the army with the rank of lieutenant-colonel in 1900 and earned a living as a military writer. Grouard was far from being opposed to traditional French military theory, and it was only after 1911, when it moved to what he regarded as curious and dangerous extremes, that he grew alarmed.

---

[200] Bonnal, 'Considérations sur la tactique actuelle', *Journal des sciences militaires*, 5 (15 Oct. 1912), 380–1; cited by Williamson, *Politics of Grand Strategy*, 219–20.

[201] Liddell Hart, *Foch*, 49–50; and esp. id. 'French Military Ideas', 144–7.

[202] See above n. 55 and related text.

[203] See esp. Grouard, *La Campagne d'automne de 1813 et les lignes intérieures* (Paris, 1897); id., *Maximes de Guerre de Napoléon Ier* (Paris, 1898); id., *La Critique de la campagne de 1815* (Paris, 1904).

Traditional and long-accepted ideas were echoed in his strategic assessment, *France and Germany, the Possible War* (1913).

Grouard's main argument was that France's only possible strategy was the defensive-offensive. Politically, she could not begin a war with an offensive, because she had to leave the first move to the Germans in order to secure the backing of her allies, Britain and Russia. Militarily, she was simply weaker than Germany and took slightly longer to mobilize.[204] In this Grouard merely restated the French strategic logic that had prevailed since the 1890s. French strategic options had not changed either. For Grouard, defensive posture by no means implied passivity. On the contrary, French defence had to be bold and active.[205] Citing Bonnal, Grouard pointed out that the Germans operated with widely dispersed armies, looking to envelop their adversary.[206] The effective Napoleonic-Jominian antidote to that strategy was, said Grouard, to keep the French forces united, make use of the French central position, and operate on interior lines to strike the enemy's armies separately as they exposed themselves.[207] The only updating required in the schemes of the defensive-offensive school from the 1890s resulted from the seriousness of the Belgian option in the present. Contrary to the later myth, however, Grouard did not differ one bit here either from his fellow military writers or from the planners in the general staff. Like both these groups, he regarded the probability of a German attack through Belgium as almost certain, but thought it would aim at outflanking the French army north of Verdun and would not extend beyond the Meuse.[208] This was the prevailing assumption in France, widely discussed in other popular books of the period like Colonel Boucher's *L'Offensive contre l'Allemagne* (1911) and *La Belgique à jamais indépendante* (1913), and Captain Sorb's *La Doctrine de défense nationale* (1912).[209] Against a German invasion through the Ardennes, Grouard suggested a French counter-offensive from the wedge formed by the junction of the Meuse and Sambre, which he believed, like Joffre, would turn the German right wing. This was exactly the course of action taken by the French Fifth Army in 1914. Grouard differed from the authors of Plan 17 in one thing only, though it was not a small one. He argued that the French must

---

[204] Id., *France et Allemagne; La Guerre éventuelle* (Paris, 1913; periodical publication from 1911), 198.   [205] Ibid. 4, 69 ff.   [206] Ibid. 85–95.
[207] Ibid. 153–70.   [208] Ibid. 98–110, 185.   [209] Ibid. 98.

not commit themselves to an early offensive but must maintain their freedom of operations until the German intentions became known. Then the bulk of the French forces should redeploy by rail to strike the decisive blow.

Returning to our original framing of the problem of French military doctrine, a brief summary is in order. Many different factors and influences interacted in producing the doctrine of the offensive on the eve of the First World War. From the mid-1880s the French discovery of German military ideas and return to Napoleon led to a marked intellectual revival. A new, prolific military school, centred around the École de guerre, emphasized active and aggressive conduct, aiming at the destruction of the enemy's main forces in battle. However, with the coming of the twentieth century, the army's newly gained confidence was badly shaken by military, domestic, and international events. The wars in South Africa and Manchuria demonstrated the strength of modern defence. The Radical campaign to republicanize the army isolated the army from the nation and diminished its popularity. Material imparity with Germany was widening steadily, while the German threat was growing alarmingly. When, after 1911, the national revival again changed the political setting, forces and ideas which had matured in the previous half-decade suggested themselves as possible solutions to the army's problems. Young middle-ranking officers in the general staff advanced the notions of superior morale and out-and-out offensive as the answer both to the problems of modern firearms and to German material superiority. In this they were expressing, and in turn were supported by, the quest for moral regeneration and by the vitalistic philosophies engulfing French culture and society. Newly appointed to high command, Joffre perceived the ideas of the 'Young Turks' as an excellent means to revitalize the army, boost its morale, and provide it with a unifying doctrine. The official adoption of the doctrine of the offensive and Plan 17 were the result.

4

From Sail to Steam:
Naval Theory and the Military Parallel
1882–1914

IMPERIALISM lay at the root of the great naval build-up of the late
nineteenth and early twentieth centuries, kindled public enthusiasm
for naval affairs, and stimulated a remarkable growth of naval
literature and ideas. While this was taking place, naval warfare
itself was being transformed by the process of mechanization which
had been going on from the middle of the nineteenth century. The
age of sail, which had begun three centuries earlier with the defeat
of the Spanish Armada, was coming to a close. Navies were
grappling with new conditions and with the uncertainties created
by rapid technological changes.

All aspects of these naval developments have been admirably
researched by historians. These include: the shifting global balance
of power at sea and the naval growth and maritime policies of each
of the Great Powers, with special reference to the two mighty
rivals—Britain and Germany; the interrelationships between
domestic politics, economics, colonial ambitions, and the new
navalism; the influence of the technological advances on naval
architecture, strategy, and tactics; and the nature and context of the
new naval theories, especially those of Mahan. If this chapter
ventures to add anything at all about the naval thinking of the
period, it will only be within the context of the general themes
developed by this book as a whole. A striking similarity existed
between naval and military ideas in the nineteenth century, and not
only because Mahan, Corbett, and other naval thinkers were deeply
influenced by the leading military theorists of their age. This sort
of influence was possible only because, for many centuries, the
major features of both military and naval warfare had been, and
continued to be, grounded in, and determined by, a common
set of technological, socio-political and economic conditions.

Furthermore, by a remarkable coincidence, both military and naval thought shared surprisingly similar strategic models: the one being French Revolutionary and Imperial might, incarnated by Napoleon; the other, no less dominating, was British naval supremacy, personified by Lord Nelson.

MAHAN AND THE SWEEP OF HISTORY

From the mid-1880s, having previously attracted very little official or public attention, naval affairs were moving centre stage in all the major countries. The prolonged dispute which erupted after 1882 over the British occupation of Egypt poisoned Anglo-French relations. For the first time in the space of a century, naval circles in France, and especially the famous Jeune école, were again looking for ways of challenging British naval supremacy. Being obliged to reckon with the threat of war against a Franco-Russian naval combination, Britain was driven on the waves of public concern to overhaul the slumbering Royal Navy and re-examine her naval policy. The Naval Act of 1889 crowned these efforts. In the following decade, the new industrial powers—the United States, Germany, and Japan—prompted by interests of world trade as well as by the pursuit of dominance, prestige, and destiny, also entered the naval arena. In all these naval powers, both old and new, the new concerns, opening horizons, and rapid growth called for, and generated, much intellectual ferment—naval visions, naval propaganda, and naval theories. It was mere coincidence that by far the most successful and influential product of this intellectual activity came from America.

The career of Alfred Thayer Mahan (1840–1914) and, inseparable from it, the circle of the 'New Navy' activists in which he operated, as well as the wider context of emerging American navalism, have all been more than thoroughly investigated.[1] In

---

[1] On Mahan himself, see in order of appearance as well as of excellence and criticism—ranging from the historically naïve to the exhaustive and from the admiring to the unsympathetic: Charles C. Taylor, *The Life of Admiral Mahan* (New York, 1920); William D. Puleston, *Mahan: The Life and Work of Captain Alfred Thayer Mahan* (New Haven, Conn., 1939); William E. Livezey, *Mahan on Sea Power* (Norman, Okla., 1947); Robert Seager II, *Alfred Thayer Mahan: The Man and His Letters* (Annapolis, Md., 1977). Robert Seager II and Doris D. Maguire ed. *Letters and Papers of Alfred Thayer Mahan*; (Annapolis, Md., 1975);

1884 Commodore Stephen B. Luce, the creator and first president of the new Naval War College, then being established at Newport, Rhode Island, offered Commander Mahan, then on duty in the Pacific station in South American waters, the chair of naval history and tactics at the college. After almost thirty years of less-than-satisfying service in the US Navy, Mahan accepted. Although he was the son of the great Dennis Mahan and was himself the author of the volume *The Navy in the Civil War, The Gulf and Inland Waters* (first publ. 1883), published as part of a series of books on the navy during the Civil War, he was scarcely qualified and little prepared for his new post. He was Luce's third choice for the job. But he was a man of intellectual bent, and he was encouraged and guided by Luce.

The self-taught and intellectually alert Luce (1827–1917) was one of the most professionally conscious and educationally minded officers in the navy. The establishment of the Naval War College was largely his own personal doing, the fruit of years of diligent campaigning. In retrospect, he viewed his Civil War experience with General Sherman as a milestone in the development of his ideas. 'You naval fellows', the general told him, 'have been hammering away at Charleston for the past three years. But . . . I will cut her communications and Charleston will fall into your hands like a ripe pear.'

After hearing General Sherman's clear exposition of the military situation [wrote Luce] the scales seemed to fall from my eyes. 'Here', I said to myself, 'is a soldier who knows his business!' It dawned upon me that there were certain fundamental principles underlying military operations which it were well to look into; principles of general application, whether the operations were conducted on land or at sea.[2]

Luce's assignment to the Artillery School at Fort Monroe and his association with Emory Upton, the champion of higher professional education in the theory of war at the US Army's military schools,

---

Mahan's autobiographical book is *From Sail to Steam: Recollections of Naval Life* (London and New York, 1907). Two brief essays by Margaret T. Sprout and Philip A. Crowl respectively can be found in Earle's and Paret's editions of *Makers of Modern Strategy*.

[2] Stephen B. Luce, 'Naval Administration III', *United States Naval Institute Proceedings* (Dec. 1903), 820; also cited by A. T. Mahan, *Naval Strategy, Compared and Contrasted with the Principles and Practice of Military Operations On Land* (London, 1911), 15.

crystallized in his mind the project which he was thereafter to pursue. In 1877 he wrote a letter to the Secretary of the Navy, raising for the first time the idea of establishing a naval war college. In the letter he explained:

As the principles of strategy are always the same and apply equally to the army on land and the army afloat—the Navy—it strikes me that our officers should be taught the Art of War very much in the same manner that our army officers are taught that branch . . . the rules of the Art should be applied to naval operations and . . . the course should be combined with the study of naval history.[3]

By 1884 Luce's relentless efforts in the Navy Department and among his fellow officers had been crowned with success. The establishment of a Naval War College was ordered and, while retaining his command of the North Atlantic Squadron, he was named its first president.[4] He had a very clear notion, reiterated both in his speeches and in his writings, of what he expected of the college. This notion derived from the positivist culture of science which had pervaded both scientific and popular consciousness in the English-speaking world from the middle of the nineteenth century.[5] Like Ardant du Picq (with whose works he was obviously unfamiliar), he sought to apply the scientific method to the infant science of maritime warfare; like Théodore Jung (with whose work he was equally unfamiliar), he offered his ideas in what amounted to a truly remarkable positivist statement. He studied his subject, albeit in a lay manner, and enlisted a heavy battery of authorities in his support. The ultimate expression of this was his lecture 'On the Study of Naval Warfare as a Science', which he twice delivered at the Naval War College—in 1885 and as the inaugural lecture of 1886:

Science is contributing so liberally to every department of knowledge and has already done so much towards developing a truer understanding of the various arts, including that of the mariner, that it seems only natural and

---

[3] Luce to R. W. Thompson, Secretary of the Navy, Aug. 1877, in Albert Gleaves, *Life and Letters of Rear Admiral Stephen B. Luce, U.S. Navy, Founder of the Naval War College* (New York, 1925), 169; Upton to Luce, ibid., p. 170; see also Luce, 'War Schools', *United States Naval Institute Proceedings*, 1883, 633–57; Roland Spector, *Professors of War: The Naval War College and the Development of the Naval Profession* (Newport, RI, 1977), 16–17.

[4] Gleaves, *Luce*, 168 ff; Spector, *Professors of War*, 20–6.

[5] See Spector, *Professors of War*, 17–20.

reasonable that we should call science to our aid to lead us to a truer comprehension of naval warfare, as naval warfare is to be practiced in the future.[6]

Quoting William Hamilton, Francis Lieber, and above all Henry Thomas Buckle for their definitions of science, which he interpreted in a strongly positivist vein,[7] Luce set out to show how the universal scientific method and standards could be applied to his chosen subject:

The grouping together of a number of important facts gathered from the accounts of naval battles will enable the naval student who has acquired the habit of generalization to lay down principles for his own guidance in war.[8]

Naval history abounds in materials whereon to erect a science, as science has been defined and illustrated, and it is our present purpose to build up with these materials the science of naval warfare. We are far from saying that the various problems of war may be treated as rigorously as those of the physical sciences; but there is no question that the naval battles of the past furnish a mass of facts amply sufficient for the formulation of laws or principles which, once established, would raise maritime war to the level of a science. Having established our principles by the inductive process, we may then resort to the deductive method of applying those principles to such a changed condition of the art of war as may be imposed by later inventions.[9]

According to Luce, it was this method of observation, accumulation, induction, generalization, and in turn deduction, which accounted for the advances in all of the sciences achieved by such great figures as Lavoisier in chemistry, Cuvier in geology, and especially Kepler and Newton in astronomy, standing on the shoulders of Hipparchus, Ptolemy, Copernicus, Brahe, and Galileo.[10] The comparative approach, argued Luce, was another scientific device of paramount importance, enriching the study of one field with the discoveries drawn from neighbouring ones by way of

---

[6] Luce, 'On the Study of Naval Warfare as a Science', *United States Naval Institute Proceedings* (1886), 527–46; reprinted in *The Writings of Stephen B. Luce*, ed. John D. Hayes and John B. Hattendorff (Newport, RI, 1975); here p. 50.

[7] Ibid. 51; the editors have provided an excellent service in compiling a brief presentation-note for each of the many authorities cited by Luce.

[8] Ibid. 54; also see Luce, 'On the Study of Naval History (Grand Tactics)', *United States Naval Institute Proceedings* (1887), 175–201; reprinted ibid.; here p. 75.

[9] Luce, 'Naval Warfare as a Science', *Writings*, 53. [10] Ibid. 51–2.

analogy. Using the comparative approach, Dalton, Matteucci, Brown-Séquard and Velpeau, Bidder and Schmidt, and Harvey achieved major breakthroughs in physiology. Max Müller advocated it in philology.[11]

Hence, we have not only comparative anatomy and comparative physiology, but comparative philology, comparative grammar, comparative religion, comparative literature, and why not we ask . . . comparative war, or a comparative study of military operations of a sea army and a land army.[12]

In history, suggested Luce, the role of naval and military commander was often filled by the same person: Cimon and Lysander, Pompey and Agrippa, Don John of Austria and Lord Howard of Effingham, Raleigh and Blake, Rupert and Monk.[13] As the two fields are intimately related, military theory can be drawn upon in developing the infant science of naval warfare:

Having no authoritative treatise on the art of naval warfare under steam . . . we must, perforce, resort to the well known rules of the military art . . . It is by this means alone that we can raise naval warfare from the empirical stage to the dignity of a science.[14]

Relying on history, which is 'philosophy teaching by example',

and knowing ourselves to be on the road that leads to the establishment of the science of naval warfare by steam, let us confidently look for that master mind who will lay the foundations of that science, and do for it what Jomini has done for the military science.[15]

Years later Luce would add: 'He appeared in the person of Captain A. T. Mahan, U.S.N.'[16]

At the age of forty-five, Mahan, as he put it, 'was drifting on the lines of simple respectability as aimlessly as one very well could'.[17] Luce's offer was to revolutionize his life and make him a world celebrity. Previously, he had shown no marked interest in the subject he was invited to teach, and he would later describe the state of his knowledge at that time as 'profound ignorance'.[18]

[11] Luce, 'Naval Warfare as a Science', *Writings*, 54–5.
[12] Ibid. 57.   [13] Ibid. 57–8; 'Naval History', ibid. 76–77.
[14] 'Naval Warfare as a Science', ibid. 55–6.
[15] Ibid. 68; 'Naval History', ibid. 74–5.
[16] 'Naval Warfare as a Science', ibid. 68, citing Luce's handwritten comment in the Naval War College, 26 July 1899; similarly, see in a letter soliciting a publisher for Mahan's *Influence* I, 5 Aug. 1889, and in a letter to Mahan 15 July 1907; Gleaves, *Life and Letters of Luce*, 268, 296.
[17] Mahan, *From Sail to Steam*, 274.   [18] Ibid. 278.

While the thought of his heredity, which he mentioned in his letter of acceptance to Luce, helped him overcome his hesitations, he was almost totally unfamiliar with his father's work.[19] He had to begin virtually from scratch, reading everything he could lay his hands on. At the English Club in Lima he came across Mommsen's *History of Rome* and was struck by the author's comments about the significance of the part played by Roman naval preponderance in determining the course and outcome of Hannibal's war.[20] Delayed at sea for almost a year and having missed the first course of the Naval War College (September 1885), he received permission to remain in New York until the following August, so that he could use the city's libraries as he worked on the preparation of his lectures.

Luce had asked him to run two lecture-courses: one dealing with naval tactics, which was mainly contemporary, and another on naval history. Mahan thought he could handle the former more easily, even though his crude ideas about naval manœuvre under steam, embodied in his manuscript 'Fleet Battle Tactics', proved to be less than satisfactory.[21] Little more than speculation and bewilderment existed regarding this subject in all navies during the 1880s. He was more worried about the course in naval history, which called for much greater scholarship. He spent his first months of study in New York in concentrated reading of both general history and the standard eighteenth- and nineteenth-century British and French naval histories, biographies, and treatises.[22] This set the historical boundaries of his work: the great age of sail and the struggle between England, Holland, and France for naval mastery from the middle of the seventeenth century to 1815.[23] By then he had also defined the main theme which was to run through his lectures. It was to be the significance of control of the sea or sea power (Mahan coined the phrase to command attention) in the history of nations, and its interdependence with other historical factors and national characteristics. He discovered fairly rapidly that this subject had never been systematically

[19] Mahan to Luce, 4 Sept. 1884, *Letters and Papers*, i. 577–8; *From Sail to Steam*, 273.

[20] Mahan to Luce, 16 May 1885, *Letters and Papers*, i. 606; *From Sail to Steam*, 277. [21] Seager, *Alfred Thayer Mahan*, 166.

[22] For the authors and works, see Mahan to Luce, 3, 14, and 19 Nov. 1885, 18 Jan, 1886, *Letters and Papers*, i. 617–19, 621–2; *From Sail to Steam*, 278–81.

[23] Mahan to Luce, 22 Jan. 1886, *Letters and Papers*, i. 622–4.

approached from such a comprehensive perspective and that it therefore offered much scope for work.[24] The question which remained unresolved and which he deliberately postponed to the end was the one Luce had impressed upon him from the beginning: what generally applicable sense could be made of all this?—'What use is the knowledge of these bygone days?'[25]

At Luce's urging, he turned to an obvious source of inspiration, military theory, which he discovered with a sense of revelation. A few years earlier, he later wrote, 'I had read carefully Napier's *Peninsular War*, and had found myself in a new world of thought, keenly interested and appreciative, less of the military narrative . . . than of the military sequence of cause and effect.'[26] In early 1886, having finished the bulk of his history reading, and having been constantly encouraged by Luce, who had sent him his paper 'On the Study of Naval History as a Science', he reported to Luce that he was finally planning to turn to the most demanding subject of naval theory. 'I will keep the analogy between land and naval warfare before my eyes,' he promised, 'I expect to begin with Jomini, etc. . . . and with an admirable system of one kind of war before me, to contribute something to the development of a systematic study of war in another field.'[27] Reading Jomini and Hamley, he found what he was looking for:

The authority of Jomini chiefly set me to study in this fashion [didactic and generalizing] the many naval histories before me. From him I learnt the few, very few, leading considerations in military combination; and in these I found the key by which . . . I could elicit, from the naval history upon which I had looked despondingly, instruction still pertinent.[28]

In September 1886, by the beginning of the second academic year at the Naval War College, the course of lectures which would become *The Influence of Sea Power Upon History* was complete.

---

[24] Ibid.; *From Sail to Steam*, 276.
[25] Mahan to Luce, 22 Jan. 1886, *Letters and Papers*, 623.
[26] Mahan, *From Sail to Steam*, 273.
[27] Mahan to Luce, 6 and 22 Jan 1886 in Gleaves, *Life and Letters of Luce*, 312, Mahan, *Letters and Papers*, i. 622–4. Also see Luce's reminding Mahan of his development and of Luce's share therein, especially the idea of the 'comparative method', suggested in his article of 1886: 15 July 1907, Gleaves, *Life and Letters of Luce*, 296.
[28] Mahan, *From Sail to Steam*, 282; also 278, and *Naval Strategy, Compared and Contrasted with the Principles and Practice of Military Operations on Land*, 17.

By the time Mahan (promoted to captain) arrived in Newport in the summer of 1886, Luce had been ordered to sea, and Mahan found himself the new president of the college. He served in this capacity from 1886 to 1889 and again from 1892 to 1893, supervising the minuscule faculty and classes, but mostly struggling to keep the college afloat in the face of a desperate shortage of funds, poor facilities, and a less-than-appreciative Navy Department. Between 1889 and 1892, when the college was suspended, Mahan used the time to prepare his lectures for publication. *The Influence of Sea Power upon History, 1660–1783* appeared in 1890, and was followed two years later by *The Influence of Sea Power upon the French Revolution and Empire* in two volumes. Success was immediate on both sides of the Atlantic, and especially in Britain. In 1893, profoundly against his wishes and despite his friends' efforts to pull strings on his behalf, Mahan was ordered to sea aboard the USS *Chicago*. As it turned out, this was a blessing in disguise. The *Chicago*'s visits of good will to English ports during 1893 and 1894 became the occasions for enthusiastic public receptions for Mahan. Dinners, formal invitations, and weekends in the country were showered upon him. The most distinguished invitations came from Queen Victoria and her guests, including Kaiser Wilhelm II; the Prince of Wales; the Prime Minister, Lord Rosebery; the leader of the Conservative party, Lord Salisbury; Lord Balfour; the First Lord of the Admiralty; and the Lord Mayor of London. Gladstone called Mahan's second *Influence* book 'the book of the age'. The press-coverage included similar superlatives. Mahan became the first foreigner received as a guest of honour at the meeting of the Royal Navy Club. The universities of Oxford and Cambridge awarded him honorary doctoral degrees in the same week.[29] These were followed in America by degrees from Harvard, Yale, Columbia, McGill, and Dartmouth College. All in all, it was his success in Britain which impressed America most and made him a famous man at home as well.

His new literary pursuits and fame opened up new prospects for Mahan. In 1896 he retired from the navy and thereafter occupied himself solely with writing. His major intellectual contribution had already been made, but he continued to publish books: *The Life of*

---

[29] Mahan, *From Sail to Steam*, 313–16; id., *Letters and Papers*, ii. esp. 105, 128–36, 203, 296–300, 312.

Nelson (first publ. 1897); *Sea Power in its Relation to the War of 1812* (1905); *Naval Strategy* (1911)—a compilation of his lectures at the Naval College; and several lesser historical and biographical works. His magazine articles on current affairs were much in demand, earned him hundreds of dollars apiece, and were later compiled and republished in book form. In these articles Mahan dealt with naval and strategic themes and called for greater American awareness of, and involvement in, world affairs, particularly in areas where the USA had major interests—the Caribbeans and Central America, China and the Far East. Official recognition was not lacking. Upon the outbreak of the Spanish–American War in 1898, Mahan was summoned to the Naval War Board, established to advise the secretary of the navy and the president. A year later he was appointed to advise the American delegation to the first Hague Peace Conference, where he was received as a world authority whose opinions carried great weight. Recognition came also from the American Historical Association which in 1902 elected him its president.

The major themes of Mahan's teaching have been noted often enough. Firstly, there was his 'philosophy of sea power' and his role as 'the evangelist of sea power'. These were grounded in his reading of naval history, in its interrelationship with modern European history. As the imperialist contest grew hotter, both philosophy and role were aimed at promoting naval expansion. Secondly, on the more strictly strategic level, there were the tenets of his theory of naval warfare.

Highlighting the historical role and significance of sea power was Mahan's most original achievement, and it won him the admiration of his contemporaries. Since his work first appeared, it has often been said that this particular notion was not novel but had been expressed centuries before by a succession of writers from Walter Raleigh and Francis Bacon onward. However, as Mahan himself put it, there is a difference between the scattered aphorisms previously issued regarding the blessings bestowed by the command of the sea and his own systematic exposition of the subject.[30] He was certainly the first to present naval history—previously written on a purely technical and operational basis—against the background of the wide sweep of historical events, interwoven and interacting with political and economic factors.

[30] Mahan, *From Sail to Steam*, 276.

Mahan's masterly history was not written, as he put it, 'after the high modern pattern'. His historical judgement was strong and balanced and he was careful to have his facts right, but the facts in themselves meant little to him. As many critics were quick to point out, both then and later, and as he himself admitted: 'Original research was not within my scope, nor was it necessary to the scheme . . . outlined'.[31] Confessing his faults as a historian in his presidential address to the American Historical Association, he went over to a brilliant attack on historical positivism, represented by the formidable figure of Lord Acton. Facts were only 'the bricks and mortar of the historian', he told his listeners. Clarity of structure and content and accessibility to readers were essential. What mattered most was historical meaning and significance.[32] Indeed, it so happened that, while Mahan's historical craftsmanship and the depth of his research improved considerably with every book he wrote, the value of his later books bore no relation to that of his earlier ones. Both the scope of his historical scene and his overriding message had been exhausted in his first two *Influence* books. It was for its historical interpretation and major thesis that his work attracted both fame and criticism.

His cardinal message was simple and compelling. Reviewing the great struggle for naval predominance between the major mercantilist powers in the age of commercial capitalism, Mahan came up with the following conclusions. It had been her naval supremacy that had given England not only security but also a commanding global position, commercial wealth, and, because of these, preponderance in Europe. Naval supremacy had given England a growing monopoly over trade, colonies, and industry. The denial of these assets to her major enemy, France, the stranglehold which England could apply to France's sea ports, and the large subsidies by which she bought and sustained European allies, ultimately destroyed the bids for European hegemony made both by Louis XIV and by Napoleon. The role which sea power played in shaping modern Europe and the modern world could thus hardly be exaggerated.

It is to Mahan's great credit that his treatment of the subject, whatever its shortcomings and omissions, is well-rounded and far from the superficially argumentative. Yet pointed criticisms both of

[31] Ibid. 277–8.
[32] Mahan, 'Subordination in Historical Treatment' (1902), in *Naval Administration and Warfare* (Boston, 1908), 245–72.

the detail and of the wider context provided by this picture have been made, rarely in Mahan's own time but to an increasing extent later on. Specifically, it has been argued that his analysis of the reasons for Britain's success did not take sufficient account of the major role played by British military forces on the Continent, from the days of Elizabeth I and Marlborough to those of the Elder Pitt and Wellington. Their role had been vital to the consolidation of successful coalitions against Britain's enemies, without which no military or political decision in Britain's favour could have been reached. Mahan, it is said, greatly exaggerated the ability of the British navy to 'strangle' single-handedly a large, rich, and fertile continental power like France, whose dependence on foreign sea-trade was far less critical than he believed.

On a more general level, it has been argued that Mahan's analysis and general conclusions were dominated by the particular characteristics of the great period which he investigated and which had, in fact, been unique in many ways. This was the so-called Columbian, Vasco da Gama, or Oceanic era, in which the coastal European nations, having mastered the technological skills for long-distance sea-voyages, acquired great wealth and power by their virtual monopoly of the world's main commercial highway. The significance of the sea, however, had not been nearly as great before the era of the sail, the compass, and the quadrant. Nor was it to remain so in the industrial age—a fact which was even more problematic for Mahan's thesis. This was argued by a number of Mahan's contemporaries: the American lawyer and historian Brooks Adams expressed these ideas in his *America's Economic Supremacy*, (1900), and they were stated even more clearly by the British geographer Sir Halford Mackinder in his lecture 'The Geographical Pivot of History' (1904). Both men pointed out that steam locomotion was opening up the vast continental masses of the Americas and Asia, previously remote and sparsely populated.[33] For the first time in history, land transportation, up till then dependent solely on human and animal muscle, was able to challenge the incontestable advantage which sea and river transportation had possessed in moving vast quantities of goods over great distances at low cost. Additionally, in the new age of industrial

[33] Brooks Adams, *America's Economic Supremacy* (New York, 1900), esp. 38–43; Halford J. Mackinder, 'The Geographical Pivot of History', *Geographical Journal*, 23 (1904), 421–37.

capitalism, domestic industrial capacity largely overshadowed overseas commerce and colonies as the main source of national wealth and naval power. If this was so, the lessons Mahan was drawing from the age of the sail and of commercial mercantilism were much less applicable to the present than he assumed.[34]

This was a significant point because it touched both upon Mahan's innermost motivation for writing his history and upon the manner in which it was received. By taking up his professorship at the new Naval College, whose future was far from secure, and by serving in a minuscule and obsolete navy which was only beginning to experience growth, Mahan was enlisted to the ranks of the gathering campaign for naval expansion. As he himself stated, the aim of his work was 'to imbue his hearers with an exalted sense of the mission of their calling, and . . . contribute to give the service and the country a more definite impression of the necessity to provide a fleet adequate to great undertakings'.[35] In this campaign, Mahan was by no means alone, nor was he even a pioneer or particularly prominent. He was typical of the 'New Navy' circle in which he moved and which, consisting as it did of young officers of middle rank, had been promulgating the creation of a strong and modern American navy since the early 1880s.[36] Only after the success of his first two *Influence* books did Mahan become one of the major and most influential figures in American navalism.

Indeed, while some early, naïve commentators tended to associate almost every expression of the new navalism with Mahan's influence, later ones took a more critical view. The facts are known well enough. The first *Influence* book had appeared in fifteen editions by 1900 and in twenty-four by 1914. The second did almost as well, being published in eleven editions by 1900 and in

---

[34] Gerald S. Graham's brilliant observations in *The Politics of Naval Supremacy: Studies in British Maritime Ascendancy* (Cambridge, 1965), 1–30, esp. 28–9, 124, have been developed by Paul Kennedy, *The Rise and Fall of British Naval Mastery* (London, 1976), *passim.*; see also Herbert Rosinski, 'Mahan and World War II' (1941), in his *Development of Naval Thought*, ed. B. M. Simpson (Newport, RI, 1977), 27–8; Bernard Semmel, *Liberlism and Naval Strategy; Ideology, Interest and Sea Power during the Pax Britannica* (London, 1986), 3–4. Earlier criticisms are summarized by William L. Langer, *The Diplomacy of Imperialsim* (New York, 1951), 418.

[35] Mahan, *Influence* II, vol. i, p. iv.

[36] See esp. Peter Karsten, *The Naval Aristocracy: The Golden Age of Annapolis and the Emergence of Modern American Navalism* (New York, 1972), 306–17, 326, *et passim*, for an excellent study of the naval mind and for pre-Mahan 'Mahanities'.

fourteen by 1914.[37] In America, the Assistant Secretary of the Navy and later President of the USA, Theodore Roosevelt, became an enthusiastic admirer and close friend of Mahan; Senator Henry Cabot Lodge amplified his views; Secretary of the Navy Tracy sought his advice;[38] Tracy's successor, Herbert, abandoned his previously hostile position and became converted to navalism upon reading Mahan's second *Influence* book; from the mid-1890s, Mahan's name and authority ranked high in Congressional deliberations over naval affairs. All the same, it is also clear that most of the people referred to above had become ardent navalists long before they had heard of Mahan. American navalism as a broad political and cultural movement had been expanding hand in hand with the country's industrial and commercial growth, was being boosted by the pressures of European colonialism, and was gathering momentum virtually independently of the work or activity of any single person. Mahan's 'philosophy of sea power' was enthusiastically received by all navalists because it defined, focused, and gave clear direction to, the ideas and notions already held by many of them. It provided them with a magnificent, magisterial demonstration of their case. Indeed, in this it also added considerable weight to their argument.[39]

Mahan's philosophy of sea power had a similar effect abroad. His works were soon translated into German, French, Japanese, Russian, Italian, Spanish, and Swedish. They were published precisely at the time when Britain was beginning to rearm in the face of the new Franco-Russian challenge to her previously undisputed maritime supremacy. As public opinion became agitated and as the government became increasingly aware of the country's relative naval decline, ancient traditions were evoked to rally support and enhance morale. Mahan's history and analysis of the

[37] *A Bibliography of the Works of Alfred Thayer Mahan*, ed. John B. Hattendorf and Lynn C. Hattendorf (Newport, RI, 1986). See also Langer, *The Diplomacy of Imperialism*, 418.

[38] Mahan made the contact by sending copies of his book to the last two names immediately upon its publication; 10 and 19 May 1890, *Letters and Papers*, ii. 10–11.

[39] A good updated summary is Crowl, 'Mahan', in Paret (ed.), *Makers of Modern Strategy*, 470–2. Harold and Margaret Sprout, *The Rise of American Naval Power, 1776–1918* (Princeton, NJ, 1966), 205–22, is probably still the most useful survey of the political scene; the authors of this pioneering study, originally published in 1939, renounced their strongly Mahanite views in their introduction to the second edition.

rise of British naval power were a major contribution in this regard and helped to set the naval build-up in an appealing historical and strategic framework.[40]

In Germany, traditionally a continental power, Mahan's role in this respect may have been even greater. In May 1894, less than a year after he had dined with Mahan at Queen Victoria's table, Kaiser Wilhelm II wrote to Poultney Bigelow of the *New York Herald*: 'I am just now not reading but devouring Captain Mahan's book and am trying to learn it by heart. It is a first-class book and classical in all points. It is on board all my ships and constantly quoted by my captains and officers.'[41] Germany's new naval orientation was the almost inevitable result of the stupendous growth of her industry and power, as well as of the mounting imperialist contest. Yet it is hardly disputed that the scale, direction, and persistence of her naval build-up were most decisively influenced by the personal interest, not to say obsession, of the Kaiser. Tirpitz, the other leading figure behind the German naval build-up, apparently needed no Mahan to crystallize his ideas regarding German naval policy. As early as 1888 and 1891, but especially in his Memorandum IX of 1894 (all composed before he read Mahan), he had already advocated the formation of a navy of battleships, to be concentrated in home waters. Still, in their campaign to create a large German navy and for the acquisition of colonies, Tirpitz and the Reich's Naval Office, in collaboration with the Colonial Society and later the Naval League, found Mahan's inspiring works an excellent weapon of propaganda. In 1898, working on the preparation of the first Naval Law, Tirpitz initiated the pubication of Mahan's first *Influence* book (already translated in a periodical series two years earlier). Of the 8,000 copies printed, 2,000 were to be distributed directly by the Naval Office itself. The second *Influence* book was also translated in 1898. Naval College professors, like Vice-Admiral von Maltzahn in *Naval Warfare* (1908), and academic propagandists, like Ernst von Halle in *Sea Power in German History* (1907), transplanted Mahan into German soil.[42]

As Mahan himself noted, his works were most widely translated

---

[40] See briefly in Langer, *The Diplomacy of Imperialism*, 422–3.
[41] C. C. Taylor, *The Life of Admiral Mahan*, 131.
[42] See esp. Tirpitz, *My Memoirs* (2 vols.; London, 1919), i. 55, 112; Volker Berghahn, *Der Tirpitz-Plan* (Düsseldorf, 1971), 145, 179–80, 424.

into Japanese, the first translation being initiated by the Club of Naval Officers in 1896. In the island empire as well, which was embarking on an imperialist and navalist course, his works provided a political and strategic rationale for policy and painted the road to destiny in vivid colours. They were placed in the libraries of middle and high schools in Japan and served as texts in all naval schools.[43]

Mahan's social Darwinist, racist, and imperialist opinions harmonized with his naval theories in much the same way that similar ideas in Germany correlated with German military ideas. In fact, his views were indistinguishable from, say, Moltke's, and indeed in both cases Christian sentiments played an important part. Close similarities suggest that Mahan was familiar with Moltke's opinions; the latter's works were published in New York in 1892–3. Moreover, it is a measure of the age in which they both lived that Mahan, like Moltke, underwent intellectual transformation; until the mid-1880s he was an anti-imperialist.[44] However, with the onset of the age of imperialism and upon taking up his research of the great sea empires, he changed completely. Here too his views were no different from those prevailing among his contemporaries in the navy.[45] Only that his opinions received world-wide circulation.

In justifying the partition of Asia, Mahan explained that 'growth is a property of healthful life'.[46] One state does not interfere in the affairs of another unless 'its stage of political development corresponds to that of childhood or decay':[47]

The claim of the indigenous population to retain indefinitely control of territory depends not upon natural right but upon political fitness . . . in such a manner to insure the natural right of the world at large that resources should not be left idle, but be utilized for the general good.[48]

'The onward movement of the world has to be accepted as a fact.'[49] Virile states compete in a process of natural evolution which inevitably breeds struggle and suffering.[50]

[43] Mahan, *From Sail to Steam*, 303; C. C. Taylor, *The Life of Admiral Mahan*, 114–15.   [44] Mahan, *From Sail to Steam*, 274.
[45] See Karsten's excellent *Naval Aristocracy*, esp. 205–31; Spector, *Professors of War*, 83.
[46] Mahan, *The Problem of Asia and Its Effects upon International Policies* (London, 1900), 29–30.   [47] Ibid. 32.
[48] Ibid. 98.   [49] Ibid. 61, 16.   [50] Ibid. 15, 46.

In the late 1890s, when Russian pressure in the Far East made the partition of China appear imminent, Mahan advocated co-operation between the three Teutonic sea-powers—Germany, Britain, and the USA—to contain Slavic Russia.[51] Analysing the differences between the two races, he regarded some as environmental and cultural and others as 'fundamental, deep seated in the racial constitution'.[52] The French, a Latino-Gallic mixture, were weaker, and there was, therefore, no third genius race competing.[53] Later, following the growth in German naval power, Mahan advocated co-operation between the two Anglo-Saxon nations against the German threat.[54]

During the two Hague Conferences, Mahan appeared as a bastion of realism. He stood fast against any limitations on war, armament, and the freedom of action at sea. From a Christian and moral point of view, he argued, war in some circumstances is righteous and even mandatory. States, like individuals, must exercise judgement and assume responsibility for their actions.[55] Furthermore, 'power, force, is a faculty of national life; one of the talents committed to nations by God'.[56] Fighting-spirit is rooted in the 'nobler qualities of bravery, courage, loyalty, patriotism', which must not be thrown out with the bath water.[57] Arbitration and an international code of law cannot always take the place,

either practically or beneficially, of the processes and results obtained by the free play of natural forces. Of those forces national efficiency is a chief element; and armament, being the representative of the national strength, is the exponent . . . It is of the first importance that the European family of states retain in full the power of national self-assertion, of which the sentiment of nationality is the spirit and armament the embodiment.[58]

Like Delbrück, whom he cited often in his last years, Mahan warned his readers that 'the consolidated Roman Empire with its Pax Romana is not a wholly happy augury for a future of peace

---

[51] Ibid. 104.   [52] Ibid. 114–15.   [53] Ibid. 105–6.

[54] Mahan, *The Interest of America in International Conditions* (London, 1910), 71–124.

[55] Mahan, 'The Power that Makes for Peace', *Some Neglected Aspects of War* (London, 1907), 97–114, esp. 100.

[56] Mahan, 'The Peace Conference and the Moral Aspect of War', *Lessons of the War with Spain and Other Articles* (Boston, 1899), 232.

[57] Mahan, 'The Power that Makes for Peace', *Neglected Aspects of War*, 8–9.

[58] Mahan, *Armaments and Arbitration, or the Place of Force in the International Relations of States* (London, 1912), 10.

dependent upon a central court and general disarmament'.[59] He became involved in a sharp literary exchange with Norman Angel, whose popular book *The Great Illusion* (1910) rejected war on the grounds that it no longer paid. He argued that, while of course being wasteful in itself, war could create the conditions for future greatness, as the British and German cases demonstrated.[60]

The second major theme in Mahan's work was his doctrine of naval warfare. Like his philosophy of sea power, this is easily summarized: one can gain command of the sea and all the benefits it entails only by destroying the enemy's main battle fleet in battle or, if the enemy shrinks from direct confrontation, by bottling up his navy in its harbours. 'Jomini's dictum that the organized forces of the enemy are ever the chief objective, pierced like a two-edged sword to the joints and marrow of many specious propositions,' he wrote.[61] 'Postponement of immediate action to "ulterior motives" ', such as attacking the enemy's commerce, never succeeded in the past and can never succeed in the future. Hence the paramount importance of battleships or ships-of-the-line in the navy. For all their importance, cruisers, or, as they were formerly called, frigates, cannot win a war. Strategic concentration of force and tactical boldness are the leading principles of naval operations.

That this was 'Jomini turned to sea' has been pointed out often enough, not least—and on many occasions—by Mahan himself. The structure of his work—as a strategic commentary on the historical narrative, developing and illustrating principles—was also derived from Jomini's *Treatise on Grand Military Operations*.[62] However, this smooth adaptation could never have been contemplated, much less carried out, if it had not been for the remarkable similarity which existed between military and naval developments in the period covered by both the *Influence* books and the *Treatise*. Deeper reasons made nineteenth-century military and naval pictures of the past, strategic models, and doctrines analogous. To demonstrate this, a brief journey through the centuries is called for, excused only by the sweep of Mahan's own *tour de force*.

That regular, state-sponsored and state-organized armies and navies appeared at much the same time is understandable enough.

[59] Mahan. 13.
[60] Ibid. 121–54; Seager, *Alfred Thayer Mahan*, 586–91.
[61] Mahan, *From Sail to Steam*, 283.   [62] Ibid.

The growth of the modern, centralized state and of a money economy from the early sixteenth century was responsible for that. The *tercios* and the *armada* which together terrorized Europe were part of the same 'Military Revolution'. So were the armies and fleets formed by the United Provinces. From the middle of the seventeenth century, all warlike activity was virtually monopolized by the state. State bureaucracy under Louvois and Le Tellier created the large regular armies of Louis XIV's France, while under Colbert it provided her with a formidable, modern, and efficient navy. During roughly the same period, a modern army and a strong regular navy were created in the England of the Lord Protector.

The similarity was no less striking in regard to weapons and battle tactics. Although introduced both on land and at sea at the outset of the sixteenth century, it took time before firearms came to dominate warfare. This was due partly to problems of technical efficiency and partly—especially in regard to artillery—to the cost and the number of pieces available. Mediterranean naval warfare throughout the sixteenth century was still carried out by fleets of galleys, which added artillery and arquebus fire to the traditional tactics of ramming and boarding.[63] In much the same way, sixteenth-century land-warfare was carried out by the old deep squares of pikemen, except that they were now supported, or more often immobilized, by the new firearms. As late as the middle of the seventeenth century, the pike still held its own on land, while the fleets of sail which dominated naval warfare in the North Sea and the Atlantic still used boarding and fire-ships as widely as they used artillery fire; in fact, boarding and the use of fire-ships were the favourite tactics of the Dutch. The deep order and the *mêlée* were the prevailing form of combat at sea. Only at the end of the seventeenth century, at the same time as the pikemen were returning their weapons for all time, did the artillery duel become the predominant form of naval warfare. The far-reaching tactical results of these parallel developments were remarkably similar.

By the late seventeenth century at sea and the early eighteenth century on land, the need to maximize fire-power led to the universal adoption of the same order of battle, the line, by all armies and navies in Europe. The complexity of manœuvring this

[63] See the fine work by John Francis Guilmartin jun., *Gunpowder and Galleys: Changing Technology and Mediterranean Warfare at Sea in the Sixteenth Century,* (Cambridge, 1974).

long, thin, and fragile formation, sometimes stretching for kilometres and dozens of kilometres both on land and at sea, proved baffling. In both cases, it called for endless drill, strict central command, clearer subdivision, and an intricate system of communication. At sea, during the Second Dutch War, the first official signal-book was introduced into the Royal Navy by the Duke of York (later King James II), and a permanent system of squadrons and flag-officers soon followed. The line also proved problematic in the offensive. The approach to the attack was made enormously cumbersome by the need to maintain formation and to refrain from exposing the leading units to devastating fire from the enemy's line. When contact was made, the shock-effect of the thin line was minor, and the chances of achieving major breakthroughs in the enemy's line were very slim indeed. At sea, in two famous incidents in 1744 and 1756, Admirals Matthews and Byng found themselves in situations which ran counter to the accepted practices, as prescribed by the Admiralty's regulations. They failed to align their fleets parallel to the French before attacking. Approaching the enemy line at an obtuse angle, their van came under heavy fire, while the rest of the British line was still too far away and unable to intervene. Matthews, who chose to proceed with the attack, suffered heavy losses and was court-martialled for misconduct. Twelve years later, Byng, who had sat as a judge at Matthews's court-marshal, failed to support his van, and then allowed the French to take Minorca. He was court-martialled and sentenced to death.

The difficulties of the attacker were compounded by the reluctance of the defender to accept battle. On land, often anxious not to waste their hard-to-replace regulars in the hazardous trial of arms, armies resorted to strongly fortified positions, from which it was extremely difficult to oust them. Similarly, the French navy in the eighteenth century was under strict orders to try as much as possible to avoid the loss of ships. With her resources divided between land and sea, France could not afford an out-and-out naval contest with Britain, and French tactics reflected this policy. Normally, while the British navy sought the attack, the French remained on the defence. They either took position to windward and thus kept out of reach; or they placed themselves to leeward, waiting to blunt the British attack during the vulnerable approach, when the British men-of-war, turning their bows to the enemy, were unable to use their broadsides effectively. The French could then receive them with full broadsides, before tacking to the rear and reforming in line, ready for another round. Their artillery fire, aimed at the sails and rigging of the British ships, served the same purpose by incapacitating them and neutralizing the attack.

The tactical impasse was complemented at the strategic level to create the famous syndrome known as the 'indecisiveness' of eighteenth-century warfare. On land, while tending not to rush into battle, generals employed a variety of other means to obtain an advantage over their rivals. First among these was the operation against the enemy's communications, which gave rise to the the so-called 'war of manœuvre'. Things were not very different at sea. Shrinking from a head-on collision with the stronger British navy, the French looked for other ways of waging naval war. The principal one was the attack on British naval communications. At sea this meant not so much military communications as seashore traffic and worldwide trade-routes. Britain's wealth was largely derived from her overseas commerce. If this could be seriously disrupted, Britain would have to accept defeat. For a century and a half, from the days of Vauban and the legendary Jean Bart to the days of Napoleon and his no less gallant raiders, French frigates and privateers, operating from Brest and Toulon as well as from Dunkirk, St Malo, Dieppe, and a host of other small ports, raided and harassed British trade. The British responded by blockading the French ports and by concentrating their merchant ships in well-protected convoys. The contest had its ups and downs. At times it became very close indeed.

The indecisiveness of eighteenth-century warfare created concern and prompted a search for radical new solutions among specialists in both the military and naval fields. In both fields, there was dissatisfaction with, and growing reaction against, the accepted linear tactics. The ideas of the famous Chevalier de Folard regarding the superior flexibility and greater shock-effect of the column were taken up in France after the humiliating failures of the French armies in the Seven Years War. Intensive debate and extensive experimentation resulted in the development of new tactics, largely associated with the teachings of Count de Guibert. These tactics relied heavily on the column, both for manœuvring and for attacking, and were to find their consummation in the Revolutionary and Napoleonic armies. France was also the centre of systematic naval theory. The creation of naval academies, the

Enlightenment spirit of enquiry and systematization, and the prestige, honours, and rewards bestowed on authors by French society and by state academies for the advancement of learning were all responsible for that. In 1697 Paul Hoste, professor of mathematics at the Royal Naval College in Toulon, wrote the first systematic treatise on sailing ships' manœuvres. Captain de Morogues, Bourde de Villehuet, and Viscount Grenier—all working under the auspices of the French Royal Academy of Sciences—elaborated on the same theme and were widely read throughout Europe.[64] Characteristically, the English, though being the greatest naval nation, shared none of the French bent for theorizing. Characteristically too, if there was any serious theorizing to be done in Britain in the Age of the Enlightenment, it was left to the Scots. During the dark days of the American War of Independence, John Clerk of Eldin, a gifted amateur and life-long enthusiast for naval affairs, was anxiously recording the successes of French evasive tactics and the repeated failures of the British in the previous fifty years to pin down the French and break through their line. In 1782, in a privately circulated essay which was later (1790) expanded and published as a book entitled *An Essay on Naval Tactics, Systematical and Historical*, Eldin acutely analyzed the tactical impasse and put forward new methods of attack.

Eldin proposed that, rather than ensuring that the two opposing fleets sailed parallel before attacking, as Admiralty regulations prescribed, the British ought to open the attack once their van had passed the enemy's rear. In that way, the approaching ships would not be exposed to the devastating fire of the whole French line. Cutting through the middle of the enemy line, they would achieve overwhelming concentration against only part of his fleet, leaving his van with the awkward alternative of either escaping and abandoning the rear to its fate or turning back to fight at a disadvantage. This was what the unfortunate Matthews had tried to do in 1744, but he had failed, owing to lack of co-ordination between his squadrons, and had thus brought about a disastrous new stiffening in naval practices. Instead of sailing in the rigid line,

---

[64] Paul Hoste, *L'Art des armées navales* (Lyon, 1697), English trans., 1762, 1834; S. F. V. B. de Morogues, *Tactique navale*, (Paris, 1763), English trans. 1767, note the academy's report in the preface; Bourde de Villehuet, *Le Manœuvrier, ou essai sur la théorie et la pratique des mouvements du navire et des évolutions navales* (Paris, 1765), English trans., 1788; Vicomte J. R. de Grenier, *L'Art de la guerre sur mer, ou tactique navale* (Paris, 1787).

suggested Eldin, the British fleet ought to be divided into separate short columns or divisions, which would be easier to handle and more flexible to manœuvre.

At the same time the French armies, at the end of the *ancien régime*, were implementing very similar ideas on land, things were also changing in the British navy. In 1782, the same year in which Eldin wrote his essay, Admiral Rodney chanced on a similar manœuvre in the course of his battle with de Grasse off the coast of Dominica (the Battle of the Saints). His fleet, still in line, cut through the French centre from leeward. Eldin later tried to suggest that Rodney had been influenced by his work, but this has been proved untrue.[65] The tactical predicament simply produced similar solutions in different minds. On the French side too, the dashing Suffren in his brilliant East Indies campaign attacked the British rear from windward off Madras two months before Rodney's manœuvre. And in 1787, observing the new developments, Grenier called for the substitution of the line by a flexible formation in short columns.

Still, the nascent revolution in tactics was able to develop as dramatically as it did only in consequence of the new conditions created by the French Revolution. This was true of both land- and sea-warfare, though in curiously opposite ways. As is well known, it was the patriotic and revolutionary *élan*, as well as the inexperience of the French troops, which made column shock-tactics so effective and so suitable for them. Yet these qualities, urged by the Revolutionary authorities and later by Napoleon, proved no substitute for technical skills and proficiency when it came to the sea. They only aggravated the condition of the French navy, already shaken by the emigration, persecution, and purges of its aristocratic officer-corps. The French navy was much weakened by the Revolution, becoming a mere shadow of its former self. If the successes of Nelson's shock-tactics, from St Vincent and the Nile to Trafalgar, are to be properly understood, this factor must be borne in mind. In 1794, at the Battle of the Glorious First of June, Lord Howe had already broken the French line in several places. In 1797 Admiral Duncan had attacked the weaker Dutch fleet in the Battle

---

[65] John Clerk of Eldin, *An Essay on Naval Tactics, Systematical and Historical* (2nd edn.; Edinburgh, 1804), xiv; persuasively refuted by the son of Rodney's flag-captain, Major-General Sir Howard Douglas, *Naval Evolutions; A Memoir* (London, 1832).

of Camperdown, breaking through the enemy line in two columns. At Trafalgar, Nelson employed similar tactics, attacking almost perpendicularly in two columns. During the approach, the head of the British columns suffered severe damage, but would have sustained even heavier losses had the French been up to their old standards. In that case, the British columns attacking the Franco-Spanish line in Iberian waters might have suffered the fate of the French columns attacking the British-Spanish line on the Iberian mainland. In another curious mirror-image of the developments on land, the attacker enjoyed a significant advantage in artillery. While reformed and improved artillery was one of the factors that contributed to the successes of the French Revolutionary and Napoleonic armies, the British cannonade, devastating at close range, was highly effective in the mêlée which was the ultimate result of the new naval tactics. In short, similar developments and conditions made possible the spectacular new battles of destruction which established French preponderance on land and British mastery at sea.

This similarity of conditions and developments also produced the remarkable resemblance which existed in the nineteenth century between military and naval theory and picture of the past. Mahan's historical interpretation, which reflected the accepted view among naval historians, was barely distinguishable from that of the military historians and theoreticians of the century. First and foremost, the Napoleonic and Nelsonian examples cast eighteenth-century warfare in an unfavourable light. Post-Napoleonic military writers rejected linear tactics and regarded the eighteenth-century 'war of manœuvre' a gross historical aberration, swept aside by Bonaparte's genius and vigour. The views of post-Nelsonian naval writers were similarily crystallized by Mahan. The cause of all mischief, he wrote, was 'the effete system to which the middle eighteenth century had degraded the erroneous but comparatively hearty tradition received by it from the seventeenth'.[66] A military theoretician like Jomini viewed Frederick the Great as a forerunner of Napoleon, but one who had none the less been unable to free himself from the methods of his time. In the same way, naval

---

[66] Mahan, *Types of Naval Officers Drawn from the History of the British Navy* (London, 1902), 56 *et passim*; *Influence I, passim*; and on many other occasions, e.g. *The Major Operations of the Navies in the War of American Independence* (London, 1913), 93; *Armaments and Arbitration* (London, 1912), 204.

writers regarded a whole line of great admirals in the glorious British naval tradition—Hawke, Rodney, Howe, and Jervis—as having 'anticipated' Nelson. Here too however, Mahan maintained that Rodney, for example, 'despite his brilliant personal courage and professional skill, which . . . was far in advance of his contemporaries . . . belongs rather to the wary, cautious school of the French tacticians than to the impetuous eagerness of Nelson'.[67]

For Mahan, French naval policy, which, owing to inferior resources, prescribed tactical and strategic restraint, was the worst of all naval mistakes. These 'unhappy prejudices' and 'false system' ensured France's ultimate defeat.[68] In avoiding battle, the French resigned the struggle for naval mastery. Just as the Austrians under Daun and Archduke Charles were reputed to have done on land, the French 'subordinated the control of the sea by the destruction of the enemy's fleets, of his organized naval forces, to the success of particular operations, the retention of particular points, the carrying out of particular ulterior strategic ends'.[69] As a single ray of light, wrote Mahan, Suffren's 'great and transcendent merit lay in the clearness with which he recognized in the English fleet, the exponent of the British sea power, the proper enemy of the French fleet'. He 'saw plainly that the way to assure those [ulterior] objects [the French were pursuing] was not by economizing his own ships, but by destroying those of the enemy. Attack, not defence, was the road to sea power in his eyes.'[70]

The *guerre de course*, resorted to by the French, was anathema to Mahan. In his view, the belief that Britain's might could be bypassed and her vulnerable lifelines attacked was an illusion and a violation of the most fundamental principle of naval warfare. This was clearly proved by the outcome of the Anglo-French conflict, in which the French were justly defeated. That the defeat basically reflected the balance of power between the two opposing navies and would probably have occurred whatever strategy the French employed, mattered little to Mahan.[71] In his opinion, rather than resort to commerce-destroying, the weaker navy should have

---

[67] Mahan, *Influence I*, 377–8. [68] Ibid. 79–80.
[69] Ibid. 339. [70] Ibid. 425.
[71] For the underlying French inferiority in money, manpower and war materials, see James Pritchard, *Louis XV's Navy 1748–1762: A Study of Organization and Administration* (Montreal, 1987). More specifically on the French lack of timber and its effect on their strategy, see Paul Walden Bamford, *Forests and French Sea Power 1660–1789* (Toronto, 1956).

waited for its opportunity, or better still, should have initiated a situation in which the enemy's navy would be divided and could be attacked in detail in a Jominian fashion.[72] Mahan, the historian who gave special attention to trade statistics, recorded the impressive numbers of British merchant ships captured by the French. British losses in each of the great wars against France—the War of the League of Augsburg, the War of the Spanish Succession, the War of the Austrian Succession, the Seven Years War, and the Revolutionary Wars—amounted to thousands, with hundreds of ships being captured each year.[73] Not unnaturally, French commerce-destroying was particularly effective during the zeniths of French power under Louis XIV and during the Revolution and Empire. During the latter period, British losses exceeded 10,000 ships. Britain's expanding and ultimately huge trade-carrying capacity enabled her to take the punishment, but Mahan was fully aware of how close Britain came to defeat in the final years before Napoleon's collapse.[74] Furthermore, in his study of the Anglo-American war of 1812, he in effect endorsed the American naval strategy of commerce-raiding as the only possible one for the weaker side and as quite effective as such.[75] Still, for him the ultimate result of Anglo-French contest was merely the confirmation of a principle. Which came first logically, the principle or the particular historical experience, was a meaningless question for him. In the tradition of the Enlightenment, which in his particular case was mixed with a deep religious faith in a divine cosmic order,[76] he believed that the universal principle is revealed in, and validated by, experience.

[72] Mahan, *Influence II*, 179–80.
[73] Mahan, *From Sail to Steam*, 282; *Influence I*, 317–19; *Influence II*, ii. 221–2; Kennedy, *The Rise and Fall of British Naval Mastery*, 53, 72, 79, 85, 93, 110, 131. Also see the pointed criticism of the gap which exists here between Mahan the historian and Mahan the dogmatic Jominian strategist in Geoffrey Sympox's excellent *The Crisis of French Sea Power 1688–1697, From the* guerre d'escadre *to the* guerre de course (The Hague, 1974), esp. 227–9.
[74] Mahan, *Influence II*, ii. 199–271.
[75] Mahan, *Sea Power in Its Relations to the War of 1812* (2 vols.; London, 1905), i. 285–9.
[76] This theme, which earlier historians had noted, was elaborated by Seager. The religious philosophy of Mahan's uncle, Milo, a distinguished ecclesiastical historian and thinker and an important influence on the young Alfred Mahan, advanced the idea that a mathematical, Pythagorian-like, divine design manifested itself in the world; Seager, *Alfred Thayer Mahan*, 4–5, 10, 445–8. Also see Mahan's own book, *The Harvest Within; Thoughts on the Life of the Christian* (London, 1909).

Finally, true application of fundamental truths was strikingly demonstrated by Nelson, whose genius embodied the principles of naval warfare in the same way that Bonaparte's embodied those of war on land. Indeed, as anyone familiar with the Napoleonic conduct of operations would not fail to recognize, the nature of both those sets of principles was almost indistinguishable. According to Mahan, Nelson possessed 'the eye of a seaman *determined on attack*'. His motto was 'first secure the victory, then make the most of it'. In May 1805 his first plan of attack in the Trafalgar campaign opened with the following words: 'The business of the English Commander-in-Chief being first to bring the Enemy's Fleet to Battle, on the most advantageous terms to himself . . . and secondly, to continue . . . until the business is decided'. He was looking for 'a close and decisive Battle . . . If the two Fleets are both willing to fight, but little manœuvring is necessary'.[77]

Given this outstanding similarity between the military and naval pictures of the past and strategic theories, it is hardly surprising that Mahan's theories experienced the very same problems which Jomini's had met in confronting changing historical conditions and technological transformation, indeed, they failed at the very same points. On land, improved firearms were transforming tactics, and steam locomotion was revolutionizing strategy. While Jomini and his disciples, steeped in the Napoleonic era and committed to immutable principles, found it hard enough to swallow the former, they could never accept the latter. At sea, steam ironclads, steel guns and armour, the torpedo, the mine, and, finally, the internal combustion engine were revolutionizing naval warfare in much the same way.[78] Yet, holding to the axiom that the details of tactics might change but that the principles of strategy were universal, and nostalgically attached to the great age of sail, Mahan was at pains to ward off anything that might threaten the foundations of his theories of sea power and naval warfare. The case of the railroad has already been mentioned. Jomini had continued to deny that it could change the eternal principles of strategy as demonstrated by Napoleon—until he was proved wrong by the Prussians. Mahan was equally insistent that the railroad could not overshadow sea-

[77] Mahan, *The Life of Nelson, The Embodiment of the Sea Power of Great Britain* (London, 1899), 294, 490, 694–5.

[78] By far the best study of these developments and of their overall significance is Marder, *The Anatomy of British Sea Power* (London, 1940); see also Bernard Brodie, *Sea Power in the Machine Age* (Princeton, NJ, 1941).

and river-transportation and thus the supremacy of naval power, because the latter would always remain cheaper. 'These distinctions', he wrote, 'are not accidental or temporary; they are of the nature of things and permanent.'[79]

Mahan had little to say about steam locomotion at sea. In any case, steam locomotion did not seem to make much difference to the principles of naval warfare, especially the dominance of the great naval battle and the supremacy of the battleship. Even here, however, when, in 1906, the British revolutionized battleship architecture with the introduction of the huge, controversial, all-big-gun HMS *Dreadnought*, Mahan opposed the new trend outright. He feared an escalating contest over size, to which no definite end could be foreseen. He thought there was no point in building ships larger than 10,000 tons (compared with the *Dreadnought*'s 18,000), the equivalents of the seventy-four-gun ship-of-the-line which had become the standard in the age of sail.[80] An escalating contest over size did develop and was not to stop before the battleship itself, more than three times larger than the original *Dreadnought* was taken out of use after the Second World War. Yet the race itself was, technically speaking, inevitable, given the fact that, in contrast to the situation with wooden sailing-ships, there was no natural limit to the size of steel hulls, or to the size of the steam or diesel engines constructed for these increasingly powerful monsters. Mahan also opposed the introduction of the single, large-calibre battery which, with the *Dreadnought*, became the standard weapon of battleships. He favoured the mixed battery which had formed the armament of battleships since the days of sail. He was not sufficiently familiar with the new developments in long-range gunnery and fire-control which had made the all-big-gun ship possible. He apprehended the very idea of long-range artillery duels as a retreat from the dashing Nelsonian tradition of hand-to-hand combat to the older, now-discarded, linear tactics. When William S. Sims, then a lieutenant-commander, answered Mahan's arguments publicly on the pages of *U.S. Naval Institute Proceedings*, it became clear, not least to Mahan himself, that the ageing authority was out of touch.[81]

[79] Mahan, *The Problem of Asia*, 37–8.

[80] Mahan, *Lessons of the War with Spain*, 41, 264–6; id., *Naval Administration and Warfare*, 141–3.

[81] Mahan, 'Reflections, Historic and Other, Suggested by the Battle of the Japan Sea', *United States Navy Institute Proceedings* (June 1906), 447–71; W. S. Sims,

However, the really serious challenges to the precepts and principles of classical naval warfare came from elsewhere. The torpedo was the most extraordinary and potent new naval weapon in the 1880s. In France, the Jeune école made it the centre-piece of its programme, envisioning swarms of small, fast torpedo-boats, which would raid and destroy mammoth but helpless British battle-fleets.[82] Whether the big battleship was doomed was a question no one ventured to answer definitely in the 1880s, not even the British Admiralty. In 1886 the parliamentary secretary to the Admiralty confessed that he might be approaching Parliament for new battleships for the last time.[83] Upon entering the Naval War College, Mahan automatically enlisted in the struggle of the 'New Navy' circle for a navy of battleships which would be able to command American waters. The old policy, which had been based on monitors and cruisers for coastal defence and commerce-raiding and which prevailed for as long as the USA was too weak to challenge the command of the seas, was now totally rejected.[84] The torpedo had many enthusiasts in the navy, but Mahan's verdict was typically belittling. In his War College lectures on tactics, he dismissed the torpedo-boat on the grounds that 'in the days of the sailing ships, which have made nearly all naval history so far', the fire-ship had proven unsuccessful, and 'there is little reason to doubt that the experience we have yet to gain in this will be like the experience the world has always had heretofore'.[85]

'The Inherent Tactical Qualities of the All-Big-Gun, One Caliber Battleship of High Speed, Large Displacement and Gun Power', ibid. (Sep. 1906), 1337–66; Mahan, *Letters and Papers*, iii. 170–1, 177–80, 193, 204; *Fear God and Dread Nought: The Correspondence of Admiral of the Fleet Lord Fisher of Kilverstone*, ed. Arthur Marder (3 vols.; London, 1956), ii. 96–7.

[82] The most complete exposition of the *Jeune école's* programme and vision, written by one of its major exponents, is Gabriel Charmes, *Naval Reform* (London, 1887); the best study is Theodore Ropp, *The Development of a Modern Navy: French Naval Policy 1871–1904* (Annapolis, Md., 1987), esp. 19–22, 155–80, 254–80; also see John Raymond Walser, 'France's Search for a Battlefleet: French Naval Policy 1898–1914' (unpub. doc. diss., University of North California, 1976), 49–50.

[83] Marder, *The Anatomy of British Sea Power*, 125; the whole chapter (pp. 119–143) is excellent on the confusion of tactical ideas in the 1880s. Also see Admiral Sir George Elliot's popular but instructive *A Treatise on Future Naval Battles and How to Fight them* (London, 1885), esp. 1–38.

[84] See the developing tendency and many statements to that effect, preceding, and unrelated to, Mahan, in Spector, *Professors of War*, 47–9; also Mahan, *Lessons of the War with Spain*, 264–80.

[85] Mahan, 'Fleet Battle Tactics', 1886, unpub. lectures, quoted in Spector, *Professors of War*, 45. Also see, more lukewarmly, *Influence I*, 110–11, 113–14.

To its French enthusiasts, the torpedo and the mine held the promise of breaking one of the most effective devices in the traditional British system of war—the blockade. Slipping out of harbour under cover of night, torpedo-boats would imperil any ship which remained within range, dozens of miles away. As the British navy discovered to its alarm during the extensive manœuvres which it conducted in 1888 to examine the problem, a close blockade to seal off the French harbours had become virtually impossible.[86] Whether this really was so, and what the consequences would be for the future of British naval mastery, were some of the most troubling questions with which naval circles in Britain grappled from the 1880s. Mahan had no doubts over the matter. The tactics which had served Hawke, Jervis, and Nelson so effectively would remain in force for as long as ships were ships and harbours were harbours. However, when war came in 1914, a close blockading of the German harbours was totally out of the question. A blockade of Germany could be imposed only by virtue of Germany's great geographical disadvantage; her routes to the open sea, unlike those of France, could be bottled up hundreds of miles away from her shores, at the two narrow entrances to the North Sea, through the Channel and the Shetlands, both of which were under British control.

When, after almost three-quarters of a century of peaceful relations, France's old rivalry with Britain was reignited by the British occupation of Egypt, the French resorted to their old strategy of commerce-destroying. They regarded it as a means of striking at Britain's oceanic lifelines, while avoiding direct confrontation with her stronger navy. The successful operations of the Confederate's commerce-raiders, notably the *Alabama*, during the American Civil War were another source of inspiration for the French. Dominating France's naval policy in the mid-1880s, the Jeune école calculated that in the late nineteenth century, when Britain was dependent as never before on imported foodstuffs to feed her populations, the revived *guerre de course* might have a deadly effect. With the price of naval insurance rocketing and with French gunboats bombarding British coastal towns, Britain might be severely shaken.

The influence of the Jeune école ebbed in the 1890s. The great

[86] Marder, *The Anatomy of British Sea Power*, 107–9.

British naval revival that followed the passage of the Naval Act of 1889—a revival which contrasted sharply with the badly conceived French construction-schemes—damaged French morale. Enthusiasm for the torpedo subsided with the introduction of the destroyer, designed to protect battle-fleets from marauding torpedo-boats. Naval analysts everywhere were on the whole agreed that in modern times commerce-destroying would be less rather than more effective than in the age of sail. Telegraph communications, which linked all the major stations of the British navy, would make it much easier to track down French raiders. The need for coaling would severely restrict their range and freedom of action. From the late 1890s, all navies were again concentrating on building battleships and preparing for major naval battles. Britain, Tirpitz's Germany, America, and Japan were taking the lead. The *guerre de course*, which had kindled imagination in the 1880s, was falling into disrepute, and Mahan's teaching, again while not creating the trend, influenced it considerably by the firmness and authoritativeness of its conclusions. Commerce-destroying, he argued, had never been, and could never become, a substitute for the command of the sea, no matter what technical means were used. This was a universal truth, repeatedly revealed in history and unaffected by changes in one detail or another.

Once again, however, the introduction of a new weapon-system, the submarine, which had been made possible by the invention of the internal combustion engine at the end of the nineteenth century, was to prove a technological change which would undermine Mahan's universal principles. That Mahan regarded the submarine as nothing more than a submerged, coast-defence torpedo-boat, possibly particularly effective and troublesome because of its peculiar quality, was nothing special; practically nobody thought otherwise before 1914, not even that progressive-minded reformer and ardent supporter of the submarine, Admiral John Fisher.[87] Mahan's theories, however, ruled out a priori the idea of a naval campaign launched by submarines.[88] And yet, in two world wars, despite having unprecedented naval superiority over its continental rival, Britain was to come closer than ever before to being defeated at sea. She was driven to that point by an enemy who used the new and deadly weapon in a large-scale, ferocious *guerre de course*.

---

[87] Ibid. 363, 367–8, 495. [88] E.g. Mahan, *Naval Strategy*, 3–4.

That Britain did not in the end lose the war at sea was not due to any inherent limitations of commerce-destroying. It was due above all to the fact that at the time of crisis she was joined—in both world wars—by a gigantic ally, the USA, whose massive resources made the struggle against Germany, at sea and otherwise, an unequal one and almost inevitable in its ultimate results. To balance the record, however, it might be noted that, while less dogmatic minds in Britain thought that the days of the wasteful and cumbersome convoy-system to protect commerce were over, Mahan held fast to the opinion that such a system was as necessary as it had been in the age of sail. Indeed, by 1917 the convoy system had been reintroduced as the most effective defence against the submarine.

When the First World War came, naval circles found themselves in a remarkably similar predicament to the one with which their army counterparts were struggling on land. While most of the new weapons and tactical developments were known, and their significance was at least partially recognized, warfare as a whole assumed an unexpected, strange, and, as it were, unsatisfactory character. Rather than leading quickly to a major battle of destruction in the North Sea, in which the fate of the naval operations would be decided in Nelsonian fashion and command of the sea established, the war turned out to be a protracted struggle of attrition. Hundreds of miles of artificial obstacles, as well as patrolling submarines, hindered movement almost as severely as on the Western front. The navy could no longer regard the enemy's shores as its front line or sail wherever it pleased in the same way that armies no longer travelled relatively open spaces in their theatres of operations. Both on land and at sea, the war became one of position. In the deadlock which emerged in the new technological environment, both the Napoleonic and Nelsonian models and the strategic theories based upon them and claiming universal validity failed to materialize.

CORBETT'S REVISIONISM FROM DRAKE TO JUTLAND

As the foremost historian of British sea-power in the late nineteenth and early twentieth centuries has noted, public interest in the navy, which was later to become such a distinctive part of British identity, barely existed before the 1880s.[89] In the age of Pax Britannica after 1815, when Britain truly ruled the waves unchallenged, the British public took the Royal Navy's policing of the world's oceans for granted. For the Victorians it was inseparable from, and as solid as, Britain's innate superiority and benevolent influence over the rest of the world.[90] Their confidence was only rarely shaken. One such occasion came in 1859, when the French launched the first ironclad, *La Gloire*, and created panic over the possibility that 'steam had bridged the English Channel'. Another came in 1866–71, when Prussia overturned the European balance of power with impressive demonstrations of military proficiency.

While industrialization and ever increasing world-trade were revolutionizing the British economy, and steam was transforming naval warfare, there was in Britain only one man who publicly gave serious consideration to the implications inherent in the new conditions for the defence of the British Isles and the Empire. Captain (later Sir) John Colomb (1838–1909) of the Royal Marines had retired from military service in 1866–7 to start a career in politics, initially in Irish local government and later in Parliament. Possibly the first strategic analyst Britain had known, his pamphlets, articles, and lectures called for a comprehensive and coherent approach to the problem of the defence of the Empire, taken as a whole. He fully appreciated the close relationship which existed between strategy and the emerging world economy, and excelled in analyzing trade statistics and in demonstrating their significance in relation to the problem of imperial defence. Many of his acute observations, the manner in which he framed the questions, and the phrases he coined gained universal currency later in the century, when naval affairs moved to the forefront of public attention. Cruelly, however, little credit was awarded John Colomb for his pioneering work over the previous decades. There was something in the man which made people regard him as a bore.[91]

While the Prussian military successes in 1866 and 1871 aroused

[89] Marder, *The Anatomy of British Sea Power*, 44–5.
[90] For British attitudes during the age of Pax Britannica, see Semmel, *Liberalism and Naval Strategy*, *passim*.
[91] The man and his work are presented in Howard d'Egville, *Imperial Defence and Closer Union: A Short Record of the Life Work of Sir John Colomb and of the Movement Toward Imperial Organization* (London, 1913); D. M. Schurman, *The Education of a Navy: The Development of British Naval Strategic Thought 1867–1914* (London, 1965), 16–35.

public concern over defence and generated the Cardwell reforms in the British army, John Colomb reminded his readers that the question of defence did not begin with the qualities of the needle-gun but with the overall organization and allocation of national forces to meet national goals. Britain's defence problems were entirely different from those of a continental power.[92] Britain was a colonial empire which had to contend with, and reconcile, the different but interrelated defence-requirements of the island-state itself, of the empire's sea-communications, and of the colonies, particularly India. According to Colomb, the public's agitation over the defence of Britain against invasion and over the schemes for military reform was characterized by a tendency to consider only one aspect of the problem in isolation. 'Supposing we had the most perfect military system the world has ever seen—every man a trained soldier, every hill-top crowned with batteries, every road swept by mitrailleuse[s], what would it avail us?' he asked.[93] Colomb was the first to point out a fact which later became the cornerstone of the argument of the so-called 'blue-water school', namely, the prospect of a major invasion presupposed that the British navy would be so overwhelmed as to lose control over Britain's home waters; however, in that eventuality no invasion would be necessary. By the late nineteenth century, Britain was becoming increasingly dependent on imported foodstuffs, which formed more than half her total consumption by the 1880s. Her problem was thus not invasion but investment;[94] or as Fisher who had little patience for the Colombs later put it: 'It is not *invasion* we have to fear if our navy is beaten, IT'S STARVATION! '[95] Impressed by the Prussians, the public focused its attention on the army and neglected the navy. Yet, no matter now strong the army was to become, its strength would in effect prove irrelevant to the protection of the British islands.

John Colomb, however, was no naval fanatic like some later 'blue water' enthusiasts. In his admirably systematic analysis of the

[92] John Colomb, The Protection of Our Commerce and Distribution of Our Naval Forces Considered (London, 1867), id., *Imperial Defence* (London, 1871), 5–6. For the background see Schurman, *Education of a Navy*, 17–19.

[93] Colomb, *Imperial Defence*, 7.

[94] See progressively in Colomb's works: *Imperial Defence*, 6–7; *Colonial Defence*, (London, 1877), 3 *et passim*; and, admirably documented with trade statistics and data on food imports, *Naval Intelligence and Protection of Commerce in War* (London, 1881), 7 *et passim*.

[95] Quoted in Marder, *The Anatomy of British Sea Power*, 65.

Empire's strategic situation, he stressed that national defence had never been the problem of the navy alone, and never would be.[96] A combined package of naval and military means was necessary to meet the Empire's varied defence-needs. While the navy blockaded the enemy's ports, protected commerce, and defended the British islands against invasion and investment, and the colonies against sea-borne expeditions, it was not able to provide full protection against naval and military raids on ports and coastal towns. For those purposes and for those only, argued Colomb, Britain needed coast-defence vessels and fortifications, garrisons and militia. Thus the work of the 'brick-and-mortar school', which had dominated during the invasion scare of 1859, may have been misguided and overdone but was not entirely misplaced. The navy, added Colomb, was insufficient to the task also in that it was unable to defend the colonies against land invasions by continental powers like Russia or the United States, and was unable to carry the war into the enemy's own territory. This, according to Colomb, was where the army ought to come in, working in close co-operation and co-ordination with the navy.[97] In retrospect, after a century of strategic debate, the wisdom of his balanced programme is vindicated by most commentators, even if its pioneering advocate has never received the credit he deserves.

Better-known and operating in an environment which was becoming increasingly concerned about naval affairs was John Colomb's elder brother, Philip (1831–99). During his long service in the navy, Philip Colomb developed a system of light-signals which the navy adopted, wrote a lively account of his period of duty in the Indian Ocean, and in 1878 won the Naval Essay Prize of the Royal United Services Institution for his paper *Great Britain's Maritime Power: How Best Developed*. He retired from the navy in 1886 and was subsequently promoted to Rear-Admiral (1887) and Vice-Admiral (1892). Only then, when he became instructor of naval strategy and tactics at the Royal Naval College at Greenwich, at almost the same time as Mahan was appointed to Newport, did the period of his scholarly and literary productivity begin.[98]

[96] Colomb, *Imperial Defence*, 8.
[97] See esp. Colomb, *Protection and Distribution*, 10–12; *Imperial Defence*, 8, 14–18, *et passim*; *Colonial Defence*, *passim*.
[98] The only study is the chapter in Schurman's excellent *Education of a Navy*, 36–56.

Philip Colomb's prize essay of 1877 was heavily influenced by his brother's opinions, whose contribution he fully acknowledged. The essay stressed the need for a comprehensive view of the empire's defence-requirements and addressed itself to Britain's new food-problem and its strategic consequences. Under the new conditions, he argued, the island's main worry was enemy blockade, not invasion.[99] He differed from his brother on one point only. He did not accept the latter's subtle analysis of the complex modality of the navy's mission. For Philip Colomb that mission amounted to the much simpler formula of blockading the enemy in its ports and protecting Britain's commercial and maritime communications.[100] This was a difference which, when developed a decade later, was to make him one of the earliest exponents and the foremost theoretician of the 'blue-water school'.

Philip Colomb's essays on Britain's strategic naval problems, written mostly in the late 1880s, appeared in book form in 1893 under the title *Essays on Naval Defence*. His theoretical-historical studies, first issued as a magazine serial, were then compiled and republished as *Naval Warfare, Its Ruling Principles and Practice, Historically Treated* (1891). Both books advance similar ideas. As British supremacy at sea was being challenged for the first time since Trafalgar, and the prospect of a naval war against a Franco-Russian coalition was looming large, Colomb returned to the great naval struggles of the past to evoke the image of Britain as an oceanic empire and mistress of the seas. In those days, Britain had been defended purely by the navy. The sea was her domain. Its communications resembled a country's inland roads. The enemy's shores were her frontiers. (This was another catch-phrase which Fisher was to make his own.)[101]

In two lectures delivered in 1888 and 1889 at the Royal United Service Institution, Colomb amazed his audience of both services, particularly the army officers, by denying the value of anything but a high-seas navy for Britain's defence. In the previous chapter we saw that, in the name of a true and shining conception of warfare, which they discovered in a more distant and glorious past, French

---

[99] Philip Colomb, *Great Britain's Maritime Power: How Best Developed* (London, 1878), 3–7; the essay was reprinted in id., *Essays on Naval Defence* (London, 1893), 31–128.   [100] Ibid. 10.
[101] Philip Colomb, *Essays on Naval Defence*, 20–3, 129–30. For Fisher see Marder, *The Anatomy of British Sea Power*, 68.

military theorists of the period were rebelling against the fixed fortifications which had been constructed in France in the previous decade. In the same way, Colomb argued that coastal defences, garrisons, and gun-boats, inherited from the panic of 1859, were virtually useless. He maintained that careful historical study showed that whenever naval supremacy had been achieved, fortifications were never put to the test; on the other hand, he argued, once naval supremacy had been lost, no fortifications were able to save major bases like Minorca or Gibraltar from a resolute enemy attack.[102] The sole aim of naval war, he argued, was command of the sea. Once this was achieved, everything else would follow.[103] Since now as before, the enemy's fleet was unlikely to challenge the Royal Navy in the open, the blockade, in its close or more distant forms, would remain the basis of British strategy even under the altered conditions of the present. While the action of commerce-raiders was now limited by coaling, and while the wasteful convoy-system might have lost its usefulness, the *guerre de course* would none the less remain the main threat.[104]

That Britain needed no Mahan to formulate the principles of naval supremacy and to articulate the ethos of her great past is evident. Yet it is equally evident that Mahan became almost at once an international celebrity, while Colomb won only modest reputation, mainly in professional circles. One reason for this was that Colomb, as one historian has put it, was 'scooped'.[105] *Naval Warfare*, which had been conceived simultaneously with Mahan's work, was published in book form only a year later. More important still, however, was the fact that Mahan's *Influence* book was more suited to the general public, more historical and less technical. It was enlightening and delighting, almost sublime. Mahan had no equal in interweaving naval history into the wider picture of general history, and, in the preface to his book, Colomb modestly bowed to the 'abler pen and deeper thinker' whose work had been published before his book left the press.[106] Having said this, however, as naval theory *per se*, Colomb's book is probably the more impressive. The main themes are the same as Mahan's

[102] Colomb, *Essays on Naval Defence*, 11–13, 149–51, 160–93.
[103] Ibid. 190, 210.   [104] Ibid. 154–9, 194–257.
[105] Schurman, *Education of a Navy*, 53.
[106] Philip Colomb, *Naval Warfare, Its Ruling Principles and Practice, Historically Treated* (London, 1891), p. viii.

but, as a systematic treatise, *Naval Warfare* is much more neatly organized.

In synthesizing the theoretical out of the historical, Colomb skilfully let every period in the chronological sequence of British naval ascendancy present a different naval theme. The struggle against Spain serves as the first, introductory chapter of the book, which deals with the nature of naval warfare. Unlike Mahan, Colomb distinguished clearly between war at sea before and during the age of sail. Before, there were naval battles, naval (or, more accurately, sea-borne) expeditions, and naval (sea-borne) raids, but no naval warfare in the later sense. This appeared only when the advent of sail produced sea-keeping ships which could remain at sea for very long periods and thus claim and maintain command over that 'vast common land'.[107] This was the reality which emerged during the Elizabethan age. It was grasped by Monson and Raleigh, who discovered the true principles of the naval art, centring on the acquisition of command of the sea.[108]

The Anglo-Dutch naval wars, says Colomb, demonstrated this new rationale. Command of the sea was the means; the destruction and protection of trade the end. The English won because of their greater naval strength and superior geographical position. The chapters in *Naval Warfare* dealing with the Anglo-French struggle examine the problem of the invasion of the British islands, which for more than a century was the main aim of French strategic planning. In Colomb's opinion, the French failed because of erroneous principles. Unless one expects strong support in the invaded country (Jacobite), no invasion can be attempted without first securing command over the water-crossings. The French tried to make do without the only means which could have led them to success—the concentration of superior naval forces in the Channel. Their ulterior purpose distracted them from the fundamental imperatives of war at sea.

Finally, in one case-study after another, Colomb examined the subject of sea-borne expeditions and came up with some significant observations. He discerned a major reason for failures in such expeditions in a duality of purpose, when a naval campaign distracted attention from the land operation. He emphasized the necessity of an adequate military force to accompany the fleet. The

---

[107] Colomb, *Naval Warfare*, 1–6; cf. Guilmartin, *Gunpowder and Galleys*, 2–3, 16, 18 *et passim*.   [108] Colomb, *Naval Warfare*, 10–24.

navy could not be expected to perform the military mission. He argued that once naval control over a local theatre of operations had been achieved, fortifications could only delay the fall of remote colonial and strategic outposts and bases.[109]

Naval Warfare was an admirably coherent and systematic exposition, clearly oriented to the present and of great didactic value. At the same time, however, it is obvious that like Mahan's *Influence* books, Colomb's book suffered from the characteristic flaws of the 'blue water' argument. In emphasizing the war at sea and the navy, it tended to downgrade, at least by omission, the role of continental operations and the army. Exalting as it did the potency of the navy, it overlooked its limitations. Bewitched by the 'Nelsonian model', it reduced the diversity of naval warfare and the complexity of historical conditions to one standard method. Like the military theories of its time, its apparently deep commitment to the past was in fact tendentious. To a large degree, both were cultivating a historical myth, nourished from the springs of national tradition at times of wavering confidence.

In the naval, as in the field of military history and theory, opposition, limited as it was, to the prevailing picture of the past and to the ruling strategic precepts drew largely on the methods and standards of modern historical scholarship. This was what Mahan respectfully called history 'after the high modern pattern', but actually regarded as somewhat pedantic and as something which he himself did not need. The growth of modern naval historical scholarship is connected with the name of Sir John Laughton (1830–1915), a Cambridge graduate in mathematics who became head of the department of meteorology and marine surveying at Greenwich when the Royal Naval College was opened there in 1873. In 1876 he started teaching naval history at the college. In 1885 he retired from the navy to become professor of modern history at King's College, London.[110]

Laughton wrote extensively in two diverging genres: popular history on the one hand, and meticulously researched chronicles on the other, particularly the hundreds of items he wrote for the *Dictionary of National Biography*. On the whole, reading him is disappointing. Although, in a seminal RUSI lecture delivered in 1874, he called for the scientific study of naval history, he in fact

---

[109] Ibid., esp. 203, 278, 375, 430.
[110] See again Schurman, *Education of a Navy*, 83–109.

propagated the historical and strategic outlook, which Mahan and Colomb were later to make their own and develop into a magnificent edifice.[111] His main contribution, however, lay elsewhere. From 1879 he had access to the Public Record Office, which later (1887) opened its gates to all scholars. In 1893 he founded the Navy Record Society, whose first secretary he became. Well-connected and eminent among all those concerned with naval affairs, Laughton initiated and presided over the vast compilation and publication of primary archival material from the navy's records.[112] One whom he persuaded to take part in this enterprise was Sir Julian Corbett.

Corbett (1854–1922) came to naval history in mid-life and from a civilian background. He took a first in law at Cambridge but, never liking the legal profession and being a man of independent means, he retired from active practice altogether in 1882. He travelled extensively, sought a literary career, and wrote a few, marginally successful novels. The popular biographies he wrote of Monk and Drake led him to join the Navy Record Society when that was founded in 1893. In 1896 he accepted Laughton's request to edit a volume of documents on the Spanish war, 1585–7. Thus began a career which was to dominate the rest of his life.[113]

Corbett's historical writings can be divided into two categories: the volumes he edited for the Navy Record Society on the development of British fighting-instructions and signals, and his histories of selected periods in British naval warfare. Both involved radically new interpretations of the past; the one of naval tactics, the other of naval strategy. In line with these came a new understanding of the present. All these themes were interrelated but, for clarity's sake, they will be treated here in succession.

In *Fighting Instructions, 1530–1816*, Corbett compiled and commented upon all printed British naval regulations which had survived and had been discovered from the earliest times. Although

---

[111] See esp. John K. Laughton, 'The Scientific Study of History', *Journal of the Royal United Services Institution*, 18, 1875, 508–27; id., *Essays on Naval Tactics* (London, 1874), 3–17; id., *Studies in Naval History* (London, 1887), *passim*.

[112] See Julian S. Corbett, 'The Revival of Naval History', 4 Oct. 1916, *Corbett Papers*, Box 4.

[113] Schurman, *Julian S. Corbett, 1854–1922* (London, 1981), cannot be bettered. See also id., *Education of a Navy*, 147–84; Peter M. Stamford, 'The Work of Sir Julian Corbett in the Dreadnought Era', *United States Naval Institute Proceedings*, 77 (1951), 61–71; and Eric J. Grove's fine Introduction to Corbett, *Some Principles of Maritime Strategy* (Annapolis, Md., 1988), pp. xi–xlv.

the book's title went back to the Elizabethan age, material pre-dating the Anglo-Dutch wars was not found, and possibly had not existed in the first place. In respect of the middle of the seventeenth century onwards, however, the *Instructions*, fragmented and incomplete as they were, provided the main primary source on the development of British, and foreign, naval tactics. Confronted with the bare evidence of the past, undisguised by later traditions and interpretations, Corbett's strong historical sense gradually came to detect a story different from the accepted one.

Tracing the succession of fighting-instructions which, since 1653, had been establishing the line as the ruling battle-formation, Corbett doubted that these instructions had been foolishly pedantic or had led to a degeneration of naval warfare in the eighteenth century. At almost the same time, in Germany, Delbrück was appealing to the relativity and inner logic of historical situations in rehabilitating eighteenth-century land-warfare, which had been discredited by the men of his own century. In a rather similar way, Corbett argued that the new discipline of the instructions and the new linear tactics had evolved over a long period of time, in response to the existing historical conditions. Increasing fire-power had necessitated a regulated system of control and manœuvre, even at the cost of individual initiative. The breaking of the enemy's line had been becoming rarer and rarer simply because increasing fire-power had been making it too dangerous a manœuvre.[114] Thus, argued Corbett, 'the manœuvre of breaking the line was abandoned by the tacticians of that era, not from ignorance nor from lack of enterprise, but from a deliberate tactical conviction gained by the experience of war'.[115]

If *Fighting Instructions* provided a historically sympathetic view of the origins and function of linear tactics, newly discovered documents, which Corbett compiled under the title *Signals and Instructions, 1776–1794* (1908), offered a fresh look over the period in which linear tactics were reformed. During the very same years that Corbett was working on the *Instructions*, Colin, researching in the French archives, was discovering that Revolutionary column-tactics had been rooted in an evolutionary process which had been gathering momentum during the last decades of the *ancien régime*. Studying British records, Corbett was independently

---

[114] Julian Corbett, *Fighting Instructions, 1530–1816* (London, 1905), 134–5, 176, 178, 183.   [115] Ibid. 184.

arriving at similar conclusions regarding naval warfare. He found out that the change from linear to column shock-tactics had not occurred in one revolutionary step, and were not an ingenious creation of people like Eldin, Rodney, Howe, or Nelson. He showed that signals for the breaking of the enemy's line had been issued by individual admirals at least as early as the 1770s, even before Rodney's famous manœuvre. These signals had been devised under the influence of the French authorities Morogues and Villehuet, whose treatises on naval tactics, composed in the 1760s, had been read by virtually everybody. Corbett suggested that Eldin's ideas provoked little attention in 1790 because reform was already in full swing within the Admiralty. In any case, he argued, the dramatic successes brought about by the new tactics were due solely to the degeneration of the French navy. Had it not been for that, Nelson's perpendicular attack at Trafalgar would have been an act of madness. Indeed, tactical instructions after Nelson recognized no dramatic change and remained in essence conservative and linear as before.[116]

Corbett's successive and voluminous studies of British naval operations from Drake to Nelson undermined the prevailing picture of the past and the accepted tenets of naval theory in an even more radical fashion than did his works on the records of British naval tactics. The similarity with Delbrück's work is striking and, in view of the resemblance which existed between the military and naval traditions that both men grew to challenge, is not really surprising. Like Delbrück, Corbett came out with a thorough revision of strategic outlook, whose implications for the present were far-reaching. For all the differences between the German academic and the Anglo-Saxon's more cavalier attitude to scholarly apparatus, in both cases their revisions stemmed from a deeply historical approach. In the process, both men profited enormously from Clausewitz's distinction between absolute and limited war and from his emphasis on the relationship between the military means and the political aim. Finally, in both cases the new ideas met with resistance and became the centre of controversy.

---

[116] Corbett (ed.), *Signals and Instructions, 1776–1794* (London, 1908), *passim*; id., *Fighting Instructions*, 313–60; id., *The Campaign of Trafalgar* (London, 1910), 347–59. On the whole, Corbett's conclusions are borne out by modern historical scholarship; see esp. John Creswell's highly knowledgeable and even more demythologizing *British Admirals of the Eighteenth Century* (London, 1972).

In *Drake and the Tudor Navy* (2 vols; 1898), Corbett's first serious historical work, questions of naval doctrine are rarely discussed and strategic judgement is rarely passed. The book is above all a historical one, and is a sound one as such, despite the author's evident admiration for his hero. In the book, however, Corbett still holds as self-evident that command of the sea is the proper aim of naval war. He began to diverge from accepted 'blue water' assumptions only with his second book, *The Successors of Drake* (1900).

In that book, Corbett dealt with the period 1596–1603, generally regarded as an anticlimax to the victory over the Armada. The victory had not led to the total destruction of Spanish naval power, or to a blockade of the Spanish ports aimed at cutting off the flow of bullion from America, as people like Drake, Hawkins, and Raleigh had recommended. The continuation of the war had seen the revival of the Spanish navy and, on the English part, the war had seemed to degenerate into mostly unsuccessful raids. For navalists both then and later, the blame for this development fell mainly on the queen's over-cautious attitude and on her continental strategy, which wasted resources and diverted attention from the naval campaign. But for Corbett the matter was far from clear-cut. He pointed out, as later historians of the period would do, that Elizabethan England had still been a relatively poor and weak country, bearing no companion with the mighty and wealthy Spanish Empire. It had probably been beyond her power and would have been too risky a policy on her part to aim at overthrowing Spain. He also pointed out that the queen had given her naval commanders many opportunities to carry out their plans. Most of these plans had failed, however, principally because the navy had not carried sufficient troops on board its ships to support its actions. Here was a lesson which Britain still had not learned. People forget that what Nelson started, Wellington ended. While talking much about sea power, they forget that its real effect is in determining the extent to which armies can be transported freely by sea.[117]

Corbett's *England in the Mediterranean 1603–1713* (2 vols.;

[117] Corbett, *The Successors of Drake* (London, 1900), esp. 1, 407–10. Also see Schurman, *Education of a Navy*, 152; R. B. Wernham, 'Elizabethan War Aims and Strategy', in S. T. Bindoff, J. Hurstfield, and C. H. Williams (eds.), *Elizabethan Government and Society* (London, 1961), 340–68; G. Mattingly, *The Defeat of the Spanish Armada* (London, 1959); Kennedy, *The Rise and Fall of British Naval Mastery*, 27–30.

1904), based on lectures he delivered in Greenwich and repeated as the Ford Lectures at Oxford, did not carry much in the way of a theoretical message. But then came Corbett's discovery of Clausewitz, which, feeding Corbett's own train of thought, proved to be enormously stimulating for him. His next historical work, *England in the Seven Years War: A Study in Combined Strategy* (2 vols.; 1907), became a case-study for a thorough-going revision of naval theory.

The main thrust of Corbett's argument was directed against what he called the narrowing of the concept of naval warfare to the winning of battles and the gaining of command of the sea. This concept he considered misleading and educationally dangerous. He maintained that command of the sea was certainly the main aim of war at sea but not the only one. An opportunity to fight a battle does not always exist, nor is battle always necessary. For example, he argued, in the Mediterranean theatre during the Spanish War of Succession, the English won without beating the enemy's fleet; their naval supremacy being recognized, they could still reap most of the advantages.[118] Hence,

we require for the guidance of our naval policy and naval action something of wider vision than the current conception of naval strategy, something that will keep before our eyes not merely the enemy's fleets or the great routes of commerce, or the command of the sea, but also the relations of naval policy and action to the whole area of diplomatic and military effort.[119]

This, he maintained, was particularly important in view of the naval myth which had grown to govern official and public opinion alike:

Of late years the world has become so deeply impressed with the efficacy of sea power that we are inclined to forget how impotent it is of itself to decide a war against great Continental states, how tedious is the pressure of naval action unless it be nicely coordinated with military and diplomatic pressure.[120]

The war with Spain came to an end only fifteen years after the defeat of the Armada; the war with Napoleon's France only ten years after Trafalgar. Truly great powers, argued Corbett, cannot

---

[118] Corbett, *England in the Seven Years War: A Study in Combined Strategy* (2 vols.; London, 1907), i. 3–5.   [119] Ibid. 5.   [120] Ibid.

be defeated solely at sea.[121] In concluding his study of *The Campaign of Trafalgar*, Corbett rejected the Mahanite view of the struggle against Imperial France. The naval victory, he argued, secured the British command of the seas and safeguarded the empire but left Napoleon as the dictator of Europe. Sea power had done all that sea power could possible do, but for Europe, whose fate was decided at Austerlitz, not Trafalgar, this was a failure.[122]

Here then we get a formula widely different from the current definitions of naval strategy . . . We begin to distinguish more clearly between the means and the end of naval policy . . . the historical method reveals that the command of the sea is only a means to an end. It never has been and never can be the end itself.[123]

Clausewitz postulated in theory what the Elder Pitt had demonstrated in practice, that war was a continuation and means of state policy and, consequently, could take different forms, either unlimited or limited.[124] This, argued Corbett, applied equally to the French, whose defensive naval strategy during the Seven Years War proved adapted to their position. Their strategy must not be dismissed only because in that particular case France lost the war.[125]

Past and present were intimately linked in Corbett's thinking. His revision of naval theory and history was stimulated by, and in turn affected, his growing role as the navy's leading intellectual. From 1901 he was writing regularly on naval affairs for the liberal journal *The Monthly Review*. Lending support to the major reforms by which Fisher, Second and later First Sea Lord, was overhauling the navy, he became one of the principal members of Fisher's circle.[126] From 1902 he was lecturing on naval history in the new war course opened at the Naval War College in 1900. From 1905 he began to lecture on naval strategy. At the same time, he became the Admiralty's chief unofficial strategic adviser.

In the war course, Corbett was trying to convey to the attending flag-officers something very different from the accepted precepts of

---

[121] Ibid. 5, 7.   [122] Corbett, *Trafalgar*, 408, 423–4.
[123] Corbett, *England in the Seven Years War*, i. 6.
[124] Ibid. i. 24, 28, 190, 336.   [125] Ibid. ii. 373–4.
[126] For their extensive correspondence see *Corbett Papers*, Box 12, only partly printed in Fisher, *Fear God and Dread Nought*.

navalism. His arguments were nothing as inspiring as the teachings of Mahan, that great pamphleteer and populizer of naval history and theory, as Corbett—sometimes admiringly, sometimes critically—referred to him.[127] Unlike Delbrück, who debated with relish against the advocates of all-out war, Corbett was operating within, and trying to influence, the naval establishment. He had to filter his ideas through, often in a roundabout way. This may have been psychologically more palatable to his audience but it also left them more bemused. They suspected his logic was leading him astray, especially as he was a civilian theoretician rather than a practical seaman. In 1906, in order to provide a clear frame of reference for his students, Corbett, in collaboration with the director of the War College, Captain Edmond J. W. Slade, issued a slim booklet entitled *Strategic Terms and Definitions used in Lectures on Naval History*, and better known as the 'Green Pamphlet'. A second, revised version of the pamphlet, *Notes on Strategy*, was issued in 1909. Corbett's book *Some Principles of Maritime Strategy* (1911) put flesh on the bare bones of the pamphlet and offered his ideas to the general public.[128]

While being in essence an *étude* on Clausewitz, Corbett's work, notwithstanding its various modest titles, was a thoroughgoing and most original revision of the accepted tenets of naval theory and indeed, more implicitly, of strategic theory as a whole. It was free of the idiosyncrasies and lingering dogmas which characterized Clausewitz's work on account of its peculiar development. At the same time, it synthesized Clausewitz's teachings and the special features of war at sea in a way which ultimately transcended even Clausewitz's later formulas, or else took them to their radical conclusions. Although for didactic reasons Corbett's arguments are often fairly involved, the work has few, if any, equals in clarity of mind, subtelty, and undogmatic thinking.

Corbett's work both tightened and loosened the connection between naval and land warfare. From the outset, he emphasized

---

[127] See e.g. Corbett, 'The Revival of Naval History' (1916), 2, *Corbett Papers*, Box 4; id., 'The Teaching of Naval and Military History' (1916), 17–18, ibid., Box 6; Grove, Introduction to Corbett, *Principles of Maritime Strategy*, p. xxx. Mahan treated Corbett with respect, and Corbett on his part refrained from criticizing Mahan's work publicly and directly, at least during the latter's lifetime.

[128] The two editions of the 'Green Pamphlet' (*Corbett Papers*, Box 6) are appended to the 1988 edn., of *Principles of Maritime Strategy*, 305–45.

that war at sea was only one branch of the phenomenon of war as a whole, to be understood in the same conceptual framework developed for land warfare by the great military thinkers of the early nineteenth century—Clausewitz and Jomini. Its proper designation was maritime rather than naval war because, both in means and ends, it extended beyond the action of navies and stood in close relationship to the development of land operations. Indeed, on the whole, war at sea took second place to war on land. While navalists everywhere exalted the marvels of commanding the seas, Corbett pointed out that 'men live upon land and not upon the sea'.[129]

It was from this simple fact, according to Corbett, that most of the crucial differences between land- and sea-warfare stemmed. Naval war, he suggested, tended to be much less decisive. While it could inflict heavy damage on some enemies, it usually lacked the means to hurt them decisively and overthrow them. Thus,

it is almost impossible that a war can be decided by naval action alone. Unaided, naval pressure can only work by a process of exhaustion. Its effects must always be slow, and so galling both to our own commercial community and to neutrals, that the tendency is always to accept terms of peace that are far from conclusive. For a firm decision a quicker and more drastic form of pressure is required. Since men live upon the land and not upon the sea, great issues between nations at war have always been decided—except in the rarest cases—either by what your army can do against your enemy's territory and national life or else by the fear of what the fleet makes it possible for your army to do.[130]

Even in regard to land strategy, argued Corbett, military writers had gone too far in emphasizing the need to overthrow the enemy totally. Corbett's interpretation of the growth of nineteenth-century military theory and of Clausewitz's development is outstanding even by today's standards. He pointed out that the conditions created by the French Revolution (which the English had in fact anticipated in their own Puritan Revolution) had brought about mass popular mobilization. It was under these conditions that military effort has been directed towards the destruction of the enemy's main forces and the complete overthrow of his powers of resistance. This mode of war had been consecrated by military

[129] Corbett, *Principles of Maritime Strategy*, 15–16.   [130] Ibid.

theorists who had taken the accidental and transient for the essential and universal and had condemned any other form of strategy as heresy. It has taken some time for Clausewitz to realize his own error and devise the concept of limited war.[131]

According to Corbett, what was true of land warfare was even truer at sea, where conditions made limited wars very much the rule. On the Continent, even the limited wars which Clausewitz described between neighbouring countries over disputed provinces tended to engulf all of the belligerents' forces and resources. By contrast, in commanding the sea, the British could, for example, effectively isolate the various theatres of war and thus conduct truly limited operations in locations of their own choosing.[132] Britain could opt for a limited involvement in a total continental war.[133] This was the principle apprehended by Francis Bacon: 'He that commands the sea is at great liberty and may take as little of the war as he will, whereas those that be strongest by land are many times nevertheless in great straits.'[134] Hence the historical divergence which existed between the continental doctrines of war and British naval doctrines.[135]

From here Corbett proceeded to reverse completely all accepted military tenets. First, he highlighted the advantages of defence, although he carefully refrained from subscribing fully to Clausewitz's formula that defence was inherently, and thus universally, stronger than attack.[136] Picking up one of Clausewitz explanations for the strength of the defence, he pointed out, for instance, that strategic defence made it possible for Britain to endure a war even in the extreme eventuality of her losing command of the sea. Losing command did not yet imply that command had passed to the enemy. In fact, disputed command, when none of the belligerents is in control of the sea, is the more common condition in naval warfare. When command is disputed—as happened, for example, during the American War of Independence—enduring is sufficient for survival.[137] Taking another instance, Corbett picked up Moltke's proposition that under existing conditions of modern firearms, the strategic offensive combined with tactical defence was the most effective form of war. Britain could, for example, utilize

[131] Corbett, 19–27.
[132] Ibid. 52–9.
[134] Ibid. 58.
[136] Ibid. 72–3.

[133] Ibid. 60–71.
[135] Ibid. 41, 51.
[137] Ibid. 91–2.

her superior sea-power to seize an isolated territorial object, which she could then defend easily against enemy counter-offensives.[138]

The implication was obvious:

it is a direct negation of the current doctrine that in war there can be but one legitimate object, the overthrow of the enemy's means of resistance, and that the primary objective must always be his armed forces. It raises in fact the whole question as to whether it is not sometimes legitimate and even correct to aim directly at the ulterior object of the war.[139]

Corbett was openly contradicting von der Goltz and Prince Kraft von Hohenlohe,[140] and silently turning Mahan on his head.

Corbett was diplomatic enough to emphasize that he did not advocate a return to the old and discredited war of manœuvre, and did not depreciate the importance of fighting and of the major battle in war.[141] At the same time, however, he was subtly warning his readers of the fallacy 'that war consists entirely of battles between armies and fleets'. This fallacy, he maintained, 'ignores the fundamental fact that battles are only the means of enabling you to do that which really brings wars to an end—that is to exert pressure on the citizens and their collective life'.[142] If battle were only a means to an end, he argued, other means might sometimes prove no less effective. Furthermore, while on land one could normally force the enemy's army to fight, at sea the enemy's fleet often hid in port, and other means for defeating it became indispensable.[143]

Finally, Corbett called into question concentration of force, the fundamental precept which completed the nineteenth-century conception of war. Concentration, he wrote, had become 'a kind of shibboleth ... Critics have come to lose sight of the old war experience, that without division no strategical combinations are possible.'[144] In the past, he argued, 'the riper and fresher our experience and the surer our grip of war, the looser were our combinations ... victories have not only to be won, but worked for. They must be worked for by bold strategic combinations, which as a rule entail at least apparent dispersal.'[145] When one's forces are kept flexibly dispersed, the enemy is left in the dark

---

[138] Ibid. 72–4.   [139] Ibid. 74.
[140] Ibid. 74–5.   [141] Ibid. 76, 86.
[142] Ibid. 97.   [143] Ibid. 155–6.
[144] Ibid. 134.   [145] Ibid.

regarding one's intentions and strength and is more easily lured into destruction.[146] The weaker French also often dispersed for sporadic action. For Corbett, this was no sign of 'constitutional ineptitude', as it had usually been regarded, but a shrewd strategy which embarrassed the stronger British navy, forced it to disperse, and gave the French the hope of winning at least minor successes.[147]

All this was revolutionary, even when expressed in Corbett's low-key manner. Thus, although *Some Principles of Maritime Strategy* was favourably accepted on both sides of the Atlantic, there was no lack of critics.[148] The anonymous 'Captain R.N.' called *Some Principles* 'the crowning mistake of Mr Corbett's career':

For some years Mr Corbett in the process of lecturing in the R.N. War College, permitted himself the indulgence of offering his audience his own views on the correctness or otherwise of the strategy adopted by naval officers in the past. His audience had usually treated his amateur excursions into the subject goodnaturedly; nevertheless his presumption has been resented, and he has apparently been deaf to the polite hints thrown out to him.[149]

More scholarly criticism came from one of Britain's leading military commentators and foremost authority on Napoleonic and Prussian strategy, the first Chichele Professor of Military History at Oxford, Spenser Wilkinson. His most unsympathetic reviews were not merely academic. His friends—Admirals Beresford, Custance, and Bridge—formed the relentless opposition to Fisher's innovations and direction of the navy. However, although that opposition was not devoid of personal and political motives, the battle was largely drawn along principled lines. Staunchly Mahanite as it was, the group attacked Fisher and his circle on almost predictable grounds in regard to battleship construction, tactics, and strategy: they fiercely objected to the *Dreadnought*; they rejected long-range gunnery, which would undermine Nelsonian tactical boldness; they regarded the offensive alone as the proper strategy, leading to decisive results, in the best British tradition. The debate which developed between Fisher's supporters and opponents was later known as the argument

---

[146] Corbett, 152.   [147] Ibid. 138.
[148] See *Corbett Papers*, Box 5 for the huge number of reactions; also Grove, Introduction, *Principles of Maritime Strategy*, pp. xxxvi–xxxix.
[149] Captain R.N., *Naval and Military Record* (1911), 821, in the *Corbett Papers*, Box 5; also Grove, Introduction, *Principles of Maritime Strategy*, pp. xxxix–xl.

between the 'historical' and the 'technological' schools. While the former appealed to the immutable lessons of history, the latter held that new technological developments and innovations had altered those lessons considerably.[150]

In three different critiques, Wilkinson denounced the harmful effect of Corbett's work. If his book were read by officers, he warned, it

must have a disastrous effect upon the Navy, for it cannot but leave their minds in doubt upon every one of the principles which the strategists of four great navies of the modern world are agreed in regarding as fundamental . . . He seems to me to assume that the teaching of the strategists . . . I have just mentioned is to be regarded as doubtful.

Taking issue with Corbett's main thesis, Wilkinson argued that 'naval warfare . . . tends to be more decisive than land warfare and approximates more to the absolute form towards which all warfare is drawn as soon as it becomes national'. He promised his readers that the German fleet was designed for a decisive battle; 'it means to take the greatest risks for the highest stakes'.[151]

However, when war came, the German High Seas Fleet did not go out to look for the expected major battle with the superior British Grand Fleet. A stalemate prevailed in the North Sea. As was happening with Delbrück's opinions, Corbett's peacetime historical teaching, which in his case had always carried a moral for the present, was suddenly becoming highly relevant. Admittedly, before the war, he had judged—like most experts—that in the age of steam and the wireless both commerce-destroying and the convoy system were becoming less effective than ever.[152] He had failed to appreciate the impact the submarine would have in this regard.[153] At the same time, however, many of the other things he had said now came true. The British navy avoided the hazardous attack on the German fleet in its home waters. But, by blockading Germany and

---

[150] A thorough study of the controversy can be found in Semmel, *Liberalism and Naval Strategy*, 134–51. For Fisher's endorsements of Mahan's doctrines so long as they were not enlisted to block (his) reform ('history is a record of exploded ideas'), see e.g. Ruddock F. Mackay, *Fisher of Kilverstone* (Oxford, 1973), 263–6.

[151] Spenser Wilkinson, 'Stragegy at Sea', *Morning Post*, 19 Feb. 1912; also 3 Aug. 1909, and *The Star, Johannesburg*, 9 Mar. 1912: *Corbett Papers*, Box 5; Grove, Introduction, *Principles of Maritime Strategy*, pp. xxxviii–xxxix.

[152] Corbett, *Principles of Maritime Strategy*, 266–71, 279.

[153] Ibid. 231–2.

completely cutting off her maritime communications, it was still fulfilling its war function. He was also right in arguing that the effects of such a blockade on a major European power would take a very long time to make themselves felt, and that this would lead to a protracted war of attrition. Only a military effort on the Continent could deliver something in the form of a decisive result.

Be that as it may, in the aftermath of Jutland, both official circles and the public at large, which had been led to expect that the British navy would swiftly dominate the North Sea in Nelsonian fashion, could only regard the British naval performance since the beginning of the war as bitterly disappointing. In reply to this criticism, in an article he wrote after Jutland, Winston Churchill drew arguments from Corbett to defend the navy and the naval policy which Fisher and himself had adopted at the beginning of the war. He reassured his readers that, by dominating German communications, the navy possessed all the advantages it could have gained from a victorious battle. By holding to its strong position, it compelled the Germans to come out and fight at a disadvantage, if they wished to break the British strategic stranglehold. Churchill did not name Corbett, who during the war was strategic adviser and official historian at the Admiralty, but others recognized the source of the doctrine he espoused. Responding to Churchill's article in a letter to *The Times*, the intellectual admiral, Reginald Custance (also without naming Corbett) pointed to the disastrous doctrine which he alleged had grown to dominate the navy in the previous ten years, as the direct cause of the dispirited British strategy.[154] In another letter to *The Times* a day later, and then in the House of Lords, the veteran imperial administrator and naval activist George Clarke, Lord Sydenham of Combe, followed up Custance. With disbelief, he quoted from Churchill's article and from the 'Green Pamphlet'.

The first duty of the navy [he said] is to capture or destroy the enemy's armed ships whenever and wherever they are accessible. Clearly in these days submarines and mines have imposed some new restrictions upon naval action, but that great principle of naval war is eternal. It applies just as much to the Battle of Salamis as to the Battle of Jutland.[155]

The controversy over British naval performance dragged on and

---

[154] Custance, Letter to *The Times*, 9 Oct. 1916, *Corbett Papers*, Box 7.
[155] 15 Nov. 1916, *Parliamentary Debates, Lords* (1916), 510–11. Also see correspondence with Corbett, 30 Nov. and 1 Dec. 1916, *Corbett Papers*, Box 7.

did not terminate with the end of the war. Corbett's official history of the war at sea had difficulties in being approved by the Admiralty. Particularly problematic was the third volume, covering Jutland, which was completed at the height of the Beatty–Jellicoe controversy. The Admiralty Board approved publication but inserted the following statement by way of preface: 'Their lordships find that some of the principles advocated in this book, especially the tendency to minimize the importance of seeking battle and forcing it to a conclusion, are directly in conflict with their views.'[156] Corbett was spared the anguish of witnessing those reservations in print. He died in September 1922, some two weeks after having submitted his manuscript.

Churchill's *World Crisis* (1923–31) rekindled the controversy. The book prompted criticism by some of Britain's leading military and naval authorities.[157] In 1931 Lord Sydenham, who, after the war, had grown increasingly critical and pessimistic regarding Britain's performance and future, again blamed Corbett's 'sea heresies' for Britain's having failed to gain any spectacular naval success during the war. Corbett was in good company; the eighty-three-year-old Sydenham compared his theories to those of Einstein, which, as he put it, also 'fog the vision'. He went on to confess that he had always been repelled by Clausewitz and 'the psycho-analysis to which he subjected himself' [*sic*!].[158] As occurred in respect of the Delbrück controversy in Germany, the argument faded away only when the Second World War finally put an end to a previous tradition of supremacy—a British one at sea and a German one on land. At almost the same time, the advent of nuclear weapons closed the curtain on the nineteenth-century Napoleonic-Nelsonian conception of unlimited war.

[156] Quoted in Grove, Introduction, *Principles of Maritime Strategy*, p. xliv.

[157] Lord Sydenham of Combe, Admiral Sir R. Bacon, General Sir W. D. Bird and Sir Charles Oman, *The World Crisis by Winston Churchill: A Criticism* (London, 1927).

[158] Lord Sydenham, 'Sea Heresies', *The Naval Review* (May 1931), 233.

5

Marxism, Clausewitz, and Military Theory 1848 to the Nuclear Age

THE affinity between Marxist thinking on war and military theory and Clausewitz's teachings is well known. Marx and Engels, busy as they were with their manifold occupations, reportedly exchanged brief admiring comments about his work. Engels in particular, the military expert of the two, was allegedly considerably influenced by Clausewitz's writings, both during the course of his military self-education and after. Lenin studied *On War* carefully and approvingly, used it repeatedly in his political pamphlets, and recommended it to party functionaries. Both Trotsky and Stalin referred to Clausewitz's work, and a host of Soviet writers on strategy followed them in this course in the nuclear age. When the Cold War began, observers in the United States did not fail to point out this Marxist 'Clausewitz connection'. Simultaneously, interest was awakened in Germany, and for reasons which in some respects did not differ much between East and West; while Clausewitz was given a new image in post-war Germany and dissociated from the Prussian and German militarist tradition, his Marxist connection helped to demonstrate the wider scope of his influence and highlighted his universal appeal. Between all these sources, over the last few decades, the relevant material from the writings of the fathers of Marxism has been diligently collected, repeatedly cited, and endlessly rehashed.

Rather than recount a familiar story, this chapter aims to do two things. First, it seeks to correct some misconceptions, especially concerning the relationship of Engels and Marx to Clausewitz. It will be argued that neither had any special interest in, or appreciation of, Clausewitz's work, and that Engels was not influenced by it to any considerable extent. Commentators have been prejudiced in their treatment of the evidence by their knowledge of Clausewitz's later successes with Marxists, especially with Lenin,[1] and by his present-day popularity. The second, more general objective of this chapter, seemingly in conflict with the previous one, is to get to the roots of the Marxist affinity with Clausewitz's work. Curiously, this primary question has, on the whole, escaped notice. The similarity between the Marxist outlook and some of Clausewitz's ideas—notably his view of war as the continuation of policy—has been widely and appropriately cited as the reason for Clausewitz's popularity with the Marxists. But this similarity itself has never been regarded as much more than an interesting coincidence. After all, what could be the point of connection between the Prussian general and the international revolutionaries?

As this chapter suggests, Clausewitz's ideas and Marxist thinking were linked by threads which ran deep into a common intellectual matrix. Both Clausewitz's thinking and Marxism, as a radical development of left-wing Hegelianism, had their roots in the great achievements of German thought in the late eighteenth and early nineteenth centuries. Prominent within that stimulating cultural environment were a pronounced historicist outlook and a powerful urge—which reached its pinnacle in the German idealist philosophy—to embrace and comprehend the nature of reality in its totality. To be sure, these notions were developed in many diverse and even conflicting directions by different currents of thought. This explains, with remarkable consistency, both the Marxists' affinity to Clausewitz's ideas and the points of criticism which qualified their basic agreement.

Engels's distinguished career as a military writer, while being one of his least familiar sides, has none the less attracted considerable scholarly attention.[2] He took up military studies very seriously in

---

[1] This prejudice goes at least as far back as the various editions, in different languages, of *Selected Correspondence, Karl Marx and Friedrich Engels* (London, 1934). A note by the editors of the Marx-Engels-Lenin Institute in Moscow (p. 100 of the English edition) already combined a brief quotation from Engels with Lenin's later endorsement of Clausewitz.

[2] See esp. Gerhard Zirke, *Der General: Friedrich Engels, der erste Militärtheoretiker der Arbeiterklassen* (Leipzig, 1957); Jehuda L. Wallach, *Die Kriegslehre von Friedrich Engels* (Frankfurt, a. M., 1968); Martin Berger, *Engels, Armies, and Revolution: The Revolutionary Tactics of Classical Marxism* (Hamden, Conn., 1977).

1851, with a view to acquiring the foundations of the discipline which, as the events of 1848–9 had demonstrated, was essential to the success of any future revolutionary action. Within a short period during which he engaged in intensive reading, he turned himself into an expert and soon became one of the most acute military observers in Europe. It has long been noted that his military writings constituted by far the greatest part of his literary output. No wonder he was nicknamed 'The General' by his friends. Throughout the 1850s, on Marx's behalf and under Marx's name, he wrote numerous articles on military affairs for the *New York Daily Tribune*, of which Marx was the London correspondent. For *The New American Cyclopaedia* (1858), published by the *Tribune*, Marx himself wrote on the marshals of the Napoleonic wars, while Engels added substantial pieces on more technical military matters.[3] In the early 1860s, again on Marx's behalf, Engels wrote on the military aspects of the American Civil War for the Viennese journal *Die Presse*.[4] To the volunteers' bulletin, the *Volunteer Journal of Lancashire and Cheshire*, he contributed ten articles on various subjects. For obvious reasons, he took interest in that militia, created after the invasion-scare of 1859. Finally, for the *Manchester Guardian* and the *Pall-Mall Gazette* respectively, he reviewed both the Austro-Prussian War of 1866 and the Franco-Prussian War 1870–1.[5]

In tracing Engels's career as a military writer, many commentators have assigned to Clausewitz a place of honour. They have based that impression primarily on two casual but much-quoted remarks which appeared in the Marx–Engels correspondence of January 1858 and which have been widely interpreted as a clear indication that Marx and Engels had a special attitude to Clausewitz's work. Those casual remarks, however, have been singled out from the fairly extensive evidence we possess regarding Engels's attitude to

---

[3] All newspaper and *Cyclopaedia* articles can be found in the complete English edition: Karl Marx and Friedrich Engels, *Collected Works* (London, 1975–), xii–xviii. Engels's military writings appeared in Russian and German, the latter version being entitled, *Ausgewählte militärische Schriften* (2 vols.; Berlin, 1958, 1964).

[4] Marx and Engels, *Works*, xviii–xix; id., *On America and the Civil War* (New York, 1972).

[5] Marx and Engels, *Works*, xviii; xx. 164–82; xxii. 9–258; *Engels As Military Critic: Articles by Friedrich Engels, Reprinted from the Volunteer Journal and the Manchester Guardian of the 1860s*, ed. Chaloner and W. O. Henderson (Manchester, 1959).

contemporary military writers, thus creating a huge distortion by omission. Furthermore, these remarks have been treated superficially and have often been magnified by prejudiced translation.

The course of Engels's military education and much other relevant material are well documented in his vast correspondence. For help in compiling a comprehensive reading-list, he approached Joseph Weydemeyer, a former Prussian officer turned revolutionary and a close friend and disciple of Marx and Engels. Explaining at some length his motivation for taking up military studies, he systematically detailed the scope of his interest, namely achieving a good overall technical command of the basics of the profession of war. He told Weydemeyer that he already possessed old Montecuccoli's works and that he had found Napier's history of the Peninsular War 'by far the best work of military history I have seen up till now'. He inquired about German stuff, naming Willisen and Clausewitz, and asked Weydemeyer what he thought about them. Finally, he inquired about Jomini. None of these authorities had he yet read. He also asked for good specialized maps for the study of modern campaigns from 1792 up to 1849.[6] After receiving Weydemeyer's reply, he added some follow-up questions and reported that he had already acquired Decker (which Marx mislaid).[7]

By April 1853 Engels had informed Weydemeyer about the substantial progress he had made in his military studies, both technical and historical. 'Prussian military literature is positively the worst there is,' he complained; after 1822, he says, it is characterized by 'repulsively pretentious pedantry ... a bogus omniscience which is the very devil'.[8] Admittedly, in this criticism Engels probably had mainly Willisen and other smaller luminaries in mind. In this, and in other, even earlier, letters to Marx, he repeatedly expressed his amusement at, and contempt for, Willisen's proverbial pedantry and mock military philosophy.[9] It appears that

---

[6] Engels to Weydemeyer, 19 June 1851, *Works*, xxxviii. 370–2.

[7] Engels to Weydemeyer, 7 Aug. 1851, ibid. 405–6.

[8] Engels to Weydemeyer, 12 Apr. 1853, ibid., xxxix. 305. Presumably, in citing the date 1822, Engels was referring to C. Decker's book, *Der kleine Krieg* (Berlin, 1822), which he had mentioned in his previous letter and which had possibly been recommended to him by Weydemeyer.

[9] Ibid. 310; Engels to Marx, 7 May 1852, ibid. 103–4: 'Willisen's book should really be called the *Philosophy* of great wars. This in itself would indicate that it contains more philosophizing than military science, that the most self-evident things

he had then not yet read Clausewitz's *On War*. However, proceeding to describe his studies of the Napoleonic campaigns, Engels added the following assessments (which are somehow never cited) of the various histories of these campaigns: '*au bout du compte* [in the final analysis] Jomini gives the best account of them; despite many fine things, I can't really bring myself to like that natural genius, Clausewitz.'[10] Jomini is by far the most cited military authority in Engels's correspondence, while Rüstow, Jomini's disciple, takes second place. But here too no mention of this inconvenient fact is to be found in the extensive literature which informs us about Engels's admiration for Clausewitz.

Even in their treatment of the famous Marx–Engels exchange of letters upon which everything rests, commentators have silently passed over the opening scene. The first letter (never cited) came from Marx. Going over their many pressing obligations for the *Tribune* and *Cyclopaedia*, he wrote to Engels: 'I sent the chaps about 8 sheets under the heading "Blücher", the same being sub-titled "The Silesian Army in the Campaigns etc.". As I had to spend so much time reading Clausewitz, Müffling, etc., some degree of compensation was called for.'[11] Engels's much-quoted comments came in reply to this, at the end of the business letter to Marx in which he discusses his progress and problems with the *Cyclopaedia* articles:

I am reading, *inter alia*, Clausewitz's *Vom Krieg*. An odd way of philosophising, but *per se* very good. On the question as to whether one should speak of the art of the science of war, he says that, more than anything else, war resembles commerce. Combat is to war what cash payment is to commerce; however seldom it need happen in reality,

are constructed a priori with the most profound and exhaustive thoroughness and that, sandwiched between these, are the most methodical discourses on simplicity and multiplicity and such like opposites. What can one say about military science which begins with the concept of art *en général*, then goes on to demonstrate that the art of cookery is also an art, expatiates on the relationship of art to science and finally subsumes all the rules, relationships, potentialities, etc., etc., of the art of war under the one absolute axiom: the stronger always overcomes the weaker.' Also see Engels to Marx, 9 May 1854, ibid. 451–2.

[10] Engels to Weydemeyer, 12 Apr. 1853, *Works*, xxxix. 305; the German original is: 'Jomini ist *au bout du compte* doch der beste Darsteller davon, das Naturgenie Clausewitz will mir trotz mancher hübschen Sachen nicht recht zusagen.'; *Marx-Engels Gesamtausgabe* (Berlin, 1975–), xxviii. 577.

[11] Marx to Engels, 31 Oct. 1857, *Works*, xl. 198; the German is '*Schadenersatz*'—compensation, indemnification.

everything is directed towards it and ultimately it is bound to occur and prove decisive.[12]

Obviously, while complimenting Clausewitz's book and indicating that he did not grasp the meaning and purpose of his obscure intellectual acrobatics any more than other readers of *On War*, both before and after, Engels picked for his friend a piece of picantry in a field which could be of interest to Marx. Marx enjoyed the cleverness of the idea. 'I hunted through Clausewitz, more or less, when doing Blücher,' he replied, 'The fellow possesses a common sense bordering on wit [*Witz*]'.[13]

Commentators who have seized upon these lines are in general guilty of two vices. The German '*Witz*' carries various meanings and some ambivalence, almost equally conveyed by the English 'wit'. While some commentators offered this most natural English equivalent, others, concerned that Marx's comment might appear as having been made in something less than absolute seriousness, chose to leave the reader no option. The recent complete edition of the Marx–Engels works has rendered '*Witz*' as 'ingenious'; another authority has 'brilliance'—both lexically possible but prejudiced interpretations.[14] Moreover, commentators have universally assumed that Marx's compliment was made in reference to Clausewitz's work in general, which he supposedly 'hunted through' when writing 'Blücher'. In fact, his comment was merely a direct response to the clever idea which Engels had cited to him from Clausewitz's *On War*. Marx himself never read *On War*. For his article on Blücher, he consulted only Clausewitz's relevant histories of the campaigns of 1812–15.[15] For all their value, there was surely nothing in those histories that was capable of prompting

[12] Engels to Marx, 7 Jan. 1858, ibid. 241–2.

[13] Marx to Engels, 11 Jan. 1858, ibid., xl. 247; where deviating from the translation of the standard English edition, I have inserted the German original in brackets; see next paragraph and note.

[14] 'Ingenious', ibid.; 'brilliance' in Bernard Semmel (ed.), *Marxism and the Science of War*, (Oxford, 1981), 66. By contrast, while confusing the order of the Marx-Engels letter exchange so that Engels's 'very good' comes more convincingly as a reply to Marx's 'common sense', Hahlweg uses the more natural translation ['wittiness']: 'Clausewitz, Lenin, and Communist Military Attitudes Today', *Journal of the Royal United Services Institute*, 105 (1960), 221; 'wit' is used by Michael E. Howard, 'The Influence of Clausewitz', in Clausewitz, *On War* (2nd. edn., Princeton, NJ, 1984), 44.

[15] See the manuscript evidence: Marx and Engels, *Works*, xl. 198, 247; Hahlweg, 'Sozialismus und Militärwissenschaft bei Friedrich Engels', in H. Pelger (ed.), *Friedrich Engels 1820–1970* (Hanover, 1971), 66.

his remark that Clausewitz was a fellow who possessed 'a common sense bordering on wit'. How much Marx really enjoyed them was already apparent to us from his letter of 31 October 1857.

But enough of this textual criticism of the Marxist holy scriptures and back to the wider picture. Commentators have long noted the rather surprising fact that most of Engels's military works were 'strictly professional' in character and virtually devoid of Marxist interpretations.[16] The course of his military education was no different. He was set upon acquiring the foundations of a profession, and he studied these systematically, along the most conventional lines, as if preparing himself for the 'ensign and lieutenant examination'.[17] Accordingly, he engaged in extensive reading of the military authorities that were accepted in his time. Among these, Clausewitz certainly held a place of honour, but outside the mainstream, while Jomini and his disciples reigned supreme. As mentioned previously, the references in Engels's writings indicate that his own hierarchy of authorities was no different.

Engels's review of the Austro-Prussian War of 1866 is a classical case in point. His intelligent articles in the *Manchester Guardian* are deservedly regarded with esteem. Yet the fact remains that he misjudged the situation in exactly the same manner as the rest of the military observers: he backed the wrong horse completely, believing in the superiority of the Austrians; he regarded the Prussian reserves as poorly motivated and inexperienced; finally, during mobilization, and especially when hostilities began, he was shocked and perplexed by the Prussian violation of the most sacred Napoleonic–Jominian principle:

Suppose a young Prussian ensign or cornet, under examination for a lieutenancy, to be asked what would be the safest plan for a Prussian army to invade Bohemia? Suppose our young officer were to answer your best way will be to divide your troops into two almost equal bodies, to send one around by the east of the Riesengebirge, the other by the west, and effect their junction in Gitschin. What would the examining officer say to this? He would inform the young gentleman that this plan sinned against the two very first laws of strategy: Firstly, never to divide your troops so that

---

[16] W. B. Gallie, *Philosophers of Peace and War, Kant, Clausewitz, Marx, Engels and Tolstoy* (Cambridge, 1978), 73; Semmel, *Marxism and the Science of War*, 8, 45–6 *et passim*; also see Trotsky, *Military Writings* (New York, 1969), 135.

[17] Engels to Weydemeyer, 7 Aug. 1851, *Works*, xxxviii. 405.

they cannot support each other, but to keep them well together; and, secondly, in case of an advance on different roads, to effect the junction at the point which is not within reach of the enemy; that, therefore, the plan prepared was the very worst of all . . . Yet this is the very plan which the wise and learned staff of the Prussian army have adopted. It is almost incredible; but it is so.[18]

Three days later, like all other experts educated on the legacy of Napoleon and Jomini, he was forced to eat his words; 'The campaign which the Prussians opened with a signal strategy blunder', he wrote, 'has been since carried on by them with such a terrible tactical energy that it was brought to a victorious close in exactly eight days.'[19]

Later in his life, in the course of his comprehensive polemic *Anti-Dühring* (1876–8), Engels devoted a few pages to outlining a Marxist view of the historical nature of war. He set out to show that war changed and assumed a new character with every change in material and, by implication, economic conditions:

At the beginning of the fourteenth century, gunpowder came from the Arabs to Western Europe, and . . . completely revolutionized methods of warfare. . . . From the outset . . . firearms were the weapons of the towns and of the rising monarchy, drawing its support from the towns . . . With the armour-clad cavalry of the feudal lords, the feudal lords' supremacy was also broken; with the development of the bourgeoisie, infantry and guns became more and more the decisive types of weapons. . . . It was not until the early part of the eighteenth century that the flint-lock musket with a bayonet finally displaced the pike in the equipment of the infantry. The foot soldiers of that period were the mercenaries of princes; they consisted of the most demoralized elements of society . . . and only held together by the whip . . . The only type of fighting in which these soldiers could apply the new weapons was the tactics of the line. . . . Like the American, the French Revolution could oppose to the trained mercenary armies of the coalition only poorly trained but great masses of soldiers, the levy of the whole nation. . . . a form had to be invented for use by large bodies of troops, and this form was found in the *column*. . . . The revolutionary system of arming the whole people was soon restricted to compulsory

---

[18] 3 July 1866, *Works*, xx. 176–7; for a similar criticism before the beginning of operations see 20 June 1866, ibid. 165–6; in *Engels as Military Critic*, the page numbers are 133–4, 123 respectively. Engels had already referred to Jomini's 'interior lines' in 1859 in analysing the strategic situation in north Italy; *Works*, xvi. 226.

[19] 6 July 1866, *Works*, 179; *Engels as Military Critic*, 136–7.

conscription . . . and in this form it was adopted by most of the large states on the continent. [With the progress of this process in the future,] the armies of princes become transformed into armies of the people.[20]

Reading *On War*, one can find remarkably similar passages, which may raise questions regarding Engels's possible sources of inspiration. The character of war, writes Clausewitz, depends on

The nature of states and societies as they are determined by their times and prevailing conditions. . . . The semi-barbarous Tartars, the republics of antiquity, the feudal lords and trading cities of the Middle Ages, eighteenth century kings and the rulers and peoples of the nineteenth century—all conducted war in their own peculiar way, using different methods and pursuing different aims.[21]

However, Engels's outline, as well as his similar review of naval developments in *Anti-Dühring*, were no more influenced by Clausewitz than had been the famous historical outline in *The Communist Manifesto* (1848). In fact, in the military passages of *Anti-Dühring*, Engels merely developed ideas which he had already articulated in his brilliant but less widely known manuscript, 'Conditions and Prospects of a War of the Holy Alliance against France in 1852' (April 1851).[22] This had been written long before he read even one line from Clausewitz—indeed even before he undertook his extensive course of reading in military literature. In the same way, it appears that Engels's historical analysis was equally uninfluenced to any significant extent by Rüstow, a fellow radical whose works Engels consulted much more than Clausewitz's. Nor, for that matter, did Engels's own work influence Delbrück's great historical enterprise, begun shortly after the publication of

[20] Engels, *Herr Eugen Dühring's Revolution in Science* (London, n.d.), 190–4.
[21] Clausewitz, *On War*, viii. 6B, 586; this is followed by an elaborate historical survey, 586–93.
[22] 'Conditions and Prospects', in Marx and Engels, *Works*, x. 556. In this work Engels also anticipated the further growth and increasing mobility of the armies of the future, beyond their bourgeois-Napoleonic stage of development. These would be made possible, he said, by growing productivity, by the improved communications offered by the railroad and the electric telegraph, and by the higher level of education enjoyed by both the officer corps and the rank and file. He wrongly believed, however, as Moltke's armies demonstrated, that all these new conditions would be able to develop only within the framework of a socialist society: ibid., 550–6. Semmel, in his useful anthology, *Marxism and the Science of War*, 8–12, 45–6, *et passim*, was evidently unaware of this early work when he argued that Engels had never offered a Marxist interpretation of military affairs before *Anti-Dühring*.

Anti-Dühring and stimulated in part by Rüstow's work. All the above-mentioned people thus expressed similar ideas in rather similar language, not because of any line of influence running between them, but primarily because of the all-pervasive effect of German historicism which stimulated them all. War, like all phenomena, had little in the way of a permanent nature. Like all phenomena, it was in a process of continuous change, affected by, and interacting with, other fields of human life. This fundamental historicist notion was the common source of Clausewitz's philosophy of war, Hegel's dialectic, together with its materialist and socialist descendants, and the great stream of nineteenth-century German historical scholarship.[23]

For Engels himself, these fundamental affinities and similarities were of little importance. The whole of German culture was permeated with various applications of the historicist idea, most of which were designated as ideological enemies of Marxism.[24] In Germany and Europe in the middle of the nineteenth century, the number of quasi-Hegelian systems alone, against which Marx and Engels directed some of their most pointed polemics, amounted to dozens at least. Engels had even less patience for military 'philosophizing', as his attitude towards Willisen and, indeed, the distinction he made in his compliment for Clausewitz, demonstrate. For Marx and Engels, philosophizing was *the* German disease. For later Marxists, however things were not quite the same. For example, by the time Lenin—never a military expert himself—was prompted by the outbreak of the First World War to study Clausewitz's *On War*, Clausewitz had already become the undisputed master of military theory in all the most important military states. At the same time, for Lenin and the public he addressed, instances of German historicism were not as commonplace as they had been for Marx and Engels two and three generations earlier. Given also Lenin's particular political preoccupations during the war years, his special interest in Clausewitz was natural. It was now left for Lenin and other leading Marxists to bring out the various themes which connected Clausewitz's theory of war and the Marxist outlook.

Lenin's contribution has been more than adequately documented.

---

[23] For the historicist idea and Clausewitz's thought and development see Gat, *The Origins of Military Thought from the Enlightenment to Clausewitz* (Oxford, 1989), 147–9, 186–9 *et passim*.
[24] For an overview see above, Ch. 2, p. 100.

Principally, it consisted in popularizing Clausewitz's formula regarding the relationship between politics and war and in giving Clausewitz the official stamp of Marxist legitimacy. The facts need not be repeated at length. During late 1914 or early 1915, while in exile in Switzerland, Lenin borrowed the first edition of Clausewitz's *On War* from the public library in Berne.[25] He was evidently much impressed by the book. As was his habit, he copied long extracts from the German text into a special notebook, underlining words, passages, and ideas of particular importance and adding numerous annotations in Russian. Apart from a few passing comments on other matters, he concentrated overwhelmingly on two themes. One was the dialectic of defence and attack; the other—far more extensive, and encompassing about two-thirds of his notebook— was the function of war as a political instrument, its overall dependence on political and social conditions, and, consequently, its continuous transformation through history. His many favourable comments on Clausewitz's formulas regarding the relationship between politics and war are much quoted. But he also seized with enthusiasm on all the passages in which Clausewitz demonstrated the historical nature of war (*On War*, i, 1, 27; vii. 30; viii. 3 and 6B). 'To each epoch—its own wars', he wrote in the margins.[26]

Lenin read Clausewitz for a purpose and put him to immediate use. With the outbreak of the First World War and the collapse of socialist solidarity, he directed all his efforts to denouncing the leaders of the Second International who, in the cause of national self-defence, had forsaken their previous commitment against war. In his pamphlets he argued that the war was nothing but a capitalist war, waged by the capitalist states and ruling classes for the advancement of their interests, and he repeatedly used Clausewitz's famous dictum as a sharp weapon. He instructed his readers that, rather than representing a break from earlier interests and political

[25] The assumption made by some historians that Lenin must have become acquainted with Clausewitz through Engels's papers, is not supported by evidence but merely deduced from the false premiss regarding Engels and Clausewitz. In his many references to Clausewitz, Lenin himself consistently connected the former's teaching with Marx and Engels only indirectly.

[26] Lenin's notebook (item no. 18674 in the archive of the Lenin Institute in Moscow) was published in Lenin's collected works: *Leninskii Sbornik* (Moscow, 1930), xii. 387–452. I have used the French translation: *Les Fondements théoriques de la guerre et de la paix en U.R.S.S.—suivi du Cahier de Lénine sur Clausewitz*, ed. B. C. Friedl (Paris, 1945), 47–78; a German edition has also been issued: *Clausewitz Werk 'Vom Kriege', Auszüge und Randglossen* (Berlin, 1957).

relations, 'War is simply the continuation of politics by other [i.e. violent] means'.[27] He again found citations from Clausewitz useful in explaining the Bolshevik position against the continuation of the war in 1917 and in advocating a strategy of deep withdrawal into the interiors of Russia in early 1918.[28] Later, he even recommended to party functionaries that they study Clausewitz.[29]

Although Lenin's appreciation of Clausewitz's work was undoubtedly genuine, the prominent supporting role he assigned to Clausewitz in his own political campaign obviously helped determine the eminently respectful way he presented Clausewitz and his ideas to his readers. Bearing this in mind, Lenin's silent amendments and extensions of Clausewitz's theses, as well as other subtle points, are as important to an understanding of the Marxist attitude to Clausewitz as were his oft-quoted praises for the 'famous', 'one of the greatest' and 'profoundest' writers 'on the history and philosophy of war'. From a Marxist point of view, Lenin's description of Clausewitz as a writer 'whose thinking was stimulated by Hegel', was at once a mark of distinction and a point of reservation.[30] On the one hand, it legitimized Clausewitz by establishing his kinship with Marxism, whose roots in Hegelian philosophy were well known. Clausewitz's work and Marxism were thus presented as distant cousins. In this context, Lenin also noted instances where Clausewitz had used dialectic.[31] On the other hand, the fact that Marxism had developed in reaction against Hegelian 'Idealism' was equally well known. Of particular importance to our case was Marx's early *Critique of Hegel's Philosophy of Right* (1843), which overturned Hegel's famous work in political philosophy (1821).

Marx rejected Hegel's central idea that the state took an impartial position, above the struggle of the particular interests in society. He argued instead that, more accurately, the state reflected and represented in the political sphere the power and interests of

[27] Lenin, 'The Collapse of the Second International' (May–June 1915), *Collected Works* (London, 1960–1970), vol. xxi. 219–20; id. 'Socialism and War' (July–Aug. 1915), ibid. 304.
[28] Lenin, 'War and Revolution' (May 1917), ibid., xxiv. 399; id., ' "Left-Wing" Childishness and the Petty Bourgeois Mentality' (Feb. 1918), ibid. xxvii. 332.
[29] V. Sorin, in *Pravda*, no. 111 (1923); cited in *Leninskii Sbornik*, xii. 390.
[30] Lenin, 'Collapse of the Second International', *Works*, xxi. 219.
[31] For the sources and nature of Clausewitz's dialectic see my *Enlightenment to Clausewitz*, 230–6.

the social ruling classes. Indeed, this idea became one of the most important articles of Marxist theory. Now Clausewitz's view (and exaltation) of the state was clearly Hegelian, which Lenin did not fail to see.[32] In his marginal annotations to the relevant passages in *On War* (viii 6B), he heavily underlined Clausewitz's position, which he cited as follows: 'politics = the representation of all interests of society as a whole'. However, Lenin's aim at that moment was not to argue with Clausewitz but rather to use Clausewitz's more general idea in his argument with Kautsky, Plechanov, and other leaders of the Second International. He therefore corrected Clausewitz silently but consistently. In all his citations of Clausewitz's dictum, he went on to explain that war continued the politics of states *and* of classes within these states.[33] On other occasions, he repeatedly stated that war was always caused by, and waged in favour of, the interests of the ruling classes in society.[34]

Where Lenin opted for low-key amendments, modern Soviet military scholars, annoyed by Western portrayals of Lenin as Clausewitz's disciple, took a direct approach. In a series of official texts on military theory, they uniformly pointed out where Clausewitz's views and Marxism diverged. While accepting his famous formula regarding the relationship between politics and war, they added that Clausewitz was an idealist who interpreted politics idealistically as the 'intelligence of the personified state' and 'representative of the interests of all of society'; he understood politics primarily as foreign relations, disregarding their domestic and economic roots.[35] Western commentators who have tended to treat these statements with amusement, as nothing but examples of

---

[32] Gat, *Enlightenment to Clausewitz*, 236–50.

[33] See the references in notes 27 and 28 above.

[34] See e.g. Lenin, 'Speech on the War before the First All-Russia Congress of Soviets', *Works*, xxv. 29–42, esp. 32–3. Also see Hahlweg, 'Lenin und Clausewitz', *Archiv für Kulturgeschichte*, 36 (1954), 382–4; id. 'Clausewitz, Lenin and Communist Military Attitudes', 222.

[35] There are several, almost identical statements of this position in works composed since the late 1950s and translated into English in the early 1970s: T. R. Kondratkov's contribution to A. S. Milovidov (ed.), *The Philosophical Heritage of V. I. Lenin and the Problems of Contemporary War* (Moscow, 1972), 39–40; presumably by the same author in B. Byely, G. Fyodorov, V. Kulakov (eds.), *Marxism-Leninism on War and Army* (Moscow, 1972), 7–8; Ye. Savkin, *The Basic Principles of Operational Art* (Moscow, 1972), 23. See also Col.-Gen. M. V. Gareev, *M. V. Frunze, Military Theorist* (Suffolk, 1988), 86.

Soviet doctrinarism, harsh rhetoric, and xenophobia, have missed the point here. The motivation behind the Soviet military writers' criticism of Clausewitz is no more important than Lenin's motivation for adopting him. In both cases, when the motivation is recognized and accounted for, the substance of the Marxist 'Clausewitz connection' remains. Both the Marxists' agreement and their differences with Clausewitz's ideas are fundamental in nature and have their roots in a common intellectual seed-bed in early nineteenth-century Germany.

Indeed, although Lenin's famous citations from Clausewitz focused attention on the relationship between politics and war, the depth of the intellectual undercurrents connecting Marxism and Clausewitz's theory of war are revealed in an even more intriguing manner in other, less noted, areas. We have seen that Lenin discovered and adopted Clausewitz as a weapon that could be used in his polemic against the leaders of the Second International. In the same way, Trotsky, Lenin's second in the revolutionary hierarchy and a leading Marxist theoretician, resorted to Clausewitz when he too found himself immersed in a controversy, albeit of a totally different nature. During the early 1920s, the young Red generals who had distinguished themselves in the Civil War—notably Frunze, in collaboration with Gusev, Tukhachevsky, and others— called for the creation of a 'Unified Military Doctrine' for the Red Army, which would reflect and express its Marxist, revolutionary, and proletarian character. At the Tenth and Eleventh Congresses of the Communist Party (1921 and 1922) and in a battle of articles which raged in the interim between those events, Trotsky, the commissar of war, opposed their idea outright. The proposals of the revolutionary generals and the details of the controversy are none of our concern here.[36] But Trotsky's articulation of the Marxist position regarding the nature of military theory has no equal and is of great interest. He rejected the notion that there was a science of war, based on eternal principles, and ridiculed the idea that Marxism prescribed or was able to offer a set of doctrines for any particular art or trade, military or otherwise. These, he

---

[36] The controversy is adequately summarized in Walter D. Jacobs's inadequately entitled book, *Frunze: The Soviet Clausewitz, 1885–1925* (The Hague, 1969), 24–88. A briefer summary can be found in Condoleezza Rice, 'The Making of Soviet Strategy', P. Paret (ed.), *Makers of Modern Strategy from Machiavelli to the Nuclear Age* (Princeton, NJ, 1986), 653–8.

maintained, were practical occupations, whose major traits were ever determined by the historical conditions prevailing in any particular period.

'There is not and there never has been a military "science",' argued Trotsky, 'What is commonly called the theory of war or military science represents not a totality of scientific laws explaining objective events but an aggregate of practical usages, methods of adaptation and proficiencies.'[37] Reviewing the so-called principles of war advanced by writers like Foch, he ridiculed them as mere trivia, both contradictory and too general to be of any practical use.[38] The dubious nature of the attempt to erect military systems based on fundamental principles, he wrote,

> was very well understood by old Clausewitz who said: 'It is not impossible perhaps to write a systematic theory of war, both logical and wide in scope. But our theory, up to the present, is far from being either. Not to mention their unscientific spirit in the attempt to make their systems consistent and complete, many such works are stuffed with commonplaces and idle chatter of every kind . . .'[39]

According to Trotsky, to attempt to turn practical military usages into a science with the aid of Marxism, which is nothing more than 'a method that analyzes the development of historical man', is 'scholastic and hopeless'.[40]

> This is the same thing as trying to construct a theory of architecture or a text book on veterinary medicine with the aid of the Marxist method. A history of war, like a history of architecture, can be written from the Marxist viewpoint, because history is a science. But the so-called theory of war, i.e., practical [military] leadership is something else again.[41]

> A scientific history of warfare explains why in a given epoch, with a given social organization, men waged war in a certain way and not differently. . . . But it is quite self-evident that a scientific history of war

---

[37] Trotsky, 'Our Current Basic Military Tasks' (1 Apr. 1922), *Military Writings*, 73.

[38] Trotsky, 'Marxism and Military Knowledge' (8 May 1922), ibid. 122–30.

[39] Trotsky, 'Military Doctrine or Pseudo-Military Doctrinairism' (5 Dec. 1921), ibid. 43. The motto of this article is also a quotation from Clausewitz: 'In the practical arts the theoretical must not be allowed to grow too high, but must be kept close to experience, their proper soil'; ibid. 31.

[40] Trotsky, 'Marxism and Military Knowledge', 8 May 1922, ibid. 110; id. 'Basic Military Tasks', ibid. 75.

[41] Trotsky, 'Basic Military Tasks', ibid. 74.

aims by its very nature to explain that which undergoes change and the reasons for these changes but not to establish eternal truths.[42]

This was the crux of the matter. Because of the historical nature of war, argued Trotsky,

All military theoreticians cannot escape from the following contradiction: In order to demonstrate the eternal character of the principles of military art they have to throw out the entire 'ballast' of living historical experience and reduce them to pleonasms, commonplaces, Euclidian postulates, logical axioms, etc. On the other hand, in order to demonstrate the importance of these principles in military affairs, they have to stuff these principles with the content of a specific epoch, a specific stage in the development of an army or in the development of military affairs.[43]

In this respect military affairs are exactly the same as political economy, the Marxist science *par excellence*:

Marxist political economy . . . is not a science of how to manage a business . . . It is the science of how in a certain epoch certain economic relations (capitalist) took shape . . . Economic laws established by Marx . . . are not eternal principles as is represented by the bourgeois Manchester school, according to which private ownership of the means of production, buying and selling, competition and the rest are eternal principles of economy . . . Doctrinaires in military affairs behave in exactly the same way with regard to military truths. . . . The army of *Landsknechts*, the regular armies of the seventeenth and eighteenth centuries, the national army called to life by the Great French Revolution—all these correspond to definite epochs of economic and political development, and they all rest upon certain technology . . . But what does military philosophy do? As a rule it looks upon the methods and usages of a preceding epoch as eternal truths, at last

[42] Trotsky, 'Marxism and Military Knowledge', ibid. 119.

[43] Ibid. 129. This is amazingly similar to Clausewitz's comments in his private notes on strategy written in 1808 and 1809, with which Trotsky could not have been familiar (the notes were published for the first time only in 1937): 'All the authors that in modern times have sought to treat this part of theory [strategy] abstractly and philosophically . . . are either simply trivial, or they get rid of triviality through one sidedness.' 'When [abstraction] must omit the living matter in order to hold to the dead form, which is of course the easier to abstract, it would be in the end a dry skeleton of dry truths squeezed into a doctrine. It is really astonishing to find people who waste their time on such efforts, when one bears in mind that precisely that which is the most important in war and strategy, namely the great particularity, peculiarity, and local circumstances, escape these abstractions and scientific systems'. Clausewitz, 'Strategy', in *Verstreute kleine Schriften*, ed. W. Hahlweg (Osnabrück, 1979), 46, 60–1; also see Gat, *Enlightenment to Clausewitz*, 174–8, 187–98; the citations are from 192–3.

discovered by mankind and destined to retain their meaning for all times and all peoples.[44]

Clausewitz, Trotsky pointed out, warned very correctly against the tendency to generalize from limited experience.

He [Clausewitz] wrote: 'What is more natural than that the revolutionary war (of France) had its own way of doing things? and what theory could have included that peculiar method? The trouble is that such a manner, originating from a special case, easily outlives its day, because it continues *unchanged*, while circumstances imperceptibly undergo complete *change . . .*'[45]

To grasp fully what Trotsky had no difficulty in perceiving, a deeper understanding of the similarity which existed between Clausewitz's and the Marxist position is again called for. This similarity was not merely coincidental. It reflected the fundamental message of German historicism, which both Clausewitz and the Marxists expressed and developed in their respective fields. Emerging as it did in the late eighteenth and early nineteenth centuries, German historicism denied that the systems and principles propounded in the eighteenth century in every branch of knowledge by the men of the Enlightenment possessed anything like the universal validity claimed for them. At best, argued historicist thinkers, these so-called universal systems and principles were only abstractions, more or less successful, of the conditions prevailing in one particular period, most commonly that of the system-builders themselves. Hence the remarkable analogy, noted by Trotsky, between the criticisms which both Marx and Clausewitz made against their respective predecessors. Marx thought that the classical political economists from Adam Smith onward, that is, the economic school of the Enlightenment, had excelled in analysing the structures, relationships, and modes of operation which had prevailed in the emerging capitalist economy, as it had begun to take shape in early modern Britain. He argued, however, that they had characteristically erred in elevating these historically conditioned features to the status of abstract, universal principles of economic science—past, present, and future. Clausewitz, for his part, argued that the military thinkers of the Enlightenment had merely reflected in their systems and principles—pretentiously regarded by them as

[44] Trotsky, 'Marxism and Military Knowledge', *Military Writings*, 119–20.
[45] Trotsky, 'Pseudo-Military Doctrinairism', ibid. 56–7.

universal—one of the many different forms that war had taken through the ages.

To be sure, Clausewitz himself was occupied during most of his life in an attempt to generalize from the limited Napoleonic experience, a mistake which he realized and began to retract only during the last years of his life. It also goes without saying that his seminal historicist notions came nowhere near the comprehensiveness and sophistication of Marx's fully developed historicism. Yet Marxists could not fail to recognize the familiarity of Clausewitz's position. Lenin himself noted this familiarity with obvious satisfaction, jotting down in his notebook on Clausewitz: 'The truth is not "in the systems".'[46] He did not dwell on the matter, however, because, as already mentioned, his main use for Clausewitz's work lay elsewhere.

The fundamental nature of the correlation which existed between Clausewitz's and the Marxist position in this regard is attested by the fact that later Marxists returned to it in exactly the same manner as Trotsky. This is significant because, whereas it can be argued that Lenin's authority secured the Marxist adoption of Clausewitz's formula regarding the relationship between politics and war, Trotsky and his works have been proclaimed as heretical by the Marxist community. All the same, basic Cold War Soviet military texts proclaim:

Many bourgeois military theoreticians maintain that the laws of military science are eternal and immutable. Military history proves them wrong, for it shows that these laws are historically conditioned, which can be seen from the fact that some laws emerge while others stop operating.[47]

Clausewitz, whose ideas, in Lenin's words, 'were fertilized by Hegel', viewed the phenomena of war and military art in their development and movement, speaking out against 'eternal principles' of military art.[48]

[46] Lenin, *Fondements théoriques de la guerre et de la paix en U.R.S.S.*, 65.

[47] Byely *et al.* (ed.), *Marxism-Leninism on War*, 315. Also see almost identically in Savkin, *Operational Art*, 2–3 and 5; p. 5 reads: 'The principles of military art bear a historical character . . . a change in objective reality . . . leads inevitably to a change in the principles.'

[48] Savkin, *Operational Art*, 23. In Soviet military literature there are many references to the 'objective laws of war' which constitute the 'science of war'. These 'laws', however, merely express and classify relationships and hierarchies which exist within war itself and, according to Marxist theory, between war and economic, social, and political reality and historical development. Soviet concepts in this regard are compiled and discussed from a rather positivist point of view in Julian Lider, *The Political and Military Laws of War: An Analysis of Marxist-Leninist Concepts* (Guildford, 1979).

Further light is shed on the common historical roots of this striking intellectual agreement by the following, outwardly unlikely, comparison: 'The most important feature of Marxist–Leninist philosophy', states a Soviet military text, 'is its *capacity of unlimited creative development and improvement.*'[49] More than half a century earlier, in Wilhelmine Germany, a leading military writer on the Prussian general staff had contrasted Jomini's principles with the German conception of military theory which had first been elaborated by Clausewitz. The enormous advantage of the German conception, he had written, 'lies in its *capacity for further development*'.[50] It would thus appear that both Prussian 'reactionary militarism' and Soviet 'proletarian revolutionism' in effect shared a common intellectual source in early nineteenth-century German historicism.

Soviet commentators could not feel entirely at ease with their strange bedfellows. In a letter he wrote in 1946, shortly after the end of the Soviet Union's desperate struggle against Nazi Germany, Stalin informed the Soviet military historian, Colonel Razin, that 'we are obliged to criticize not only Clausewitz but also Moltke, Schlieffen, Ludendorff, Keitel, and other bearers of military ideology in Germany'. He went on to dismiss the relevancy of Clausewitz's military teaching to the present, but he did that in a quite revealing manner; he argued that history had rendered that teaching increasingly irrelevant for practical purposes, in the same way that it had rendered large parts of Marx's theory itself irrelevant. Stalin, too, was employing the historicist idea:

What must be noted in particular about Clausewitz is that he is, of course, obsolete as a military authority. Strictly speaking, Clausewitz was the representative of the hand-tool period of warfare. But we are now in the *machine* age of warfare. The machine age undoubtedly demands new military ideologists. It is ridiculous to take lessons from Clausewitz now . . . We do not regard Marx's theory as something completed and untouchable; we are convinced, on the contrary, that it had merely laid the cornerstone of that science, which Socialists *must* move further in all directions, unless they want to be left behind by life . . .[51]

[49] Byely *et al.* (ed.), *Marxism-Leninism on War*, 293; italics in the original.
[50] Caemmerer, *Strategical Science*, 54; italics in the original.
[51] Stalin's letter was published in Feb. 1947 in the magazine *Bolshevik*, and is cited in B. Dexter, 'Clausewitz and Soviet Strategy', *Foreign Affairs*, 29 (1950), 44–5; see also R. Garthoff, *Soviet Military Doctrine* (London, 1953), 55–6.

A later Soviet military authority referred to the same problem with greater refinement:

As the dialectic of Hegel was one of the sources for the forming Marxist philosophy, so the military works of Clausewitz, regardless of their class limitations, were one of the sources for the development of bourgeois military theory . . . as in the philosophy of Hegel, the strongest aspect of the works by Clausewitz was the dialectical approach to the phenomena of objective reality and the viewing of a number of complex phenomena in war and military art in their relationship and development. For this reason, it is inadmissible, along with the reactionary elements, to disregard the progressive features in the works of Clausewitz merely because he was the military ideologist of the manufacturing period of the conduct of war, just as we do not completely discard the philosophy of Hegel and Feuerbach.[52]

In conclusion, the main point of all the above is worth emphasizing. When all due allowances have been made, one may say that the West, and the English-speaking countries in particular, have been dominated, in their ethos and their conception of knowledge, primarily by the legacy of the Enlightenment and by its positivist descendants in the nineteenth and twentieth centuries. Thus, although in the nuclear age the West has embraced Clausewitz and almost made him its own, its actual insight into, and affinity with, his intellectual world are, in effect, fairly superficial. Quite the opposite is true, however, of both Marxism and the Prussian-German military school of the nineteenth century. Needless to say, there are great differences in this regard between the two. The Prussian military school shared Clausewitz's admiration for the state and, with the change in Germany's position, progressed from the brand of patriotism which had characterized his generation to more aggressive forms of nationalism. Marxists, for their part, could only regard Clausewitz's devotion to the state and to his country as either naïvely idealist or downright chauvinist. At the same time, however, both the Germans and the Marxists could not fail to respond with special awareness to Clausewitz's historicist notions, comprehensive approach to the phenomenon of war, and rejection of all systems. In the Prussian-German case, this response reflected a clear recognition and enthusiastic reaffirmation of key elements embedded in German national culture. In the Marxist case too, different as it may be,

---

[52] Gareev, *Frunze*, 86.

there has been recognition that, going back to the formative period of the early nineteenth century, Clausewitz's ideas had derived from the very same currents of thought which a little later stimulated the development of Marxism. Hence, even if not intimate, these historical and intellectual family-ties are nevertheless still detectable in the genetic code of Marxist theory.

Conclusion

WITHIN the time-span dealt with in this book, the nineteenth century may be viewed as an age of epigoni. By and large, after the great theoretical statements made by military writers like Jomini and Clausewitz in the aftermath of the Napoleonic wars, nothing fundamental seems to have changed in the way people in the Western world in the nineteenth century viewed war and military theory. Works like du Picq's *Battle Studies* and Bloch's *La Guerre future* stand out for their originality among military writings of that century, but none of them became epoch-making in their influence, as had the works of Jomini and Clausewitz.

How is this conspicuous fact to be explained? If we disregard the naïve notion that geniuses and great theories appear at certain times and places just by accident, then the historical preconditions which account for their development must be sought out. New ideas emerge during periods of revolutionary change or at times of crisis, in response to great historical challenges. They express human effort to come to grips with new developments and integrate them within meaningful intellectual frameworks. The edifices thus created then dominate until they themselves are rendered inadequate by new paradigmatic changes.

The stimulating cultural activity of the Enlightenment and the Romantic period expressed precisely these kinds of formative developments. During those periods, men attempted to work out the implications of the scientific revolution for the study of human-related subjects, war included. The two fundamental positions which grew out of this intellectual process underlie the modern outlook and still vie for supremacy to this day in the humanities and social sciences. Similarly, the advent of national, all-out war, which first emerged in all its fury during the wars of the Revolution and Empire, also marked a historical junction. Men's efforts to come to terms with the new phenomenon during, and in the wake of, the Napoleonic era produced the military theories which were to dominate the nineteenth century. Almost anything written about war later that century followed the paradigmatic notions worked out by the generation which had lived through the cataclysmic change. Mahan, to name one of the century's few great successes, won fame for responding to the challenge raised by the imperialist contest and by the ensuing naval race. But in terms of theory he merely applied long-established intellectual and strategic categories to a previously neglected subject.

It was none the less in the naval sphere that the ruling strategic precepts of the nineteenth century were challenged. Corbett argued that the fundamental features of naval warfare were in many ways different from those of land warfare. Furthermore, he suggested that the parameters of British policy had been historically different from those which the leading continental powers such as France and Prussia-Germany had used, and upon which the prevailing theory of war had been based. From this starting-point, he proceeded to turn nineteenth-century military theory on its head, reversing almost each and every one of its sacred tenets and articles of faith.

Indeed, it is no coincidence that Britain was the country which provided the background for the emergence of a new strategic outlook, once new historical preconditions developed. The strategic paradigm which had dominated the nineteenth century fell into crisis when the First World War failed to produce a quick and decisive result and, assuming a Moloch-like character, left both victors and vanquished almost equally exhausted. After the war, reflecting the general change of opinion about international relations and war, and building on distinctively British cultural and political traditions, people like Liddell Hart were to apply Corbett's revolutionary theses to produce a comprehensive reformulation of military theory. This involved a total rejection of both all-out war and the strategic theory which went with it. In inter-war Britain, new challenges and new cultural perspectives were again to give rise to new grand theories.

SELECT BIBLIOGRAPHY

Primary Sources

American State Papers, Military Affairs, i (Washington, DC, 1832).

ARDANT DU PICQ, C. J. J. J., *Études sur le combat* (Paris, 1880); 2nd edn. ed. Ernst Judet, Paris, 1903; trans. as *Battle Studies* (Harrisburg, Pa., 1947).

BALCK, WILHELM, *Modern German Tactics* (London, 1899). First publ. German 1892.

BERENHORST, GEORG HEINRICH VON, *Betrachtungen über die Kriegskunst* (3rd edn.; Leipzig, 1827).

BERNHARDI, FRIEDRICH VON, *Delbrück, Friedrich der Große und Clausewitz* (Berlin, 1892).

—— *On War of To-Day* (2 vols; London, 1912).

—— *Britain as Germany's Vassal* (London, 1914; trans. of *Unsere Zukunft*).

—— *Germany and the Next War* (New York, 1914).

—— *Vom Kriege der Zukunft* (Berlin, 1920).

—— *Denkwürdigkeiten aus meinem Leben* (Berlin, 1927).

BERTHAUT, J. A., *Principes de stratégie, étude sur la conduite des armées* (Paris, 1881).

BIGGE, WILHELM, *Feldmarschall Graf Moltke* (Munich, 1901).

BISMARK, FRIEDRICH WILHELM VON, *Lectures on the Tactics of Cavalry* (London, 1827, 2nd edn. 1855).

BLEIBTREU, CARL, *Napoleon'sche und Moltke'sche Strategie* (Vienna, 1901).

BLOCH, JEAN, *La Guerre future* (6 vols.; Paris, 1898).

—— *Is War Now Impossible?* (London, 1899).

BLUME, WILHELM VON, *Strategie: Eine Studie* (Berlin, 1882).

—— *Moltke* (Berlin, 1907).

BOGUSLAWSKI, ALBRECHT VON, *Die Nothwendigkeit der Zweijährigen Dienstzeit* (Berlin, 1891).

—— *Der Krieg in seiner wahren Bedeutung für Staat und Volk* (Berlin, 1892).

—— *Die Parteien und die Heeresreform* (Berlin, 1892).

—— *Volkskampf—nicht Scheinkampf: Ein Wort zur politischen Lage im Innern* (Berlin, 1895).

—— *Betrachtungen über Heerwesen und Kriegführung* (Berlin, 1897).

BONNAL, HENRI, *Les Maîtres de la guerre: Frédéric II, Napoléon, Moltke, d'après des travaux inédits de M. le général Bonnal*, ed. Léonce Rousset (Paris, 1899).

—— *De la méthode dans les hautes études militaires en Allemagne et en France* (Paris, 1902).

—— *La Récente Guerre sud-africaine* (Paris, 1903).

—— *De Rosbach à Ulm* (Paris, 1903).

—— *L'Art nouveau en tactique* (Paris, 1904).

—— *La Manœuvre d'Iéna 1806* (Paris, 1904).

—— *La Manœuvre de Saint–Privat* (3 vols.; Paris, 1904–12).

—— *La Manœuvre de Landshut 1808–1809* (Paris, 1905).

—— *La Manœuvre de Vilna 1811–1812* (Paris, 1905).

—— *Sadowa: A Study* (London, 1907).

BOUCHER, ARTHUR, *L'Offensive contre l'Allemagne* (Paris, 1911).

—— *La Belgique à jamais indépedante* (Paris, 1913).

BOURDE DE VILLEHUET, JACQUES, *Le Manœuvrier, ou essai sur la théorie et la pratique des mouvements du navire et des évolutions navales* (Paris, 1765). (Eng. trans. publ. 1788).

BRUCE, H. A. (ed.), *Life of General Sir William Napier* (London, 1864), written anonymously by Patrick MacDougall.

BYELY, B., FYODOROV, G., KULAKOV V. (eds.), *Marxism-Leninism on War and Army* (Moscow, 1972).

CAEMMERER, R. VON, *The Development of Strategical Science during the 19th Century* (London, 1905).

CAMON, HUBERT, *Clausewitz* (Paris, 1911).

CARDOT, LUCIEN, [writing as Loukiane Carlovitch] *Éducation et instruction des troupes* (3 vols.; Paris, 1896–7).

—— *Hérésies et apostasies militaires de notre temps* (Paris, 1908).

CHARMES, GABRIEL, *Naval Reform* (London, 1887).

CHERFILS, MAXIME, *Cavalerie en campagne* (2nd. edn.; Paris, 1893).

CHURCHILL, WINSTON, S., *The World Crisis* (6 vols.; London, 1923–31).

CLAUSEWITZ, CARL VON, *Politische Schriften und Briefe*, ed. Hans Rothfels (Munich, 1922).

—— *Principles of War* (Harrisburg, Pa., 1942).

—— *On War*, trans. Michael E. Howard and Peter Paret (Princeton, NJ, 1976), (2nd edn. 1984).

—— *Verstreute kleine Schriften*, ed. W. Hahlweg (Osnabrück, 1979).

COLIN, JEAN, *L'Éducation militaire de Napoléon* (Paris, 1900).

—— *The Transformation of War* (London, 1912).

COLOMB, JOHN, *The Protection of Our Commerce and Distribution of Our Naval Forces Considered* (London, 1867).

—— *Imperial Defence* (London, 1871).

—— *Colonial Defence (London, 1877).*

—— *The Defence of Great and Greater Britain* (London, 1880).

—— *Naval Intelligence and Protection of Commerce in War* (London 1881).

—— *Imperial Federation: Naval and Military* (London, 1886).

COLOMB, PHILIP, *Naval Warfare, Its Ruling Principles and Practice, Historically Treated* (London, 1891).

—— *Essays on Naval Defence* (London, 1893).

CONRAD VON HÖTZENDORF, FRANZ VON, *Aus meiner Dienstzeit, 1906–1918* (5 vols.; Berlin, 1921–5).

CORBETT, JULIAN S., The Corbett Papers, The National Maritime Museum, Greenwich.

—— *Drake and the Tudor Navy* (2 vols.; London, 1898).

—— *The Successors of Drake* (London, 1900).

—— *England in the Mediterranean, 1603–1713* (2 vols.; London, 1904).

—— (ed.), *Fighting Instructions, 1530–1816* (London, 1905).

—— *England in the Seven Years War: A Study in Combined Strategy* (2 vols.; London, 1907).

—— (ed)., *Signals and Instructions, 1776–1794* (London, 1908).

—— *The Campaign of Trafalgar* (London, 1910).

—— *Some Principles of Maritime Strategy* (Annapolis, Md., 1988).

CULMANN, FRÉDÉRIC, *Deux tactiques en présence* (Paris, 1904).

—— *Tactique d'artillerie: Le Canon de tir rapide dans la bataille* (Paris, 1906).

DAHN, FELIX, *Moltke als Erzieher* (Breslau, 1892).

DANY, JEAN, 'La Littérature militaire d'aujourd'hui', *La Revue de Paris* (Mar.–Apr. 1912), 611–24.

DARRIEUS, GABRIEL, *La Guerre sur mer: Stratégie et tactique* (Paris, 1907).

DAVELEY, RENÉ, *L'Esprit de la guerre navale* (3 vols.; Paris, 1909–10).

DEBENEY, MARIE-EUGÈNE, *La Guerre et les hommes* (Paris, 1937).

DECKER, CARL VON, *Ansichten über die Kriegführung im Geist der Zeit* (Berlin, 1817).

—— *Grundzüge der praktischen Strategie* (2nd. edn.; Berlin, 1841).

—— *Der kleine Krieg* (Berlin, 1822).

DELBRÜCK, HANS, *Historische und politische Aufsätze* (Berlin, 1886).

—— *Die Strategie des Perikles erläutert durch die Strategie Friedrichs des Großen* (Berlin, 1890).

—— *Erinnerungen, Aufsätze und Reden* (Berlin, 1902).

—— *Numbers in History* (London, 1914).

—— *Krieg und Politik* (3 vols; Berlin, 1918–19).

—— *Ludendorff, Tirpitz, Falkenhayn* (Berlin, 1920).

—— *Ludendorffs Selbstporträt* (Berlin, 1922).

—— *Government and the Will of the People* (New York, 1923). First publ. in German 1914.

—— *Vor und nach dem Weltkrieg, politische und historische Aufsätze, 1902–1925* (Berlin, 1926).

DELBRÜCK, HANS, *History of the Art of War within the Framework of Political History* (4 vols; London, 1975–85). First publ. in German 1920.

DERRÉCAGAIX, V. D., *Modern War* (Washington, DC, 1888).

—— *la Guerre et l'armée* (Paris, 1901).

DILKE, CHARLES W., 'The French Armies', *The Fortnightly Review*, 1 Nov. 1891.

DOUGLAS, HOWARD, *Naval Evolutions: A Memoir* (London, 1832).

DRAGOMIROV, M. I., *Manuel pour la préparation des troupes au combat* (3 vols.; Paris, 1886–8).

—— *Principes essentiels pour la conduite de la guerre: Clausewitz interprété par le Général Dragomiroff* (Paris, 1889).

ELDIN, JOHN CLERK OF, *An Essay on Naval Tactics, Systematical and Historical* (2nd. edn.; Edinburgh, 1804).

ELLIOT, GEORGE, *A Treatise on Future Naval Battles and How to Fight Them* (London, 1885).

ENGELS, FRIEDRICH, *Selected Correspondence, Karl Marx and Friedrich Engels* (London, 1934).

—— *Ausgewählte militärische Schriften* (2 vols.; Berlin, 1958, 1964).

—— *Engels as a Military Critic: Articles by Friedrich Engels Reprinted from the Volunteer Journal and the Manchester Guardian of the 1860s*, ed. H. Chaloner and W. O. Henderson (Manchester, 1959).

—— *On America and the Civil War* (New York, 1972).

—— and MARX, KARL, *Collected Works* (1975–).

—— *Herr Eugen Dühring's Revolution in Science* (London, n.d.).

—— *Marx-Engels Gesamtausgabe* (Berlin, 1975–).

FISHER, JOHN, *Fear God and Dread Nought: The Correspondence of Admiral of the Fleet Lord Fisher of Kilverstone*, ed. A. Marder (3 vols.; London, 1956).

FOCH, FERDINAND, *De la conduite de la guerre* (2nd edn., Paris, 1909).

—— *The Principles of War* (London, 1920). First publ. in French (1903).

—— *Foch Talks*, ed. C. Bugnet (London, 1929).

—— *Marshal Foch: His own Words on Many Things*, ed. Raymond Recouly (London, 1929).

—— *The Memoirs of Marshal Foch* (New York, 1931).

FREDERICK, CROWN PRINCE OF PRUSSIA, *The War Diary of the Emperor Frederick III, 1870–1871* (London, 1927).

FREYTAG-LORINGHOVEN, HUGO BARON VON, *Die Heerführng Napoleons und Moltkes* (Berlin, 1897).

—— *Der Infanterie-Angriff in den neuesten Kriegen: Ein Beitrag zur klärung der Angriffsfrage* (Berlin, 1905).

—— *Die Macht der Persönlichkeit im Kriege: Studien nach Clausewitz* (Berlin, 1905).

—— *Krieg und Politik in der Neuzeit* (Berlin, 1911).

—— *Deductions from the World War* (London, 1918).

—— *A Nation Trained in Arms or a Militia* (London, 1918).

—— *Generalfeldmarschall Graf von Schlieffen* (Leipzig, 1920).

GALLIÉNI, GAËTAN, *Les Carnets de Galliéni* (Paris, 1932).

GAREEV, M. A., *Frunze, Military Theorist* (Suffolk, 1988).

GAY DE VERNON, S. F., *A Treatise on the Science of War and Fortifications* (2 vols.; New York, 1817).

The General Staff, War Office (ed.), *The Operations of Large Formations* (London, 1914).

GILBERT, GEORGES, *Essais de critique militaire* (2nd edn.; Paris, 1890).

—— *Sept études militaires* (Paris, 1892).

—— *Lois et institutions militaires* (Paris, 1895).

—— *La Guerre sud-africaine* (Paris, 1902).

GOLTZ, COLMAR VON DER, *The Conduct of War* (London, 1899). First publ. in German 1895.

—— *The Nation in Arms* (London, 1906).

—— *Von Rosbach bis Jena* (Berlin, 1906). Earlier version *Rosbach und Jena*, 1883.

—— *Kriegsgeschichte Deutschlands im Neunzehnten Jahrhundert* (Berlin, 1910), i.

—— *Jena to Eylau* (London, 1913).

—— *Denkwürdigkeiten* (Berlin, 1929).

GOLTZ, FRITZ VON DER, *Moltke* (Berlin, 1903).

—— *Die gelbe Gefahr im Licht der Geschichte* (Leipzig, 1907).

GRANDMAISON, F. J. L. L. DE, *Dressage de l'infanterie en vue du combat offensif* (Paris, 1906).

—— *Deux conférences faites aux officiers de l'état-major de l'armée (février, 1911); La Notion de sûreté et l'engagement des grandes unités* (Paris, 1911).

GRENIER, J. R. DE, *L'Art de la guerre sur mer, ou tactique navale* (Paris, 1787).

GROUARD, A., *La Perte des états et les camps retranchés; Réplique au général Brialmont* (Paris, 1889).

—— *Fallait-il quitter Metz en 1870?* (Paris, 1893).

—— *Stratégie, objet, enseignement, éléments* (Paris, 1895).

—— *La Campagne d'automne de 1813 et les lignes intérieures* (Paris, 1897).

—— *Maximes de guerre de Napoléon Ier* (Paris, 1898).

—— *Comment quitter Metz en 1870? Avec une note sur le rôle de la fortification* (Paris, 1901).

—— *La Critique de la campagne de 1815* (Paris, 1904).

—— *France et Allemagne; La Guerre éventuelle* (Paris, 1913; periodical publ. from 1911).

GUILLON, E., *Nos écrivains militaires* (2 vols.; Paris, 1898).

HALLECK, HENRY W., *Elements of Military Art and Science, or Course of Instruction in Strategy, Fortification, Tactics of Battles etc.* (New York, 1846).

HAMILTON, ALEXANDER, *The Works of Alexander Hamilton*, ed., H. C. Lodge (New York, 1886).

HAMLEY, EDWARD BRUCE, *The Operations of War* (London, 1866).

HOSTE, PAUL, *L'Art des armées navales* (Lyon, 1697). Eng. trans. 1762, 1834.

IDEVILLE, H. D', *Memoirs of Marshal Bugeaud. From his Private Correspondence and Original Documents* (2 vols.; London, 1884).

JÄHNS, MAX, *Feldmarschall Moltke* (3 vols.; Berlin, 1894–1900).

JAURÈS, JEAN, *L'Armée nouvelle* (Paris, 1913).

JOFFRE, JOSEPH, *The Memoirs of Marshal Joffre* (2 vols.; London, 1932).

JOMINI, ANTOINE HENRI, LLOYD, H. E., TEMPELHOFF, G. F., *The History of the Seven Years War* (London, n.d. [1808?]).

—— *Histoire critique et militaire des guerres de la révolution* (15 vols.; Paris, 1820–4).

—— *An Exposition of the First Principles of Grand Military Combinations and Movements, Compiled from the Treatise upon Great Military Operations*, ed. J. A. Gilbert (London, 1825).

—— *Summary of the Art of War* (New York, 1854; another edn. Philadelphia, 1862).

—— *Treatise on Grand Military Operations*, trans. Colonel S. B. Holabird (2 vols.; New York, 1865).

—— *Life of Napoleon*, trans. Major-General H. W. Halleck (4 vols.; New York, 1864).

JUNG, THÉODORE, *La Guerre et la société* (Paris, 1889).

—— *Stratégie, tactique et politique* (Paris, 1890).

—— *La République et l'armée* (Paris, 1892).

KEIM, AUGUST, *Graf Schlieffen* (Berlin, 1921).

KRAFT ZU HOHENLOHE-INGELFINGEN, *Letters on Artillery* (Woolwich, 1887).

—— *Letters on Cavalry* (London, 1889).

—— *Letters on Infantry* (London, 1889).

—— *Letters on Strategy* (London, 1898). First publ. in German 1887.

KRAUSS, ALFRED, *Moltke, Benedek und Napoleon* (Vienna, 1901).

LANGLOIS, HIPPOLYTE, *L'Artillerie de campagne en liaison avec les autres armes* (2 vols.; Paris, 1892).

—— *Questions de défense nationale* (Paris, 1906).

—— *Lessons From Two Recent Wars, The Russo-Turkish and South African War* (London, 1909).

—— *The British Army in a European War* (London, 1910).

LAUGHTON, JOHN K., *Essays on Naval Tactics* (London, 1874).

—— 'The Scientific Study of History', *Journal of the Royal United Services Institution*, 18 (1875), 508–27.

—— *Studies in Naval History* (London, 1887).

LEER, H. A., *Vorträge über Strategie* (Vienna, 1868).

—— *Positive Strategie* (Vienna, 1871).

LEHAUTCOURT, PIERRE, 'Le Colonel Ardant du Picq', *La Revue de Paris* (May–June 1904), 347–66.

LENIN, V. I., *Collected Works* (London, 1960–70).

—— *Les Fondements théoriques de la guerre et de la paix en U.R.S.S.— suivi du Cahier de Lénine sur Clausewitz*, ed. B. C. Friedl (Paris, 1945).

LEWAL, J. L., *La Réforme de l'armée* (Paris, 1871).

—— *Le Maréchal de Moltke, organisateur et stratège* (Paris, 1891).

—— *Introduction à la partie positive de la stratégie* (Paris, 1892).

—— *Stratégie de marche* (Paris, 1893).

—— *Stratégie de combat* (2 vols.; Paris, 1895–6).

LINCOLN, ABRAHAM, *The Collected Works of Abraham Lincoln*, ed. Roy P. Basler (New Brunswick, 1953).

LUCE, STEPHEN B., 'War Schools', *United States Naval Institute Proceedings*, (1883), pp. 633–57.

—— 'Naval Administration III', *United States Naval Institute Proceedings* (Dec. 1903).

—— *The Writings of Stephen B. Luce*, ed. J. D. Hayes and J. B. Hattendorff (Newport, RI, 1975).

LUNDENDORFF, ERICH, *My War Memories, 1914–1918*, (London, 1919).

—— *Kriegführung und Politik* (Berlin, 1922).

—— *Der totale Krieg* (Munich, 1935).

MACDOUGALL, PATRICK, *The Theory of War, Illustrated by Numerous Examples from Military History* (London, 1856).

—— (publ. anonymously), *Life of General Sir William Napier*, ed. H. A. Bruce (London, 1864).

MACKINDER, HALFORD J., 'The Geographical Pivot of History', *Geographical Journal*, 23 (1904), 421–37.

MAHAN, ALFRED THAYER, *The Influence of Sea Power upon History, 1660–1783* (London, 1890), cited in the text as 'Influence I'.

—— *The Influence of Sea Power upon the French Revolution and Empire* (2 vols.; London, 1892), cited in the text as 'Influence II'.

—— *The Navy in the Civil War, The Gulf and the Inland Waters* (London, 1898).

—— *Lessons of the War with Spain and Other Articles* (Boston, 1899).

—— *The Life of Nelson: The Embodiment of the Sea Power of Great Britain* (London, 1899).

—— *The Problem of Asia and Its Effects upon International Policies* (London, 1900).

MAHAN, ALFRED THAYER, *Retrospect and Prospect: Studies in International Relations, Naval and Political* (London, 1902).

—— *Sea Power in Its Relation to the War of 1812* (2 vols.; London, 1905).

—— *Types of Naval Officers Drawn from the History of the British Navy* (London, 1902).

—— 'Reflections, Historic and Other, Suggested by the Battle of the Japan Sea', *United States Naval Institute Proceedings* (1906), 447–71.

—— *From Sail to Steam: Recollections of Naval Life* (London and New York, 1907).

—— *Some Neglected Aspects of War* (London, 1907).

—— *Naval Administration and Warfare* (Boston, 1908).

—— *The Interest of America in International Conditions* (London, 1910).

—— *Naval Strategy, Compared and Contrasted with the Principles and Practice of Military Operations on Land* (London, 1911).

—— *Armaments and Arbitration, or the Place of Force in the International Relations of States* (London, 1912).

—— *The Major Operations of the Navies in the War of American Independence* (London, 1913).

—— *Letters and Papers of Alfred Thayer Mahan*, ed. Robert Seager II and Doris D. Maguire (3 vols.; Annapolis, Md., 1975).

—— *Admiral Farragut* (New York and London, 1920).

—— *A Bibliography of the Works of Alfred Thayer Mahan*, ed. John B. Hattendorf and Lynn C. Hattendorf (Newport, RI, 1986).

MAHAN, DENIS HART, *An Elementary Treatise on Advanced Guard, Out-Posts and Detachment Service of Troops . . . with a Historical Sketch on the Rise and Progress of Tactics* (New York, 1847).

MAILLARD, L., *Éléments de la guerre* (Paris, 1891).

MARCHAND, A., *Plans de concentrations de 1871 à 1914* (Paris, 1926).

MARMONT, A. F. L. V. DE, *De l'esprit des institutions militaires* (Paris, 1846).

MAYER, Émile, *Nos institutions militaires* (Paris, 1901).

—— *Comment on pouvait prévoir l'immobilisation des fronts dans la guerre moderne* (Paris, 1916).

—— *Autour de la guerre actuelle* (Paris, 1917).

—— *La Psychologie du commandement, avec plusieurs lettres inédites du Maréchal Foch* (Paris, 1924).

—— *Trois maréchaux: Joffre, Galliéni, Foch* (Paris, 1928).

MESSIMY, ADOLPHE-MARIE, *Mes souvenirs* (Paris, 1937).

MILOVIDOV, A. S. (ed.), *The Philosophical Heritage of V. I. Lenin and the Problems of Contemporary War* (Moscow, 1972).

MITCHELL, JOHN, *Thoughts on Tactics and Military Organization* (London, 1838).

—— *The Fall of Napoleon* (3 vols.; London, 1845).

—— *Biographies of Eminent Soldiers of the Last Four Centuries* (London, 1865).

MOLTKE, HELMUTH, C. B.. VON, *Gesammelte Schriften und Denkwürdigkeiten* (8 vols.; Berlin 1891–3); trans, as:

—— *Letters of Field-Marshal Count von Moltke to his Mother and Brothers* (New York, 1892).

—— *Moltke, His Life and Character, Sketched in Journals, Memoirs, a Novel and Autobiographical Notes* (New York, 1892).

—— *Essays, Speeches and Memoirs of Field-Marshal Count Helmuth von Moltke* (2 vols.; New York, 1893).

—— *Field-Marshal Count Helmuth von Moltke as a Correspondent* (New York, 1893).

—— *Militärische Werke* (17 vols.; Berlin, 1892–1912).

MOLTKE (the younger), HELMUTH VON, *Betrachtungen und Erinnerungen* (Hamburg, 1914).

MOROGUES, S. F. V. B. DE, *Tactique navale* (Paris, 1763). Eng. trans. 1767.

NAPIER, WILLIAM, 'Traité des grandes opérations militaires', *The Edinburgh Review*, 35 (1821), 377–409.

—— *History of the War in the Peninsula and in the South of France from the Year 1808 to the Year 1814* (6 vols.; London, 1828–40).

—— *Six Letters in Vindication of the British Army, Exposing the Calumnies of the Liverpool Financial Reform Association* (London, 1849).

NAPOLEON, *Mémoires pour servir à l'histoire de France sous Napoléon, écrits à Sainte Hélène*, ed. C. G. F. T. Montholon (Paris, 1823).

NÉGRIER, FRANÇOIS DE, *Lessons of the Russo-Japanese War* (London, 1906). First publ. in the *Revue des deux mondes*, 15 Jan, 1906.

PERCIN, ALEXANDRE, *1914: Les Erreurs du haut commandement* (Paris, 1920).

—— *Le Massacre de notre infanterie, 1914–1918* (Paris, 1921).

PIERRON, ÉDOUARD, *Stratégie et grande tactique, d'après l'expérience des dernières guerres* (Paris, 1887).

—— *Comment s'est formé le génie militaire de Napoléon Ier?* (Paris, 1889).

—— *La Stratégie et la tactique allemandes au début du XXe siècle* (Paris, 1900).

Reichsarchiv, *Der Weltkrieg, 1914–1918; Kriegsrüstung und Kriegswirtschaft* (Berlin, 1930).

ROGNIAT, A. DE, *Considérations sur l'art de la guerre* (Paris, 1816).

—— *Réponse aux notes critiques de Napoléon* (Paris, 1823).

RÜSTOW, WILHELM, *Der deutsche Militärstaat, vor und während der Revolution* (Osnabrück, 1971).

—— *Der Krieg und seine Mittel* (Leipzig, 1856).

Rüstow, Wilhelm, *Die Feldherrkunst des neunzehnten Jahrhunderts* (2 vols.; Zurich, 1857).
—— *Geschichte der Infanterie* (Gotha, 1857).
—— *Der Krieg von 1805 in Deutschland und Italien, als Anteilung zu kriegshistorischen Studien* (Zurich, 1859).
—— *The War for the Rhine Frontier 1870* (3 vol.; London, 1871).
—— *Strategie und Taktik der neuesten Zeit* (3 vols.; Zurich, 1872–4).
Saint-Cyr, Gouvion, *Mémoires pour servir à l'histoire militaire sous le directoire, le consulat et l'empire* (4 vols.; Paris, 1831).
Savkin, Ye., *The Basic Principles of Operational Art* (Moscow, 1972).
Schäfer, Dietrich, *Zu Moltkes Gedächtnis. Rede* (Jena, 1901).
Scherff, von, *The New Tactics of Infantry* (London, 1873).
—— *Von der Kriegführung* (Berlin, 1883).
—— *Die Lehre vom Kriege* (Berlin, 1897).
Schlichting, S. W. L. von, *Taktische und strategische Grundsätze der Gegenwart* (3 vols; Berlin, 1897–9).
—— *Moltkes Vermächtniß* (Munich, 1901).
—— *Moltke und Benedek* (Berlin, 1909).
Schlieffen, Alfred von, *Gesammelte Schriften* (4 vols; Berlin, 1913).
—— *Briefe*, ed. E. Kessel (Göttingen, 1958).
Schmerfeld, Ferdinand von (ed.), *Die deutschen Aufmarschpläne, 1871–1890* (Berlin, 1929).
Sims, W. S., 'The Inherent Tactical Qualities of the All-Big-Gun, One Caliber Battleship of High Speed, Large Displacement and Gun Power', *The United States Naval Institute Proceedings* (1906), 1337–66.
Sorb, *La Doctrine de défense nationale* (Paris, 1912).
Sprout, Harold and Margaret, *The Rise of American Naval Power, 1776–1918* (2nd edn.; Princeton, NJ, 1966).
Sydenham of Comb, Clarke George, Lord, 'Sea Heresies', *The Naval Review*, (May 1931).
—— Bacon, R., Bird, W. D., Oman, C., *The World Crisis by Winston Churchill: A Criticism* (London, 1927).
Theobald, J. von, *Die Kunst der großen Kriegsoperationen nach den besten Quellen frey bearbeitet* (Stuttgart, 1820).
Thoumas, *Les Transformations de l'armée française* (2 vols.; Paris, 1887).
Tirpitz, Alfred von, *My Memoirs* (2 vols.; London, 1919).
Treitschke, Heinrich von, *Politics* (2 vols; London, 1916).
Trochu, Louis, *L'Armée française en 1867* (20th edn.; Paris, 1870).
Trotsky, Leon, *Military Writings* (New York, 1969).
Valentini, Georg Wilhelm von, *Die Lehre vom Krieg* (2nd edn.; Berlin, 1833).
Verdy du Vernois, *Studien über den Krieg* (4 vols.; Berlin, 1891–1909).

WALDERSEE, ALFRED VON, *Denkwürdigkeiten*, ed. H. O. Meisner (3 vols.; Berlin 1923).

WILKINSON, SPENSER, *The Early Life of Moltke* (Oxford, 1913).

WILLISEN, KARL WILHELM VON, *Theorie des großen Krieges* (Berlin, 1840).

—— *Der italienische Feldzug des Jahres 1848* (Berlin, 1849).

YATES, EDWARD, *Elementary Treatise on Strategy* (London, 1852).

—— *Elementary Treatise on Tactics* (London, 1853).

COMMANDANT Z . . ., Montéchant, H., *Les Guerres navales de demain* (Paris, 1891).

Secondary Sources

ADAM, JULIETTE, *Le Capitaine Georges Gilbert* (Paris, 1924).

AMBROSE, STEPHEN E., *Halleck: Lincoln's Chief of Staff* (Baton Rouge, La, 1962).

ARNOLD, JOSEPH, 'French Tactical Doctrine 1870–1914', *Military Affairs*, 42 (1978), 61–7.

ARON, RAYMOND, *Clausewitz, Philosopher of War* (London, 1986).

ASTON, GEORGE, *The Biography of the Late Marshal Foch* (London, 1929).

BAMFORD, PAUL WALDEN, *Forests and French Sea Power, 1660–1789* (Toronto, 1956).

BAUER, REINHARD, 'Hans Delbrück', in B. Schmitt (ed.), *Some Historians of Modern Europe* (Chicago, 1941).

BÉDARIDA, FRANÇOIS, 'L'Armée et la république: Les Opinions des officiers français en 1876–78', *Revue historique* (1964), 119–64.

BERGER, MARTIN, *Engels, Armies, and Revolution: The Revolutionary Tactics of Classical Marxism* (Hamden, Conn., 1977).

BERGHAHN, VOLKER, *Der Tirpitz-Plan* (Düsseldorf, 1971).

BEST, GEOFFREY, *War and Society in Revolutionary Europe* (Leicester, 1982).

BOND, BRIAN, *The Victorian Army and the Staff College, 1854–1914* (London, 1972).

—— *War and Society in Europe, 1870–1970* (London, 1984).

BOWDITCH, JOHN, 'The Concept of Élan Vital: A Rationalization of Weakness', in E. M. Earle (ed.), *Modern France* (Princeton, NJ, 1951).

BRODIE, BERNARD, *Sea Power in the Machine Age* (Princeton, NJ, 1941).

BUCHOLTZ, ARDEN, *Hans Delbrück and the German Military Establishment: War Images in Conflict* (Iowa, 1985).

CALLEO, DAVID, *The German Problem Reconsidered* (New York, 1978).

CARRIAS, E. *La Pensée militaire française* (Paris, 1960).

—— *La Pensée militaire allemande* (Paris, 1948).

CASE, LYNN M., *French Opinion on War and Diplomacy during the Second Empire* (Philadelphia, 1954).

CHALMIN, PIERRE, *L'Officier français de 1815 à 1870* (Paris, 1957).

CHARLTON, D. G., *Positivist Thought in France during the Second Empire, 1852–1870* (Oxford, 1959).

CHICKERING, ROGER, *Imperial Germany and a World without War: The Peace Movement and German Society, 1892–1914* (Princeton, NJ, 1975).

—— *We Men Who Feel Most German: A Cultural Study of the Pan-German League* (Boston, 1984).

COCHENHAUSEN, F. VON (ed.), *Von Scharnhorst zu Schlieffen, 1806–1906: Hundert Jahre preußisch-deutscher Generalstab* (Berlin, 1933).

COLE, RONALD, H., ' "Forward with the Bayonet! ": The French Army Prepares for Offensive Warfare, 1911–1914' (unpub. diss., University of Maryland, 1975).

CONTAMINE, HENRI, *La Revanche* (Paris, 1957).

COOLIDGE, LOUIS A., *Ulysses S. Grant* (Boston, 1922).

CRACKEL, THEODORE J., 'The Founding of West Point: Jefferson and the Politics of Security', *Armed Forces and Society*, 7 (1981), 529–43.

CRAIG, GORDON, *The Politics of the Prussian Army* (Oxford, 1955).

—— *The Battle of Königgrätz* (London, 1964).

—— *Germany, 1866–1945* (Oxford, 1978).

CRESWELL, JOHN, *British Admirals of the Eighteenth Century* (London, 1972).

CUNLIFFE, MARCUS, *Soldiers and Civilians: The Martial Spirit in America, 1775–1865* (London, 1969).

DANIELS, EMILE, 'Delbrück als Politiker', in id. (ed.), *Am Webstuhl der Zeit* (Berlin, 1928).

DEIST, WILHELM, 'Die Armee in Staat und Gesellschaft, 1890–1914', in M. Stürmer (ed.), *Das kaiserliche Deutschland: Politik und Gesellschaft, 1870–1918* (Düsseldorf, 1970), 312–39.

—— *Flottenpolitik und Flottenpropaganda, 1897–1914* (Stuttgart, 1976).

—— 'Zur Geschichte des preußischen Offizierkorps, 1888–1918', in H. H. Hofmann (ed.), *Das deutsche Offizierkorps, 1860–1960* (Boppard am Rhein, 1980).

DEMETER, KARL, *The German Officer-Corps in Society and State, 1650–1945* (London, 1965).

DEMIRHAN, PERTEV, *General-Feldmarschall Colmar von der Goltz* (Göttingen, 1960).

DEWEY, JOHN, *German Philosophy and Politics* (New York, 1915).

DEXTER, BYRON, 'Clausewitz and Soviet Strategy', *Foreign Affairs*, 29 (1950), 41–55.

DONALD, DAVID, 'Refighting the Civil War', in id., *Lincoln Reconsidered* (New York, 1956).

—— (ed.), *Why the North Won the Civil War* (Baton Rouge, La., 1960).

DRONBERGER, ILSE, *The Political Thought of Max Weber* (New York, 1971).

DÜLFFER, JOST, *Regeln gegen den Krieg? Die Haager Friedenskonferenzen von 1899 und 1907* (Frankfurt a. M., 1981).

——, and HOLL, KARL (eds.), *Bereit zum Kreig: Kriegsmentalität im wilhelminischen Deutschland, 1890–1914* (Göttingen, 1986).

DUPUY, R. E., *The Story of West Point, 1802–1943* (Washington, DC, 1943).

EARLE, E. M. (ed.), *Makers of Modern Strategy from Machiavelli to Hitler* (Princeton, NJ 1943).

EGVILLE, HOWARD D', *Imperial Defence and Closer Union: A Short Record of the Life Work of Sir John Colomb and of the Movement Toward Imperial Organization* (London, 1913).

ELTING, JOHN R., 'Jomini: Disciple of Napoleon', *Military Affairs*, 28 (1964), 17–26.

État-Major de l'Armée, *Les Armées françaises dans la grande guerre* (Paris, 1936).

FARRAR, L. L., *The Short-War Illusion* (Oxford, 1973).

—— *Arrogance and Anxiety: The Ambivalence of German Power, 1848–1914* (Iowa City, 1981).

FISCHER, FRITZ, *Germany's Aims in the First World War* (New York, 1967). First publ. in German 1961.

—— *War of Illusions* (London, 1975).

FOERSTER, WOLFGANG, *Graf Schlieffen und der Weltkrieg* (2nd ed.; Berlin, 1925).

—— *Aus der Gedankenwerkstatt des deutschen Generalstabs* (Berlin, 1931).

FORMAN, SIDNEY, *West Point* (New York, 1950).

FÖRSTER, STIG, *Der doppelte Militarismus: Die deutsche Heeresrüstungs-politik zwischen Status-quo-Sicherung und Aggression, 1890–1913* (Stuttgart, 1985).

FORTESCUE, JOHN W., *Historical and Military Essays* (London, 1928).

—— *A History of the British Army* (London, 1930), vols. xi–xiii.

FOSSATI, W. J., 'Educational Influences in the Career of Marshal Ferdinand Foch of France' (unpub. doc. diss., University of Kansas, 1976).

FREEMAN, DOUGLAS S., *R. E. Lee* (4 vols.; New York, 1934).

FRIEDBERG, AARON L., *The Weary Titan: Britain and the Experience of Relative Decline, 1895–1905* (Princeton, NJ, 1988).

GALLIE, W. B., *Philosophers of Peace and War: Kant, Clausewitz, Marx, Engels and Tolstoy* (Cambridge, 1978).

GAMELIN, M., *Manœuvre et victoire de la Marne* (Paris, 1954).

GARTHOFF, RAYMOND, *Soviet Military Doctrine* (London, 1953).

GAT, AZAR, 'Clausewitz on Defence and Attack', *Journal of Strategic Studies*, 10 (1988), 20–6.

—— *The Origins of Military Thought from the Enlightenment to Clausewitz* (Oxford, 1989).

GAULLE, CHARLES DE, *France and Her Army* (London, 1945).

GAYL, FREIHERR VON, *General von Schlichting* (Berlin, 1913).

GIRARDET, RAOUL, *La Société militaire dans la France contemporaine, 1815–1939* (Paris, 1953).

GLEAVES, ALBERT, *Life and Letters of Rear Admiral Stephen B. Luce, U. S. Navy, Founder of the Naval War College* (New York, 1925).

GODWIN-AUSTIN, A. R., *The Staff and the Staff College* (London, 1927).

GOERLITZ, WALTER, *The German General Staff* (London, 1953).

GORCE, PAUL-MARIE DE LA, *The French Army: A Military-Political History* (London, 1963).

GRAHAM, GERALD S., *The Politics of Naval Supremacy: Studies in British Maritime Ascendancy* (Cambridge, 1965).

GRIFFITH, P. G., *Military Thought in the French Army, 1815–1851* (Manchester, 1989).

GROENER, WILHELM, *Das Testament des Grafen Schlieffen* (Berlin, 1927).

—— *Der Feldherr wider Willen* (Berlin, 1930).

GUILMARTIN JUN., JOHN FRANCIS, *Gunpowder and Galleys: Changing Technology and Mediterranean Warfare at Sea in the Sixteenth Century* (Cambridge, 1974).

HAHLWEG, WERNER, 'Lenin und Clausewitz', *Archiv für Kulturgeschichte*, 36 (1954), 30–59, 357–87.

—— 'Clausewitz, Lenin and Communist Military Attitudes Today', *Journal of the Royal United Services Institute*, 105 (1960), 221–5.

HANSON, VICTOR D., *The Western Way of Warfare: Infantry Tactics in Classical Greece* (Oxford, 1990).

HARRIES-JENKINS, GWYN, *The Army in Victorian Society* (London, 1977).

HARSH, JOSEPH L., 'Battlesword and Rapier: Clausewitz, Jomini and the American Civil War', *Military Affairs*, 38 (1974), 133–8.

HERTZ, FREDERICK, *The German Public Mind in the Nineteenth Century* (London, 1975).

HERWEGH, MARCEL, *Guillaume Rustow: Un grand soldat, un grand caractère* (Paris, 1935).

HERZFELD, HANS, *Die deutsche Rüstungpolitik vor dem Weltkrieg* (Bonn, 1923).

HILLGRUBER, ANDREAS, *Germany and the Two World Wars* (London, 1981). First publ. in German 1967.

—— 'Hans Delbrück', in H.-U. Wehler (ed.), *Deutsche Historiker* (Göttingen, 1972).

HINTZE, OTTO, 'Delbrück, Clausewitz und die Strategie Friedrichs des

Großen', *Forschungen zur Brandenburgischen und preußischen Geschichte*, 33 (1920), 131–77.

—— *The Historical Essays of Otto Hintze*, ed. Felix Gilbert (New York, 1975).

Höhn, Reinhard, *Sozialismus und Heer* (Berlin, 1959).

Holmes, T. R. E., *Four Famous Soldiers* (London, 1889).

House, Jonathan, 'The Decisive Attack, A New Look at French Infantry Tactics on the Eve of World War I', *Military Affairs*, 40 (1976), 164–9.

Howard, Michael E., *The Franco-Prussian War* (London, 1961).

—— (ed.), *The Theory and Practice of War* (London, 1965).

—— 'Wellington and the British Army', in id. *Studies in War and Peace* (London, 1970).

—— *War in European History* (London, 1976).

Hughes, H. Stuart, *Consciousness and Society: The Reorientation of European Social Thought, 1890–1930* (London, 1959).

Hull, Isabel, *The Entourage of Kaiser Wilhelm II* (Cambridge, 1982).

Iggers, Georg, *The German Conception of History* (Middletown, Conn., 1968).

Irvine, Dallas, 'The French and Prussian Staff Systems before 1870', *Journal of the American Military Institute* 2 (1938), 192–203.

—— 'The French Discovery of Clausewitz and Napoleon', *Journal of the American Military Institute*, 4 (1942), 143–61.

Jacobs, Walter D., *Frunze: The Soviet Clausewitz, 1885–1925* (The Hague, 1969).

Jany, Kurt, *Die königlich-preußische Armee und das deutsche Reichsheer, 1807 bis 1914* (Berlin, 1933).

Jauffret, Jean-Charles, 'L'Organisation de la réserve à l'époque de la revanche, 1871–1914', *Revue historique des armées* (1989), 27–37.

John, Hartmut, *Das Reserveoffizierkorps im deutschen Kaiserreich, 1890–1914* (Frankfurt a. M., 1981).

Jones, Archer, 'Jomini and the Strategy of the American Civil War: A Reinterpretation', *Military Affairs*, 34 (1970), 127–31.

—— Connolly, Thomas L., *The Politics of Command; Factions and Ideas in Confederate Strategy* (Baton Rouge, La., 1973).

—— Hattaway, Herman, *How the North Won* (London, 1983).

Karsten, Peter, *The Naval Aristocracy: The Golden Age of Annapolis and the Emergence of Modern American Navalism* (New York, 1972).

Kehr, Eckart, *Schlachtflottenbau und Parteipolitik, 1894–1901* (Berlin, 1930).

—— *Economic Interest, Militarism and Foreign Policy: Essays*, ed. G. Craig, (Berkeley, Calif., 1977).

Kelley, Alfred, *The Descent of Darwin: The Popularization of Darwinism in Germany, 1860–1914* (Chapel Hill, NC, 1981).

KENNEDY, PAUL, *The Rise of the Anglo-German Antagonism, 1860–1914* (London, 1914).

—— *The Rise and Fall of British Naval Mastery* (London, 1976).

—— (ed.), *The War Plans of the Great Powers, 1880–1914* (London, 1979).

—— *The Rise and Fall of the Great Powers* (London, 1988).

KESSEL, EBERHARD, *Moltke* (Stuttgart, 1957).

—— *Militärgeschichte und Kriegstheorie in neuerer Zeit*, ed. Johannes Kunisch (Berlin, 1987).

KITCHEN, MARTIN, *The German Officer Corps, 1890–1914* (Oxford, 1968).

KLOSTER, WALTER, *Der deutsche Generalstab und der Präventivkrieg-Gedanke* (Stuttgart, 1932).

KRAUSE, MICHAEL D., 'Anglo-French Military Planning before the First World War (1905–1914): A Study in "Military Diplomacy" ' (unpubl. diss., Georgetown University, 1968).

KRUMEICH, GERD, *Armament and Politics in France on the Eve of the First World War: The Introduction of the Three Years Conscription* (London, 1984).

KUHL, H. VON, *Der deutsche Generalstab in Vorbereitung und Durchführung des Weltkrieges* (Berlin, 1920).

LANGER, WILLIAM L., *The Diplomacy of Imperialism* (New York, 1951).

LIDDELL HART, B. H., *Foch, The Man of Orleans* (London, 1931).

—— 'French Military Ideas before the First World War', in M. Gilbert (ed.), *A Century of Conflict 1850–1950* (London, 1966), 135–48.

LIDER, JULIAN, *The Political and Military Laws of War: An Analysis of Marxist-Leninist Concepts* (Guildford, 1979).

LIVEZEY, WILLIAM E., *Mahan on Sea Power* (Norman, Okla., 1947).

LOTTMAN, HERBERT R., *Pétain: Hero or Traitor?* (New York, 1985).

LUVAAS, JAY, *The Education of an Army: British Military Thought, 1815–1940* (London, 1965).

MACKAY, R. F., *Fisher of Kilverstone* (Oxford, 1973).

MARDER, ARTHUR, *The Anatomy of British Sea Power* (London, 1940).

—— *From the Dreadnought to Scapa Flow* (5 vols.; London, 1961–9).

MATTINGLY, G., *The Defeat of the Spanish Armada* (London, 1959).

MAY, ERNEST R. (ed.), *Knowing One's Enemies: Intelligence Assessment before the Two World Wars* (Princeton, NJ, 1984).

MICHON, GEORGES, *La Préparation à la guerre: La Loi de trois ans (1910–1914)* (Paris, 1935).

Militärgeschichtliches Forschungsamt (ed.), *Handbuch zur deutschen Militärgeschichte, 1648–1939* (4 vols.; Munich, 1979).

MILLER, STEVEN E. (ed.), *Military Strategy and the Origins of the First World War* (Princeton, NJ, 1985).

MITCHELL, ALLAN, *Victors and Vanquished: The German Influence on Army and Church in France after 1870* (London, 1984).

MOMMSEN, WOLFGANG J., *Max Weber and German Politics, 1890–1920* (London, 1984).

MONTEILHET, J., *Les Institutions militaires de la France (1814–1924)* (Paris, 1926).

MOSSE, GEORGE L., *The Crisis of German Ideology* (London, 1966).

—— *Toward the Final Solution: A History of European Racism* (London, 1978).

NA'AMAN, SHLOMO, *Lassalle* (Hanover, 1970).

NICHOLS, J. ALDEN, *Germany after Bismarck: The Caprivi Era* (Cambridge, Mass., 1958).

PARET, PETER, *Clausewitz and the State* (Oxford, 1976).

—— (ed.), *Makers of Modern Strategy from Machiavelli to the Nuclear Age* (Princeton, NJ, 1986).

PELGER, H. (ed.), *Friedrich Engels, 1820–1970* (Hanover, 1971).

PETTER, WOLFGANG, ' "Enemies" and "Reich Enemies": An Analysis of Threat Perceptions and Political Strategy in Imperial Germany, 1871–1914', in Wilhelm Deist (ed.), *The German Military in the Age of Total War* (Worcester, 1985), 22–39.

POLIAKOV, LÉON, *The Aryan Myth: A History of Racist and Nationalist Ideas in Europe* (London, 1974).

PORCH, DOUGLAS, *Army and Revolution: France 1815–1848* (London, 1974).

—— *The March to the Marne: The French Army, 1871–1914* (Cambridge, 1981).

—— 'Clausewitz and the French, 1871–1914', in M. Handel (ed.), *Clausewitz and Modern Strategy* (London, 1986).

PRITCHARD, JAMES, *Louis XV's Navy, 1748–1762: A Study of Organization and Administration* (Montreal, 1987).

PULESTON, WILLIAN D., *Mahan: The Life and Work of Captain Alfred Thayer Mahan* (New Haven, Conn., 1939).

RALSTON, DAVID, *The Army of the Republic: The Place of the Military in the Political Evolution of France, 1871–1914* (Cambridge, Mass., 1967).

REVOL, J., *Histoire de l'armée française* (Paris, 1929).

RICHMOND, HERBERT, *Statesmen and Sea Power* (Oxford, 1947).

RINGER, FRITZ K., *The Decline of the German Mandarins: The German Academic Community, 1890–1933* (Cambridge, Mass., 1969).

RITTER, GERHARD, *The Schlieffen Plan* (London, 1958). First publ. in German 1956.

—— *The German Problem* (Columbus, Oh., 1965).

—— *The Sword and the Scepter* (4 vols.; Miami, Fla., 1969), German original 1954.

Röhl, John, Sombart, Nicolaus (eds.), *Kaiser Wilhelm II: New Interpretations* (Cambridge, 1982).

Ropp, Theodore, *The Development of a Modern Navy: French Naval Policy, 1871–1904* (Annapolis, Md., 1987).

Rosinski, Herbert, *The German Army* (London, 1939).

——— *The Development of Naval Thought*, ed. B. M. Simpson (Newport, RI, 1977).

Roskill, S. W., *The Strategy of Sea Power* (London, 1962).

Rüdt von Collenberg, Ludwig, *Die deutsche Armee von 1871 bis 1914* (Berlin, 1922).

Ryan, Stephen, *Pétain the Soldier* (London, 1969).

Schmidt, F. J., Molinski, K., Mette, S., *Hans Delbrück, Der Historiker und Politiker* (Berlin, 1928).

Schulte, Bernd-Felix, *Die deutsche Armee, 1900–1914: Zwischen Beharren und Verändern* (Düsseldorf, 1977).

Schurman, D. M., *The Education of a Navy: The Development of British Naval Strategic Thought, 1867–1914* (London, 1965).

——— *Julian S. Corbett, 1854–1922* (London, 1981).

Seager II, Robert, *Alfred Thayer Mahan: The Man and His Letters* (Annapolis, Md., 1977).

Sedgwick, Alexander, *The Third French Republic, 1870–1914* (New York, 1968).

Semmel, Bernard, (ed.), *Marxism and the Science of War* (Oxford, 1981).

——— *Liberalism and Naval Strategy: Ideology, Interest and Sea Power during the Pax Britannica* (London, 1986).

Serman, William, *Les Origines des officiers française, 1848–1870* (Paris, 1979).

Setzen, Joel A., 'The Doctrine of the Offensive in the French Army on the Eve of World War I' (unpub, diss., University of Chicago, 1972).

Shand, Alexander I., *The Life of General Sir Edward Bruce Hamley* (2 vols.; London, 1895).

Showalter, Dennis, *Railroads and Rifles: Soldiers, Technology and the Unification of Germany* (Hamden, Conn., 1975).

Simon, W. M., *European Positivism in the Nineteenth Century* (New York, 1963).

Snyder, Jack, *The Ideology of the Offensive* (Ithaca, NY, 1984).

Spector, Ronald, *Professors of War: The Naval War College and the Development of the Naval Profession* (Newport, RI, 1977).

Spiers, Edward M., *The Army and Society, 1815–1914* (London, 1980).

Stadelmann, Rudolf, *Moltke und der Staat* (Krefeld, 1950).

Stamford, Peter M., 'The Work of Sir Julian Corbett in the Dreadnought Era', *United States Naval Institute Proceedings*, 77 (1951), 61–71.

Steinberg, Jonathan, *Yesterday's Deterrent: Tirpitz and the Birth of the German Battle Fleet* (London, 1965).

STERN, FRITZ, *The Politics of Cultural Despair* (Berkeley, Calif., 1961).

STONE, NORMAN, *The Eastern Front, 1914–1917* (London, 1975).

STRACHAN, HEW, *European Armies and the Conduct of Wars* (London, 1983).

—— *Wellington's Legacy: The Reform of the British Army* (Manchester, 1984).

—— *From Waterloo to Balaclava: Tactics, Technology and the British Army, 1815–1854* (Cambridge, 1985).

STROMBERG, RONALD, *Redemption by War: The Intellectuals and 1914* (Lawrence, Kan., 1982).

STUART, REGINALD C., *The Half-Way Pacifist: Thomas Jefferson's View of War* (Toronto, 1978).

—— *War and American Thought from the Revolution to the Monroe Doctrine* (Kent, Oh., 1982).

SULLIVAN, A. T., *Thomas-Robert Bugeaud* (Hamden, Conn., 1983).

SWIFT, EBEN, 'The Military Education of Robert E. Lee', *Virginia Magazine of History and Biography*, 35 (1927), 97–108.

SYMPOX, GEOFFREY, *The Crisis of French Sea Power, 1688–1697, From the* guerre d'escadre *to the* guerre de course (The Hague, 1974).

TANENBAUM, JAN KARL, *General Maurice Sarrail, 1856–1929* (Chapel Hill, NC, 1974).

TAYLOR, A. J. P., *The Struggle for Mastery in Europe* (Oxford, 1954).

TAYLOR, CHARLES C., *The Life of Admiral Mahan* (New York, 1920).

TESKE, HERMANN, *Colmar Freiherr von der Goltz* (Göttingen, 1957).

THIMME, ANNELISE, *Hans Delbrück als Kritiker der Wilhelminischen Epoche* (Düsseldorf, 1955).

THOMAS, WILLIAM, *The Philosophic Radicals* (Oxford, 1979).

THRALL, MIRIAM, *Rebellious Frazer's: No. 1 Yorke's Magazine in the Days of Maginn, Thackeray and Carlyle* (New York, 1934).

TRAVERS, T. H. E., 'Technology, Tactics and Morale: Jean de Bloch, the Boer War, and British Military Theory, 1900–1914', *Journal of Modern History*, 51 (1979), 264–86.

TROELTSCH, ERNST, 'The Idea of Natural Law and Humanity in World History', app. to O. Gierke, *Natural Law and the Theory of Society, 1500–1800* (Cambridge, 1934).

TUCHMAN, BARBARA, *The Guns of August* (New York, 1962).

VAGTS, ALFRED, *A History of Militarism* (London, 1959).

WALLACH, JEHUDA L., *Das Dogma der Vernichtungsschlacht* (Frankfurt a. M., 1967).

—— *Die Kriegslehre von Friedrich Engels* (Frankfurt, a.M., 1968).

WALSER, JOHN RAYMOND, 'France's Search for a Battlefleet: French Naval Policy, 1898–1914', (unpub. doc. diss., University of North California, 1976).

WEBER, EUGEN, *The Nationalist Revival in France, 1905–1914* (Berkeley, Calif., 1959).

WEBER, MAX, *Economy and Society* (New York, 1968).

WEHLER, HANS-ULRICH, *The German Empire* (Leamington Spa, 1985). First publ. in German 1973.

WEIGLEY, RUSSEL F., *History of the United States Army* (Bloomington, Ind., 1967).

—— *The American Way of War: A History of United States Military Strategy and Policy* (London, 1973).

WERNHAM, R. B., 'Elizabethan War Aims and Strategy', in S. T. Bindoff, J. Hurstfield, and C. H. Williams (eds.), *Elizabethan Government and Society* (London, 1961).

WHITTON, F. E., *Moltke* (London, 1921).

WILLIAMS, T. HARRY, 'The Return to Jomini: Some Thoughts on Recent Civil War Writing', *Military Affairs*, 39 (1975), 204–6.

WILLIAMSON, SAMUEL, *The Politics of Grand Strategy: Britain and France Prepare for War, 1904–1914* (Cambridge, Mass., 1969).

WOHL, ROBERT, *The Generation of 1914* (Cambridge, Mass., 1979).

ZANIEWICKI, WITOLD, 'L'Impact de 1870 sur la pensée militaire française', *Revue de Défense Nationale*, 26 (1970), 1331–41.

ZIRKE, GERHARD, *Der General: Friedrich Engels, der erste Militär-theoretiker der Arbeiterklassen* (Leipzig, 1957).

INDEX